*Sex and Society in the World of
the Orthodox Slavs, 900–1700*

Sex and Society in the World of the Orthodox Slavs, 900–1700

EVE LEVIN

Cornell University Press

ITHACA AND LONDON

This book has been supported by a grant from the National Endowment for the Humanities, an independent federal agency.

First published 1989 by Cornell University Press
First printing, Cornell Paperbacks, 1995

Printed in the United States of America

Library of Congress Cataloging-in-Publication Data

Levin, Eve, 1954–
Sex and society in the world of the orthodox Slavs, 900–1700 / Eve Levin.
    p.   cm.
  Bibliographical: p.
  Includes index
  ISBN 0-8014-2260-4 (alk. paper)
  ISBN 0-8014-8304-2 (pbk. : alk. paper)
    1. Sex customs—Europe, Eastern—History. 2. Slavs—Sexual behavior—
History. 3. Orthodox (Orthodox Eastern Church)—Europe, Eastern—Sexual
behavior—History. 4. Sex—Religious aspects—Orthodox Eastern Church—
History. I. Title.
HQ18.E852L48   1989   306.7'0947—dc19   89-30075

Cloth printing   10 9 8 7 6 5 4 3 2 1

Paperback printing   10 9 8 7 6 5 4 3 2

Contents

Illustrations

Preface

This book delves into a hitherto unexplored area of inquiry, the social context of sexuality among the medieval Orthodox Slavs. These people inhabited a territory stretching from the Adriatic into Siberia; within this vast region, three great kingdoms—Serbia, Bulgaria, and Russia—emerged to shape their political identifications. The wars and revolutions of the past century so strengthened the Slavs' sense of nationality that scholars have usually defined their parameters accordingly, writing about *Russian* spirituality, *Serbian* iconography, *Bulgarian* patristics. I do not deny the existence of national distinctiveness, even in the premodern period, but the cultural affinities far exceed the discrepancies. Throughout the medieval period, Orthodox Christianity reinforced and preserved the underlying cultural unity. The first conversions in the ninth century mark the beginning of the Middle Ages in the East; the rapid influx of Western and secular influences under Peter the Great marks the end. During this time, Bulgarians, Russians, and Serbs shared a common Byzantine inheritance in religion, literary language, the arts, and teachings on sexuality.

The medieval Orthodox Slavs regarded sexuality as a public rather than a private matter, and a religious rather than a secular one. It was fraught with spiritual and practical consequences for the community as well as the individual. Thus an understanding of medieval Slavic sexuality requires explorations of ecclesiastical and family structure, theology and canon law, church sacraments and judicial procedures. I hope that this book will illuminate these aspects of Slavic history, which have too long remained in shadow.

Like most historians, I am wary of using my knowledge of the past as an excuse for pontificating about the present. Yet I cannot avoid an awareness that many issues of medieval Slavic sexuality also cause concern today. Ours is not the first society to grapple with the problems of divorce, or premarital sex, or homosexuality, or rape. As we reexamine our policies and ethical standards in regard to sexuality, the medieval Orthodox Slavs offer an instructive lesson. They were European, but they lacked the concepts of Roman law and romantic love which molded the modern ideas of sexuality. They were Christian, but their laws and practices diverged sharply from the Roman Catholic and Protestant traditions of the West. The medieval Slavic experience reveals some of the diversity possible within Western civilization, presenting for consideration alternatives that are unfamiliar but not entirely alien. The early Slavs, like so many of our forebears, regarded righteousness in sexual conduct as the primary measure of an individual's moral worth. They discovered, too, that strict standards did not forestall wrongdoing. Although the Orthodox Slavs' view of sex as evil, unhealthy, and abnormal seems to invert our own, they shared with modern society a willingness to talk frankly about it. And while medieval Slavic Orthodox society was religious in a way that the modern world has long abandoned, its policies on sex were shaped as much by practical considerations as by theological ones. Consequently, my book is not the story of religious dicta imposed and resisted, but rather a tale of the interplay of the ideals of ethical conduct and the realities of human behavior. Whether it contains a moral for modern society I leave to my readers.

I have used the International system of transliteration for Church Slavonic, Russian, and Bulgarian. The letter *jat* in nineteenth-century Russian was transliterated as *e*. Modern Serbian is rendered in the form established for Serbo-Croatian in the Latin alphabet.

I have been extremely fortunate in the help I have received in the preparation of this book. Several institutions provided financial and administrative assistance. Grants from the International Research and Exchanges Board and the Fulbright-Hays Commission enabled me to conduct research in the Soviet Union. A grant from the United States Information Agency for an academic exchange between the Resource Center for Medieval Slavic Studies at Ohio State University and the Serbian Academy of Sciences and Arts and the National Library of Serbia funded research in Yugoslavia. Grants from the College of Humanities and the Office of Research and Graduate Studies at Ohio State University made it possible for me to travel to Bulgaria. A postdoctoral research fellowship provided by the Joint Committee on Eastern Europe of the American Council of Learned Societies and the Social Science Research Council funded leave time to finish the writing. Additional financial assistance was provided by the Center for Medieval and Renaissance Studies, the Resource Center for Medieval Slavic Studies, the

Department of History, and the College of Humanities at Ohio State University. I benefited from the opportunities provided by the Summer Research Laboratory sponsored by the Russian and East European Center at the University of Illinois every year from 1980 through 1986. I am also grateful for the assistance of the staffs of libraries and archives: the Hilandar Research Library and the Main Library at Ohio State University; the Slavic Reading Room at the University of Illinois; in Moscow, the Central State Archive of Ancient Acts (TsGADA) and the State Historical Museum (GIM); in Leningrad, the Saltykov-Ščedrin Library, the Library of the Academy of Sciences, and the Institute of Old Russian Literature (Puškinskij Dom); the Novgorod State Museum; in Belgrade, the Manuscript Divisions of the Library of the Serbian Academy of Sciences and Arts and the National Library of Serbia.

Many individuals decisively influenced my thinking. First among them is Natal'ja Lvovna Puškareva, who initially suggested that I pursue this topic and who has conscientiously commented on my conclusions. Predrag Matejić, curator of the Hilandar Research Library, located for me many of the sources used in this book and shared his insights about their contents. John G. Ackerman and two readers for Cornell University Press made many valuable suggestions for improvements. Barbara Salazar expertly edited the manuscript. In addition, I benefited from the suggestions and assistance of Gordana Babić, Helen Hundley, Valentin Lavrent'evič Janin, Sandra Levy, Cheryl M. Mansky, Mateja Matejić, Brenda Meehan-Waters, Petar Milich, Jennifer Parkhurst, Dušan Sindik, Elizabeth Todd, William Wolf, Christine Worobec, and Mirjana Živojinović. Dimitrije Stefanović and his family helped to make my stay in Belgrade both pleasant and productive. Margaret and Timothy Phillips, my sister and brother-in-law, performed similar services in Urbana.

Parts of this project were presented at the following conferences: Midwest Slavic Conference, Columbus, Ohio, May 4–6, 1984; Central Slavic Conference, Columbia, Missouri, October 19–20, 1984; Midwest Slavic Conference, South Bend, Indiana, April 19–20, 1985; Fourth Summer Colloquium on Old Bulgarian Studies, Sofia, Bulgaria, August 14–23, 1985; and AAASS National Conference, Boston, November 5–8, 1987. I am grateful to the participants for their questions and recommendations.

Assistance with translations was provided by my father, Saul Levin, for Greek and Latin, and by Irene Katele, for Italian and Lithuanian. Finally, I thank my colleagues in the Department of History at Ohio State University for their unfailing collegiality, intellectual stimulation, and encouragement.

Columbus, Ohio

EVE LEVIN

Abbreviations

BAN-L	Library of the Academy of Sciences, Leningrad
BAN-S	Bulgarian Academy of Sciences, Sofia
BNL	Bulgarian National Library, Sofia
Dečani	Dečani Monastery, Yugoslavia
DKU	Ja. N. Ščapov, *Drevnerusskie knjažeskie ustavy* (Moscow, 1976)
GBL	Lenin Library, Moscow
GIM, Sin.	State Historical Museum, Moscow, Sinodal'nyj Collection
GPB	Saltykov-Ščedrin Library, Leningrad
Hil.	Hilandar Monastery, Mount Athos, Greece
Kiev	Slavonic books from Kiev at University of Toronto
Koll. Pereca	Perec Collection at Puškinskij Dom, Leningrad
Kormčaja	V. N. Beneševič, *Drevne-slavjanskaja kormčaja XIV titulov bez tolkovanij* (St. Petersburg, 1906)
L.	Leningrad
Lavra	Great Lavra Monastery, Mount Athos, Greece
M.	Moscow
NBS	National Library of Serbia, Belgrade
Nov. Mus.	Novgorod State Museum
PD	Institute of Old Russian Literature (Puškinskij Dom), Leningrad
Peć	Peć Monastery, Yugoslavia
Pinež.	Pinežskoe Collection at Puškinskij Dom, Leningrad
PRP	*Pamjatniki russkogo prava*, 8 vols. (Moscow, 1953)
PSRL	*Polnoe sobranie russkix letopisej*, vols. 4, 5, 8 (St. Petersburg, 1848, 1859; Leningrad, 1925)
RIB	Russkaja istoričeskaja biblioteka, vols. 2, 6, 12, 14, 25 (St. Petersburg, 1875, 1908, 1890, 1894, 1908)
Rila	Rila Monastery, Bulgaria

SANU	Serbian Academy of Sciences and Arts, Belgrade
Sinai	Mount Sinai Monastery, Egypt
Sintagmat	Stojan Novaković, *Matija Vlastara Sintagmat* (Belgrade, 1907)
SOCH	Serbian Orthodox Church of Hungary, Szentendre
Sof. b-ka	Sofijskaja Biblioteka Collection at Saltykov-Ščedrin Library, Leningrad
Solov.	Soloveckij Monastery Collection at Saltykov-Ščedrin Library, Leningrad
SPb.	St. Petersburg
SPbDA	St. Petersburg Ecclesiastical Academy Collection at Saltykov-Ščedrin Library, Leningrad
Stoglav	D. E. Kožančikov, ed., *Stoglav* (St. Petersburg, 1863)
TsGADA	Central State Archive of Ancient Acts, Moscow
Uppsala	Uppsala University Library, Sweden
VAT-Bor.	Vatican Library, Borgiani Illirici Collection
vyp.	*vypusk* (part)
ZSL-K	*Zakon Sudnyj Ljudem: Kratkoj redakcii* (Moscow, 1961)
ZSL-P	*Zakon Sudnyj Ljudem: Prostrannoj i svodnoj redakcii* (Moscow, 1961)

*Sex and Society in the World of
the Orthodox Slavs, 900–1700*

Introduction

The Problem

The dispassionate scrutiny of sexuality is an innovation of the twentieth century; in earlier times silence cloaked that area of the human psyche. Sigmund Freud first formulated the theory that sexual desires are inherent in human beings, that the external manifestations of these desires are affected by societal constraints, and that behaviors apparently unrelated to sexuality may have their roots in sexual matters. Freud's successors have disputed the extent to which individual sexuality can justly be said to influence overtly nonsexual aspects of society. In Freud's wake, however, psychologists, sociologists, anthropologists, physicians, and recently historians have studied sexuality in the same manner as any other aspect of human life. It has become possible to examine sexual behavior without intending either to advise individuals on how to expand their repertoire of techniques or to preach adherence to a moral code.[1]

Some scholars of sexuality have viewed the sexual realities of a given time and place primarily as manifestations of universal and indomitable biological or psychological characteristics. Others argue that society, culture, and history shape sexual behavior.[2] The strongest proponent of

1. See the ground-breaking studies of modern American sexuality produced by the research group headed by Alfred C. Kinsey, *Sexual Behavior in the Human Male* (Philadelphia, 1948) and *Sexual Behavior in the Human Female* (Philadelphia, 1953). Much of the study of sexuality is still classified as relating to women or to family history. For a general bibliography of academic works on sexuality, see Gerald L. Soliday et al., eds., *History of the Family and Kinship: A Select International Bibliography* (Millwood, N.Y., 1980). This bibliography includes works on Eastern Europe, but few in native languages.

2. A brief discussion of this literature and its implications for historians may be found in Jeffrey Weeks, *Sex, Politics, and Society: The Regulation of Sexuality since 1800* (New York, 1981).

the latter view is Michel Foucault, whose *History of Sexuality* empha-
sizes the abstract and complex interaction of social forces and sexual
behavior.[3] Those who accept this premise alternately view social constraints on sexual expression as civilization's only safeguard against
sexual savagery or as the fettering of human potential for spiritual and
emotional development through sex.

Most historians have preferred to avoid taking sides in the debates on
the nature of sexuality by discussing sexual norms and behavior con-
cretely. Vern Bullough, who examined both Eastern and Western societies, has produced the best general history of sexuality.[4] The strength
of his study lies in its forswearing of stereotypic and simplistic characterizations of the structures and purposes of sexual life in the past. Although wide-ranging, Bullough's study gives no more than a fleeting
glance at the medieval Slavs.

Historians reveal their various theoretical premises in evaluations of
the effectiveness of official norms, expectations, and laws in altering
actual sexual behavior. This debate comes through strongly in the literature about sexuality in medieval and early-modern Western Europe.
Some scholars work from the premise that the authorities who established rules enjoined specific sexual conduct, and that the result is the
"repressive" standards of the Western tradition. Others presume that
the bulk of the population was amoral in sexual matters, and that conduct was little influenced by rules and laws. It is not surprising that the
adherents of the former position tend to be scholars of prescriptive
sources, such as law and books of penance, while adherents of the latter
view investigate records of behavior, such as court cases and parish
records.[5] There is enough truth to both presuppositions to sustain the
conclusions of researchers on both sides of the issue.

The quality of publications on sexuality in medieval and early-modern
Europe is impressively high. James A. Brundage has contributed the
most comprehensive treatment of Roman Catholic canon law.[6] Penitential literature has also been studied for its information on sexuality,

3. Michel Foucault, *The History of Sexuality*, vol. 1: *An Introduction* (New York, 1980).
4. Vern L. Bullough, *Sexual Variance in Society and History* (New York, 1976).
5. The debate is summarized and evaluated in G. R. Quaife, *Wanton Wenches and Wayward Wives: Peasants and Illicit Sex in Early Seventeenth-Century England* (New Brunswick, N.J., 1979), 178–248. See also two articles by J.-L. Flandrin: "Repression and Change in the Sexual Life of Young People in Medieval and Early Modern Times," in Robert Wheaton and Tamara K. Harevin, eds., *Family and Sexuality in French History* (Philadelphia, 1980), 27–48, and "Sex in Married Life in the Early Middle Ages: The Church's Teaching and Behavioural Reality," in Philippe Ariès and André Béjin, eds., *Western Sexuality: Practice and Precept in Past and Present Times* (New York, 1985), 115–129.
6. James A. Brundage, *Law, Sex, and Christian Society in Medieval Europe* (Chicago, 1987).

although primarily for the early Middle Ages.[7] We have had volumes on the treatment accorded violators of sexual prescriptions by ecclesiastical courts in early-modern England and in Renaissance Venice, and numerous articles have appeared on specific aspects of sexuality.[8] Homosexuality has attracted special attention.[9] A study of sexual expression in medieval Greece and the Byzantine empire is still in the future, although the empire's canon law on marriage has been investigated.[10] Unfortunately, few scholars have examined marriage and sexuality among the Slavs who converted to Roman Catholicism.[11]

Medieval Western Europe provides the most informative model for the study of sexuality among the Orthodox Slavs: the two societies were roughly similar in political organization, social stratification, economic resources, and technological level; many of the types of sources available are similar, as are the unavoidable gaps in information; and the Orthodox Slavs shared a common early Christian tradition with Western Europe, including Neoplatonic asceticism. The Orthodox Church in medieval Slavic countries, like the Roman Church in Western Europe,

7. Pierre J. Payer, *Sex and the Penitentials: The Development of a Sexual Code, 550–1150* (Buffalo, 1984); J.-L. Flandrin, *Un Temps pour embrasser: Aux origines de la morale sexuelle occidentale (VIe–XIe siècle)*, (Paris, 1983).

8. Martin Ingram, *Church Courts, Sex, and Marriage in England, 1570–1640* (New York, 1987); Quaife; Guido Ruggiero, *The Boundaries of Eros: Sex Crime and Sexuality in Renaissance Venice* (New York, 1985). Some of the best works on sexuality are contained in the volume edited by James A. Brundage and Vern L. Bullough, *Sexual Practices and the Medieval Church* (Buffalo, 1982). Other excellent articles include three in *Proceedings of the Fifth International Congress of Medieval Canon Law, Salamanca, 21–25 September 1976*, Monumenta Iuris Canonici, ser. C: Subsidia, 6 (Vatican, 1980): James A. Brundage, "Carnal Delight: Canonistic Theories of Sexuality," 361–385; Christopher N. L. Brooke, "Aspects of Marriage Law in the Eleventh and Twelfth Centuries," 333–344; and Jean Gaudemet, "Recherche sur les origines historiques de la faculté de rompre le mariage non consommé," 309–331; and Pierre J. Payer, "Early Medieval Regulations Concerning Marital Sexual Relations," *Journal of Medieval History* 6 (December 1980): 353–376; Elizabeth M. Makowski, "The Conjugal Debt and Medieval Law," *Journal of Medieval History* 3 (June 1977): 99–114.

9. John Boswell, *Christianity, Social Tolerance, and Homosexuality* (Chicago, 1980); Michael Goodich, *The Unmentionable Vice: Homosexuality in the Later Medieval Period* (Santa Barbara, 1979); Arno Karlen, "The Homosexual Heresy," *Chaucer Review* 6 (Summer 1971): 44–63. This interest in homosexuality doubtless springs from the study of this topic in connection with ancient Greece—a society that was frank if not objective in its presentation of sex. See Kenneth J. Dover, *Greek Homosexuality* (Cambridge, Mass., 1978); Eva C. Keuls, *The Reign of the Phallus* (New York, 1985); Felix Buffière, *Eros adolescent: La Pédérastie dans la Grèce antique* (Paris, 1980); as well as Foucault, *History of Sexuality*, vol. 2: *The Use of Pleasure* (New York, 1985) and vol. 3: *The Care of Self* (New York, 1986); and Paul Veyne, "Homosexuality in Ancient Rome," in Ariès and Béjin, *Western Sexuality*, 26–35.

10. Jean Dauvillier and Carlo de Clercq, *Le Mariage en droit canonique oriental* (Paris, 1936); R. Guilland, "Les Noces plurales à Byzance," *Byzantinoslavica* 9 (1947–48): 9–30.

11. John M. Klassen has studied some of these issues among the medieval Czechs; see his "Marriage and Family in Medieval Bohemia," *East European Quarterly* 19, no. 3 (1985): 257–274, and "The Development of the Conjugal Bond in Late Medieval Bohemia," *Journal of Medieval History* 13, no. 2 (1987): 161–178.

regulated sexual behavior, primarily through private confession and a system of ecclesiastical courts. By teaching the requirements of righteous conduct in an atmosphere that emphasized guilt, clerics could hope that their communicants would internalize the established moral standard.[12] The Orthodox Slavs represent a branch of the same European and Christian culture that has dominated Western civilization. A study of sexuality in Eastern Europe makes evident the broad range of possibilities within the Western tradition.

The similarities between Roman Catholic Western Europe and Orthodox Eastern Europe must not be overemphasized, however. The social structure of the Orthodox Slavs differed from that of Western Europeans in its lack of a feudal hierarchy. The Serbian, Bulgarian, and Russian monarchies did not practice subinfeudation or grant fiefs, although the *pronija* in the Balkans and the *pomest'e* in Russia were service-dependent to some degree. In place of feudal bonds, lineage and family status determined the range of political opportunity.[13] The prevalence of ancestral landholding was coupled with partible inheritance for sons, if not for daughters, and a substantial economic role for widows. These considerations profoundly affected Orthodox Slavic conceptions of the purpose of marriage and the acceptability of extramarital sex.

The tradition of Roman law lost force in the East, especially outside of Byzantine territory. Though the canon laws of the Eastern and Western churches shared a common base, they diverged sharply. The writings of Augustine and the decisions of the Council of Elvira, which inspired later Western ecclesiastical thinking on sexuality, never gained recognition in the East. The final split between the two churches occurred in 1054, that is, before the period of intellectual revival in the West and the greatest development of the Western traditions of canon law. As the rift between the churches became more pronounced, the flow of ideas between Roman Catholic and Orthodox Slavs declined. To a certain extent the Roman Catholic Slavs—Poles, Czechs, and Croats, could bridge the gap between Western Catholics and their Orthodox neighbors. Interaction occurred most notably in the seventeenth century in the Ukraine, where Uniates and Orthodox lived in close proximity.[14] Dis-

12. On confession in medieval Western Europe, see Thomas N. Tentler, *Sin and Confession on the Eve of the Reformation* (Princeton, 1977).

13. The power of family ties is well documented for Russia; see Nancy Shields Kollmann, "Kinship and Politics: the Origin and Evolution of the Muscovite Boyar Elite in the Fifteenth Century" (Ph.D. diss., Harvard University, 1980); Nancy Shields Kollmann, *Kinship and Politics: The Making of the Muscovite Political System, 1345–1547* (Stanford, 1987). I am not aware of similar research on medieval Serbia and Bulgaria.

14. William K. Medlin, "Cultural Crisis in Orthodox Rus' in the Late 16th and Early 17th Centuries as a Problem of Socio-cultural Change," in Andrew Blaine, ed., *The Religious World*

course was limited, however, by theological hostility between the two churches and by political rivalries between Slavic states (especially between Croatia and Serbia in the Balkans and between Poland and Russia in the north). Language made a difference as well. The Roman Catholic Church insisted on the use of Latin, which few Slavic Orthodox churchmen understood.

The institutional structure of the two churches differed also. Unlike the Roman Catholic Church, the Orthodox Church preserved the ancient institution of married clergy. Consequently, the body of canon law dealing with sexuality in the lives of Orthodox priests has no direct analogue in the West. In the Orthodox world, autocephalous national churches became the rule, and each provided the liturgy in the vernacular. This type of organization limited the degree of control that the Byzantine church could exercise over the Slavs. The use of the vernacular similarly contributed to the independence of Slavic churches, because as a rule Greek hierarchs did not study Slavic or oversee the content of Slavic texts. As a result of these structural features, canon law tended to diverge among the Slavic states in response to native conditions and values, especially in the regulation of sexual expression.

Byzantine culture influenced every area of Slavic religious life, without crushing ethnic distinctiveness. The Byzantine church and empire provided a model for the developing Serbian, Bulgarian, and Russian societies. In accepting Orthodoxy, the medieval Slavs became part of the Ecumenical Church, based in Constantinople. They adopted the forms of Orthodox observance and the styles of Byzantine art and architecture. They granted the divine inspiration of the teachings of the Church Fathers, making no formal distinction between the prelates of the early church councils and the most notable of Byzantine hierarchs. They granted the authority of Byzantine canon law and extended their reverence of it to Byzantine secular law, which they included in their ecclesiastical collections. Yet medieval Slavic society cannot justly be characterized as merely imitative.[15] The Slavs adapted the Byzantine artistic style to accommodate their own aesthetic sense; they adapted Byzantine teachings to fit their own concepts of propriety. In the multiplicity of conflicting canons, Slavic hierarchs could select what made sense to

---

of Russian Culture (The Hague, 1975), 173–188. Anti-Russian bias and typographical errors in dates mar Stephen M. Horak, "The Kiev Academy: A Bridge to Europe in the 17th Century," *East European Quarterly* 2, no. 2 (1968): 117–137.

15. The relationship between Byzantine and Slavic cultures has been the subject of a considerable literature. For some of the most insightful and accessible expressions of this concern, see D. S. Likhachev, "The Type and Character of the Byzantine Influence on Old Russian Literature," *Oxford Slavonic Papers* 13 (1967): 14–32.

them and reinterpret laws to match their needs. And when the Byzantines proposed to lead the Orthodox Church into concessions to the Latin heretics in the Union of Florence in 1439, the Slavs uncompromisingly rejected them. The fall of Constantinople in 1453 seemed to the Slavs to vindicate their view. Still, the authority of Greek customs was such that Patriarch Nikon of Russia could declare as late as the seventeenth century that he was a Russian by birth and a Greek by faith.

Greek influence in the Slavic world did not cease with the translation of ecclesiastical texts and the establishment of strong local churches. For example, the Byzantine patriarchate strove to retain control over the appointment of metropolitans for Slavic states, although frequently that power was only nominal. Matthew Blastares' reference index of Byzantine canon and civil law was translated into Slavonic at the behest of Stefan Dušan of Serbia for use in his territory. Hesychasm, the Byzantine mystical movement, enjoyed a wide following among Slavic clerics, and inspired a renaissance of the arts in late-fourteenth-century Russia. As the Turks conquered large portions of the Balkans, Greek (and also South Slavic) churchmen sought protection and employment in Russia. The monastic complex on Mount Athos in Greece served as a meeting ground for ideas from various parts of the Orthodox world. Through the Slavic monasteries on Mount Athos (St. Panteleimon, Zograf, and Hilandar), Greek practices continued to spread to Slavic Orthodox countries long after those countries had first accepted baptism. Equally important was the transmission of texts and practices among the Slavic states which these monasteries—and particularly the Serbian monastery, Hilandar—facilitated.[16]

Orthodox faith and Slavic ethnicity united the Serbs, Bulgarians, and Russians, despite political divisions and differing historical experiences. They shared a common written language, a common corpus of canon law, a common body of didactic literature, laid over the same base of folk culture. In the absence of linguistic and cultural barriers, the transfer of ideas within Slavia Orthodoxa occurred easily and rapidly.[17] A

16. I. Mansvetov, *Mitropolit Kiprian v ego liturgičeskoj dejatel'nosti* (M., 1882), 62 and *passim*.

17. This phenomenon has been discussed extensively. See vol. 19 of *Trudy otdela drevnerusskoj literatury* (1963), subtitled *Russkaja literatura XI–XVII vekov sredi slavjanskix literatur*, esp. V. P. Adrianova-Peretc, "Drevnerusskie literaturnye pamjatniki v jugoslavjanskoj pis'mennosti," 5–27; V. Mošin, "O periodizacii russko-južnoslavjanskix literaturnyx svjazej X–XV vv.," 28–106; I. Dujčev, "Centry vizantijsko-slavjanskogo obščenija i sotrudničestva," 107–129; and P. Dinekov, "Iz istorii russko-bolgarskix literaturnyx svjazej XVI–XVIII vv.," 318–329. See also Bonju St. Angelov, "Iz istorijata na ruskoto kulturno vlijanie v Bŭlgarija (XV-XVIII v.)," *Izvestija na Instituta za Bŭlgarska istorija* 6 (1956): 291–325; Ivan Snegarov, *Duxovno-kulturni vružki meždu Bŭlgarija i Rusija prez srednite vekove (X-XV v.)* (Sofia, 1950). The term "Slavia Orthodoxa" was coined by Riccardo Picchio; see, e.g., "Models and Patterns in the Literary Tradition of Medieval Orthodox Slavdom," in Victor Terras, ed., *American Contributions to the Seventh International Congress of Slavists*, vol. 2 (The Hague, 1973), 439–467.

few examples will suffice to illustrate this process. The *prolog*, a calendar of daily readings of saints' lives and instructional tales, was developed by a joint effort of Russian, Bulgarian, and Serbian clerics.[18] The *vita* of the Slavic saint Paraskeva, written by the Bulgarian patriarch Evtimij, appeared in the *Velikij Čet'i-Minej*, a sixteenth-century collection prepared under the direction of Metropolitan Makarij of Russia. In one manuscript of the text, she was described as a credit to the "Bulgarian" people; in another, to the "Serbian" people.[19] Thus all three national traditions claimed St. Paraskeva. Metropolitan Kiprian of Russia, one of the most active and effective medieval Slavic prelates, was from the same family as the equally noted patriarch Evtimij of Bulgaria. The nomocanon attributed to the Serbian saint Sava was recopied in Bulgaria for the patriarch of Trnovo around 1226; a copy was sent to Russia in 1262 at the request of Metropolitan Kirill II. This version of the nomocanon came to predominate throughout the Slavic Orthodox community.[20] Bulgarian, Serbian, and Russian Orthodoxy were three branches of the same tradition, growing intertwined from the same root. Nowhere is this interconnection more evident than in canon law on sexuality, where the vast majority of materials exist in all three recensions.

Cultural and religious unity notwithstanding, the Slavic Orthodox states were dissimilar in numerous ways. Each state received influences from directions other than Byzantium. None of the Slavic Orthodox states was internally homogeneous; all contained non-Slavic and non-Orthodox peoples. Serbia experienced considerable contact with Italian cities through the trade along its Adriatic coast; it also had a substantial Roman Catholic constituency. The medieval Balkan peninsula was also home to Albanians, Vlahs, and Jews. The original ruling class in the First Bulgarian Empire consisted of Turkic horsemen from the Eurasian steppe, who were assimilated only after many decades. Historians debate the degree of influence of the Scandinavian founders of Russia's ruling dynasty, but steppe influences were strong. Russia even more than Serbia and Bulgaria was a multinational state from its inception, containing within its borders a variety of Finno-Ugric tribes. As these peoples did

---

18. A. I. Rogov, "Russko-bol'garskie kul'turnye svjazi v konce XII–XIII vv.," *Etudes balkaniques* 17, no. 3 (1981): 86–91.

19. *Velikija minei četii, sobrannyja vserossijskim mitropolitom Makariem; Oktjabr', dni 4–18* (SPb., 1874), 1021–1042.

20. A. Pavlov, *Pervonačal'nyj slavjano-russkij Nomokanon* (Kazan, 1869), 66. For a brief study of the manuscript tradition, see A. Solovjev, "Svetosavski nomokanon i njegovi novi prepisi," *Brastvo* 26 (1932): 21–43. Metropolitan Kirill II was a Greek by birth, but apparently he took up residence in Russia before his appointment to the metropolitanate; he was ordained in Kiev rather than in Byzantium. See E. Golubinskij, *Istorija Russkoj Cerkvi*, vol. 1 (M., 1901), 318.

not share the dominant Slavic culture, we need not dwell on them here.[21]

The geographical locations of Bulgaria and Serbia put them much more firmly in the Byzantine orbit than Russia. During the reigns of strong rulers, both Bulgaria and Serbia laid claim to the Byzantine imperial title and Byzantine territory. The Bulgarian tsars Symeon in the tenth century and Ivan Asen II in the thirteenth century both nearly succeeded, as did the fourteenth-century Serbian ruler Stefan Dušan, who declared himself to be "emperor of the Serbs and the Greeks." Russian rulers did not attempt to assume Byzantine imperial authority until after the empire collapsed; claims to Byzantine territory arose only in the eighteenth century.

Foreign invasions also left their separate marks on Orthodox Slavic states. Of the three, only Bulgaria experienced a period of direct Byzantine rule, from 1018 to 1185. The Mongols conquered Russia in 1238–1240 and continued to hold suzerainty over it until 1480. The penetration of the Turks into the Balkans in the late fourteenth century ended Bulgarian and Serbian independence. Both invasions caused extensive destruction, and the overlords continued to drain each region economically for centuries. The effects on the intimate lives of Slavic Orthodox men and women were more gradual and indirect. Some authors blame the Mongols and the Turks for an undocumented "decline of morals" among the conquered peoples, but this view is based exclusively on stereotypes fed by ethnic and religious hostility.[22] Neither the Mongols nor the Turks attempted to force their Slavic subjects to assimilate the culture of their overlords. The Mongols even more than the Turks were absentee rulers, governing through a handful of envoys and the native leaders, backed by military force when necessary. Foreign rule affected sexual behavior primarily by strengthening the power and prestige of the church, which had sole charge in the enforcement of sexual standards. Turkish rule of the Balkans had one additional consequence for sexual behavior: a significant minority of the Slavic population adopted Islam, which offered a different approach to sexuality.[23] As it is Orthodox

21. A partial exception is made for the Vlahs, who adopted Orthodoxy and for centuries used the Slavonic liturgy of either the Serbian or the Russian recension.

22. For an example of the stereotype of pernicious Mongol influence repeated, see Mikhail Stern with August Stern, *Sex in the USSR* (New York, 1980), 9; for a refutation, see Charles J. Halperin, *Russia and the Golden Horde* (Bloomington, Ind., 1985), esp. 104–119. For the Turks, see, e.g., John Macdonald, *Czar Ferdinand and His People* (New York, 1971), 8–9.

23. On the religious diversity in the Balkans after the Turkish conquest and the absorption of Christian beliefs and practices into Balkan Islam, see Speros Vryonis, Jr., "Religious Changes and Patterns in the Balkans, 14th–16th Centuries," in Henrik Birnbaum and Speros Vryonis, eds., *Aspects of the Balkans: Continuity and Change* (The Hague, 1972), 151–176.

attitudes and practices that concern us here, we need not linger over the Muslim population of medieval Bulgaria and Serbia.

The division of Orthodox Slavs into three national groups—the Serbs, the Bulgarians, and the Russians—represents a simplification of a complex political history. These designations do not reflect shifting borders or political fragmentation. Nor do they speak to the question of the emergence of an independent national consciousness by a segment of the population, as in the case of the Macedonians and the Ukrainians. The justification for the use of only three national designations lies in the language and orthography of the primary sources, which divide into only three recensions. Even these categorizations are subject to dispute. Most of the oldest texts were of the Bulgarian tradition, regardless of where they were produced. Numerous manuscripts in the "Serbian" recension were in fact produced in Bulgarian territory. Many texts from twelfth- and thirteenth-century Bulgaria and from seventeenth-century Serbia were in fact in the Russian recension.[24] Further subdivisions are possible, but they would be inexact and disputable. Certain "Bulgarian" manuscripts were produced in Macedonian territory; "Russian" materials include those produced in Novgorodian territory, Belorussia, and the Ukraine. The Ukraine was particularly fertile in the production of ecclesiastical books in the seventeenth century; materials produced there were used throughout Muscovy.

The Slavic world adopted Christianity later than most of Western Europe, coming into the fold only in the ninth, tenth, and eleventh centuries. As the Reformation had little direct effect on the Orthodox, it cannot serve to demarcate periods of their history. Although the date of the Turkish conquest is properly used as a dividing point in studies of the political history of the South Slavs, it is less appropriate for investigations of society and culture, which changed little under Turkish rule. It is also inapplicable to Russia. For Russia, the dramatic change in regulations of sexual behavior occurred as a result of the adoption of Western practices under Peter the Great. The Russian church at that time was preeminent among Orthodox Slavs, owing to its status as the one such institution that was not held captive by the infidels. The changes the Russian church adopted spread steadily to the Serbs and Bulgarians. For that reason, it is appropriate to focus on the eight hundred years between A.D. 900, shortly after Christianity began to be adopted among Slavic states, and 1700, when the last premodern Russian patriarch died. During this period the constants in the treatment of sexual matters far exceeded any changes.

24. B. Angelov, 300; Rogov, 86–91.

The sexual norms of medieval Slavic Orthodox society have not previously received much scholarly attention. Few investigations touch even
obliquely on sexual behavior. Overt discussion of sexuality was deemed
inappropriate in the nineteenth-century academic milieu, as elsewhere in
those years. Works on "marriage"—the only polite referent for sex—
concentrated on its economic, legal, and ritual aspects.[25] References to
the conjugal relationship within marriage were couched in the delicate
euphemisms of religion and morality, as though Victorian standards
were universal among civilized peoples. Sexual activity outside of marriage could be mentioned only obliquely, with due condemnation. Maxime Kovalevsky's work was typical of this approach to the study of
sexual mores. After discussing Slavic pagan marriage customs for a total
of ten pages, he concluded: "I hope I have now given an amount of
information sufficient to answer the purpose I have in view, which is no
other, than to show that, in a low state of morality, communal marriage
between near relations and endogamy, went hand in hand amongst the
early Slavs with a considerable degree of independence among the weaker sex."[26] Thus Kovalevsky equated sexual license, incest, immorality,
barbarism, and women's rights, all hopefully consigned to the distant
Russian past.

Most often, sexuality was simply omitted, as it was from Golubinskij's massive *Istorija Russkoj Cerkvi*. The histories of the Bulgarian
and Serbian churches share this deficiency.[27] The twentieth-century émigré scholar George P. Fedotov was little more inclined to pursue this

25. V. T. Baldziev, "Studija vŭrxu našeto personalno supružestvenno pravo," *Sbornik za
narodni umotvorenija, nauka i knižnina* 4 (1891): 156–193, 5 (1891): 187–203, 7 (1892):
111–158, 8 (1892): 194–215, 10 (1894): 236–267; Konstantin Alekseev, "Ob otnošenie
suprugov po imuščestvu v drevnej Rossii i v Pol'še," *Čtenija obščestva istorii i drevnostej
rossijskix pri Moskovskom universitete*, bk. 2 (1868), 1–108; Aleksandr Dobrjakov, *Russkaja
ženščina v do-mongol'skij period* (SPb., 1864); Vitalij Jakovlevič Šul'gin, *O sostojanii ženščin v
Rossii do Petra Velikogo* (Kiev, 1850); K. D. Kavelin, "O sostojanii ženščin v Rossii do Petra
Velikago: Istoričeskoe izsledovanie Vitalija Šul'gina" (1850), in *Sobranie sočinenij*, vol. 1
(SPb., 1897), 1030–1044; I. E. Zabelin, "Ženščina po ponjatijam starinnyx knižnikov," *Russkij vestnik* 9 (1857): 5–46; A. P. Ščapov, "Položenie ženščiny v Rossii po do-Petrovskomu
vozzreniju" (1873), in *Sočinenija*, vol. 2 (SPb., 1908), 105–153; D. N. Dubakin, *Vlijanie
xristianstva na semejnyj byt russkago obščestva* (SPb., 1880); S. S. Šaškov, *Istorija russkoj
ženščiny* (SPb., 1879); Marija Nikolaevna Ditrix, *Russkaja ženščina velikoknjažeskago vremeni* (SPb., 1904). Elaine Elnett's *Historic Origin and Social Development of Family Life in
Russia* (New York, 1926) follows very much in the vein of Russian scholars of the nineteenth
century, marred by significant inaccuracies.
26. Maxime Kovalevsky, *Modern Customs and Ancient Laws of Russia* (London, 1891).
27. See, e.g., Svetozar Niketić, "Istorijski razvitak Srpske crkve," *Glasnik srpskog učenog
društva* 27 (1870): 81–163; 31 (1871): 45–88; Djoko Slijepčević, *Istorija srpske pravoslavne
crkve*, vol. 1: *Od pokrstavanja Srba do kraja XVIII veka* (Munich, 1962); Jordan Nikolov,
"Pravoslavnata cŭrkva prez epoxata na feodalizma (IX—XIV v.)," in *Pravoslavieto v Bŭlgarija
(Teoretiko-istoričesko osvetlenie)* (Sofia, 1974), 101–124; Todor Sŭbev, *Samostojna narodnostna cŭrkva v srednovekovna Bŭlgarija* (Sofia, 1987); K. Dinkov, *Istorija na bŭlgarskata
curkva (četiva)* (Sofia, 1954).

aspect of the history of the Orthodox Church. He noted the predominance of sexual subjects in the penitential literature of the medieval Russian church, "passing in review all the dark realms of vice, natural and unnatural, with disgusting details, as if the seventh commandment were the only one in the Decalogue."[28] By dismissing the medieval concern with sex as a perversion of true Christianity, Fedotov, like his predecessors, freed himself of the need to discuss it. This omission is surprising, especially when we consider that sexual behavior was a central part of the church's area of competence and concern, as evidenced by the very sources these historians cited.

After the October Revolution, sexual morality continued to be a forbidden subject. To the disappointment of the Bolshevik feminist Aleksandra Kollontai and others of her kind, the Revolution did not usher in a drastic revision of the established "bourgeois" sexual morality. Under Stalin and his successors, the study of sexual behavior in the Russian past remained taboo. Studies of marriage, with emphasis on legal rights and property arrangements, appeared occasionally, but sexuality per se was still not discussed.[29] B. A. Romanov cited rules governing sexual behavior—still mostly in the context of marriage—in his investigation of the church's restriction of folk custom.[30] N. L. Puškareva was a little more forthcoming in an article intended for the popular audience.[31] Marxist historians had to be suspicious of psychoanalytic underpinnings of studies of sexuality in the West, so inconsistent with a materialistic interpretation of history. They also had difficulty perceiving women as a distinct group worthy of study, because women do not represent a single economic class. This attitude was shared by the scholarly communities of postwar Bulgaria and Yugoslavia.

For post-Stalin émigrés, writing about sex represented a statement of emancipation from the constraints of Eastern-bloc socialism. In his book on sexuality in the Soviet Union, Mikhail Stern blames all sexual deviance on the oppression of the Soviet state. In order to condemn modern Soviet society more roundly, he offers a thirteen-page historical sketch in which he characterizes medieval Russia as "stranded in the backwaters of European civilization," "at only one remove from barbarism"—a state of affairs he attributes to the insufficiency of the "civilizing and repressive influences of the Church."[32] Stern's harsh judgment is

28. George P. Fedotov, *The Russian Religious Mind*, vol. 1 (1946; Belmont, Mass., 1975), 238.

29. Ja. N. Ščapov, "Brak i sem'ja v drevnej Rusi," *Voprosy istorii*, 1970, no. 10: 216–219.
30. B. A. Romanov, *Ljudi i nravy drevnej Rusi*, 2d ed. (L., 1966), 166–167, 174–176, 182–212.

31. N. L. Puškareva, "Ni svjaščennika čtjat, ni boga sja bojat . . . ," *Nauka i Religija*, 1986, no. 1: 15–18.

32. Stern, 7–19.

based on slim evidence, the product of hostility rather than research. Even such an unsatisfactory polemical overview of sexuality in the medieval Balkans is lacking.

Scholars in the West were less hampered by semiofficial disapproval of investigations into historical sexuality. But because Eastern European scholars of the Slavic past did not address that subject, their Western counterparts did not think to do so either. Western scholars were also deterred by the lack of available primary sources. When students of women and marriage in the modern period felt obliged to provide background material, they would include a few scant pages based heavily on flawed nineteenth-century histories, folklore, and foreign travelers' reports, with peculiar emphasis on wife-beating.[33] Specialists on the medieval period who turned their attention to the status of women generally preferred to restrict themselves to questions of women's legal rights, economic and political roles, and literary images.[34]

Thus this book fulfills a double purpose. First, it examines sexuality among the medieval Orthodox Slavs for the first time, using sources that have not previously been tapped. Use of theoretical discussions, literary images, canon law, and penitential materials in conjunction with records of actual behavior permits the development of a comprehensive depiction of sexuality in the Slavic Orthodox world. While not primarily comparative, this exposition will note comparisons with Byzantine and Roman Catholic law, in order to place the Slavic experience in the wider European context. Second, I seek to illuminate the relationship between prescriptive teachings and actual sexual behavior. The medieval Slavic cases suggest an interaction between canon law and actual practice. The

33. For the least successful examples of this sort of study, see William M. Mandel, *Soviet Women* (Garden City, NY., 1975), 12–14; Fanina W. Halle, *Woman in Soviet Russia* (London, 1933), 1–20; Bernard I. Mursten, *Love, Sex, and Marriage through the Ages* (New York, 1974), 445–446. Somewhat more effective is Dorothy Atkinson, "Society and the Sexes in the Russian Past," in Atkinson et al., *Women in Russia* (Stanford, 1977), 3–24.

34. See, e.g., the special issue of the journal *Russian History*, 1983, no. 2, devoted to the question of women in medieval Russia; Joan D. Grossman, "Feminine Images in Old Russian Literature and Art," *California Slavic Studies* 11 (1980): 33–70; L. R. Lewitter, "Women, Sainthood, and Marriage in Muscovy," *Journal of Russian Studies* 37 (1979): 3–11; Susanne J. McNally, "From Public Person to Private Prisoner: The Changing Place of Women in Medieval Russia" (Ph.D. diss., SUNY-Binghamton, 1976); two articles in *Recueils de la Société Jean Bodin pour l'histoire comparative des institutions* 12 (1962): Stanislaw Roman, "Le Statut de la femme dans l'Europe orientale (Pologne et Russie) au moyen âge et aux temps modernes," 389–403, and Alexandre Eck, "La Situation juridique de la femme russe au moyen âge," 404–420; Susan Mosher Stuard, "Women in Charter and Statute Law: Medieval Ragusa/Dubrovnik," in Stuard, ed., *Women in Medieval Society* (Philadelphia, 1976), 199–208; Peter Laslett and Marilyn Clarke, "Houseful and Household in an Eighteenth-Century Balkan City: A Tabular Analysis of the Listing of the Serbian Sector of Belgrade in 1733–1734," in Peter Laslett and Richard Wall, eds., *Household and Family in Past Time* (New York, 1972), 375–400; Carsten Goehrke, "Die Witwe im Alten Russland," *Forschungen zur osteuropäischen Geschichte* 38 (1986): 64–96.

church succeeded to a large degree in inculcating its moral values concerning sex, but it did so precisely because these values corresponded so well with societal needs and popular notions of propriety. The medieval Slavic Orthodox system of sexual morality was strong enough and flexible enough to survive centuries of political upheaval and foreign conquest, to leave its mark on modern Slavic culture and society.

Approach

All researchers make assumptions that affect their interpretations of the facts. My first assumption is that sexuality can be examined apart from family structure or the status of women, to which it has traditionally been connected. Marriage is an integral part of the structure of the family, and sexual intercourse plays an important role in the marital relationship. Attitudes toward women and their role in a society are frequently tied up with attitudes toward sexuality, because women differ from men primarily in their functioning in sexual relations and reproduction. But the organization of the family does not rest primarily on sexual interaction. Thus sexuality per se can be considered apart from economic, social, and political activities. Furthermore, it is a bias—not peculiar to modern scholarship—to relate sexuality more to the study of women than to the study of men, who of course are equally involved.

A second set of assumptions concerns the nature of sexuality. Modern Western society has accepted as axiomatic the proposition that sexuality is innate. The medieval Orthodox Slavs rejected this view. They believed that the desire for sex came from outside the human being, and was not part of God's original creation. They saw sexuality as an evil inclination originating with Satan, dangerous to the individual and to society, best kept within strict bounds if it could not be eliminated altogether.

Modern society also considers that sexual feelings naturally go hand in hand with love. There are several corollaries to this presupposition. First, the pleasure that results from sexual activity will vary with the degree of emotional attachment between partners. Sexual activity that involves no affection, as in prostitution, is to be disdained as inferior and bestial. Sexual activity that does involve affection cannot be totally wrong, even if it violates other commitments. These ideas may be traced to the troubadours of the twelfth century. In their conception, incidentally, romantic love did not occur in marriage, which was arranged to advance political goals. The idea that the permanent sexual union of marriage properly results from a permanent emotional bonding developed somewhat later. In the West, romantic love has seven centuries of tradition behind it; is it any wonder that we, like the Lamarckian scientists of the past, have labeled this acquired characteristic as inherent?

The example of the medieval Orthodox Slavs reveals our mistake. Having missed the genesis of romanticism, they denied that love, an emotion of generosity and devotion, could be connected to sexual desire. The medieval Slavs could scarcely conceive that sexual activity might be more fulfilling physically or emotionally with one partner than with another. We see this view expressed in an episode told of the Russian saints Peter and Fevronia. In order to discourage the sinful advances of one of her husband's boyars, Fevronia commanded him to draw a bucket of water from each side of the boat. She then asked him whether the water in the two buckets tasted different. When he said it did not, she made her point: all women are alike sexually, so a man might as well be content with his legal wife.[35]

The psychological and medical sciences have not yet achieved a verdict on the extent to which sexuality is inherent in human biology. Certainly anatomical distinctions are genetic, but the vast variation among individuals in sexual desires and sexual behavior indicates that very little in sexual behavior is instinctive. For the nonce it is sufficient to say that the modern approval of sexual activity between responsible and caring adults would be as alien to medieval Slavic society as their view is to ours.

A third set of assumptions concerns the adoption and enforcement of sexual values. If we eschew the idea of a universal morality ingrained in the makeup of human beings, then sexual values must be acquired. Each society has generally accepted standards of conduct. The norms of sexual conduct are transmitted to each generation through formal teaching and the examples of elders and peers. Involving as it does the intimate behavior of the majority of people, sexuality cannot be regulated according to an alien standard imposed by a few leaders. Nor will rules totally in opposition to other societal needs survive for long. Conversely, rules and customs concerning sexual expression must serve the end of social stability.

At first glance the frequency with which sexual standards were violated seems to contradict this assertion of the general acceptance of the church's sexual ethic.[36] Certainly medieval churchmen constantly de-

---

35. N. K. Gudzij, *Xrestomatija po drevnej russkoj literature XI–XVII vekov* (M., 1962), 239.

36. Daniel H. Kaiser takes this position, arguing that there was "a collision between the traditional, pagan order and the norms of Christianity." The frequency of violations of rules on marriage and pagan observances indicates to Kaiser that "the Church did not wage an especially effective struggle against the traditional order": *The Growth of the Law in Medieval Russia* (Princeton, 1980), pp. 164–170. The prerevolutionary Russian scholar N. M. Gal'kovskij took

cried violations. Transgression of the law, however, is not the same as rejection of its norms. People never observe their society's rules on sexual expression as strictly as the enforcers of those rules think they should. Devotion to moral principles is no protection against breaches of the sexual standard, as the Puritans in New England discovered.[37] No matter how wide the range of permitted sexual behaviors in a society, the limits are continually violated. Sexual misconduct is as common to the human condition as taxation, and as inevitable. The parameters of sexual norms are seen more clearly in the severity of the official and public responses to transgressions than in the frequency of those transgressions.

Deviance helps a society to define the limits of acceptable behavior. Peter Laslett made this point forcefully: "The function of deviance from the viewpoint of the established order is to draw a thick, black line around what is permissible. . . . An effective social rule must be capable of being broken if it is to be effective. Those who defy it do something to confirm its importance, and this may be so even if they are numerous."[38]

John Boswell, too, has perceptively commented on the significance of sexual misconduct: "Deviance in sexual matters in cultures organized by sexually created relationships is much like heresy in theologically dominated societies or political dissent in politically organized communities."[39] In order to define unacceptable behavior, Boswell argues, a clan/tribe society promulgates detailed rules for governing sexual conduct. Adherence to those rules is important. Sexual behavior, which in modern society is generally defined as private, has a public significance in such societies.[40] The confusion engendered by undefined sexual ties in that situation can be as disruptive as conflicting national loyalties in the modern day. Such societies limit legitimate sexual contact to recognized and regulated institutions in order to avoid chaos. Other forms of sexual expression do not cease, of course, but they do not enjoy societal protection. Deviations can be punished with more or less severity, depending on the challenge each represents to social stability.

There are two problems in applying Boswell's insight to the medieval

---

the same view in *Bor'ba Xristianstva s ostatkami jazyčestva v drevnej Rusi*, vol. 1 (Kharkov, 1916), esp. 142–149.

37. Edmund S. Morgan, "The Puritans and Sex," *New England Quarterly* 15 (1942): 591–607.

38. Peter Laslett, *Family Life and Illicit Love in Earlier Generations* (New York, 1977), 102–103.

39. Boswell, 33.

40. In modern societies, life-threatening sexually transmitted diseases, such as the current acquired immune deficiency syndrome (AIDS), may alter the conception of sexual behavior as primarily a private matter.

Slavic Orthodox world. The first problem involves the categorization of medieval Slavic society as structured by familial units rather than by theological identification. At the time that the Slavs adopted Christianity, their society was in the process of evolving from a clan/tribal organization into socially stratified states. Slavic rulers adopted Orthodoxy for their people in part because it provided a pattern for reformulating and codifying the existing unwritten rules of personal conduct, and an institution to regulate it. With the establishment of the church, it might be expected that theological dissent would become the primary focus of concern. Indeed, religious opposition began early in the history of the Slavic Orthodox churches. The Bogomil heresy arose in Bulgaria in the tenth century and spread to Serbia.[41] The Strigolnik heresy posed a similar threat to the authority of the Russian church and state in the thirteenth century.[42] Despite the introduction of the new organizational structures of church and state, medieval Slavic society still depended on familial and quasi-familial bonds. Consequently, rules for sexual behavior continued to be important, as the penitential materials reveal. And it is not accidental that the early heresies challenged the Orthodox Church on sexual matters. The Bogomils made a special point of attacking the institution of marriage.[43] The Strigolniki denied the validity of confession, which was used to enforce conformity in sexual behavior.[44]

The second problem concerns the adoption of a repressive sexual standard by the Orthodox Slavs. Family-based societies are numerous in world history, and their sexual standards are far from uniform. They may share the trait of an elaborate and prominent set of rules on sexual conduct, but they differ considerably in the details of the behavior they permit and outlaw. Many societies with strong family structures encourage and even exalt sexual expression. The Slavs, however, like most of their Germanic and Romance neighbors, adopted a negative view of sexuality.

Explanations for the hostility toward sexuality which characterizes the dominant forms of Christianity in both Eastern and Western Europe center on assumptions about the nature of Christianity and the circumstances of its adoption by European peoples. Medieval Christianity carried a strong strain of sexual asceticism as an inheritance from Neo-

41. On the Bogomils, see Dmitri Obolensky, *The Bogomils* (Cambridge, Eng., 1948).

42. Ann M. Kleimola, "Law and Social Change in Medieval Russia: The Zakon Sudnyj Ljudem as a Case Study," *Oxford Slavonic Papers,* n.s. 9 (1976): 17–27.

43. Henri-Charles Puech and André Vaillant, *Le Traité contre les Bogomiles de Cosmas le prêtre* (Paris, 1945), 262–264. The Orthodox Church did not respond with broad accusations of sexual misconduct against the Bogomils, perhaps because it was sufficiently damning to decry their view of marriage.

44. S. I. Smirnov, *Drevne-russkij duxovnik* (M., 1913), 256–280.

platonic philosophy and the Messianic Judaism of the first century.⁴⁵
Many of the Church Fathers considered physical sensation a distraction
from spiritual awareness. Of all physical sensation, sexual intercourse
was the most dangerous; this was what tempted Adam and Eve to sin
and so led to their expulsion from Eden. Sexual activity, if not eliminated altogether, had to be confined to marriage and to its one divinely
ordained purpose, procreation.⁴⁶ Sexual behavior was closely associated
with morality. Indeed, at times the two were virtually synonymous,
especially for women: rigid adherence to the established standard of
sexual conduct became the touchstone of moral integrity; unchastity
signified immorality of the worst sort.⁴⁷

Given the strength of the antisexual attitude in the mainstream of
Christianity, it would be easy to attribute the heritage of repression to
the church. Modern critics who make Christianity the explanation for
Western sexual morality tend to couch their observations in terms of
blame rather than credit; they invert the judgment of their predecessors,
who lauded Christianity for bringing morality to the heathen. In both
cases, the commentators ascribe to the church a power it could not have.
No system of ethical teachings can reconstruct the sexual standard of a
society by itself, independent of existing mores and societal imperatives.
The Christian sexual standard was not so much imposed from above as
it was inculcated with the dissemination of information about Christian
faith and practice. As often as popular sexual ethics changed to fit with
Christian teachings, the church's regulations on permissible and imper-
missible behavior altered to fit popular mores. Where the norms of the
church fitted badly with local mores, as in Iceland, they fell by the
wayside.⁴⁸ Among European societies, however, that of Iceland was an
exception. As little as sexual asceticism accords with modern tastes, it
had wide appeal in the medieval world.

Furthermore, Christianity is not innately hostile to sexuality. Within
the framework of Christian theology, a multitude of systems of sexual
ethics have been promoted, ranging from a requirement of universal

45. Bullough, 74–76, 159–189. Foucault traced the ascetic strands in Greek philosophy in
vols. 2 and 3 of his *History of Sexuality*. See also Boswell, 120–141, for a discussion of
antisexual tendencies in the late Roman Empire.
46. Brundage, *Law, Sex, and Christian Society*, 152.
47. John Bugge, *Virginitas: An Essay in the History of a Medieval Ideal* (The Hague, 1975);
Bullough, 154–196.
48. Jenny M. Jochens, "The Church and Sexuality in Medieval Iceland," *Journal of Medieval
History* 6 (December 1980): 377–392; Grethe Jacobsen, "Sexual Irregularities in Medieval
Scandinavia," in Brundage and Bullough, 72–85. Jochens describes the efforts of two medieval
bishops, Thorlakr (1176–1193) and Guðmunðr (1201–1237), to alter existing patterns in
sexual behavior. Though Icelanders admired both for their piety and the Althing later sainted
them, their programs of moderate reform in sexual behavior failed to gain any ground.

abstinence to the encouragement of promiscuous indulgence. Most Protestants repudiated celibacy, regarding it as unnecessary and undesirable. For many modern Christians, the physical world reflects the goodness of God's creation and must not be rejected. Sex is blameless: Adam and Eve's sin consisted not in engaging in sex but in disobeying God. Sexual intercourse need not be restricted to procreation, because sexual bonding is in accordance with the divine plan. And while marriage may remain the most appropriate sphere for sexual expression, many churches acquiesce in certain extramarital liaisons. The diversity of Christian sexual standards indicates that the theological tenets of Christianity do not dictate a negative attitude toward sexuality.

It would be a grave mistake to grant the appellation "Christian" only to a single set of norms, adopted and propagated by an official ecclesiastical institution. Numerous churches claim to be the sole correct representation of Christian belief, and they have widely divergent sexual norms. Within the Slavic Orthodox world, there was more than one institutional organization. In different periods there were autocephalous churches in Bulgaria, Russia, and Serbia. Although they agreed on all major tenets of faith and practice, they differed in minor ways. Even within a given church a diversity of opinions can be held—by both clergy and laity—concerning any matter of faith and practice, including sexual matters. While medieval Slavic bishops and abbots may have been well informed about traditions of canon law, priests often shared the belief systems of their uneducated parishioners. The historian who reserves the designation "Christian" or "Orthodox" for the dominant opinion of the hierarchy, labeling opposing views as heterodox, heretical, or pagan, deprives the opponents of their Christian identity. Heretics never consider themselves to be other than true Christians; the most ignorant peasants believe themselves and their customs to be Christian by definition. I use the term "heretical" to refer to a view officially condemned by the established church—that is, the institution that eventually predominated; I do not intend it as a judgment on the validity of either view. The designation "pagan" is restricted to customs or beliefs that unambiguously originated in the pre-Christian religious traditions of the Slavs.

Socialist critics of Christianity as the source of Western hostility toward sex indict its institutional structure more than its theology. The classic Marxist theorists Friedrich Engels and August Bebel regarded both sexual repression and sexual licentiousness as consequences of the exploitive structure of society. The church represented the interests of the ruling class, but the main culprit was the state. The "liberation" of sexuality after the Communist revolution would take the form of hetero-

sexual monogamous unions of variable duration, based on spiritual
love. Aleksandra Kollontai purged this view of its lingering elements of
gender inequality, arguing that socialism would properly provide wom-
en with the hitherto denied opportunity for sexual fulfillment.[49]

It is indisputable that social structures place limits on sexual expression, as they restrain other types of activity, but limitation is not the
same as repression. Complex institutions of power do not necessarily
discourage sexual activity in general; witness the modern United States.
Conversely, many primitive societies with little in the way of political
infrastructure allow little variety in acceptable sexual behavior; witness
ancient Israel. Social stratification dictates different rights, responsibilities, privileges, and limitations for men and women, the differences
depending on rank as well as gender, but it does not in itself dictate that
sexuality be regarded negatively, as ancient India illustrates.[50] A total
absence of social, economic, and political constraint, even if it were
possible, would not necessarily lead to the sexual morality that Engels,
Bebel, and Kollontai envisioned. Romantic love, as we know, is neither
universal nor innate. In the final analysis, the political system, the social
structure, and the economic base influence but do not determine the
final shape of a society's sexual standard.

Feminists less devoted to the idea of revolution have tended to be
more vociferous in their indictment of Christianity as the culprit in
sexual repression. By identifying the Deity as male, by promoting a
patriarchal vision of the universe, by denying women leadership roles,
the church denied the female. Consequently society glorified violence
and celibacy, the "male" characteristics, and deprecated sensuality and
fertility, the "female" characteristics. Sexual repression became inevitable.[51]

The flaws in this view should be obvious. Violence may be traditionally associated more with men than with women and fertility more
with women than with men, but neither is inherently exclusive to one
sex. Women have repeatedly shown themselves capable of brutality, and
men frequently take an active interest in reproduction. Sensuality and
celibacy reflect two ends of a continuum of sexual behavior common to

49. Barbara Evans Clements, *Bolshevik Feminist: The Life of Aleksandra Kollontai* (Bloomington, Ind. 1979), 48–59, 73–74, 226–228.

50. Bullough, 245–274.

51. For an expression of this view, see Mary Daly, *The Church and the Second Sex* (New
York, 1968), esp. chap. 2; Pauline Stafford, *Queens, Concubines, and Dowagers* (London,
1983), esp. 26–27. For this view applied specifically to medieval Russia, see Mary Matossian,
"In the Beginning, God Was a Woman," *Journal of Social History* 6 (Spring 1973): 337–338;
Joanna Hubbs, *Mother Russia: The Feminine Myth in Russian Culture* (Bloomington, Ind.,
1988).

both sexes. The denigration of sexuality by medieval Christianity was nearly as repressive to men as to women. The ideals of conduct were equivalent. And if men were often permitted greater leeway in their violations of the sexual standard, they were deemed just as guilty of sin.

Misogyny is not an essential aspect of Christianity, however prevalent it may have been in its history. Just as Christianity admits of alternative views on sexuality, it admits of a variety of views of the sexual identity of the Divine, the organization of the universe, and women's roles within the institutional structure of the church. Even in the ancient and medieval worlds, the alternative standards of sexual conduct and gender roles did not go entirely unexplored; their failure to predominate cannot be blamed on Christian theology or institutional structure.[52] Furthermore, other religious systems, such as Islam, encourage sexuality while still severely restricting women's autonomy.[53]

Finally, it is a mistake to assume that sexual restraint had no appeal for medieval women. In an era of inequality between the sexes, to promote the sensual was to impose sexually on women, without regard for their needs or wants. In premodern society, heterosexual sex was inseparable from childbearing. The divorcing of sex and reproduction is a phenomenon brought about by modern medicine. Sexual activity may now be enjoyed for the pleasure it brings, without serious concern about pregnancy. The Orthodox Slavs, like other medieval peoples, lacked the technology to prevent unwanted births and to guarantee that women would survive pregnancy. Any sexual activity carried substantial dangers for women, if not for men. In this context, mere physical pleasure might well have seemed too insignificant a reward for the risks sex entailed. By making procreation the sole justification for sexual activity, Christianity taught that the risks of sex should be undertaken only in pursuit of a valued goal. For medieval women, the antisexual aspect of Christianity was more liberating than constrictive.

Other than an awareness of sexuality and a few physiological absolutes, nothing about human sexuality is universal. The method of copulation, the selection of a partner, the psychological mood of the participants, the spiritual implications of their union, and the societal environment and purposes of sexual contact vary among individuals and among cultures. Each society has its written and unwritten rules, its rituals and structures, governing sexual behavior.

52. There are numerous works on the female component of Christianity, many prepared for devotional purposes. For an example of a historical work, see Jean LaPorte, *The Role of Women in Early Christianity* (New York, 1982). On alternatives to homophobia, see Boswell, 6–13, 171–210.

53. Bullough, 205–232; B. F. Musallam, *Sex and Society in Islam: Birth Control before the Nineteenth Century* (New York, 1983).

Sources

The study of sexuality in societies of the past presents difficulties that scholars who focus on the present do not face. Long-dead populations may not be surveyed to find out what they do, how they feel, and what they think proper. Except in the case of relatively recent history, statistical evidence of sexual behavior is exceptionally rare. Very few sources from premodern Slavic Orthodox states provide information on actual sexual conduct. Parish registers in which births, marriages, and deaths were recorded—the bases of many studies of sexuality in the early modern West—do not survive even in scraps, nor are there analogous state documents.[54] Thus a statistical study is not possible.

Records of actual behavior—even nonstatistical ones—are scarce. Chronicles and histories contain some scraps of information, usually about high-ranking individuals. Because such records were composed or at least copied by churchmen, the ecclesiastical viewpoint on sexuality predominates, and historical fact might be rewritten to enhance the moral lesson. Information about sexual exploits tends to be anecdotal and incomplete, but still can indicate the application or nonapplication of legal regulations.

The best source of information on actual behavior consists of the records of ecclesiastical courts. Unfortunately, records of this sort, which have been used to such good advantage in studies of the early modern West, are virtually untapped among the Orthodox Slavs. Other than three volumes from the archiepiscopal courts of northern Russia in the seventeenth century, few cases have been published.[55] Because nearly all issues of sexual behavior came under the purview of the church, the more extensive and better-known secular court records are of little use in this regard. As limited as available court cases are, they demonstrate the application of prescriptive norms to real situations. Furthermore, they tell not only the accusation but often the violator's response to it. The court records depict a society in which laymen are familiar with the general contours of ecclesiastical sexual norms and accept their validity even as they transgress them.

The accounts of eyewitnesses—foreigners who traveled to the Slavic

54. The Moscow Synod of 1666 ordered the keeping of parish records of baptisms and marriages, as well as a current census of parishioners; see *Dejanija moskovskix soborov 1666 i 1667 godov* (M., 1893; The Hague 1970), 39v–41r. This seems to have been the first order of its kind in the Slavic Orthodox world.

55. *Akty xolmogorskoj i ustjužskoj eparxij*, RIB, 12, 14, 25 (SPb., 1890, 1894, 1908). It would be reasonable to assume that many more court records survive, at least in Russia and perhaps among the South Slavs as well. To the best of my knowledge, however, no scholar or archivist has noted their existence.

Orthodox world in the Middle Ages—have gained the most attention in Western studies of popular culture. These travelers witnessed sexual behavior as it occurred, and they asked their informants about rules and standards. At the same time, the foreign travelers saw only limited aspects of the host society; usually they were barred from the most intimate ones. The foreigners brought with them their own conceptions of sexual morality. Consequently, they tended to misunderstand what they saw and to condemn what they did not understand. In the interest of diverting their readers, they accentuated sexual peculiarities; the odd sexual habits of alien peoples are a perennial favorite topic among tourists.[56]

Ethnography provides another sort of eyewitness account of popular culture. The traditions of nineteenth-century peasants were observed at firsthand. Past historians often assumed that the peasantry had preserved ancient custom unchanged through the centuries, and consequently based many of their conclusions about medieval popular life on ethnographic reports. Their assumption was unwarranted. Although peasant cultures tend to be conservative, they are hardly unchanging. The dramatic political, economic, and legal changes of the nineteenth century left their marks on every aspect of peasants' lives, including their marriage customs, sexual behavior, stories, and songs. Consequently, ethnography and folklore cannot provide reliable indications of medieval practices. The traditional epic poetry can be traced more reliably to the Middle Ages, but oral transmission made it susceptible to later interpolations.[57] Folk customs can serve at best only to confirm practices attested to by medieval documents.

Secular sources contribute little information about sexuality, because most matters concerning morality and family came under the authority of the church. In some areas of the law on sexual expression, however, the line between secular and ecclesiastical powers was not firmly drawn. Rape, for example, involved both sexual impropriety, a church matter, and assault, a state concern.[58] Violation of the bonds of marriage

---

56. For a discussion of the observations of foreign travelers, see Hana Hynkova, "Putepisni izvori ot XV i XVI v. za bita i kulturata na Bŭlgarskija narod," *Sbornik za narodni umotvoreni-ja i narodopis* 55 (1976): 145–273; Charles J. Halperin, "Sixteenth-Century Foreign Travel Accounts to Muscovy: A Methodological Excursus," *Sixteenth Century Journal* 6 (October 1975): 89–111.

57. For texts of these epics, see Ju. I. Smirnov and V. G. Smolickij, *Novgorodskie byliny* (M., 1978); N. S. Tixonravov and V. O. Miller, *Russkija byliny: Staroj i novoj zapisi* (1894; The Hague, 1970); Jovan Brkić, *Moral Concepts in Traditional Serbian Epic Poetry* (The Hague, 1961).

58. Ustav of Prince Rostislav of Smolensk, in *DKU*, 144; Beneševič, *Sbornik pamjatnikov po istorii cerkovnogo prava* (Petrograd, 1915), 89, 105. Infanticide became a matter for shared jurisdiction in the sixteenth century. In the west, the Fourth Lateran Council of 1215 made

through illegal divorce had a secular aspect as well as an ecclesiastical one: divorce could disrupt the system of familial alliances. For that reason, some secular codes, such as the Serbian Lekin Zakonik, include provisions on marriage and divorce.[59] Inheritance similarly had secular ramifications, which resulted in the appearance of regulations both in the Pravosud'e metropolič'e and in such secular codes as Russkaja Pravda.[60] Orthodox prelates might call upon secular authorities to enforce unpopular aspects of canon law when church methods failed,[61] but state authorities usually declined to enforce ecclesiastical rulings. Indeed, princes were sometimes the most blatant violators of canon law. Although such powerful rulers as Stefan Dušan of Serbia and Ivan IV of Russia had extensive influence with the church, they did not use it to transfer jurisdiction over sexual matters to secular authorities. Consequently, even secular influences on sexual regulations are expressed in ecclesiastical sources.

The bulk of extant medieval documents related to sexuality are ecclesiastical.[62] Literary texts fit into several broadly defined genres: sermons and instructive lessons, *vitae* of saints and excerpts from the writings of the Church Fathers, didactic tales and stories for entertainment. The sermons and lessons imparted Christian virtues, explaining the sort of conduct that was appropriate to believers. Citations of Scripture and of the writings of the Church Fathers were included in order to add authority. St. John Chrysostom was the favorite Slavic sermonist, although not all the lessons attributed to him were actually his. The *vitae* of the saints provided examples of the way Christians should live. In many cases, literary formulas overshadow historical fact, but that does not reduce their value as a source for medieval Slavic moral standards.[63] On the

---

provision for the church to recruit the power of the state to impose conformity in sexual matters, particularly homosexuality; see Goodich, 51. In seventeenth-century England, the ecclesiastical authorities similarly shared jurisdiction with the secular magistrates in certain matters of sexual misconduct, particularly rape, homosexuality, and bestiality; see Quaife, 41.

59. Stojan Novaković, *Zakonski spomenici srpskix država srednjega veka* (Belgrade, 1912), 98–103.

60. M. N. Tixomirov, "Pravosud'e metropolič'e," in *Arxeografičeskij ežegodnik za 1963 god* (M., 1964), 32–55; "Russkaja Pravda," in *Pamjatniki russkogo prava*, vol. 1 (M., 1953), 117–119.

61. See, e.g., "Episkopskoe poučenie knjaz'jam i vsem pravoslavnym xristianam," in RIB, 6:852–853.

62. Medieval Slavic primary sources have not been heavily published or widely disseminated. No general bibliography exists. Furthermore, published versions intended for devotional rather than scholarly purposes lack the critical apparatus that permits dating and verification of the text. Manuscripts survive in considerable numbers, but they are scattered in libraries and archives over two continents. The existence of microfilm copies has made their contents much more accessible.

63. L. A. Dmitriev made this point in *Žitijnye povesti russkogo severa kak pamjatniki literatury XIII–XVII vv.* (M., 1973), esp. 3–10. Oswald P. Backus, "Evidences of Social

contrary, the more often a formula was repeated, the more sure the historian can be that churchmen were trying to instill in their listeners the value it expressed. The excerpts from the lives of the saints which were read at church services were perhaps of greater importance than the full versions of the *vitae*, for they reached a wider audience. These excerpts, like the didactic tales, were usually written in a lively style, complete with vivid descriptions and direct speech. The authors made no attempt to be realistic. The plot lines were often complex, and elements of the supernatural abounded. Their moral lessons, however, were straightforward. Righteous conduct, generosity, and reverence for ecclesiastical personnel were rewarded; evildoing, disrespect, and immorality resulted in disaster unless one truly repented. Stories intended purely for entertainment were relatively few—or, at least, few survive to this day. They are recognizable by their inversion of the church's precepts: misconduct results in success, while virtue is equated with gullibility.

The Slavic narrative tales often were translations or reworkings of foreign originals. Byzantine ecclesiastical literature was the major source. A few texts, usually didactic tales, entered the Orthodox Slavic literary tradition from Western Europe. Most of these Western borrowings were either very ancient or very recent. Until the schism between the Roman Catholic and Orthodox churches solidified, the Slavs were willing to accept accounts of Western Christians into their corpus of ecclesiastical writings. In the seventeenth century, Western tales again made their way into Orthodox books, cleansed of their overt Catholic teachings if not of their Western European geographical references. The most notable collection of such tales is the *Velikoe Zercalo*, which was widely distributed in Russia.[64] Slavic authors also composed original texts, following Greek models more or less loosely. Frequently clerical writers drew on Byzantine and biblical themes and images in addition to Slavic ones. Originality was not a medieval virtue; whole passages might be borrowed from an earlier text, with neither reference citation nor apology. Or an original work might be attributed to a revered earlier author.

The copyists rarely mentioned whether the pieces they included were translations, retellings of foreign works, or original Slavic compositions. The medieval churchman did not distinguish among them; all were imbued with sanctity, and all could be instructive to Christians, regard-

---

Change in Medieval Russian Religious Literature," in Andrew Blaine, ed., *The Religious World of Russian Culture* (The Hague, 1975), 75–99, attempts to use literary sources for social history, with mixed results.

64. For a history and reprinting of this collection, see O. A. Deržavina, *'Velikoe Zercalo' i ego sud'ba na russkoj počve* (M., 1965).

less of ethnic identity. Distinctively Slavic features become evident in the selection of texts for inclusion in collections, even when each component is of foreign origin. The compilers of miscellanies chose materials that fitted central themes, or those they considered most valuable. The editors of *prologi, mineja,* and other calendars indicated the saints to be accorded special honor by including their *vitae* and prayers in praise of them; others were mentioned only in passing or not at all. Additions, deletions, and "corrections" were frequently made to texts to bring them into line with native perspectives. At the same time, as all ecclesiastical materials were considered to be in some way sanctified, churchmen were reluctant to abandon them totally or to alter them beyond recognition.

Most important for the study of sexuality are law codes, penitential writings, and related materials. Their use as a source of information about sexual behavior is problematical. By their nature, prescriptive texts tell about standards of conduct and established penalties for violations—excellent for learning about ecclesiastically based norms but less informative about popular reactions to them. Even prescriptive texts, however, contain clues about how widely their provisions were accepted.

Of all prescriptive materials, canonical questions and responses best reflect the concerns of the lower clergy and their parishioners. The most famous are the questions of the twelfth-century Novgorodian Kirik to Bishop Nifont, but there are many others, often appearing in compendia without title or attribution. The question-and-answer format is not a literary device used to form a coherent argument in Socratic fashion; each question stands alone, usually unrelated to those that precede and follow. Most of the questions concern pragmatic matters of Orthodox observance, as asked by laymen and their priests. In these inquiries the historian can glimpse the popular conception of Orthodox sexual morality.

The diversity in the manuscript tradition of medieval Slavic prescriptive texts gives further clues about the population's acceptance of sexual norms. In addition to marking changes and selections, the copyist (and later users of the book) made marginal notes to indicate provisions that experience indicated were particularly important. Given the possibilities for alteration, the consistency in the sexual standard of the manuscript tradition assumes more than ordinary significance: it must reflect a consensus among the clergy at all levels, including those who lived and worked among the laity.

As in the case of narrative literature, Slavic churchmen drew heavily on the codes compiled by their Byzantine predecessors. Slavic canonists, like other Orthodox believers, accepted the rulings of the the seven Ecumenical Church councils as binding. They also granted authoritative status to some of the Church Fathers, particularly to St. Basil and St. John the Penitent. The rulings of numerous other Greek hierarchs became known in the Slavic Orthodox community, most often through Slavonic translations of the compilations of Byzantine legal scholars. Selections from Byzantine secular law were also included in Slavic canons. To this corpus were added the codes of native origin and the rulings of local prelates and councils.

The diverse sources of canon law did not always agree, and here native selectivity became decisive. The Slavic copyists who compiled the manuscripts of canon law for use in the local parishes had to decide which of numerous conflicting statements to include. The larger reference books destined for bishops' courts and monastic libraries might well contain a wide variety of opinions, including articles intended for a society structured differently from that of the medieval Slavs. From the perspective of Slavic hierarchs, Byzantine practices were worth knowing, even if they were not directly applicable locally, because of the prestigious place the Greeks held in the earthly hegemony. Parish service books (*trebnici*), intended as practical guides for priests, contained abbreviated codes with few conflicting opinions.[65] Through this selectivity patterns emerge, suggesting dominant and minority traditions in canon law. As in the case of narrative literature, it made little difference to the medieval churchman whether a canon originated in Byzantium or among the Slavs; in either case it could be considered authoritative. From the perspective of the study of social norms, the origin of a rule matters less than its acceptance by the society.

Considerable scholarly effort has been devoted to tracing the transfer of Byzantine canon law to the Slavs and its dispersion in the Slavic world. The results of this research are impressive, although numerous gaps and debatable points remain.[66] The nineteenth-century Russian scholar A. Pavlov was perhaps the most prolific; his works include several that trace the development of the nomocanon, the basic reference

---

65. The Slavic *trebnik* contained the material from the Greek Euchologion relating to perennial services and sacraments. The *služebnik* contained the special services for the year, while the *molitvennik* consisted of a collection of prayers. The distinctions among the types of service books were hazy and the contents varied. Mansvetov, 8–65, discusses the evolution of the *trebnik*.

66. The best survey in English is Kaiser's, esp. chap. 2. Kaiser does not attempt to explore the Serbian and Bulgarian branches of canon law, except insofar as they relate to Russia. The Soviet scholar R. G. Pixoja has worked on the social context of Russian penitential law, but I had access only to the abstract of his dissertation, "Cerkov' v drevnej Rusi (konec X–pervaja polovina XIII v.): Drevnerusskoe pokajannoe pravo kak istoričeskij istočnik" (Sverdlovsk, 1974).

code.[67] V. N. Beneševič, also a noted scholar, published commentaries on Orthodox canon law and the medieval Slavic text of the nomocanon, which he called *kormčaja*.[68] P. Ivan Žužek traced the history of the *kormčaja* as a collection of texts of canon law centering around the nomocanon.[69] The contents of a text called "nomocanon" or "*kormčaja*" were not strictly set. The core of the nomocanon consisted of selections from the codes of the sixth-century Byzantine canonist John Scholasticus. The nomocanon usually contained the decisions of the ecumenical councils, selected rules by patriarchs and other hierarchs, and excerpts from secular law. Texts produced by Slavic authors were frequently appended to the translated Byzantine portion. Three Slavonic versions circulated in the medieval period. The first was probably produced by the Cyrillo-Methodian mission to the Slavs, based on the text in ascendancy in the Greek church at the time. The second, sometimes called the "Nomocanon of Fourteen Titles," attributed falsely to Patriarch Photios of Constantinople, was also translated into Slavonic; it circulated in Russia before the importation of the more accurate Serbian version. This new version, attributed to the Serbian saint Sava, circulated in the Slavic Orthodox world from the early thirteenth century.[70] Manuscripts of the nomocanon may be further distinguished by the presence or absence of lengthy interpretive explanations of the laws.

The nomocanon was not the only collection of Byzantine laws to circulate among the medieval Orthodox Slavs. The Zakon Sudnyj Ljudem, composed of selected articles of Byzantine secular and canon law, has a complicated and debated history. The code was originally formulated either for the western Slavs or for the Bulgarians soon after the adoption of Christianity; there is strong evidence to support the contention that it was followed, at least in part, in the first Bulgarian empire. The only surviving manuscripts of the code are from Russia. It has been published in three redactions, and a competent English translation is available.[71]

Another major Byzantine compilation to enter the Slavic repertoire was the syntagma of Matthew Blastares. First published in Greek in

67. A. Pavlov, *Nomokanon pri Bol'šom Trebnike* (Odessa, 1872; M., 1897); *Pervonačal'nyj slavjano-russkij Nomokanon.*

68. *Kormčaja;* V. N. Beneševič, *Sinagoga v 50 Titulov i drugie juridičeskie sborniki Ioanna Sxolastika* (SPb., 1914).

69. P. Ivan Žužek, *Kormčaja Kniga: Studies on the Chief Code of Russian Canon Law,* Orientalia Christiana Analecta, no. 168 (Rome, 1964).

70. Pavlov, *Pervonačal'nyj slavjano-russkij Nomokanon;* J. Vasica, "Collectio 87(93) Capitulorom dans les nomocanons slaves," *Byzantinoslavica* 20 (1959): 1–8.

71. ZSL-K; ZSL-P; Horace W. Dewey and Ann M. Kleimola, *Zakon Sudnyj Ljudem (Court Law for the People),* Michigan Slavic Materials, no. 9 (Ann Arbor, 1973). The evolution of the text in Russia is discussed in Kleimola, "Law and Social Change."

1335, it appeared in Slavonic in 1347–1348 and received wide distribution in Serbia under Stefan Dušan. It also influenced subsequent compilations. The Serbian scholar Stojan Novaković published a text and commentary of the syntagma, as well as a collection of other sources of medieval Serbian law.[72] Sergej Troickij, a postrevolutionary Russian émigré to Yugoslavia, amended Novaković's contribution on the syntagma.[73]

A considerable number of monuments of canon law produced by Slavic authors have survived and been published. Most are Russian; there are fewer Serbian texts and still fewer Bulgarian ones.[74] The major medieval Russian codes of canon law for the study of sexuality are the so-called Code of Jaroslav of the twelfth century and the decisions of the Stoglav Council of 1551 and of the councils of 1666 and 1667.[75] The fourteenth-century Code of Stefan Dušan carried analogous authority in Serbia; it covers both ecclesiastical and secular matters.[76] The Bulgarian code of equivalent stature, the Sinodik of Tsar Boril, contains little information on sexuality.[77]

The penitential materials provide the historian with information about sexuality in its social context. The numerous Slavic versions of these questions were only loosely based on the Greek originals. A. Almazov published many examples of these questionnaires as an appendix to his study of the rite of private confession.[78] Lists of questions for confession and the associated lists of regulations on penances exhibit an amazing diversity. Regional differences are apparent: South Slavic versions of the questions tend to concentrate on incest, while Russian questions center on the method of sexual intercourse. Even within a recension there is much variation. No two of the texts I have consulted are identical. Apparently the copyist—often the parish priest himself—felt

72. *Sintagmat*; Stojan Novaković, *Zakonski spomenici srpskix država srednjega veka* (Belgrade, 1912).

73. Sergije V. Troicki, *Dopunskie članci vlastareve sintagme*, Srpska akademija nauka, Posebna izdanja, vol. 268; Odeljenje društvenih nauka, vol. 21 (Belgrade, 1956).

74. The publication of these materials is extraordinarily scattered. The major sources for Russian canon law are Beneševič, *Sbornik pamjatnikov po istorii cerkovnago prava* and *Pamjatniki drevne-russkago kanoničeskago prava*, RIB, 6 (SPb., 1908). Novaković's collection *Zakonski spomenici* includes some canon law in addition to secular materials. There is no analogous Bulgarian volume.

75. For Jaroslav's Ustav and other princely charters to the church, see *DKU*; *Stoglav*. The attribution of the code to the eleventh-century grand prince Jaroslav is almost certainly spurious because the code seems to have been developed a century later.

76. The best publication is *Zakonik cara Stefana Dušana* (Belgrade, 1975). There is an English translation with commentary by Malcolm Burr, "The Code of Stephan Dušan," *Slavonic and East European Review* 28 (1949–50): 198–217, 516–539. It is based on Stojan Novaković's publication *Zakonik Stefana Dušana* (Belgrade, 1898).

77. M. G. Popruženko, "Sinodik carja Borila," *Bǔlgarski starini* 8 (1928).

78. A. Almazov, *Tajnaja ispoved' v pravoslavnoj vostočnoj cerkvi* (Odessa, 1894).

free to alter his sources. He emphasized the sins he expected to find among his congregants, and selected rules that coincided with his own ideas of propriety.[79] Despite wide variation among the texts, they display a consistency in purpose. In every version, the majority of questions address matters of sexual sin; except in a few seventeenth-century Russian questionnaires, the priest began the ritual with inquiries about sexual activity. Taken as a whole, the rite of confession emphasized to believers that their righteousness in the eyes of God was determined more by their sexual behavior than by their faith, good intentions, or ethical conduct.

Penitential materials reveal how the church's ideas of sexual righteousness were transmitted to the laity. In the absence of mandatory schooling and even regular church attendance, the sacrament of penance with its emphasis on confession—required of every believer—provided a method for the priest to educate his congregants. By asking penitents about sexual sins, the priest taught them what sorts of sexual activities were prohibited. This aspect of confession was emphasized by a change in the style of Slavic questionnaires in the late sixteenth century. In the earlier penitentials, the questions were positive ("Did you do . . . "); later, they became negative ("Did you not do . . . "). The grammatical construction used indicated the speaker's hope that the action had not been committed. The rite of confession also included a homily by the priest, in order to explain to the penitent what sort of conduct was expected by God and the church.[80] Certain Orthodox clerics recommended a first confession for boys at age fourteen and for girls at age twelve—in other words, just as they began to assume adult responsibilities. Others recommended confession for children as young as eight or ten, hoping to instill respect for the canons at an early age. One tradition lowered the recommended age to seven for girls and nine for boys.[81]

Orthodox clerics shared the concern of their Roman Catholic counterparts that the level of detail in penitential questions would merely inspire in the penitent ideas on new ways to sin. For that reason, occa-

79. Pavlov, *Nomokanon pri Bol'šom Trebnike* (M., 1897), 1–29 and *passim*. Jean-Louis Flandrin discusses the use of penitentials as a source of information about Christianity as the ordinary layman lived it. He also notes that the early medieval emphasis on sexual behavior in the penitentials gradually was abandoned in the West from the twelfth century on. See *Un Temps pour embrasser*, 6–7, 128–136. See also Brundage, *Law, Sex, and Christian Society*, 153.

80. Almazov, 3:255–271, contains a selection of confessional homilies.

81. SANU 123(28), f. 61r; Nikolaj Tixonravov, *Pamjatniki otrečennoj russkoj literatury*, vol. 1 (SPb., 1863), 295; I. I. Sreznevskij, *Svedenija i zametki o maloizvestnyx i neizvestnyx pamjatnikov*, 3 vols. (SPb., 1867), 2:310.

sional texts recommend that the confessor skip sections that were clearly not pertinent to a given individual. Detailed questions about sexual sins, for example, were reserved for adults. Occasional marginal notes tell the confessor not to put a question to members of certain groups. In one manuscript, a marginal note, "Don't ask virgins!" stands next to a question about sexual intercourse after communion.[82] The special penitential questionnaires for children limit inquiries about sexual activities to those they might reasonably have experienced—masturbation, exploration of sexuality with their friends, and rape.[83] In that way the confessor might avoid the risk of instilling evil thoughts in his spiritual children, but he also missed the opportunity to teach them right from wrong. For the most part, Slavic hierarchs advised that confessors ask about all sins, despite any embarrassment the priest or the penitent might feel. Hierarchs feared an unconfessed sin more than a potential one.

For adults, the main purpose of confessing sexual sins was to admit guilt and reaffirm the validity of the sexual standard. They accomplished this purpose by reciting their sins and performing the penance imposed by the priest. Absolution carried the prerequisite of a full confession.[84] While all sins required spiritual care, churchmen had long acknowledged that not all sins were equally grievous. The severity of the penance reflected the seriousness of the offense.

The average priest did not consult the major compendia of canon law in order to determine penances for his parishioners. Instead, he would refer to the abbreviated code attached to the penitential service, termed "nomocanon," like the complete version in the *kormčaja*. The confessional questions in many Russian codes were accompanied by brief notes on recommended penances. The major sources of this penitential version of the nomocanon were the rules of St. Basil and of St. John the Penitent, but they were revised freely and were supplemented by articles taken from other codes.[85] In general, the Slavs preferred the shorter

82. Kiev 191, f. 164r.
83. Almazov, 3:169, 205–206, 256.
84. E.g., Dečani 68, ff. 265v–266r. The most complete study to date of the Slavic tradition of confession is Smirnov, *Drevne-russkij duxovnik*. Smirnov discounts Russian innovation in the regular church (2) but includes a fascinating study of the Strigolnik custom of confessing to the Earth (256–276). See also a tale in Deržavina, chap. 96.
85. S. I. Smirnov published a number of codes of this type, along with other texts of canon law: *Materialy dlja istorii drevnerusskoj pokajannoj discipliny*, Čtenija obščestva istorii i drevnostei rossijskix pri Moskovskom universitete, no. 3 (M., 1912). The code of St. John the Penitent has been published in Greek, Slavonic, and Georgian parallel texts. See N. A. Zaozerskij and A. S. Xaxanov, *Nomokanon Ioanna Postnika v ego redakcijax: Gruzinskoj grečeskoj i slavjanskoj*, Čtenija obščestva istorii i drevnostej rossijskix pri Moskovskom universitete, no. 2 (M., 1903). For connections between the Greek and the Slavonic versions of the penitential nomocanon, see Pavlov, *Nomokanon pri Bol'šom Trebnike*, and N. Suvorov, "Verojatnyj sostav drevnejšago ispovednago i pokajannago ustava v vostočnoj cerkvi," *Vizantijskij vremennik* 8, nos. 3–4 (1901): 357–434.

penances of the code of St. John to the recommendations of St. Basil. Texts that combine the two codes first cite St. Basil, then follow his recommendation by the phrase "but we say . . . ," indicating preference for the rules of St. John. Texts that recommend only the lower penances are quite common; in fact, those sets of penitential questions accompanied by recommendations for penances always were based on the rules of St. John rather than on those of St. Basil.[86] Yet, Slavic churchmen did not feel comfortable simply dismissing the venerable St. Basil's instructions and imposing on sinners substantially lower penances.[87] They justified the reduced penances on the grounds that they would be accompanied by fasts and prayers, in addition to exclusion from communion—although these provisions were also implicit in the rules of St. Basil.

Penances usually consisted of some combination of exclusion from communion, prohibition of full participation in services and entry into the church building, fasts, and prayers accompanied by prostrations. The structure of penances varied. Penitents could be barred from communion but suffer no other disability. Or they could be instructed to fast for a period. The usual penitential fast consisted of abstention from meat and milk products (called a "dry" fast) on Mondays, Wednesdays, and Fridays. The usual requirements for penitential prayer consisted of recitation two or three times daily of the Fiftieth Psalm, the Lord's Prayer, and prayers for mercy accompanied by prostrations in the number the confessor directed. Persons who could not fulfill the indicated fasts or prayers because of health or employment could substitute other penances.[88]

The penitent could earn a substantial decrease in the length of the

---

86. Priests who needed to use a code with only the penances according to St. Basil could consult instructions for converting them to those of St. John:

St. Basil	St. John
20 years	4 years fast, 300 prostrations
15 years	3 years fast, 250 prostrations
10 years	2 years fast, 200 prostrations
7 years	1 year + 2 months fast, 150 prostrations
6 years	1 year fast, 100 prostrations
4 years	1 year exclusion, 3 months fast
3 years	1 year exclusion, 2 months fast
2 years	1/2 year exclusion, 2 months fast
1 year	1 month fast, 8 prostrations

(From Hil. 304, ff. 115v–119v.; SANU 123[28], ff. 9v–10r). In fact, the formula for converting penances was not followed regularly. Slavic copyists substituted higher or lower penances to suit the native standard of behavior, sometimes attributing them to St. John the Penitent. In one manuscript tradition, a mistake was made, and this alternative penitential code was attributed to the more famous St. John Chrysostom; see BNL 246(103), f. 154r.

87. See, e.g., the question raised about the validity of using St. John's code, in Peć 77, f. 253r.

88. Suvorov, 383–385.

penance by undertaking additional pious observances: extra fasting, perhaps adding a day of abstinence to those required or refraining from consuming meat, cheese, eggs, butter, fish, wine, or spirits on all week-days. Additional recitations of prayers with accompanying prostrations also served to demonstrate contrition, and could earn the penitent a shortened term. Charity to the poor and regular attendance at the liturgy could also mitigate the length of a penance. A year of exclusion from communion could be replaced by attendance at the liturgy thirty times; a year of fasting could be replaced by 150 masses. Fifteen readings of the Psalter served as the equivalent of a year of penance. The wealthy had the option of fulfilling their penances through donations: ninety *nogaty* or sixty dinars substituted for a year of penance.[89] The penitent could also earn a significant reduction in his penance by taking monastic vows, although that was an extreme step.[90] Ultimately, each year of the original penance could be reduced to a month of fasting, prayer, and charity. A truly contrite sinner had the option of rapidly restoring himself to full participation in the church.

While the penitential codes recommended certain penances, in fact the priest enjoyed a great deal of leeway in selecting the length and stringency of penances. Priests were authorized to take individual limitations and capabilities into consideration when assigning penances. For example, peasants, who engaged in hard physical labor, were not assigned the same strict fasts as persons in the upper classes.[91] A pregnant woman could not be directed to kneel, perform prostrations, or undergo stringent fasts, lest she miscarry her unborn child.[92] In matters of sexual sin, penances were often lower for "young" people—those under the age of thirty—than for older persons, who were expected to show restraint.[93] A distinction was made between a person who committed a sexual sin only once and a persistent offender, especially if the sin was not viewed as a serious one.[94] The confessor was directed to consider other extenuating circumstances, such as constraint because of fear, force, or poverty, in determining the penance.[95] The penance might also be reduced if

89. Smirnov, *Materialy*, 157–159.
90. Kiev 127: 242–244; Smirnov, 157–159. It is difficult to determine the relative value of money in the medieval period, but it is clear that these amounts would be substantial though not impossibly great for a peasant and of minimal importance to a wealthy merchant or aristocrat.
91. "Poučenie arxiepiskopa Ilji," art. 18, in RIB, 6:364–366.
92. "Poučenie arxiepiskopa Ilji," art. 16, in RIB, 6:363–364.
93. Sinai 17(17), f. 171r; Hil. 301, ff. 124v–125r; *Izbornik 1076 goda* (M., 1965), 591–592. The *Izbornik* was a Russian copy of a Bulgarian collection of the previous century.
94. Sinai 17(17), f. 171v; Hil. 378, ff. 66v–67r.
95. Rila 1/20(48), ff. 144v–145r, 185v–186r.

the penitent sinned unknowingly—if, as one text put it, "he is not wise, that is to say, illiterate."[96]

When circumstances dictated, the priest could reduce the penance for a sincerely repentant sinner to a very short period, regardless of the seriousness of the offense. A miracle attributed to the Hilandar icon of the Virgin provides a case in point. The heroine of the tale had committed two of the most grievous sins in the nomocanon: incest with her son and murder of the infant who resulted from this illicit affair. A demon in the form of a self-righteous monk accused her publicly of these crimes. On the night before her trial, she confessed her guilt to her priest. Seeing her sincere contrition, he assigned her a penance of only that single night of prayer and fasting. When she faced her accuser the next morning, the Virgin miraculously appeared and silenced him, saving the woman public humiliation.[97]

Regardless of extenuating circumstances, however, the sinner still had to undergo some sort of penance. The healing of the ailing soul required some overt form of contrition, and the community had to be protected from the deleterious effects of the misdeed. In spiritual terms, sinners had "given the human race over to Satan,"[98] regardless of their underlying motivation. In practical terms, the community had to be reassured that violations of its norms did not go unpunished.

The penitential materials speak to the degree to which the laity internalized the church's dicta about sex: the effectiveness of confession and penance required cooperation between individual and community.[99] The enforcement of sexual standards depended largely on the willingness of the parish priest to inquire, the sinner to confess, and the community to report suspected violations.

If the system was to work, priests had to be convinced of their obligation to insist that their parishioners account for their sexual activity. Priests were warned not to refrain from asking probing personal questions out of embarrassment, and to constrain their parishioners to make a complete confession. And if the priest should hear of an unconfessed sin, it became his duty to bring the sinner to repentance. Canon law

96. SANU 124(29), f. 56v. On literacy in medieval Russia, see Simon Franklin, "Literacy and Documentation in Early Medieval Russia," *Speculum* 60, no. 1 (1985): 1–38, and my article "Novgorod Birchbark Documents: The Evidence for Literacy in Medieval Russia," in *Medieval Archaeology*, ed. Charles Redman (Binghamton, N.Y., 1989), 127–137. I know of no discussion of literacy in the medieval Balkans.

97. BNL 740(168), ff. 102r–105r.

98. Peć 77, ff. 204r–205v.

99. Smirnov, *Drevne-russkij duxovnik*. On the development of private confession as a Christian sacrament, see Tentler, *Sin and Confession*, 1–89 and 223. Tentler notes that sexual behavior was not a major concern of Roman Catholic confessors in the period of his study.

forbade the sacraments to a known fornicator or adulterer. If a priest served communion to such a person, he, not the violator, shouldered the burden of sin.[100] Similarly, priests were forbidden to perform Christian burial for persons who died while committing major sins, including brigandage and adultery.[101] Because of the role confession played in the maintenance of discipline, a priest who neglected to demand confessions of his parishioners endangered the social order and was subject to stern ecclesiastical penalties.[102]

The use of confession and penance to enforce sexual standards implies general cooperation on the part of the laity. However, the system also contained methods for dealing with the recalcitrant. Persons who failed to confess were denied participation in the religious life of the community. Confession was an absolute prerequisite for access to communion. It was required of believers once a year, before Easter, and was expected at least four times a year, during the major fasts. If a sinner made a confession but refused to fulfill the penance, the confessor could increase its length and severity. Failure to obey the spiritual father was equated with disobedience to the Scriptures and disdain for God's judgment.[103] The ultimate penalty was excommunication—exclusion from the rites of the church and ostracism by society.

Thus it was the community, more than the priest and the church, that ultimately constrained the individual to acknowledge the validity of the sexual standard. The church fostered a sense of mutual responsibility, which reverberated strongly in a society accustomed to bonds of joint surety (*poruka*).[104] A sermon attributed to St. John Chrysostom urged the faithful not to be shy about confronting sinners: "If you see your friend fornicating, say to him, 'This is an evil thing you are doing.' Do not be ashamed and do not blush, for that thing is evil. . . . This is friendship, for brother to help brother, so that the city will be firm. It is not eating and drinking together that makes friends; brigands and murderers do that, too."[105] Privacy, even in matters of sexual behavior, was a concept alien to medieval Slavic society, as it was to the medieval and early modern West.[106] For the welfare of the community and all its

---

100. Voprosy Ilji, art. 1, in RIB, 6:57–58.

101. Hil. 302, f. 15v. See the forthcoming works of Christine Worobec on Russian and Ukrainian peasant shaming procedures in the nineteenth century.

102. The traditional rules on confession were enshrined in the decisions of the Moscow Council of 1666, *Dejanija moskovskix soborov*, 42v.

103. Smirnov, *Drevne-russkij duxovnik*, 42–45.

104. On the medieval Russian system of joint surety, see Horace W. Dewey and Ann M. Kleimola, "Suretyship and Collective Responsibility in Pre-Petrine Russia," *Jahrbücher für Geschichte Osteuropas* 18 (1970): 337–354.

105. Hil. 302, ff. 94v–95r.

106. Quaife makes this point (16) about seventeenth-century England.

members, each person had the responsibility of overseeing the conduct of his fellows.

The Slavs developed a negative view of sexuality in theory and a broad system of constraints on its manifestations in practice. Given their dependence on cooperation and community support, standards of sexual behavior could not have been imposed in the face of massive popular opposition. So the church's rules must have been acceptable to the lay community.[107] Once accepted, this approach to sexual matters became self-perpetuating and extraordinarily tenacious. It had its own internal logic, and its ramifications extended far beyond the domain of intimate relations. Orthodox theology endowed the existing standard of sexual conduct with the authority of God, which could outweigh even practical considerations. Most of the constraints, however, had an obvious social utility, establishing legitimate expectations and promoting stability in the family and the community.

107. Ingram arrives at a similar conclusion in regard to early modern England; see 30–33, 167, 280–281.

CHAPTER I

The Ecclesiastical
Image of Sexuality

T he Orthodox Slavs inherited an elaborate cosmology
from their Byzantine teachers. In the eight centuries between the Crucifixion and the mission to the Slavs, the
Greek church had developed answers to the mysteries of
the human condition, including human sexuality. A wealth of *vitae*,
tales, sermons, prayers, and responses promoted a view of sexuality as
something alien to Christian life—a manifestation of the imperfection of
the world.

The first source of information for Orthodox believers was Scripture,
but in those pre-Protestant days there was no imperative to locate and
explain every biblical reference. Christianity developed in the milieu of
other belief systems, which shaped and challenged its concepts. The
official Byzantine attitude toward sexuality was influenced by Neoplatonic asceticism, institutionalized in the lives and teachings of the
early desert fathers, and by dualistic heresies, which challenged the Byzantine church to match their otherworldliness.

Neoplatonic philosophy emphasized the incongruity between the spiritual and the physical, in the universe as a whole and in the human
individual. The weakness of men's physical nature limited their ability to
achieve fulfillment of the spirit. Women's reproductive function tied
them more intimately to the physical world and made them even less
capable of spiritual growth. Sexual contact involved indulgence of the
physical side of human nature to the exclusion of the spiritual. Gnosti-
cism and its Manichean stepchild concurred with the Neoplatonic dichotomy between the physical and the spiritual and its denigration of
the spiritual capacity of women. Gnostic theology held that the physical
world was evil—according to some sects, the creation of Satan. Evil
entered the world through woman's initiation into sexual knowledge.

Most sects eschewed bodily pleasures of any sort; sexual activity, as the original sin, was the most pernicious.[1]

The mainstream Orthodox Church ultimately rejected the Gnostic and Manichean belief in the wickedness of the physical world and affirmed that it was God's creation, and thus by nature good, however corrupted it might have become. But Orthodox theologians retained the belief that men's physical nature interfered with their attainment of spiritual salvation. They also retained a strong belief that women were more flawed and less spiritual than men. Sexuality, according to Gregory of Nyssa, one of the most revered fathers of the Orthodox Church, was antithetical to the original state of human nature. The great St. John Chrysostom echoed this sentiment; it was through the Devil's seduction of Eve that the perfection of creation was destroyed.[2] The logical consequence of this point of view should have been an overt condemnation of sexual activity. Indeed, Manichean heretics generally espoused such a view—but the Orthodox did not. They embraced a more moderate position: while virginity was admirable, sexual activity in marriage was a tolerable alternative, given the sinful state of the world.

By the time of the mission to the Slavs, Orthodox attitudes toward sexuality were already established. In the Slavic world they had to vie with two other systems: the established Slavic paganism and the radical Bogomil heresy.

Slavic Paganism

It should be remembered that Christianity arrived fairly late in the Slavic world. The adoption of Orthodoxy in Bulgaria and Russia was based blatantly on political imperatives; in all three Slavic Orthodox countries, it was the rulers who decided to promote the new faith. The level of knowledge about Orthodoxy outside the urban centers remained low for several centuries; beneath a veneer of Christian beliefs and terms, pagan practices continued. In addition, the Slavic Orthodox states included a substantial non-Slavic and non-Christian population: Albanians in Serbia, Cumans in Bulgaria, Vlahs in both, and Finnic and

---

1. Bullough, *Sexual Variance*, 150–167, 170–172, 182–185; Brundage, *Law, Sex, and Christian Society*, 12–49, 80–87; John T. Noonan, Jr., *Contraception: A History of Its Treatment by the Catholic Theologians and Canonists*, 2d ed. (Cambridge, Mass., 1986), 56–72.
2. Bugge, 7–20, 23. Augustine disagreed with this interpretation of Scripture, arguing that Adam and Eve were created as sexual beings, but their sexuality was pure and untainted by passion. See also Makowski, 100. In general, Roman Catholic canon law conceded that sexuality was normal and natural, but accorded it no intrinsic positive value. See Brundage, "Carnal Delight," 363–364.

Turkic peoples in Russia. These peoples clung to their pagan leaders (termed "sorcerers" by Orthodox clerics) and provided continuing support for non-Christian customs. The church could not prevent interaction between believers and the unbaptized, especially when the Orthodox rulers made alliances with them. Furthermore, no clear lines were drawn between pagans and Christians. The bulk of the Slavic population readily accepted a Christian identity. Because they were Christians, their traditions and customs—whatever their origin—had to be Christian by definition.

Pre-Christian Slavic sexual mores are difficult to determine, as virtually all sources of information are of later Christian origin. Such reports deserve a skeptical reading, because they obviously owe much to the motifs of the didactic literature, which connects paganism with sexual license. Most scholars of medieval Slavic marriage customs have made the mistake of accepting the medieval clerics' views uncritically, believing them to be an accurate portrayal of pre-Christian sexual morality rather than part of a diatribe on the sinful state of paganism. Pre-Revolutionary commentators generally shared the medieval opinion of pagan sexual morality, including the belief that paganism was primarily female.[3] At least two feminist scholars of recent years similarly accepted the medieval description of pre-Christian sexual customs, but praised them as a glorification of the female and the sensual. Because female deities had a prominent place in the pantheon (it was argued), Russian paganism was a more "organic" religion than Christianity, one that reflected the rhythm of the seasons and the movement of sun and moon, which was incorporated in women's bodies. It was assumed, more than proven, that this religious system bestowed upon women equal or superior status.[4]

In fact, Slavic paganism was neither so licentious nor so liberated. Patriarchal monogamy and exogamy were the rule at the time Christianity appeared on the scene. Wedding customs then as in the nineteenth century reflected much earlier conjugal structures—endogamy, communal marriage, and bride abduction—but these structures were already little more than ceremonial remnants. Marriage was a socially recognized institution, and entrance into it was marked by public celebration and the transfer of property. There is no evidence that young women—or young men—enjoyed freedom of choice in selecting a spouse.

The case of the early Russian princess Rogneda is often invoked in

---

3. See, e.g., S. Smirnov, "Baby bogomerzkija," in *Sbornik statej posvjaščennyx Vasiliju Osipoviču Ključevskomu* (M., 1909), 217–243.
4. Matossian, 325–343; Hubbs, 12–22, 35.

support of the view of marital choice. According to the legend recounted in the Primary Chronicle, Prince Vladimir approached Rogneda's father, Rogvolod, to propose a marriage with his daughter. When Rogvolod asked his daughter for her consent to the match, she refused, casting aspersions on Vladimir's ancestry. Vladimir later disrupted her wedding to his half-brother Jaropolk, murdered Rogvolod, and abducted and raped Rogneda. The medieval narrator fully approved of Vladimir's actions. Far from demonstrating approval of individual choice of a spouse, this tale points out the impropriety of a young woman's opposition to the will of her parents and of a powerful suitor. Norse custom demanded that parents ask their daughter's consent to a proposed marriage; custom also dictated that the daughter respond by deferring to their wishes. The names Rogneda (Ragnheid) and Rogvolod (Ragnvald) are Scandinavian; thus the entire legend may be no more than a transplanted Norse myth.

Beliefs about the power of female virginity are evidenced by myths of *vily* and *rusalki*, maidens who died as virgins and then populated forests and rivers in the form of spirits who lured men to their deaths. Maidenly virginity may have been powerful, but this strength was meant to be released and used, not preserved intact. Among the pre-Christian Slavs, marriage seems to have been well-nigh universal. The pre-Christian custom of presenting material evidence of the bride's virginity after the wedding night was preserved in peasant marriage celebrations into the nineteenth century. Incest within the family living as a unit was taboo, and there is considerable evidence for the existence of the *zadruga*, or joint extended family. Although some members of the elite practiced polygamy, it is doubtful that the average farmer could afford the luxury of multiple wives.

Certain Slavic pagan rites involved sex, particularly as part of the worship of *vily*, the thunder god Perun, the god Xors, the household goddess Mokoš, and fertility deities.[5] The pagan pantheon included several levels of fertility deities. Newest and most prominent—at least in Russia—were Rod and his multiple consorts, called Rožanicy. As his name suggests, Rod personified the eternity of the clan, whose perpetuation depended on reproduction. Phallus-shaped idols representing Rod and other male fertility deities decorated pre-Christian homes. Celebrations of Rod and Rožanicy were partially subsumed in holidays in honor of the Virgin Mary, in particular the Nativity of the Virgin, on Septem-

---

5. Smirnov, "Baby bogomerzskija," 224. The most complete examinations of Slavic paganism are in B. A. Rybakov's *Jazyčestvo drevnyx slavjan* (M., 1981) and *Jazyčestvo drevnej Rusi* (M., 1987). These works contain a wealth of information, but the author's interpretations are often open to dispute.

ber 8. The celebration included a feast with foods representing fruitful-
ness: bread, cheese, and honey.[6] The connection between the Virgin and
the pagan gods seems to have been their miraculous fertility. The deity
Lado represented an earlier stratum of belief. The vocative form of the
name leaves Lado's gender indeterminate; in surviving references, modi-
fying adjectives are found in both male and female forms. Celebrations
of Lado coincided with the summer solstice and the Orthodox veneration of the Nativity of John the Baptist; the resulting hybrid was
the holiday of Ivan Kupalo or Rusalia. Observance included bonfires,
mixed-sex bathing, dancing, and ritual sex. The central theme of the
holiday was the rebirth of light and the resurrection of latent fertility.[7]
Still older than Lado was the cult of the Moist Mother Earth, the promoter of fertility in crops, livestock, and humans. Both men and women
took part in rituals intended to help them share in the Earth's fertility.
Men might pantomime sexual intercourse with the Earth, while married
women laid themselves prone on the ground.[8] The Earth seems not to
have been personified in the period immediately before Christianization,
but veneration of the Earth may have been a remnant of the prehistoric
cult of the Great Mother Goddess. Thus the fertility deities were both
male and female; so were the participants in the rituals to honor them.

Numerous clerics described the pagan rituals that survived into their
time, emphasizing the drinking, dancing, and other licentious practices
associated with the celebrations. Despite their inflammatory language, it
is possible to reconstruct a core of truth concerning the nature of these
pagan celebrations. The purpose of the ritual sex was generative; the
sympathetic magic of relations between a man and a woman guaranteed
the fertility of nature.[9] Monastic commentators viewed ritual sex as

6. Voprosy Kirika, art. 33, in RIB, 6:31; Rybakov, *Jazyčestvo drevnyx slavjan*, 468–469;
Rybakov, *Jazyčestvo drevnej Rusi*, 234–236, 245–247; Gal'kovskij, 2:43, 86–89, 93–94,
296–297. Rybakov attempts to distinguish between rituals directed toward Rod and those
associated with Rožanicy. Although his argument that these deities had separate origins is
convincing, Russian paganism almost always paired them. Hobbs (15) argues unconvincingly
that the god Rod never existed in Slavic paganism but was created by the Orthodox Church to
provide patriarchal deities for the Slavic family.

7. *Stoglav*, Quest. 24, 141; Popruženko, art. 42, 44; Gal'kovskij, 2:296–297, 303–304;
Dubakin, 52–55; Rybakov, *Jazyčestvo drevnyx slavjan*, 285–294, 314–317, 376–378;
Rybakov, *Jazyčestvo drevnej Rusi*, 158–159, 234, 662–663. Rybakov believes that·Lado was
exclusively a female deity, but the example he cites in Lithuanian uses masculine forms.

8. Almazov, 3:151, 279.

9. See excerpts from a sixteenth-century Serbian manuscript published by Stojan Novaković,
"Apokrifi kijevskoga rukopisa," *Starine* 16 (1884): 94; V. G. Družinin, *Neskol'ko neizvestnyx
literaturnyx pamjatnikov iz sbornika XVI-go veka*, Letopis' zanjatij imperatorskoj arxeografičeskoj kommissii za 1908 god (SPb., 1909), 82; Dimitar Angelov, "Man through the
Middle Ages of Bulgaria," *Bulgarian Historical Review* 10, no. 2 (1982): 79–80. Angelov cites
the complaints of Kliment Oxridski and Patriarch Evtimij about pagan festivals.

wild, orgiastic, and scandalous, but when religious observances included sexual rites, they were usually carefully structured and directed by the officiating priests. When sexual activity was given a cosmic significance, individual preference and pleasure became inconsequential. Ritual sex was hardly synonymous with freedom of sexual expression.

Byzantine writings predisposed Slavic clerics to relate non-Christian religion and sexual impropriety. The Slavic version of the writings of Efrem Sirin read: "Woe to the profligate and the drunkards with him; woe to adulterers and witches."[10] A tale from the Bulgarian patristics described the interrelationship of paganism, sexual misconduct, and the Devil. It told of a monk whom the Devil led into illicit sex with a woman relative. When he later went to confess his sin to a second monk, the latter responded that he already knew of it. The confessor had taken shelter from a storm in a pagan temple, and there heard the demons gloating over their betrayal of the holy man.[11]

Medieval Slavic ecclesiastical writers could not believe that their pagan forebears adhered to Christian sexual standards; at that time, they served the Devil and had no knowledge of Christian propriety. Indeed, churchmen attributed to them all manner of sexual violation.[12] Because pagans did not practice the Christian sacrament of marriage—the one limitation on unbridled sexuality[13]—it was assumed that they yielded fully to demonic temptation. The author of the eleventh-century Russian Primary Chronicle ascribed polygamy and incest to many of the pagan East Slavic tribes.

These Slavic tribes preserved their own customs, the law of their forefathers, and their traditions, each observing its own usages. For the Polyanians retained the mild and peaceful customs of their ancestors, and showed respect for their daughters-in-law and their sisters, as well as for their mothers and fathers. For their mothers-in-law and their brothers-in-law they also entertained great reverence. They observed a fixed custom, under which the groom's brother did not fetch the bride, but she was brought to the bridegroom in the evening, and on the next morning her dowry was turned over.

The Derevlians, on the other hand, existed in bestial fashion, and lived

10. Sreznevskij, 1:43, based on a fifteenth-century Volhynian manuscript.

11. Svetlina Nikolova, *Pateričnite razkazi v bŭlgarskata srednovekovna literatura* (Sofia, 1980), 167–168.

12. *Pamjatniki drevnerusskoj cerkovno-učitel'noj literatury*, vyp. 3 (SPb., 1897) 39, 239.

13. Certain Orthodox thinkers acknowledged a second limitation on sexuality, circumcision as practiced by the Jews. See the *vita* of Constantine the Philosopher in Marvin Kantor, *Medieval Slavic Lives of Saints and Princes* (Ann Arbor, 1983), 56. Numerous medieval scholars, including the Jewish philosopher and physician Maimonides, believed that circumcision reduced sexual desire.

like cattle. They killed one another, ate every impure thing, and there was no marriage among them, but instead they seized upon maidens by capture. The Radimichians, the Vyatichians, and the Severians had the same customs. . . . There were no marriages among them, but simply festivals among the villages. When the people gathered together for games, for dancing, and for all other devilish amusements, the men on these occasions carried off wives for themselves, and each took any woman with whom he had arrived at an understanding. In fact, they even had two or three wives apiece.[14]

The author's disdain for the sexual customs of the pre-Christian Slavs does not come as a surprise; accusations of sexual immorality among pagans were a stock in trade of the Orthodox polemicist. Marriage in the Christian form obviously did not exist; pagan festivals, with their dancing, drinking, and ritual sex obviously did. The Pol'jane, who were the direct ancestors of the Kievan audience, alone escaped condemnation. To them he attributed the "proper" sexual customs of his time, which he labeled as "Christian." These customs included a patriarchal family structure, arranged marriage, and prohibition of sexual relations within the *zadruga*—the mirror image of the other tribes' violations. In exempting the Pol'jane from his tirade against the pagans, the author was probably motivated by a desire not to cast aspersions on his listeners' direct ancestors. But for the most part, sexual impropriety was part of paganism—a state the Slavs had mercifully left behind them.

Slavic Orthodox writers did not distinguish between witchcraft, an inverted and transmuted form of Christianity, and the paganism surviving from the pre-Christian era. From the perspective of the church, both involved worship of the Devil. Demonic cults, naturally, featured the Devil's own favorite tool for human destruction, sexuality.

Evil women, condemned for their speech and overt sexuality, were also pagan; the adjective most often applied to them, *zlojazyčny*, meant both "evil-tongued" and "evil and pagan." A sermon attributed to St. John Chrysostom warned that men who get involved with lustful women "not only receive eternal and deathless death, but perish from the evilest evil"—sorcery and witchcraft.[15] All pagan observances were condemned; when they involved sex, they were that much worse.

Nor could the clergy be counted upon to refrain from participation in pagan rituals. The 1274 church council at Vladimir in Russia accused

14. Samuel H. Cross, ed. and trans., *The Russian Primary Chronicle* (Cambridge, Mass., n.d.), 56. See also "Slovo nekoego xristoljubca," in *Pamjatniki drevnerusskoj cerkovno-učitel'noj literatury*, vyp. 3, 225.

15. GPB FnI44, f. 133r–v.

certain priests of engaging in "sorcery." Metropolitan Ioann II of Russia protested strongly against the holding of pagan feasts in monasteries.[16] Such violations could occur because the Slavic clergy often shared the popular perception of their traditional customs as Christian.

In short, the sexual standard of the pagan Slavs did not consist of unbridled indulgence in the sensual, despite the complaints of Orthodox clerics. Traditional Slavic society recognized the institution of marriage. Relics of capture rituals, with their illusion of free choice of spouses, were giving way to rites formally transferring the bride and her property from her parents' family to her husband's. Polygamy was permitted but was not widespread. Divorce and remarriage occurred; there is no evidence concerning any constraints that might have operated. Religious rituals in which sex played a part seem to have been among the popular observances, but these practices did not imply general freedom in sexual expression.

Heresy

The second alternative to Orthodoxy, heresy, emerged among the South Slavs almost from the moment of the adoption of Christianity. The Bogomil heretics of the Balkans adopted a dualistic theology akin to the versions the Orthodox Church had already condemned. They believed the world and humankind to be the creations not of God but of his elder son, Satan. Therefore, everything in the material world except the human soul was evil. Although Bogomil theology seems to have had little to commend it to the masses of the population, it actually gained considerable support. First, by labeling the world as the realm of the Devil, the Bogomils denied the legitimacy of secular and ecclesiastical authorities. Thus Bogomilism provided a justification for civil disobedience, such as refusal to pay taxes and to join the army. Second, Bogomil leaders gained notoriety for their feats of self-denial among a population already tutored to regard such activities as signs of saintliness. They observed an uncompromising asceticism, consuming no meat or alcoholic spirits and denying the propriety of sexual activity.[17]

Orthodox polemicists objected primarily to the heretical belief that true Christianity forbade marriage. Certain of the heretics in fact did discourage marriage, even more strongly than Orthodoxy. The Bogomils taught that it was Satan, not Jesus, who authorized the drink-

16. "Opredelenie vladimirskogo sobora," in RIB, 6:90–99; "Kanoničeskie otvety Ioanna II," art. 29, in ibid., 16–17.

17. The most complete study of the Bogomils is Obolensky's.

ing of wine, the eating of meat, and the taking of wives. Thus married persons could rightly be described as servants of Mammon.[18] The Bogomils required men to separate from their wives when they entered the sect.[19] Orthodox writers responded by quoting the authorizations of marriage in the New Testament (I Tim. 4:1–5) and the revered St. John Chrysostom: "Many in the desert and the mountains, thinking about worldly things, have perished, and many in the cities, living with wives, have been saved." Even if the heretics practiced the Orthodox virtue of celibacy, they charged, it was not in the proper monastic form. Indeed, according to Kozma Presviter, the heretics even took their wives with them on pilgrimages, negating the proper distinction between married and monastic life.[20]

Other heretics similarly were criticized for disparaging marriage. One of the major accusations the Slavic Orthodox hierarchs directed against the Roman Catholics concerned their insistence on clerical celibacy. Not only was priestly celibacy unnecessary, the Orthodox argued, but it represented an impossible standard; Latin priests ended up consorting with prostitutes instead of marrying lawfully. Furthermore, the Latins tolerated improper marriages, they charged, including multiple remarriages and unions between spiritual kin.[21] Old Believer heretics in seventeenth-century Russia prohibited marriage, believing that the world had fallen under the sway of the Antichrist.[22]

There were hints about other improper practices among heretics, but Slavic Orthodox churchmen were reluctant to launch wholesale accusations of sexual licentiousness.[23] For example, the Byzantine patriarch Kalistos, in his life of St. Feodosij, told of the heretic nun Irina in Salonika. She appeared to live in purity, he wrote, but in fact was defiled. He gave no details, perhaps because he knew none. The Orthodox author simply could not conceive of a heretic actually living a pure

18. Ju. K. Begunov, *Kozma Presviter v slavjanskix literaturax* (Sofia, 1973), 331–332; Hil. 167, ff. 233v–234r; N. A. Kazakova and Ja. S. Lur'e, *Antifeodal'nye eretičeskie dviženie na Rusi XIV–načala XVI veka* (M–L., 1955), 304.

19. Edina Bozoky, ed., *Le Livre secret des cathares* (Paris, 1980), 167.

20. Begunov, *Kozma Presviter*, 355, 351.

21. Attributed to Patriarch Filaret, Kiev 191, ff. 368r–374v. Other complaints include shaving the beard, use of organ music in the liturgy, and bringing dogs into the church. The Roman Catholic Church of the later Middle Ages was more lenient than the Orthodox Church on remarriage and consanguinity, but it had not always been so. Western canon law from the period before the Fourth Lateran Council restricted multiple remarriages and unions among kinsmen in a manner analogous to that in the East. See Brundage, *Law, Sex, and Christian Society*, 140–141, 356.

22. Ja. L. Barskov, *Pamjatniki pervyx let russkago staroobrjadčestva* (SPb., 1912), 82–83, 121.

23. Their reluctance contrasts sharply with attitudes in Western Europe in the same period. See Vern L. Bullough, "Postscript: Heresy, Witchcraft, and Sexuality," in Brundage and Bullough, 206–217.

life; therefore any apparent purity had to be a sham. In the same *vita*, two heretic preachers, Lazar and Kirill, paraded in Trnovo in the nude, wearing only a gourd on their genitals, encouraging castration and the abandonment of marriage. The saint argued against them, citing Jesus' blessing of the wedding at Cana, his prohibition of divorce, and the apostolic confirmation of marriage.[24] Anna Comnena hinted at unsavory sexual practices among the Bogomils but declined to describe them, because "what is the talk of the vulgar had better be passed over in silence."[25]

Because heretics were believed to be in league with the Devil, it would seem to follow logically that they would also be guilty of sexual violations. In fact, Byzantine sources translated into Slavonic did castigate heretics for advocating bigamy and illicit sex.[26] Slavic clerics, however, accused heretics not of excessive license but of excessive asceticism, and wrote darkly of the Bogomils' denial of marriage and recommendation of self-castration.

The facts about the sexual conduct of heretics remain shrouded by Orthodox myths. Although many of the Bogomil leaders certainly outdid the Orthodox in acts of asceticism, it cannot be assumed that all heretics observed a strict sexual propriety. On the contrary; many heretics joined the movement not out of strong religious belief but out of hatred for the oppressive taxation and servitude imposed by their governments and supported by the Orthodox Church. Besides, in the struggle against heresy, religious leaders have rarely felt obliged to restrict themselves to truthful statements. Had Slavic Orthodox clerics felt that accusations of sexual impropriety were an appropriate means of attacking heretics, they would not have hesitated to use them. Thus we cannot assume, as even so eminent a historian as Dmitri Obolensky has done, that the heretics observed a strict sexual propriety.[27]

The Origin of Sexuality

In the Slavic Orthodox conception, the original, perfect creation was devoid of sexuality. God may have created woman as a distinct entity from man, but her role was nonsexual. Eve was intended as Adam's companion and helpmate, and their relationship was to be one of ex-

---

24. V. N. Zlatarski, "Žitie i žizn' prepodobnago otca našego Feodosij," *Sbornik za narodni umotvorenija, nauka, i knižnina* 20, no. 5 (1904), 19–21.
25. Anna Comnena, *The Alexiad*, trans. Elizabeth A. S. Dawes (New York, 1967), 415.
26. Hil. 378, f. 171v; NBS 48, f. 364r.
27. Obolensky, 186–187, 201, 251–252.

clusively spiritual love. Through greed, intemperance, and disobedience, sin entered the world, and sexual desire was born.[28]

Orthodox Slavic churchmen did not carefully distinguish between impurity and sin in regard to sexuality. Many primitive peoples, including the Hebrews and apparently the early Slavs, accepted the notion that sexual activity or manifestations of sexuality (such as menstruation and nocturnal emissions) caused ritual impurity, even when no transgression of law or sinful thought had occurred. Sex was ritually defiling, making a person ineligible for contact with the divine.[29] In the Slavic Orthodox view, all sexual thoughts and activity constituted association with the Devil and were sinful. Consequently the line between ritual impurity and sin was blurred.

Iconography reflected this view of the origin of sexuality. Medieval Slavic pictures of Paradise depict Adam and Eve without sexual characteristics. It is only after the Fall that the symbols of sexuality appears. In some Russian iconographical traditions, large, pendulous breasts are the mark of sexual desire. The serpent is occasionally portrayed as female, with large breasts (fig. 1).[30] Adulterers, men as well as women, are depicted with prominent breasts (figs. 2 and 3). Loose hair on women is also a sign of sexual licentiousness, particularly in South Slavic iconography. Illustrations of the biblical scene of the temptation show Eve with her hair long and loose (fig. 4). A Bulgarian woodcut in the eighteenth-century collection of the priest Punčo (done in traditional style) depicts Eve's transformation to an industrious wife: still nude, but with her hair modestly covered (fig. 5).

Sexuality was evidence of the imperfection of the world. Consequently, the closer human beings came to reflecting the perfection of heaven, the less sexuality would be in evidence. Slavic clerical writers stopped short of espousing the Bogomils' belief that sex originated when Satan seduced Eve,[31] but they did explicitly accept the notion that the Devil was the source of sexual desire (*blud*). They believed that Satan

28. See V. I. Savva, S. F. Platonov, and V. G. Družinin, *Vnov' otkrytyja polemičeskija sočinenija XVII veka protiv eretikov*, Letopis' zanjatij imperatorskoj arxeografičeskoj komissii za 1905 god, vol. 18 (SPb., 1907), 167.

29. For a discussion of ritual impurity in relation to sexuality in the ancient and early Christian traditions, see Brundage, *Law, Sex, and Christian Society*, 2, 53, 81, 92.

30. The Church Slavonic word for "serpent" could be either *zmij* (masculine) or *zmija* (feminine); see Tixonravov, *Pamjatniki otrečennoj russkoj literatury*, 1:1–17. The Greek term for "serpent," as used in the Genesis passage, is always masculine.

31. See "Tajnata kniga Ioanna," in Jordan Ivanov, *Bogomilski knigi i legendi* (Sofia, 1925), 78; Obolensky, 227–228. For an interpretation of this legend from the perspective of the Albigensian heresy, see Bozoky, 35, 75, 115–116, 135–136, and *passim*. The Bogomil version of creation is heavily indebted to earlier Gnostic and Manichean beliefs.

1. The Fall. Both Eve and the serpent are depicted with large breasts to symbolize sexuality. Icon, "The Symbols of Faith" (Novgorod, mid–seventeenth century). Reproduced from V. G. Brjusova, *Russkaja živopis' 17 veka* (Moscow, 1984), no. 115, by permission of Iskusstvo Art Publishers.

2. The Damned. The ranks of the damned include fornicators, adulterers, brigands, witches, sorcerers, drunkards, slanderers, heretics, and Arians. Notice that the male figure at center front has breasts, to indicate sexuality. Miniature, Russian, from an Old Believer collection (seventeenth–eighteenth century), courtesy of Hilandar Research Library, Ohio State University, and Uppsala University Library (Uppsala Slav-71).

48

3. The Torment of Prostitutes. Both women have the large breasts that symbolize sexual desire. Fresco at Rostov (1680s). Reproduced from V. G. Brjusova, *Russkaja živopis' 17 veka* (Moscow, 1984), p. 123, by permission of Iskusstvo Art Publishers.

sent sexual impulses to distract men and women from God and their salvation.[32]

The didactic literature consistently portrayed sexual desires as of Satanic origin. In one story, an elder praying for the salvation of a monk saw a vision of a "spirit of lust" sitting nearby and mocking him. The elder then called the monk forth to confess the guilty thoughts thus personified.[33] The demon of sexuality generally assumed female form,

32. See Hil. 458, f. 184v; 227, f. 110r; 477, f. 224v; 485, f. 59r. Similar ideas were not unknown in the West, although there were stronger voices to counter them, see Tentler, 165–166.

33. TsGADA, F. 381, no. 163, f. 42r. A passage from the life of St. Andrej *jurodivyj* on the same theme was included in many versions of the nomocanon. In response to the saint's question, a demon replies that he gains his strength when humans commit idolatry, sorcery, murder, sodomy, and adultery. See Hil. 305, ff. 22v–23r.

4. The Fall. Eve has long, loose hair, a symbol of sexual license. Fresco at Zograf Monastery, Mount Athos, Greece, courtesy of Hilandar Research Library, Ohio State University.

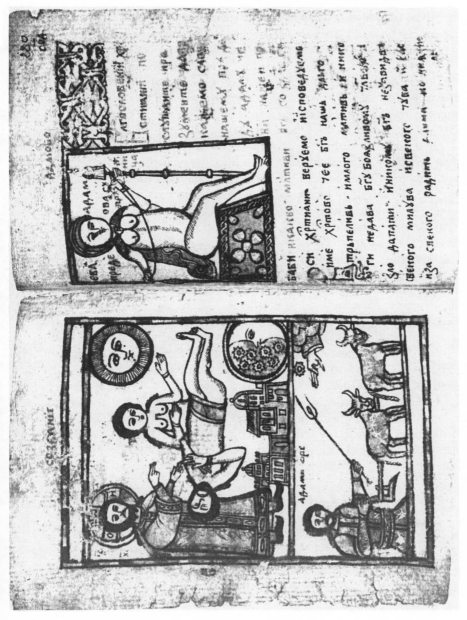

5. Eve as Wife. Among the South Slavs, loose hair symbolized sexuality. Once Eve is properly married, she covers her hair. Woodcut from the book of the priest Punčo (Bulgarian, eighteenth century). Reproduced from *Bŭlgarija prez vekovete* (Sofia, 1982), p. 95, no. 9, by permission of Jus Autor.

as in the *vita* of Archbishop Ioann of Novgorod. In order to distract the saint from prayer—or at least to discredit him in the eyes of his parishioners—Satan sent a demon in the form of a prostitute.[34] Sometimes it took divine intervention to rescue men from demons of lust—in one case, a miracle-working icon of the Virgin.[35] Demons in male form occasionally appeared to tempt men into homosexual lust.[36]

It was possible, but very rare, for a saintly woman to be depicted as tormented by a demon in male form. In the one tale with this reverse motif, the heroine was the repentant former concubine of a priest, and thus vulnerable to sinful thoughts.[37] In another, a young bride was raped repeatedly by demons, who forced her to bear blue demonic children for them. The reason for her torment, it was eventually discovered, was that the drunken priest who baptized her had left the rite incomplete.[38] A woman who was not truly Christian was naturally vulnerable to Satanic temptation.

In saints' lives and tales, the demon in female form was virtually interchangeable with the woman of evil character. Sermons attributed to St. John Chrysostom and the *Pčela*, a collection of didactic aphorisms, warned about the faults of "evil" women: their talking, their paganism, their sexuality, their bad housekeeping.[39] These traits were interconnected. Because "evil" women were not responsive to Christian teachings on purity and salvation, they actively accepted sexual urges from the Devil. Because they were "evil tools of the Devil," they sought to prevent men's salvation by giving them bad advice, by making their home lives miserable, and by leading them into sin.[40] "A woman dancer is the bride of Satan, the wife of the Devil, with every man looking at her. This woman is defiled and shameless before her husband. You bear the image of God, but you consort with your wife in dancing—and still you enter the church! Tell me, is that how you glorify God?"[41]

34. PD, Pinež 2, ff. 163v–165r; *Pamjatniki literatury drevnej Rusi, XIV–seredina XV veka* (M., 1981), 458. An example of this motif in translated Byzantine literature is found in TsGADA, F. 381, no. 163, f. 22r–v.
35. BNL 740(168), ff. 46r–48v.
36. TsGADA, F. 381, no. 173, ff. 132v–133r.
37. BNL 740(168), ff. 48v–49v.
38. *Pamjatniki starinnoj russkoj literatury* (SPb., 1860–1862; The Hague, 1970), 1:153–161.
39. TsGADA, F. 381, no. 173, ff. 118v–119r; BNL 309, ff. 129v–131v. The Russian *slovo* of Daniil Zatočnik replicates this theme; see *Slovo Daniila Zatočnika po redakcijam XII i XIII vv, i ix peredelkam, podgotovil k pečati M. N. Zarubinim* (L., 1932). For secondary literature see, e.g., I.E. Zabelin, "Ženščina po ponjatijam starinnyx knižnikov," *Russkij vestnik* 9 (1857): 5–46; and M. D. Kagan-Tarkovskaja, "Slovo o ženax dobryx i zlyx v sbornike Evfrosina," in *Kul'turnoe nasledie Drevnej Rusi* (M., 1976), 382–386.
40. Evgenija I. Demina, *Tixonravovskij Damaskin: Bolgarskij pamjatnik XVII v.* (Sofia, 1971), 229–230; Lavra GL-9, ff. 280–281v.
41. "Poučenie filosofa, episkopa belgorodskago," in *Pamjatniki literatury drevnej Rusi, XII vek* (M., 1980), 404.

One aphorism warned: "Do not pay attention to an evil woman. Honey flows from the mouth of a fornicating woman."[42] It was believed that women were innately more sexual than men and more susceptible to the Devil.[43] Through the power of their sexual attractiveness, evil women could cause the downfall of the most pious and blessed of men:

> There is no head like the head of a snake, and there is no evil like the evil of women. O Evil Devil, this is your oldest tool! Because of a woman, in the beginning, Adam was driven from Paradise. Because of a woman, the most gentle David committed the murder of Uriah. Because of a woman, the wise Solomon was driven into adultery. Because of a woman, the most manly Samson was stripped and given into captivity. Because of a woman, the full-wisdomed [i.e., abstinent] Joseph was cast into prison. Because of a woman, John [the Baptist], who was the light unto all, was beheaded. . . . Because of a woman, angels were cast out of Heaven. Because of women, everyone is dirtied, everyone is killed, everyone is dishonored, everyone is insulted.[44]

There was no limit to the harm an evil woman could do. One Bulgarian tale told of a wicked wife who murdered her husband and seven sons in order to pursue an adulterous affair.[45]

Unless a man had the patience of a saint, resistance to feminine evil required extraordinary measures. In one tale, a pious monk burned off his fingers in a candle flame while trying to resist an evil woman's wiles.[46] The *vita* of the Serbian archbishop Maksim told of the attempt of a flirtatious Turkish maiden to attract the attention of the youthful saint during his visit to the sultan's court. When she asked him playfully, "Who am I like?" the saint replied crushingly, "Like the one who led Adam and Eve from Paradise"—that is, the Devil in the shape of a serpent.[47]

Some of the heroes of these stories were unable to ward off temptation. In one tale, a monk renounced his vows and his baptism because of his attraction to the daughter of a pagan priest. It was only when he was

42. GPB FnI44, f. 132v.

43. In this belief, Orthodox theologians agreed with their Roman Catholic counterparts; see Brundage, "Carnal Delight," 375–378. Christian thinkers here reversed the position of Roman writers, who characterized men as more highly sexed than women.

44. Hil. 278, ff. 237r–239v. For a similar sixteenth-century Russian text, see Nikolaj Tixonravov, *Letopisi russkoj literatury i drevnosti* (M., 1863), 145–147; for an original thirteenth-century text on a similar theme, see "Poslanie Jakova černorizca ko knjazju Dmitriju Borisoviču," in *Pamjatniki literatury drevnej Rusi, XIII vek* (M., 1981), 456–458.

45. Nikolova, 215–216.

46. TsGADA, F. 381, no. 163, ff. 112r–113v; a similar tale is told in Nikolova, 168–169.

47. Stojan Novaković, *Primeri književnosti i jezika staroga i srpsko-slovenskoga* (Belgrade, 1904), 345. Archbishop Maksim came from the ruling Nemanjid family; his official reason for visiting the Turkish court was to see his kinswoman Mara, wife of the sultan.

unable to achieve his desire with the girl that he repented of his double sin of lust and apostasy.[48] The Devil, not satisfied with a single act of illicit fornication, created an insatiable desire. In the seventeenth-century tale of Savva Grudcyn, the hero "remained for a long time like cattle in that unsated fornication."[49]

Men were not the only victims of female sexuality. One Russian folktale depicted the Devil himself trapped by desire for an evil woman, who managed to outwit him. The author concluded: "Such is the cleverness of women! Even the Devil himself is put to shame by an evil woman!"[50] Thus a woman's sexuality was perceived as stronger than a man's will and self-control. The male heroes of religious tales were not held responsible for their sins; the fault lay with the women who led them into irresistible temptation.

Certain Orthodox polemicists were suspicious of even good women. Part of the problem was that women were so susceptible to evil. According to a sermon attributed to St. John Chrysostom, a single drink and a kiss from another man could change a devoted wife into a whore. At the first taste of lust, he wrote, a woman no longer had any shame and would commit any sin.[51] Woman was regarded as a lesser creation than man; it was difficult for women to overcome the tendency to sin.[52] Good women were rare. According to the author of the extremely misogynistic "Parable about Feminine Evil," not one woman in a thousand was virtuous.[53]

Even the most chaste of women was a potential danger to a man's salvation, especially if her status was that of a potential sex partner—that is, wife or maiden, rather than mother or nun. The mere presence of a woman, regardless of her actions or her character, sufficed to tempt men. Because lust originated with the Devil, any woman, even a pious virgin or a chaste wife, could inadvertently serve as his tool. "The beginning of sin comes from women": not only original sin, apparently, but also the temptation to sin.[54] Thus a man's the safest route to salvation lay where no woman lurked:

Do not give a woman your soul, so that she does not invade your fortress. Do not look at a prostitute, lest you fall into her bonds. Do not look at

48. TsGADA, F. 381, no. 163, ff. 140v–141r; a similar tale is told in Nikolova, 169–170.
49. Gudzij, 402.
50. Tixonravov, *Letopisi russkoj literatury i drevnosti*, 84.
51. I. E. Zabelin, "Iz knigi 'Zlatoust,'" in *Opyty izučenija russkix drevnostej i istorii*, vol. 1 (M., 1872), 179–188.
52. Angelov, "Man through the Middle Ages of Bulgaria," 38–52.
53. "Pritča o ženskoj zlobe," in *Pamjatniki starinnoj russkoj literatury*, 1:461–470.
54. TsGADA, F. 381, no. 163, f. 180r–v.

virgins lest you be tempted. Avert your eyes from a beautiful woman and do not glance at another's beauty. From a woman's goodness many have perished, and from her friendship a fire flares up. Do not speak with a woman at a feast, lest your soul become inclined toward her.[55]

Any sort of association between men and women was fraught with danger; the best solution was simply to stay away from each other (fig. 6). If even such great and godly men as Joseph, David, and Solomon fell prey to desire at a woman's glance, how could lesser men hope to escape?[56]

Instructional tales drove home this teaching. A monk named Julian was awakened to sexual desire by the chance visit of a woman recluse, who asked for water in the desert. Foreshadowing the coming temptation, the author regarded this request as unreasonable. Sure enough, the Devil later incited Julian to seek her out and indulge his passions. He was rescued by a vision of the bodies of men who had died by following their desires: "Their bodies are in Hell and their souls in Gehanna, for the sake of these sins," he was told in forceful fashion.[57] The woman in this case was a saintly hermit, modeled on St. Mary of Egypt, but even she could figure as the temptress in an allegory of lust defeated. One legend had even the great St. John Chrysostom yielding to the temptation inspired by too much wine and the presence of a young woman.[58]

Although the Devil could encourage sin among those who did not have the spiritual strength and knowledge to resist, he could not compel a person to engage in it.[59] Man's innate weakness made him vulnerable to Satanic machinations.[60] Ecclesiastical authors advised their readers (primarily monks) on methods of avoiding sexual temptation: fasting, abstinence from alcohol, silence, vigilance, prayer, and most of all, avoidance of women.[61] One author warned: "Wine, women, wealth, and health are not naturally sins, but from them it is naturally easy for one to become inclined toward perilous sins. For that reason, a man

55. TsGADA, F. 181, no. 332, ff. 56v–57r; GPB Fn144, f. 146r–v; TsGADA, F. 381, no. 163, f. 180r–v. The text is a reworking of chap. 9 of the book of Sirach in the Apocrypha.
56. GBL, F. 304, no. 12, ff. 125v–128v.
57. TsGADA, F. 381, no. 163, ff. 190v–191r.
58. Thomas Butler, ed., *Monumenta Serbocroatica* (Ann Arbor, 1980), 140–148, from a fifteenth- or sixteenth-century Croatian Glagolitic manuscript. In a similar tale in Hil. 278, ff. 80v–81r, when a monk talks with a woman visitor, talk leads to laughter, then to holding hands and lustful thoughts; thus seemingly innocent conversation ends by conjuring up a demon.
59. *Izbornik 1076 goda*, 529–530.
60. Bullough traces this belief about male weakness in the face of sexual temptation to postexilic Judaism; see *Sexual Variance*, 74–76.
61. Hil. 278, f. 277r; 485, ff. 59v–60r, 238r; 458, f. 183v.

6. The Feast of the Righteous and the Dishonorable. The feast of the righteous (center) consists of an exclusively male gathering and sober discussion, while an angel presides. At the feast of the dishonorable (below) men and women drink together as musicians play. The demon at the left with large breasts brings a man and woman together, while the tiny demon at the center fills a wine bowl with excrement. Woodcut, Russian (seventeenth–eighteenth century), from Ol'ga Baldina, *Russkie narodnye kartinki* (Moscow, 1972), p. 149.

must preserve himself staunchly from all of these worthless things, especially from drunkenness and from women."[62]

Of course, Orthodox clerics were not teetotalers; the consumption of wine was right and appropriate in some circumstances. After all, Jesus turned water into wine for the wedding party at Cana, and Paul advocated use of wine for medicinal purposes. However, Orthodox clerics took the same dim view of drunkenness as of illicit sexual activity; it is not surprising that they thought the two interrelated. A sermon attributed to Basil the Great recommended drinking four cups of wine as an aid to conversation and understanding; seven cups led the drinker into blasphemy, bloodshed, adultery, shame, and dancing.[63] Overindulgence in food, too much sleep, or a sense of superiority also led men into illicit sexual desire.[64] Clearly, a man who felt sexual desire was regarded as a victim of external oppression; at worst, he had made himself susceptible by concessions to physical sensation.

Even if a man cleared his conciousness of lust through self-restraint, fasting, and prayer, the Devil could incite evil desires during sleep. The evidence of this unconscious temptation to sin, according to Orthodox authors, was the nocturnal emission of semen. The Devil, they believed, sent images of women to the sleeping man in order to probe sinful thoughts.[65]

The authors of these diatribes against sexuality and the temptation of women sometimes thought to remind their readers that women were also capable of saintliness. After all, Scripture did not condemn *all* women, only wicked ones. And if one woman, Eve, was blamed for the introduction of sin into the world, another woman, Mary, brought salvation. If it appeared that there were more evil women than good women, it was because virtue may remain hidden, while wickedness must be conspicuous.[66] Despite the polemics about female evil, the average Orthodox believer heard a great deal of good about women. Mary received adulation as Virgin, Mother of God, Queen of Heaven, and intercessor. Women saints filled the church calendar, and were presented as models of piety and virtue for both men and women to emulate. Sermons about "good women" existed, though often they served merely as an excuse for further castigation of female evil. Virtuous women were completely

62. Družinin, 72.

63. Sreznevskij, 3:322, 324.

64. Hil. 468, ff. 223v–224r; Lavra GL-36, ff. 70r, 102v–103r. The latter text consists of a Slavic interpolation in a translation of the Greek "Answers to Father Anastasius."

65. Hil. 468, f. 226r.

66. BNL 324(520), ff. 40v–43v. In one place the copyist mistakenly wrote *bludnici* (prostitutes) instead of *vdovici* (widows); perhaps the error reflects his own doubts about the message of the sermon.

7. The Blessed. Women who preserve their virginity appear among the pious saints, emperors, apostles, patriarchs, and martyrs. Even blessed women yield first place in the front row to men. Miniature, Russian, from an Old Believer collection (seventeenth–eighteenth century), courtesy of Hilandar Research Library, Ohio State University, and Uppsala University Library (Uppsala Slav-71).

nonsexual, either virgins or devoted mothers. The rare wife-saint, while attentive to her husband, never earned praise for providing him with physical affection.

The Value of Virginity

Given this attitude toward sex and women, it is not surprising that monastic celibacy was considered the superior lifestyle. A sermon attributed to St. John Chrysostom states:

> There are three orders among men: virginity, marriage, and fornication. Virginity is great and exalted. Marriage is not the same, but without sin. Adultery and fornication lead one into torment. But he who wishes to maintain his virginity must preserve from sin not only his body but also his thoughts. If he is aroused by thoughts, he should marry under the law, and not sin. If he can preserve both his thoughts and his body, that is better: virginity may be compared to the purity of the angels.[67]

The Slavs concurred with enthusiasm. Through virginity, according to one sermon, men most closely approximate the angelic life (fig. 7).[68] Patriarch Evtimij of Bulgaria illustrated the power of virginity by recounting a tale about a celibate priest who brought a dead child back to life in order to complete his baptism.[69] Individuals who could not manage to practice abstinence in their youth had the option of taking up celibate life in old age. Deathbed monastic vows were much more common in the Slavic Orthodox world than in Western Europe.

The term for living in sexual abstinence in Church Slavonic was *celomudryj,* literally "full wisdom." It was applied equally to individuals living celibately as monks or nuns and to married couples who rejected the conjugal relationship. Monastic life, with its perpetual prayer and isolation from the distractions of the mundane world, was considered superior even to sexual abstinence in the home; Church Slavonic terminology consistently identified monastic vows as the taking on of "angelic form."

For men, avoidance of sex was a necessary part of spiritual preparation for salvation. Sexual activity, even in an exclusive marriage, was too much of a distraction from the spirit. For women, the weaker vessels,

67. Begunov, *Kozma Presviter,* 370.
68. GBL F. 304, no. 12, ff. 108v–109v.
69. Emil Kaluzniacki, *Werke des Patriarchen von Bulgarien Euthymius* (1901; London, 1971), 224.

VIRGINITY Below

Tourful

Marriage

sexual purity was in itself an achievement worthy of high praise.[70] Certain women saints, including a large percentage of those most popular in Slavic Orthodox countries, were lauded for their virginity.[71] Saintly women preferred death to defilement; as a rule, they got their wish, becoming martyrs with their virginity intact.[72] Even a lawful marriage was to be despised and avoided in favor of virginity.[73]

Slavic copyists so valued virginity that occasionally they attributed it falsely to favorite saints. Thus the prayers in one manuscript lauded St. Thekla ("the equal of the Apostles") as a virgin, though her *vita* described her as married.[74] Even such famous former prostitutes as Mary Magdalene and St. Pelagia of Antioch were occasionally transformed into virgins.[75]

The outstanding example of the ideal of virginity was of course Mary. Although the Eastern Orthodox churches tended to emphasize her maternal aspect (as in the Greek *Theotokos* and the Slavic *Bogorodica*), she was honored as highly for her chastity, as "most pure and immaculate." Mary surpassed the achievement of virgin saints; she was not only virgin but also bride and mother. "As a virgin you gave birth, not tried by marriage, and you remained a virgin," proclaimed one prayer. This doctrine led to epithets that convey a completely different sense to modern ears; "unwed mother," for instance.[76] Other characterizations, although defensible in theological terms, sound vaguely incestuous: "Mother of God, your bridegroom is made flesh in your womb."[77] Having been impregnated by the Holy Ghost, Mary was able to achieve the exalted rank of motherhood without defilement by sexual intercourse.[78]

70. Roman Catholic canonists also regarded female chastity as exceptionally praiseworthy, because women's virtue was easily corrupted. See Brundage, "Carnal Delight," 378, "Prostitution in the Medieval Canon Law," in Brundage and Bullough, 152–153.

71. Of 239 women saints in Russian calendar of the fourteenth and fifteenth centuries, 41 (21%) were specifically identified as virgins. Of the 33 women saints whose popularity is demonstrated by the inclusion of special prayers, 17 (52%) were virgins.

72. Cf. St. Pelagia of Antioch (not to be confused with the reformed prostitute of the same name), St. Ganania, St. Lukia, St. Irene, St. Theodora, St. Antonina: TsGADA, F. 381, no. 173, ff. 2r, 39v, 108r, 122r–123r; no. 163, ff. 39r, 96v–97r; no. 162, f. 46r–v. The only exception is St. Efrasia, a slave who was forced into sexual intercourse with her master (ibid., no. 163, f. 134r–v).

73. See, e.g., the tales of maidens who cut out their eyes or mutilate their faces rather than accept a nobleman's proposal of marriage: BNL 740(168), ff. 35v–42v.

74. TsGADA, F. 381, no. 45, f. 154r; the text in ibid., no. 131, ff. 18v–19r, does not make this mistake. *Vita*: GPB, Sof. b-ka no. 1324, f. 3r–v; Sreznevskij, 3:499.

75. TsGADA, F. 381, no. 45, f. 234r–234v; no. 173, f. 170r; no. 163, ff. 38v–39r; GIM, Sin. 707, f. 348r; GPB, Sof. b-ka, no. 1324, ff. 15r–16r; BAN-L, no. 16.14.14, ff. 61r–66v; PD, Koll. Pereca, no. 21, f. 82v.

76. TsGADA, F. 381, no. 131, ff. 55v, 6r; no. 133, f. 2r.

77. BAN-L, 16.14.14, ff. 80v–81r.

78. Little work has been done on the nonpolitical aspects of the cult of Mary among the Orthodox Slavs. See D. T. Strotmann, "Quelques aperçus historiques sur le culte marial en Russie," *Irénikon* 32 (1959): 178–202.

Of course, Mary also had an earthly husband, Joseph, whom Slavic texts usually identified as her "fiancé" (*obručnik*) to make clear that their relationship was not sexual. Although the Orthodox Slavs did not particularly draw on this nuptial model, they did accept its basic principle: the ideal marriage was one that was never consummated (see fig. 8). Because sex was considered defiling, even as part of a Christian marriage, saintly individuals preferred to live in abstinence with their spouses. A tale tells of a pious shepherd and his wife who slept separately and always appeared before each other completely clothed. The shepherd told the narrator, "I have never defiled my wife."[79] Spouses who chose to live together as brother and sister were hardly depicted as unfeeling; on the contrary, the love one couple felt for each other was so strong and pure that they choose to die at the same time and enter heaven together.[80] Sexual desire and love were viewed as antithetical emotions, even within the domain of Christian marriage. A man who truly loved and honored his wife would not want to expose her to the Satanic dangers of sexual intercourse.[81]

Even when spouses consummated their marriage in the beginning, it was considered a sign of piety to renounce further marital relations. Juliana Lazareveskaja, a seventeenth-century Russian saint who was presented as a model for a Christian life "in the world," decided not to engage in sex again, and imposed this decision on her reluctant husband.[82]

Although the Byzantines adopted the theme of the unconsummated marriage, it found a much more extensive use in Slavic literature. It was central to the extremely popular *vita* of St. Alexis Man of God, especially in its later (fourteenth-to-fifteenth-century) Slavic revised version.[83]

79. TsGADA, F. 381, no. 163, f. 73r. See also no. 173, ff. 110r–111v, for a similar tale about a bootmaker. Among abstinent saintly couples are Galaktion and Epistemia (ibid., no. 162, f. 103r–v) and Chrysanthus and Daria (ibid., f. 73r–v, no. 45, f. 211r). Perhaps because of the inherent unlikelihood of a chaste marriage, one manuscript changes Darija to Darin, a man (GIM, Sin. 707, f. 299v). The Apocryphal Acts of the Apostle Thomas also includes this theme, depicting Jesus counseling newlyweds to remain virgin; see Bugge, 60. For a discussion of the tradition of chaste marriages in the ancient Stoic tradition, see Brundage, *Law, Sex, and Christian Society*, 20; and in the Roman Catholic Church, JoAnn McNamara, "Chaste Marriage and Clerical Celibacy," in Bullough and Brundage, 22–33.

80. BNL 740(168), ff. 120v–123r. See also the tale of Peter and Fevronia in Gudzij, 240.

81. Compare the Slavic view of the dichotomy between sexual desire and love with that of a second-century Church Father, Clement of Alexandria: "A man who marries for the sake of begetting children must practice continence so that it is not desire he feels for his wife, whom he ought to love, and so that he may beget children with a chaste and controlled will": Noonan, *Contraception*, 77.

82. Gudzij, 348.

83. Sreznevskij, 2:1–18. Because Sreznevskij's twelfth-century manuscript source was defective, it is not possible to determine whether that version of the *vita* included a miraculous birth. The fifteenth-century version adds a concise reiteration of the circumstances of his birth in his mother's prayer for his well-being after the saint's disappearance from his wedding. The popular verse version (in the style of seventeenth-century *byliny*) makes the miraculous concep-

8. The Celibate and the Chaste Married. The married women in the lower picture
are bareheaded, to indicate that they are still virgins. Miniature, Russian, from an
Old Believer collection (seventeenth–eighteenth century), courtesy of Hilandar
Research Library, Ohio State University, and Uppsala University Library (Uppsala Slav-71).

marriage w/o consummation + piety

Patriarch Evtimij used the motif of the unconsummated marriage extensively in his *vitae*. He depicted St. Philothea as convincing her husband that they should live in chastity. Her major argument was moral: they should remain pure in this transient life in order to be worthy of life everlasting with Christ, and to avoid the Devil's traps. She also had a more practical set of arguments: pregnancy is uncomfortable, childbirth is dangerous, child care is burdensome, and children often disappoint their parents.[84]

Lack of sexual activity between saintly couples, remarkably enough, did not prevent them from having children. A Bulgarian tale from the sixteenth century depicts the pious tsar Foka as marrying the maiden Teofana only in order to produce an heir, but then not consummating the marriage. Children were not born in this case because Teofana committed adultery and then arranged for her lover to kill her husband. The author implied that it was Teofana's sinfulness rather than her husband's virtue that prevented the birth of a child.[85] According to the *vita* of St. Dmitrij Donskoj, he and his wife, Princess Avdot'ja, lived without sexual intercourse but produced a large number of children.[86] Nor was their case unique. In Slavic *vitae*, numerous saints were the products of miraculous conceptions by pious parents.

The origin of this motif may be found in the biblical stories of Abraham and Sarah, Elkanah and Hannah, Joachim and Anna, and Zacharias and Elizabeth. The parents were pious and faithful, but were unable to have a child. After the husband and wife prayed—in most cases, in separate locations—a vision appeared to them heralding the birth of the desired child. This miraculous child became a saint, noted for his holy life and good works. The Slavs made an important revision of this classic story: they omitted the words to the effect that "Abraham knew his wife Sarah." On the contrary, the saint was "born of the promise."[87] In other words, the Slavic texts implied that no sexual

tion a major theme. A Serbian version of the fourteenth century was similar to the fifteenth-century Russian one; see Novaković, *Primeri književnosti i jezika*, 464–472.

84. Kaluzniacki, 81–85. Patriarch Evtimij draws this theme from a popular tale of his time, that of St. Amoun. One version of the tale is found in Hil. 278, f. 16r. Hussite writers in late-medieval Bohemia advised young women against marriage on similar grounds, suggesting that husbands could be brutal and children worrisome. See Klassen, "Development of the Conjugal Bond," 176.

85. Jordan Ivanov, *Starobŭlgarski razkazi* (Sofia, 1935), 307–309. In a curious transference of motifs, Tsar Foka's method of choosing a wife was to ask candidates to try on a small slipper (not glass, however).

86. *Plotigodija ne tvorxu*, Novgorod IV chronicle, Akademičeskij manuscript, in *PSRL*, vol. 4, pt. 1 (Petrograd, 1915), 351–366.

87. TsGADA, F. 381, no. 45, ff. 228r–229r. One manuscript goes even further: the first prayer under the title for the nativity of John the Baptist includes the phrase "born of a virgin" (*ot děvy roditisja*) and "conception without seed" (*bezsemenne začatie*)—descriptions rightly reserved for Jesus alone.

contact was necessary for conception; prayer alone produced a child.

This theme appears repeatedly in Patriarch Evtimij's lives of St. Ilarion, bishop of Moglen; St. Nedela; and the Byzantine empress Theophano.[88] Perhaps the eminent Bulgarian patriarch inspired later Slavic hagiographers. In any event, a number of *vitae* from the fifteenth and sixteenth centuries featured the identical motif, even when the miraculous birth did not square with other information in the text. In the interrelated *vitae* of Aleksandr Svirskij, Aleksandr Oševenskij, and Efrem Perekomskij, the parents had previously had children. Still, the saint was conceived as a result of his parents' prayers. To celebrate the happy event, the parents vowed to live without sexual relations for the rest of their lives.[89] The 1469 version of the life of Constantine the Philosopher by Vladislav Grammaticus attributed the same sentiment to the saint's parents. Consequently, the saint was characterized as "a good offshoot from a good root."[90] The *vita* of Bishop Nifont of Novgorod describes his miraculous conception, even though earlier the author disavowed any knowledge of his parents. The hagiographer explains the anomaly thus: "It is known that a great child is born of honorable and saintly parents."[91]

This phrase provides the key to the widespread use of the motif of miraculous birth among the Orthodox Slavs. A truly pious couple, worthy of bearing and rearing a child destined for sainthood, would have practiced the ideal, unconsummated marriage. Sexual intercourse, even in marriage, meant defilement, a yielding to Satan, which was unthinkable for the parents of a saint. On the other hand, procreation fulfilled God's command, and bearing a child brought a woman honor. There was a definite sense that children were a normal and appropriate part of marriage. Prayers for newlyweds expressed the hope that they would have children—along with the hope that they would preserve themselves from lust and obscenity.[92] Thus hagiographers faced a dilemma: the

88. Kaluzniacki, 28–29, 150–151. A shortened version of the life of St. Theophano is found in TsGADA, F. 381, no. 163, f. 100r–v.

89. For the *vita* of Aleksandr Svirskij, see GIM, Sin. 997, f. 1144r; Aleksandr Oševenskij, PD, op. 24, no. 18, f. 22r; Efrem Perekomskij, Nov. Mus., no. 10923, f. 40r. The miraculous birth attributed to the thirteenth-century Avraamij Smolenskij was doubtless the result of a later rewriting; see *Pamjatniki literatury drevnej Rusi, XIII veka*, 68. The commentary by D. M. Bulanin (533–535) dates the text to the thirteenth century. V. O. Ključevskij, in his *Drevnerusskija žitija svjatyx kak istoričeskij istočnik* (M., 1871), 52–58, also attributes the first version to the period soon after the saint's death, but notes that it underwent significant revision later. All manuscripts of the *vita* date to the sixteenth or seventeenth century; see Nikolaj Barsukov, *Istočniki russkoj agiografii* (SPb., 1882), 8–10.

90. Kantor, 27.

91. *Pamjatniki starinnyx russkoj literatury*, vyp. 4, 1–9.

92. Most *trebnici* include a marriage ceremony; e.g., Hil. 169, ff. 47v–54r; BNL 251(200), ff. 17r–24r; Kiev 49, ff. 53r–72v. Peculiarly enough, in about half of the South Slavic manu-

[handwritten note at top: not when cereal that produces children But GOP]

birth of a child, especially a saint, was good, but the sexual intercourse essential to the child's conception was evil. The miraculous conception resolved the difficulty—children were born of prayer and faith in God, not of Satanic activities.

That the birth of children into the world was good seemed obvious—God, not Satan, was the author of all creation. God commanded his creatures to "be fruitful and multiply"; the bearing of children was nothing but obedience to the Highest. Orthodox polemicists wrote disdainfully of the Bogomils' belief that children were small demons. According to one Orthodox author, "God condemned not childbirth but fornication."[93] The laws of biology would seem to require sexual intercourse as a prerequisite to the birth of a child, but this necessity too Orthodox theologians saw as a consequence of the Fall. St. John Chrysostom wrote that, had Adam and Eve not sinned, God would have found some other way to multiply the species. Even in the flawed present world, he argued, it was not intercourse that produced children, but rather the word of God.[94]

Thus procreation, in the Slavic Orthodox view, officially did not result from sexual intercourse. In fact, Orthodox churchmen knew very well the relationship between sex and conception, but this admission was possible only in cases of illicit intercourse. Under canon law, the birth of a child out of wedlock served as proof of sexual misconduct, and didactic tales are filled with illegitimate births. And such tales could also present an alternative to barrenness more practical than prayer and abstinence: in the tale of Akir, the pious couple prayed for a child, in accordance with the ecclesiastical model; instead of a miraculous conception, the husband received a divine vision instructing him to adopt his sister's son.[95]

[handwritten note in right margin: Sex ≠ Childbr]

---

scripts I have seen, one of the most overt references to childbearing in marriage was altered: in the phrase *zakonom s"pregyi i jaže o njem' čedorodstvo tvore,* "lawfully united in order to bear children," the word *čedorodstvo* has been replaced by *čjudorodstvo,* so that the phrase now means "lawfully united in order to make a miracle of birth." See Hil. 169, f. 55v, Hil. 167, f. 320r; BNL 246(103), f. 67v, for examples of the first case; and Rila 2/1(51), f. 42r; BNL 612(17), f. 61r; and BNL 251(200), f. 24r, for examples of the second.

93. Cf. Popruženko, 45–46; N. M. Petrovskij, "Pis'mo patriarxa Konstantinopol'skago Feofilakta carju Bolgarii Petru," *Izvestija otdelenija russkago jazyka i slovesnosti imperatorskoj Akademii nauk* 18, no. 3 (1913): 370. See also Angelov, *Bogomili,* 32–35. Angelov notes that the Bogomils paid little heed to this belief in practice. Historians who attribute a high standard of morality and social conscience to the Bogomils have great difficulty reconciling their admiration with the Bogomils' belief in the evil of children. Victor N. Sharenoff, for example, entirely dismissed the Orthodox statements to this effect: "this statement . . . cannot be true, because the Bogomils called themselves Christians and strictly followed the law of Jesus": "A Study of Manichaeism in Bulgaria with Special Reference to the Bogomils" (Ph.D. diss., Columbia University, 1927), 50.

94. Bugge, 17; Bullough, 324.

95. Ivanov, *Starobŭlgarski razkazi,* 237–245; *Xristomatija po starobŭlgarska literatura*

This curious dichotomy in Slavic Orthodox thinking is comprehensible in the context of medieval Slavic epistomology. First, Christian theology demanded acceptance of the idea that at least one birth, that of Jesus Christ, did not result from a sexual union. Thus Orthodox thinkers could not insist that sex was the sine qua non of procreation. Second, Orthodox Slavs, lacking exposure to even the sketchy scientific knowledge available in the medieval world, did not know the details of the physiology of procreation. They were aware that a woman's menstruation marked her failure to conceive. A sixteenth-century Serbian medical codex included procedures to remedy female infertility, but ecclesiastical penitential codes condemned such efforts as witchcraft.[96] The herbal potions recommended, incidentally, would hardly prove effective.

Finally, Orthodox Slavs shared the widespread medieval notion that a child's character was determined by the circumstances of his or her conception. Thus they felt, despite the protestations of their more learned hierarchs, that a child conceived in defiance of church canons on Friday, Saturday, or Sunday would necessarily grow up to be a thief, brigand, or adulterer.[97] Similarly, in the popular perception, a man of illegitimate birth was not considered an appropriate candidate for the priesthood. The Russian author of the *vita* of the saints Boris and Gleb proposed in all seriousness that their murderer-brother Svjatopolk inherited his evil character from the rape and incest that resulted in his birth:

> The third [brother] was Svjatopolk, who conceived this evil murder. His mother, a Greek, was formerly a nun, and Jaropolk, Volodimir's brother, took her, and because of the beauty of her face he unfrocked her, and begot of her this accursed Svjatopolk. But Volodimir, who was still a pagan, killed Jaropolk and took his wife, who was pregnant; and of her was born this accursed Svjatopolk.[98]

(Sofia, 1967), 226–227, 246–250; "Povest' o premudrom Akire," in *Pamjatniki starinnoj russkoj literatury*, 1:359–370.

96. NBS I-14, f. 270r; Hil. 302, f. 22v; Relja Katić, *The Chilandar Medical Codex N. 517* (Belgrade, 1980), 368. A Serbian codex from c. 1690 reveals a fairly sophisticated understanding of the physiology of conception, but it cannot be determined how early such information became known among the South Slavs. See V. Jagić, "Opisi i izvodi iz nekoliko južnoslovinskih rukopisa: Srednovječni liekovi, gatanja i vračanja," *Starine* 10 (1878): 96–99. Smirnov, "Baby bogomerzskija," 232, quotes a report of an article in Voprosy Kirika, forbidding women to seek the advice of a wisewoman on how to conceive.

97. "Nekotoraja zapoved'," art. 10, in Smirnov, *Materialy*, 29; Voprosy Kirika, art. 74, in RIB, 6:61. People consulted horoscope texts to determine astral influences on the day of birth. See Angelov, "Man through the Middle Ages," 70–71.

98. Kantor, 167. The Novgorod I Chronicle similarly attributed Svjatopolk's wicked character to his birth, but altered the explanation somewhat: "For an evil root grows evil fruit, as his mother had been a nun, and secondly, Vladimir lay with her not in marriage": *Novgorodskaja*

Similarly, in the sixteenth century, Prince Kurbskij complained that his enemy, Ivan the Terrible, was born as a result of the efforts of sorcerers and witches to help his parents conceive.[99]

Fictional tales took up the theme. The author of the "Parable about Feminine Evil" recounted the story of a good man whose depraved wife bore seven sons, each more evil than the last.[100] A seventeenth-century tale told of the harlot Jezebel, who conceived a daughter in lust. The girl grew to be an adulteress, "full of evil" and "a vessel for demons," the prototype of the Great Whore of Babylon of the Apocalypse, as depicted in Russian Old Believer texts of that period (fig. 9). God was so angered by her wickedness that he commanded that the earth swallow her whole. Her obscenity still emerged, growing up in the form of the "evil herb" tobacco.[101]

Another possible result of the parents' immorality was loss of the child, whom the parents had shown themselves unworthy to have. A miscarriage had to have been the result of the woman's sinfulness. She was required to confess her sins and do penance.[102] Service books included an extensive set of prayers for purification:

> Lord our God, who was born of the Ever-Virgin Mary, the Holy Mother of God, and who lay as a baby in a cradle: Today, out of your great clemency, have mercy on this your servant N., who has fallen into the sin of willful murder, and aborted that which was conceived within her. Forgive her her willful and unwilling sins, and preserve her from all Satan's deceptions. Purify her of obscenity and heal her sickness . . . for we are born in sin and lawlessness, and we are all defiled before you.[103]

Similarly, if a child died soon after birth, the parents were considered to be at fault. In the case of infanticide, this was certainly true, but Slavic canons blurred the distinctions between deliberately killing a newborn, neglecting it so that it died of natural causes, and permitting it to die unbaptized.[104] But even if the child died of natural causes and its parents

---

pervaja letopis' staršego i mladšego izvoda (M./L., 1950), 125–127; see also Sofijskij I Chronicle, *PSLR,*, vol. 5 (L., 1925), 43–47. In order to make Svjatopolk's claims to the throne as illegitimate as possible, the author of the *vita* denied that he was the son of Vladimir. The chronicle account is doubtless more accurate on this point.

99. Smirnov, "Baby bogomerzskija," 231.

100. "Pritča o ženskoj zlobe," in *Pamjatniki starinnoj russkoj literatury*, 1:468. The author of the parable previously had argued that the man alone contributes to the conception of children, in order to explain how the biblical patriarchs could be married and still be godly. Evidently the contradiction did not strike him.

101. "Legenda o proisxoždenii tabaka," in ibid., 427–435.

102. SANU 125(154), f. 25v.

103. Peter Mogila, *Trebnik* (Kiev, 1646), 32–33; a similar prayer is found in NBS I-39, f. 217r–v.

104. See my "Infanticide in Pre-Petrine Russia," *Jahrbücher für Geschichte Osteuropas* 34, no. 2 (1986): 215–224.

9. The Great Whore, garishly dressed, rides the seven-headed beast of the Apocalypse. Miniature, Russian, from an Old Believer collection (seventeenth–eighteenth century), courtesy of Hilandar Research Library, Ohio State University, and Uppsala University Library (Uppsala Slav-70).

were grief-stricken, they still could be held accountable. After the birth of a child, the mother prayed that the child's life be preserved, lest she "be like a dissolute prostitute," that is, a woman who engaged in sex merely for pleasure.[105]

If evil persons were born of sexual violation and saintly persons were born of chastity, it followed that the average human being, neither depraved nor virtuous, would be born of a relationship neither demonic nor angelic—namely, marriage.

The Theology of Marriage

The institution of marriage presented a problem to Orthodox theologians. Its whole purpose seemed to be only to channel sinful sexual desires, especially once procreation had been removed as a justification. Indeed, marriage did not exist before the expulsion from Eden, and in itself served as evidence of the flawed nature of the world.[106] Illicit sex could be condemned without hesitation; licit sex seemed to be a contradiction in terms. The *Lestvica Ioanna Lestvičnika*, a handbook of spirituality for monks, stated at the beginning that it was possible (in theory) to live a pious life in the world with women, provided one was content with one's wife. A sermon included in the Russian *prolog* argued to a doubtful audience that a virtuous life was possible in marriage. After all, Abraham, Isaac, and Jacob were all both godly and married. But, the preacher warned, they lived chastely with their wives according to the law, and did not engage in fornication with others or look for prostitutes. Once exposed to the temptations of the world, even righteous men could be seduced into sexual sin: David committed murder and adultery for the sake of Bathsheba, and the most wise Solomon perished of a surfeit of women.[107]

Because Orthodox theologians could not justify marriage on the basis of procreation, the defense of the institution was complicated. They did not know of St. Augustine's cleverly constructed thesis of the "conjugal debt"—that spouses "owed" each other cooperation in the channeling of dangerous sexual desires. Nor could they accept the Western notion that marital sex could be condoned, at least in the absence of the lustful

---

105. Hil. 172, f. 124r–v.

106. See "Povest' o gore i zločastii," from the second half of the seventeenth century, in Gudzij, 886.

107. TsGADA, F. 381, no. 39, f. 12v; no. 173, ff. 209v–210v. The author clearly did not take note of the fact that the biblical patriarchs practiced polygamy and concubinage.

pursuit of pleasure rather than duty.[108] The dualist Bogomil heresy offered a logical but unacceptable solution: all sex was evil, marriage an abomination, and the birth of children a victory for the Devil.[109] It was in reaction to the dualistic heretics that Slavic Orthodox clerics formulated their strongest defense of procreation, marriage, and sexual activity. Ultimately, Orthodox theologians had to fall back not on logic but on an appeal to Scripture.

Despite the importance they attached to sobriety, fasting, and abstinence, Orthodox writers affirmed that drinking wine, eating meat, and engaging in marital relations were permitted under God's law. The venerable St. Paul had so decreed, and Orthodox canons anathematized those who disagreed.[110] St. Paul's support of marriage, however, was weak at best; himself celibate, he offered marriage as an inferior alternative for those who could not sustain continence. A more positive statement of divine approval of marriage was found in Jesus' transformation of water into wine at the marriage at Cana. That Jesus attended the wedding and worked a miracle to assist in its celebration proved that Christian marriage was indeed a blessed state.[111] It was not accidental that these two passages from the New Testament formed the central readings in Orthodox marriage services in the medieval period. Depictions of the marriage at Cana served as a model for pictures of real weddings (compare figs. 10 and 11). Western ideas of the purposes of marriage reached the Slavic Orthodox Church only in the mid-seventeenth century, filtered through Uniate seminaries in the Ukraine. The service book of Peter Mogila included a paraphrase of the Augusti-

108. The passage from the New Testament (I Cor. 7:3–5) was known in the Orthodox world (it appears in, e.g., BNL 684, f. 164r), but a theory of marriage was not derived from it. For a summary of Augustinian and canon law on sexuality in the Roman Catholic Church, see Brundage, "Carnal Delight," 361–385, and *Law, Sex, and Christian Society*, 2, 89–93, 241–242. Brundage notes that canonists were not enthusiastic about marriage, seeing it primarily as a cure for fornication and not desirable in its own right. Bullough notes (324) a passing remark in a sermon of St. John Chysostom permitting intercourse between spouses even when conception could not occur in order to prevent illicit fornication, but grants that it seems to be offhand, rather than part of a well-developed philosophy of marriage. In any case, it does not appear that the Slavs picked up on this comment.

109. Puech and Vaillant, 262–264; Hil. 167, ff. 233v–234r. The Western patristic scholar John Henry Newman concisely voiced the main-line Christian ambivalence: "Marriage is a sin which it is sinful to repent of": quoted in Christopher N. L. Brooke, "Marriage and Society in the Central Middle Ages," in R. B. Outhwaite, ed., *Marriage and Society: Studies in the Social History of Marriage* (London, 1981), 17–34.

110. See, e.g., a segment of the "Slovo stgo. Daniila o mirstem' žitii i o černeč'stve," included in the sixteenth-century Dubenskij Sbornik (Sreznevskij, 3:318); Hil. 378, ff. 173v–174r.

111. See, e.g., Begunov, *Kozma Presviter*, 282; Patriarch Evtimij to Metropolitan Anthim of Wallachia (1370–1389), in Kaluzniacki, 247. See also Angelov, "Man through the Middle Ages," 34–35.

10. The Marriage at Cana. Fresco at Kalenić Monastery, Yugoslavia (Serbian, 1407–1413). Reproduced by permission of the National Museum of Belgrade.

71

11. The Wedding Feast of Andrei, Son of Vladimir Monomax. Notice the structural similarity to the fresco of the marriage at Cana (fig. 10). Miniature, Russian (sixteenth century), from *Drevnerusskaja knižnaja miniatjura iz sobranija gosudarstvennoj publičnoj biblioteki imeni M. E. Saltykova-Ščedrina* (Leningrad, 1980), by permission of Aurora Publishers.

nian formula, justifying marriage on the grounds of procreation, child rearing, marital affection, and the prevention of adultery.[112]

Orthodox writers could not bring themselves to confront the issue of sex in marriage directly, even to refute heretical teachings. All statements legitimizing marital relations were in the negative. Orthodox polemicists anathematized those who condemned "a good Christian woman sleeping with her husband."[113] They criticized those men who castrated themselves to avoid sexual desire, "insulting the procreative organ, which God gave to men for the birth of children."[114] They advised married couples not to deny each other, except by mutual consent and to preserve the purity of the sacraments.[115] Even when they made concessions for married couples, however, hierarchs characterized marital sexual expression as dirty and evil: "A person sometimes may not be able to restrain himself for God's sake, but he ought to restrain himself on these days, and not always wallow like a pig in a pen. From such unrestrained passions a wicked and evil seed is born."[116]

The halfhearted defense of marital sex did not alter the overwhelming impact of the antisexual teachings of the church. Marital relations were justified only as a sort of dispensation, granted by an infinitely merciful but totally inscrutable God for the benefit of a humanity susceptible to sin.

Although Orthodox clerics were certainly prepared in practice to make allowances for the human capacity for sin, they were reluctant to acknowledge a compromise with sin as part of God's order. They could not accept the notion that sexual activity, which was so clearly iniquitous outside of marriage, could possibly be right and proper within it. The ecclesiastical lesson about the dubious nature of marital sex was not lost on the medieval Slavic lay population. The popular mind made the leap that the church so carefully avoided, and labeled even marital sex as

112. Mogila, 359. These justifications for marriage are so much part of the Western tradition that even completely secular works, such as the Kinsey reports, accept them with little revision. On Augustine's justification of marriage, see Brundage, "Carnal Delight," 364.

113. Peć 77, f. 263r–v.

114. Zlatarski, 20–24. The penance for castrating a son for sale as a slave was three years; see "Nekotoraja zapoved'," art. 41, in Smirnov, *Materialy*, 31. Other canons condemned self-castration as a form of suicide; see Peć 77, ff. 159r–160r.

115. Hil. 302, f. 21v. Usually authors paraphrase I Cor. 7:1–9; see, e.g., Begunov, *Kozma Presviter*, 371.

116. Kiev 49, f. 671. In response to a question from Tsar Boris of Bulgaria, Pope Nicholas I (858–867) also discouraged marital sex, especially at holy times: "For when the male and the female have converse together, it is hard for the ambush of the ancient fiend not to be there"; see *Izvori za bŭlgarskata istorija*, vol. 7, *Latinski izvori za bŭlgarskata istorija* (Sofia, 1960), 98. St. John Damascene dissented from this view; he gave his approval to enjoyment in the conjugal relationship, but the Orthodox Slavs ignored this part of his teachings. See Brundage, *Law, Sex, and Christian Society*, 38.

sinful. Serbian epics record the use of the phrase "by sin" (*po grehu*) to identify a parent or child by birth; a "parent without sin" (*roditelj bezgrešni*) was a godparent.[117]

The Consequences of Sexual Sin

A person who fell from sexual purity had the option of contrition and repentance. As inspiration for sinners in the real world, ecclesiastical literature provided multitudes of examples of redemption. A person—most often a woman—who repented of the defilement of her chastity could earn salvation if she rejected further sexual activity. In one tale, a virgin nun yielded to the blandishments of a young singer instigated by the Devil. Finding herself pregnant, she repented of her sin, and prayed to God to take away the "conception of lust" on the grounds that if she killed herself from shame, the child would die as well. Her prayer was answered by the death of the infant, and the nun spent the next thirty years in prayer and fasting to atone for her sin. The author so valued her contrition that he termed her "like a virgin."[118]

The heroine did not need to be the unfortunate victim of a single lapse; the redemption of a prostitute to a life of chastity and salvation was a favorite theme of instructional tales. Sometimes a pious monk persuaded the prostitute to abandon her life of sin; sometimes heavenly powers intervened directly. Angels came to rescue the soul of a nun-turned-prostitute who died at the very gates of the convent where she sought readmission. In a seventeenth-century Russian version of the popular Western tale of Beatrice, the Virgin Mary herself guided the former nun's return from a life of prostitution. For a former prostitute, the only path to salvation lay in complete rejection of sexual activity; a Christian marriage was not an option.[119]

---

117. For texts of some of the epics related to this topic, see Brkić, 46–69. Brkić recognized the implication of the term *po grehu* but was at a loss to explain it. He rejected the idea that the Orthodox Church could have been the source of this view of marital sexuality, and he was also reluctant to assign responsibility to the Bogomils.

118. TsGADA, F. 381, no. 173, ff. 80v–81r; Hil. 278, f.134r–v. Notice the lack of criticism for wishing for the child's death, although "cursing one's womb" to cause an abortion was a violation of canon law; see art. 56 of "Zakon o kaznex," in A. S. Pavlov, "'Knigi zakonnyja' soderžaščija v sebe v drevne-russkom perevode vizantijskie zakony zemledel'českie, ugolovnye, bračnye i sudebnye," *Sbornik otdelenija russkago jazyka i slovestnosti imperatorskoj akademii nauk* 38, no. 3 (1885): 75.

119. TsGADA, F. 381, no. 163, ff. 20v, 63v, and no. 173, ff. 63r–64v, 161v; Deržavina, 207–209. In Western Europe in same periods, pious men were encouraged to redeem prostitutes from their life of sin by marrying them; see Vern L. Bullough, "The Prostitute in the Early Middle Ages," in Brundage and Bullough, 41. This theme does not appear in Slavic Orthodox stories until the seventeenth century, when it was imported from the West; see Deržavina, 201.

Men could also fall into sexual sin and later win redemption, but this motif was less common. One tale featured a pious but weak-willed cleric. The Devil drowned him in a river while he was on his way home from a sinful encounter, and demanded his soul in the Court of Judgment. But the Virgin came to the cleric's defense, arguing that he had been reciting prayers to her at the moment of his accident. The cleric thus escaped death and damnation, and was returned to earth as a monk. Thenceforth he devoted his life to praise of the Mother of God.[120]

If one committed sexual sins and did not repent of them, Orthodox clerics predicted dire consequences, in this world and the next. The author of *Domostroj*, a sixteenth-century Russian guide to household management, indicted sexual offenses and sorcery together:

> And God, who is good and loves mankind, will not abide in men such evil morals and customs and improper doings. Like a Father who loves His children, He will save us through suffering, and will lead us to salvation, punishing us for the multitude of our sins, but not giving us over to death. He does not want the death of the sinner, but awaits his repentance, so that he will return to Him and live with Him. If we do not return to Him and do not repent our evil deeds, for our sins He will lay upon us sometimes famine; sometimes plague, or fire, or flood; or captivity and annihilation at the hands of the pagans; the ruination of cities and God's churches; the destruction of everything holy; the plundering of every regiment; false accusations by others; sometimes confiscation of property because of the Tsar's wrath, or punishment without mercy, a mournful death; murder by bandits, and pillage, and theft; judicial expropriation and torture; or drought; or excessive rainfall, intemperate summers, harsh winters, cruel frosts, barren land; murrain of cattle, and wildlife, and birds, and fish; and an abundance of every sort of need; poverty leading to a miserable, sudden and early death for parents, women, and children; suffering from manifold serious illnesses; and an evil end.[121]

And if these social ills were not enough, the sinner could also bring upon himself a whole catalogue of diseases, from broken bones to constipation. The Russian thinker Joseph of Volokolamsk explained the connection between fornication and illness: a fornicator destroyed the original purity of the body, which was God's temple; consequently, God aban-

---

120. BNL 740(168), ff. 131r–132r.
121. *Domostroi* (Letchworth, 1971), 20–28. The authorship of *Domostroj* is disputed, although it is traditionally ascribed to the Kremlin archpriest Silvester. Similar sentiments are expressed in the record of the contemporary Moscow Church Council; see *Stoglav*, 53. English moralists in the early modern period also shared the belief that divine wrath would result from sexual violations; see Ingram, 153–154.

doned him, and illness took over.[122] Nor was it necessary to commit the major sexual sin of adultery or sodomy in order to bring about these disasters; even seemingly lesser violations such as engaging in sexual intercourse on holy days, sufficed to bring down God's retribution.

Toleration of illicit sexual activity by others could result in widespread suffering. In one Old Believer tale, a demon washed away his pollution after a visit to a whorehouse by using water in uncovered vessels in Christian homes. This water then caused illness among the believers. The moral is clear: the presence of immorality in the community brings affliction even to the righteous.[123]

The Acceptance of the Ecclesiastical Image

There is every indication that the Slavs accepted the general outlines of this ascetic vision of sexuality without objection. They selected, translated, and recopied the Byzantine religious texts, and wrote original pieces in the same vein. They did not seek alternative guides for sexual expression, although such guides were certainly available. The ancient scientific studies of nature, such as those of Aristotle and Galen, remained unknown in the Slavic Orthodox world. The more permissive Islamic view of sexuality failed to alter Slavic Orthodox teachings on the subject, despite centuries of coexistence in the Balkans. Scandinavian practicality in sexual matters had equally little influence in Russia. And despite centuries of political interaction between the Slavic Orthodox and Roman Catholic states, key Western concepts of sexuality, such as Augustine's conjugal debt and the idea of courtly love, remained unknown in the East until the middle of the seventeenth century.

Slavic enthusiasm for the Byzantine ecclesiastical sexual standard was indicated by more than copying of Byzantine texts and failure to copy materials from other sources. The Slavs did not adopt the full range of Byzantine canons, but rather selected writings they found to be most appropriate to their own societies and sense of propriety. The Slavs might select one or another of the multitude of Byzantine canons; they might ignore some canons, add others, and alter details. The differences occurred in the details of acceptable and unacceptable conduct, the relative seriousness of offenses, and the severity of punishment. The Slavs did not, during the medieval period, challenge the Byzantine concepts of sin and sexuality.

122. "Poslanie starca Iosifa (Volockago)," in *Pamjatniki starinnoj russkoj literatury*, 4:192–193.
123. Tixonravov, *Letopisi russkoj literatury i drevnosti*, 89–90.

The Slavs' acceptance of Byzantine sexual standards may perhaps be explained in three ways. First, the Byzantine tradition seemed rich, complete, and consistent to the less cultured Slavs, and, more important, it was imbued with the spiritual truth of their new Christianity.[124] By the time the Slavic peoples were secure in their Orthodoxy, threats from the Mongols, the Turks, and the Roman Catholic West made them cling to their established faith as a matter of cultural and national identity. Even the fall of Constantinople did not cause the Slavs to question the validity of the Byzantine model. On the contrary, it presented a poignant example of the dire consequences of rejecting essential aspects of their faith, and made righteousness, measured partially in sexual purity, even more important.

Second, Byzantine Christianity shared with Slavic pagan traditions the conviction that proper sexual conduct was essential to the proper ordering of the universe. Sexual behavior was not primarily a matter of personal ethics for the individuals involved. Rather, it determined the benevolence or hostility of supernatural powers, and thus was rightfully of concern to the religious authorities and the community. The Orthodox and pagan systems shared beliefs in the patriarchal structure of the family and the potency of female sexuality. In this context, it is not surprising that individual pleasure in sexual intercourse never became an issue; personal satisfaction was of little consequence in comparison with the cosmic significance of the act itself. But despite the common ground between Slavic paganism and Orthodox Christianity, discrepancies emerged in the details of the Slavic Orthodox rules on marriage and sexual conduct.

Third, the Slavic Orthodox sexual ethic contained a great understanding of and sympathy for human weakness to balance the consciousness of inescapable sin. Under canon law, despite the belief that the Devil originated sexual desires, individuals who committed sexual violations were responsible for their own actions. "The Devil made me do it" might be an acceptable excuse in saints' lives and tales, but not in private confession. In real life, persons who experienced sexual urges were considered to have made themselves vulnerable to them by distraction or lack of faith. A person who yielded to such urges through illicit activity bore responsibility for the sin. At the same time, Orthodox confessors did not probe attitude and intention. Sex acts were judged on objective criteria, the circumstances of intercourse, rather than the attitudes and intentions of the penitent. Thus sex for pleasure was no more sin-

---

124. Georges Florovsky, "The Problem of Old Russian Culture," in Michael Cherniavsky, ed., *The Structure of Russian History* (New York, 1970), 126–139, esp. 136–137.

ful than sex for procreation—a striking departure from the Roman Catholic position. Penitential literature conceded the sinfulness of lustful thoughts—after all, did not Christ say that lusting after a woman was akin to committing adultery with her? However, clerics were not prepared to impose the same penance for lechery and adultery. In practice, the church strove to regulate actions more than words or thoughts.

Although sexual desire was perceived to be of demonic instigation, the church did not regard all expressions of sexuality as equally sinful.[125] As we shall see, there was a hierarchy of sins, whose seriousness could be measured by the length and severity of the recommended penances. The priest's role was to guide the penitent to a full confession, to pray with him or her for forgiveness, and to impose a healing penance. And although didactic literature taught that women were more susceptible to sexual sin, to the detriment of their own and their husbands' souls, most provisions of canon law authorized identical penalties for men and women offenders.

That sexual standards would be violated frequently Orthodox thinkers did not doubt, but the human propensity to sin was no justification for altering God's eternal and immutable dicta. Recognition of the human capacity for sin did not alter the church's high ideal of sexual conduct, but it did foster an attitude of compassion for those who fell short of it. For the sake of their souls, sinners had to undergo instruction and penances, but the clergy expected repeated and frequent sexual violations and made allowances for them. The church recognized that men and particularly women were weak and the Devil was strong; even the dispensation of marriage would not suffice to forestall less licit forms of sexual activity.

125. The Orthodox Church did not adopt the Roman Catholic categories of mortal and venial sins.

CHAPTER 2

Marriage

The Orthodox Church was ambivalent about marriage. On one hand, it officially approved. When Jesus blessed the wedding at Cana, he established once and for all divine approval of the institution. The image of the marital union inspired theological metaphors: Jesus "betrothed" himself to his church; the Virgin Mary was the "bride" of God. Marriage in this metaphorical sense signified a chaste and abiding union between two unequal parties. The male deity, omnipotent and compassionate, deigned to affiance himself to the female, exalting her above the ranks of ordinary mortals.

But this sort of spiritual union was a far cry from the physical consortium of human husbands and wives, which the church regarded with great suspicion. In the flawed real world, the celibate monastic life was glorified; marriage was the inferior alternative for the spiritually weak. "Virginity is the most greatly revered. For Christ did not damage the seal of virginity when he was born of the Virgin, but respected her virginity. Virginity is higher and much more honorable than marriage; as the angels are higher than humans and as Heaven is higher than Earth, so much is he who is not married higher than he who is married."[1] The sexual aspect of marriage was particularly distressing. In theory detached from reproduction, sexual activity served only Satan's purposes. While marriage might be adjudged the proper setting for conjugal relations and the birth of children, the sexual act involved remained tainted. Orthodox clerics were concerned lest their Bogomil rivals be proved

---

1. Luke Chrysovergus, patriarch of Constantinople, to Grand Prince Andrej Bogoljubskij (c.1100), in RIB, 6:70.

right in their assertion that marriage was nothing more than a license to sin.[2]

Living without marriage in the world, Orthodox clerics realized, represented even more of a license to sin. Many were adamant: a supervised monastery was the only appropriate residence for the celibate; persons living "in the world" should be married, or grievous sin would result. This philosophy was reflected in the requirement that parish priests be married. A few hierarchs went so far was to order that single lay people marry. "If you have spiritual children who are unmarried," one Russian hierarch wrote to his priests in the sixteenth century, "you should get them married; bachelors should not live without wives."[3]

The Adaptation of Canon Law

Ecclesiastical sources gave only one explanation of the marital canons: they reflected God's law, and were intended to preserve society from sin. From a historical perspective, rather than the metaphysical, laws regulating marriage must reflect social realities and standards.

The Slavic churches strove to regulate marriage, both in its forms and in the relationship between spouses. Byzantine Orthodoxy offered a ready-made set of rules for sexual relationships.[4] The Slavs' reverence for the divine authority of Orthodox canons and the secular laws of the Christian Roman Empire did not alter the fact of their incomplete suitability for medieval Slavic society. The conflict between Orthodox law and preexisting societal needs and standards was resolved more easily in practice than in theory. The Slavic churches had the task of resolving these differences, merging the Slavic pre-Christian tradition and the newly acquired Christian dicta into a unified and enforceable system.

Churchmen were reluctant to alter established canons; they did not doubt that the canons reflected immutable, divine commandments, yet they could not help noticing that they were often contradictory. The rules of the ecumenical councils did not match those established in the civil law of the Byzantine empire, the mimesis of the Heavenly Kingdom.

2. See Sava Kosanović, ed., "Beleška o bogomilima," *Glasnik Srpskog učenog društva* 37 (1873): 181, for a sample of Orthodox criticism of the Bogomil view of marriage. Some Roman Catholic canonists in the same period were equally unenthusiastic about marriage; see JoAnn McNamara, "Chaste Marriage and Clerical Celibacy," in Brundage and Bullough, 22–33; Brundage, "Carnal Delight," 364 and *passim*.
3. "Three Spiritual Instructions to Clergy and Laity," in RIB, 6:917–919.
4. Dauvillier and Clercq, who provide the best study of Orthodox canon law on marriage, subsume the Slavic churches under the Byzantine, and their treatment of Slavic policies is spotty.

The dictates of the venerable St. Basil were incompatible with those of the equally venerable St. John the Penitent. In selecting among the multiplicity of Orthodox sources, Slavic churchmen could draw on their own sense of justice and propriety, which was determined as much by their Slavic traditions as by their Orthodox ones. Furthermore, the clergy could innovate in their rulings to a limited extent, on the assumption that the customs of the Slavs, as a Christian people, were by definition Christian. The result of these efforts was a system of regulations that reflected both the realities of Slavic marital practices and the ideals that the Orthodox hierarchy was trying to inculcate.

The Slavic principalities placed the regulation of marriage under the exclusive control of the church. This practice should not be interpreted as an alienation of the rights of the secular state, because the secular government had not previously regulated sexual behavior. The princes were still instrumental in the establishment of policy, as indicated by the fact that their names were attached to the various codes governing familial relations. Instead of using secular authority to judge cases involving marriage and sexual behavior, the princes decided to mandate that ecclesiastical authorities act in their stead. The princes reserved the right to share jurisdiction in cases of rape, which involved both violence and sex, as well as in matters concerning inheritance.

The Slavs were monogamous and exogamous long before they adopted Christianity, but their customs did not coincide precisely with ecclesiastical canons. They had rituals to mark the transition from single to married life. Christianity added another ceremony, marking marriage as one of the sacraments of the church. It offered a set of rules on how, when, why, and with whom a marriage could be formed—rules that were justified not by practicality but by God's commands. A Christian theoretical understanding of the meaning of the marital union linked Scriptural teachings and symbolism to Orthodox ceremony and canon law.

The primary purposes of marriage among the medieval Slavs were economic and political rather than moral and religious. Marriage was a fundamental part of the clan and family structure that dominated medieval Slavic society. With each union, financial resources were pooled and political activities coordinated. Familial interests took precedence over individual preference. Arranged marriages were the rule and politically motivated dissolutions were acceptable. The emotional and physical bond between husband and wife was of interest only insofar as it affected the rest of the family.[5]

5. On the political purposes of marriage in medieval Russia, see Kollmann, *Kinship and Politics,* esp. 121–145. No study with comparable detail has been done on other periods of

At first glance, the church's rules seem to have ignored the most important aspects of marriage in medieval Slavic culture, because canon law said little about the political and economic aspects of marriage. Certain provisions of Byzantine secular law entered the compendiums of the Slavic Orthodox churches from the Procheiron and Justinianic Code, but they are found primarily in *zakonici* and nomocanons, which were intended as reference books for the upper clergy, and not in the abridged codes in parish manuals. With a few exceptions, Slavic rules were the same for all social classes. Native Slavic canon law had little to say about the economic arrangements surrounding a marriage. The church neither required a dowry nor forbade the *věno*, or bride-price. The church restricted its intervention in the economic aspects of marriage to suggestions and a few regulations.[6]

The failure of the Slavs to adopt Byzantine rules on the political and economic aspects of marriage must be balanced against their general acceptance of Byzantine regulations of the conjugal relationship itself, albeit with substantial revision. The Byzantine rules were developed for a complex, urbanized, aristocratic society, in which political alliances did not necessarily follow familial lines. Among the Slavs, the extended family and clan remained the basic unit of political and economic activity, and social stratification was neither so complex nor so rigid as in Byzantium. Property was much more likely to be measured in land than in monetary income. Furthermore, the Slavs had a tradition of female independence in economic matters; women, regardless of marital status, could own property in their own right. Byzantine rules on marital agreements, dowries, marital gifts, and interclass unions were not applicable to Slavic society.[7]

Byzantine rules governing the form of marriage and conduct within it fit Slavic society much better. Protection of the family unit was accorded high priority. A society based on familial structures needs to have clear rules on what constitutes a marriage, who may marry whom, and what behaviors are necessary and appropriate in conjugal relationships and

---

Russian history or on the South Slavs. Georges Duby, *Medieval Marriage: Two Models from Twelfth-Century France* (Baltimore, 1978), and Brooke, "Aspects of Marriage Law," 333–344, discuss the interrelationship of the secular and the ecclesiastical purposes of marriage in the medieval West. On the relationship between love and family interests in that milieu, see Flandrin, *Sexe et l'Occident*, 7–15.

6. Tsar Boris specifically asked Pope Nicholas I whether Christian law permitted economic arrangements surrounding weddings. See *Izvori za bŭlgarskata istorija*, 7:98.

7. Byzantine law known in medieval Serbia prohibited marriage between a woman and her former slave, and between a male aristocrat and a dancer, actress, or prostitute. See *Sintagmat*, 144. The financial and political aspects of marriage are discussed in, e.g., Ja. N. Ščapov, "Brak i sem'ja," 216–219; Dubakin; Elnett; Kovalevsky.

detrimental outside of them. Thus canon law emphasizing the form in which a marriage was celebrated, the choice of marriage partners, and general sexual conduct in fact reflected societal imperatives in addition to the church's teachings about righteousness and sin.

The Form of Marriage

Orthodox canons established before the adoption of Christianity by the East and South Slavs defined a legal marriage as one confirmed by a church ceremony (*blagoslovenie* or *venčanie*). The definition of marriage established in Western Europe, based on the Roman criteria of consent and marital affection, ceased to apply in Byzantium before the baptism of the Slavs. Civil marriage did not exist.[8] And the Slavs never picked up the Byzantine and Roman category of concubine—that is, a woman in a legally recognized conjugal relationship that fell short of marriage.[9] Consequently, canon law regulating the formation and dissolution of marriages diverged sharply between the Roman Catholic West and the Slavic Orthodox East.[10]

The requirement of church marriage was not practical in Slavic states in the first centuries after the official adoption of Christianity. There was a shortage of priests, especially in the Russian countryside, and an overtly pagan population remained. Consequently, older methods of solemnizing marriages persisted, in particular ceremonies featuring the formal

8. Pavlov, *Nomokanon*, 172–173.

9. Byzantine civil law acknowledged ancient endorsement of concubinage but forbade it to contemporaries on moral grounds. See Procheiron, art. 18, in Pavlov, "'Knigi zakonnyja,'" 84–85. The author of one text, clearly viewing marriage as the only socially acceptable conjugal relationship, recommended that a man should marry the woman he kept as his concubine, if she were honest; see NBS 688, f. 59v. An additional article of the syntagma demands that a man either marry his concubine or break the relationship; otherwise, he is to be excluded from the church: Troicki, 78. On the evolution of the category of concubine in the Roman Catholic Church, see Brundage, "Concubinage and Marriage."

10. On the sources of Orthodox canon law, see Dauvillier and Clercq, 1–9. The list of Serbian, Bulgarian, and Russian sources is incomplete. See also Brundage, *Law, Sex, and Christian Society*, 87–88, 94–98, 114–117. The difference between Orthodox and Catholic methods of celebrating marriages and judging their validity was an issue even in the ninth century, as revealed in Pope Nicholas' answers to Tsar Boris of Bulgaria: *Izvori za bŭlgarskata istorija*, 7:67–69. After describing the Catholic ceremony, Nicholas asserted the Catholic position: "Merely the consent of those whose union is in question suffices. If this consent alone is lacking in a marriage, all the rest having been celebrated is in vain, including sexual intercourse." A marriage ceremony could not be required, Nicholas argued, because some people were too poor to afford a celebration. For a discussion of the Roman Catholic definition of marriage by consent, see Brundage, *Law, Sex, and Christian Society*, 260–267, 331–336; and Charles Donahue, Jr., "The Policy of Alexander the Third's Consent Theory of Marriage," *Proceedings of the Fourth International Congress of Medieval Canon Law, Toronto, 21–25 August 1972*, Monumenta Iuris Canonici, ser. C: Subsidia, vol. 5 (Vatican, 1976), 251–281.

transfer of the bride and her property to her husband's house. This sort of common law marriage, a public wedding with familial support, was popularly viewed as legitimate. Only clandestine unions and those formed through individual choice were regarded as invalid. Church and state tacitly accepted prevailing custom, at least at first.

Churchmen acknowledged that a couple joined by common law were husband and wife without making an issue of the lack of a church ceremony. Indeed, in the Code of Jaroslav, canon law formally recognized common-law marriage by levying a fine on a couple who later divorced without justifiable cause.[11] Archbishop Ilja of Novgorod in the twelfth century included instructions on the ceremony priests should use to confirm an irregular union in a church ceremony. The couple were not to be condemned or ordered to separate. Instead, they and their children, if any, were brought into the church, where the usual *venčanie* service for marriage was recited. The officiating priest assigned a penance as atonement for the earlier sin.[12] The children of such irregular but permanent unions were uniformly regarded as legitimate before the sixteenth century; unlike the offspring of informal unions, they were allowed to inherit.[13] This principle held even in the case of the most suspicious unions, such as that of the twelfth-century prince Jaroslav "Osmomysl'" of Galič. He was married to Olga, the daughter of the powerful prince Jurij Dolgoruki, but kept a common law wife, Anastasija. It was Anastasija's son, Oleg, who immediately succeeded his father to the princely seat; the offspring of the legal union, Vladimir, became prince of Galič only later.[14]

The imposition of ecclesiastical marriage took centuries, especially in Russia. The eleventh-century metropolitan Ioann II condemned "those who marry without the benediction, and repudiate their wives, divorce them and join with others," and urged priests under his authority to try repeatedly to teach such sinners the error of their ways. He noted that proper marriage was confined largely to the upper ranks of society.[15] In the fifteenth century, Metropolitan Fotij made the elimination of common law marriage a crusade. He characterized noncclesiastical marriage as a form of illicit fornication, and even labeled it as *dušegublenie*, "destruction of a soul," in the same category as manslaughter and infanticide. Anyone who had married without priestly blessing was to be

11. Jaroslav's Ustav, art. 19, in *DKU*, 95.
12. Instruction of Archbishop Ilja (1166), art. 19, in RIB, 6:367.
13. "Russkaja pravda," art. 98, in *Pamjatniki russkogo prava*, 1:118.
14. N. de Baumgarten, *Généalogies et mariages occidentaux des rurikides russes du Xe au XIIIe siècle*, Orientalia Christiana, vol. 9 (Rome, 1927).
15. Canonical Answers of Ioann II, art. 15, in RIB, 6:7–8.

placed under penance for three years. Couples who refused to marry in church were to be denied access to ecclesiastical rites. He also called for "great civil penalties" for offenders, although there is no evidence that secular authorities complied. However, Fotij did not wish to put any obstacle in the way of couples who wished to conform; those who obeyed their priest's order to marry in accordance with church law were to be given communion.[16] Metropolitan Iona, in 1456, echoed the same concerns that Fotij had voiced in 1410. Iona also excoriated parish priests for allowing their parishioners to evade canon law and even abetting them in doing so.[17]

By the sixteenth century, Russian church authorities had withdrawn recognition from common law marriages. "Be it known to you that nobody may take a wife without the *venčanie*, neither the rich nor the poor, neither the lowly nor the enslaved. Without the *venčanie*, the wedding is illegal, profane, and impure."[18] One method of eliminating common law marriage was to refuse to uphold it, by permitting free divorce: "If a man comes to live with a woman without church marriage, or a woman with a man, and there were no prayers said in church by the priest, and they then want to divorce, either the husband from the wife, or the wife from the husband, they may be divorced, because without that [blessing] they lived in adultery."[19] The Moscow Synod of 1667 instructed priests to require such improperly married couples to confirm their marriages in church or risk excommunication and civil penalties.[20] Under seventeenth-century Russian secular law, the children of illicit unions were forbidden a paternal inheritance, even if their parents later married.[21] The persistent issuance of new rulings indicates that church dicta failed to secure universal compliance. A printed *trebnik* in 1651 acknowledged the continuing existence of common law marriages, despite regulations prohibiting them.[22] Penitential question-

16. Metropolitan Fotij to Novgorod (1410), in RIB, 6:272–273; "Instruction of Metropolitan Fotij . . . on Responsibilities of Clergymen" (c. 1431), in ibid., 512–513. In calling for the assistance of secular authorities in enforcing ecclesiastical marriage law, Fotij was echoing the syntagma of Matthew Blastares which quoted art. 26 of the Sixth Ecumenical Council; see *Sintagmat*, 173. See also "Pravilo o cerkovnom ustroenii," arts. 28–29, in Smirnov, *Materialy*, 92–93.
17. Metropolitan Iona to Vjatka (c. 1456), in RIB, 6:605–606. The problem persisted even into the nineteenth century in Russia. I. S. Belliustin complained that the local nobility pressured priests to agree to sanctify improper unions: *Description of the Clergy in Rural Russia* (Ithaca, 1985), 135–137.
18. Smirnov, *Materialy*, 115.
19. *DKU*, 206, from a sixteenth-century manuscript of the "Stat'i o razvodax."
20. *Dejanija moskovskix soborov*, 14v–15r.
21. "Sobornoe Uloženie carja Alekseja Mixajloviča 1649 goda," chap. 10, art. 280, in *Pamjatniki russkago prava*, 6:143.
22. Kiev 191, f. 153v.

naires routinely inquired whether the parishioner was properly married in church.[23]

South Slavic churchmen also granted backhanded recognition to common law marriage. In fourteenth-century Serbia, Stefan Dušan insisted on church marriage (*venčanie*); his statement that a popular celebration (*svadba*) was insufficient to make a marriage valid indicates that church marriage had not yet been fully established.[24] According to a fifteenth-century *trebnik*, however, it was worse to force a man and a woman in a common law marriage to separate than to permit them to stay together and impose the penance for illicit fornication. The rationale was that otherwise the woman might later enter into a second, adulterous marriage with another man.[25]

The church had two major objections to common law marriage. First, it removed the selection of the spouse from ecclesiastical purview, permitting unions that were forbidden under canon law. Because the church regarded proper sexual conduct to be a matter of community welfare, the institutionalization of offensive unions was an affront to God and a threat to society.[26] Second, common law marriage did not consist of the casual establishment of a joint household; it usually was concluded through a pagan ceremony, which posed a direct threat to the authority of the church. Pagan rites involved dancing, which was specifically forbidden by the Church Fathers as not in keeping with the solemnity of the occasion. Pagan fertility rites, such as bringing brides to water and cutting cheese, represented to clerics nothing less than an invocation of the sexual power of the Devil. These rites were conducted by *skomoroxi*, the surviving remnant of the class of pagan priests.[27] Ritualized abductions also came under the church's strong condemnation. Any priest who sanctified a union concluded by removal of the bride from her family's home was deposed from his rank; any layman who engineered such a union was anathematized.[28]

---

23. Almazov, 3:145, 160.

24. Code of Stefan Dušan, Atonski *prepis*, art. 2–3, in *Zakonik cara Stefana Dušana*, 164; discussed in Nikola Krstić, "Razmatranja o starim srbskim pravima," *Glasnik društva srbske slovesnosti* 11 (1859): 222–224. See also NBS 48, f. 182v.

25. Peć 77, f. 212r–212v.

26. In the medieval and early-modern West, the church upheld the definition of marriage by the consent of the partners in part to limit the power of families and feudal suzerains while increasing the authority of the church. See Donahue, 251–281; Ingram, 189–218.

27. Decisions of the Vladimir church council of 1274, in RIB, 6:99. See also Rybakov, *Jazyčestvo drevnej Rusi*, 152–154, 513. For a discussion of the roles of the *skomoroxi* in conducting weddings, see Russell Zguta, *Russian Minstrels* (Philadelphia, 1978), 12–13.

28. Examples of this provision are very numerous in the sources. See Chalcedon Canons, art. 27, in *Kormčaja*, 124; Hil. 300, f. 21v; BNL 251(200), f. 130v. Byzantine law included civil penalties for the abduction of women of any rank or marital status. See Pavlov, "'Knigi zakonnyja,'" 67; *Sintagmat*, 105, quoting canons of the Fourth Ecumenical Council, art. 26, and of the Sixth Ecumenical Council, art. 92. Abduction is discussed further in chap. 5.

[handwritten: Consummation Not Required for Valid Wedding]

Pagan marriage rituals proved to be more tenacious than the church had anticipated. Although ultimately the church prevailed upon the population of all classes to accept the necessity of a Christian marriage ceremony, it did not succeed in eradicating earlier forms. Instead, the church ceremony became merely one part of the ritual surrounding the taking of a bride. The Stoglav Council of 1551 registered a complaint against combining ecclesiastical and pagan rituals in the performance of marriages.[29] Hierarchs were very uneasy about permitting Orthodox priests to participate in the popular rituals surrounding weddings. Their participation would bring them into association with *skomoroxi* and would lend tacit support to drinking and dancing. At the same time, the priest could be a restraining influence, a constant reminder of the Christian nature of the occasion. The Moscow Synod of 1667 advocated a compromise between these two points of view, and authorized priests to ride in a wedding parade, although they were forbidden to acknowledge it as an Orthodox procession by carrying a cross.[30] Despite the church's objections, ritual abduction remained part of the popular wedding. The twelfth-century Russian *Kormčaja* condemned a widow who wished to remarry through a capture ritual, but more for the desire to take a second husband than for the pagan method she chose.[31] Ceremonial abductions were reported in sixteenth-century Bulgaria and among Ukrainian Cossacks of the mid–seventeenth century.[32]

The consummation of a marriage had no part in the ecclesiastical celebration. The church denied that sexual intercourse constituted a form of marriage ("Coition is not marriage," wrote St. Basil, "nor is it the beginning of marriage"),[33] and canons did not require consummation for a marriage to be considered valid and binding. As we have seen, the unconsummated marriage was held up as an example to be emulated. At the same time, the traditional customs surrounding the celebration of a wedding, including escorting the new couple to bed and examining the bedclothes for blood the following morning, were designed to guarantee that the conjugal union was established.[34]

---

29. *Stoglav*, 135–136.
30. *Dejanija moskovskix soborov*, 15.
31. GIM, Sin. 227, f. 193v.
32. See the reports of the Frenchman Ogier Chiselin de Brusbecq, in Bistra A. Cvetkova, ed., *Frenski putepisi za Balkanite XV–XVIIIv.* (Sofia, 1975), 124, and Guillaume Le Vasseur, sieur de Beauplan, "A Description of the Ukraine," in *A Collection of Voyages and Travels* (London, 1732), 537.
33. St. Basil's Rule, art. 26, in *Kormčaja*, 486. Similar sentiments are expressed in *Sintagmat*, 161.
34. Foreign travelers witnessed displays of the proofs of virginity, a custom that survived into the twentieth century. See Samuel Collins, *The Present State of Russia* (London, 1671), 8; Le Vasseur, 538.

Nonconsummation was not grounds for annulment. When one wife, Mar'ica, was unable to consummate her marriage, her husband, Marcko Vasil'ev *syn* (son) Moxin, petitioned the episcopal court of Ustjug for a divorce, charging that she had abandoned him. Mar'ica, conscious of her reputation, denied the charge. The court decided that it was in the best interest of all concerned to send Mar'ica to live in a convent. Although in effect Marcko received a divorce because of his wife's physical disability, he had to request the dissolution on the grounds of desertion, the equivalent of presumed adultery. In another case, Matrena Klimatova *doč'* (daughter) ran away from her husband, Stenka. Before he and his father could locate her, she had borne an illegitimate child to one man and had entered into an illegal second marriage with another. After her arrest, Matrena justified her actions to the court on the grounds that Stenka and his father had beaten her, that she and Stenka had not had sexual intercourse, and that she did not love him. None of these justifications was acceptable in the eyes of the church. The court ruled that nonconsummation did not justify the dissolution of the first marriage. Matrena was returned to Stenka, and the two were ordered to cohabit and consummate their marriage.[35]

The two cases together suggest that churchmen understood consummation to be a normal part of marriage, even though canon law did not require it. When consummation was desired but not possible, as in the first instance, the court found a way to dissolve the marriage. The only reason for dissolution that accorded with canon law was the wife's physical disability. The court could not acknowledge the husband's sexual needs overtly by annulling the marriage on the grounds of nonconsummation, or even by authorizing him to remarry. By placing the wife in a convent, however, the court in effect opened the way for the husband to contract a second union. When nonconsummation led to adultery, as in the second case, the court could order the couple to engage in conjugal relations with each other in order to prevent further sin. Although the church preached the virtues of the nonconsummated marriage, in practice it facilitated consummation for those who were unable to remain abstinent.[36]

35. Nos. 190 and 180 in RIB, 12:911–913, 856–860.

36. In the Roman Catholic Church, consummation became an essential component of a valid marriage, although only after several centuries of debate. See Gaudemet, 309–331; James A. Brundage, "The Problem of Impotence," in Brundage and Bullough, 135–140; Makowski, 106–107; Donahue; Brundage, *Law, Sex, and Christian Society*, 136–137, 188–189, 235–242, 260–267, 331–336.

Betrothal and Wedding

The ecclesiastical marriage service consisted of two parts, the betrothal (*obručenie*) and the wedding (*venčanie*). Both were public ceremonies, to be performed only in the church. Secret or private weddings were invalid.[37] The emphasis on public ceremonies might be understood as analogous to the twentieth-century desire to eliminate secret treaties and private governmental meetings: the public wedding announced the existence of a marital alliance. Canon law did not allow the omission of betrothal entirely, but it was permissible to perform the ceremonies sequentially on the same day. Byzantine custom generally included a betrothal months or even years in advance of the wedding, but Slavic custom was more mixed. Many of the manuscripts of the betrothal and wedding rites reveal the two ceremonies as entirely separate, the betrothal ending with a benediction and dismissal of the congregation. Many other manuscripts end the betrothal ceremony with the order to continue with the wedding service, if it was to take place the same day. A few manuscripts combine the two services completely, under one heading, indicating that no prior betrothal took place.[38]

Once a betrothal was made in church, it was almost as difficult to break as a marriage. Permission to dissolve the betrothal had to be sought from the bishop, metropolitan, or patriarch.[39] Under canon law, a man or woman who was betrothed to one person but married another was guilty of adultery.[40] If a couple managed to break their betrothal after a church ceremony, they were considered previously married, and suffered the disabilities attached to that position. Possibly this rule was motivated by both idealistic and practical considerations. The church held that a vow made before God and witnesses should be upheld; a

37. Procheiron, art. 20, in Pavlov, "'Knigi zakonnyja,'" 85; *Sintagmat*, 161; Hil. 171, f. 277r; NBS I-14, f. 244v. In the West, clandestine marriages were discouraged but were still valid; in Sicily, where there was a strong Greek tradition, Orthodox rules applied, and a priestly benediction was required for a valid marriage. See Brundage, *Law, Sex, and Christian Society*, 189–190, 442.

38. Of twenty-two *trebnici* from the fourteenth to the seventeenth century which I surveyed, six contain completely separate betrothal and marriage services, nine contain services that could be performed either separately or on the same occasion, and seven contain combined services to be performed together. The same pattern emerged in the Byzantine church in that period; see Dauvillier and Clercq, 35. The custom of having separate betrothal and marriage ceremonies was known in ancient Rome; perhaps the Byzantine custom originated there. See Jean Gaudemet, *Sociétés et mariage* (Strasbourg, 1980), 15–45.

39. See Grigorij Kotošixin's explanation of the procedure in Fedor Buslaev, *Russkaja xrestomatija: Pamjatniki drevnej russkoj literatury*, Slavistic Printings and Reprintings, vol. 222 (1904; The Hague, 1969), 305–312.

40. "Questions and Answers . . . on Pastoral Practices," art. 8, in RIB, 6:858.

formal promise to marry was binding upon both parties. Second, it is likely that betrothals in the medieval Slavic world, as elsewhere, were informally regarded as bestowing permission to enter into sexual relations. The church did not approve of premarital intercourse between fiancés, and subjected violators to penances ranging from forty days to four years.[41] The frequency with which this prohibition is repeated indicates how frequently it was violated.

In theory a betrothal was as binding as a marriage, and could be broken only for the same reasons. In fact, a whole range of additional justifications for breaking betrothals are found in Slavic canon law. Many of the rules clearly reflect Byzantine practice; hence it is not surprising that the South Slavs, and particularly the Serbs under Stefan Dušan, seem to have recorded the rules on betrothals most frequently.[42]

Byzantine rules forbade betrothals of children under the age of seven; promises made for children under that age were not binding. The Slavic churches did not issue this rule themselves, and betrothals at earlier ages were recorded. The betrothal could be broken if the children turned out to be unsuitable as marriage partners. For men, unsuitability could take the form of "obscenity" and "dishonor"—vague terms that could be used to reject any person with an unacceptable lifestyle. One ruling, however, rejected the notion that the bride could break off a betrothal because her husband-to-be kept a mistress.[43] A woman's unsuitability could take the form of obvious infertility or, conversely, her pregnancy by another man. However, canon law held the betrothal to be binding if the bride-to-be had been raped or seduced.[44]

Canon law also recognized that changing political and economic circumstances could make a planned marriage disastrous for the family. For that reason, a betrothal could be called off if either party suffered confiscation of property. The church did not permit betrothals to drag on indefinitely, leaving the young couple neither married nor free. After four years, a betrothal was not considered binding unless there was good reason for the delay. Justifications included the illness of bride or groom, the death of a parent, the groom's absence on princely service, and great distance between the residences of the two families. The church also permitted the breaking of a betrothal if either party apostasized from Orthodoxy. Byzantine rules, recorded only rarely in Slavic translation, authorized the father of the bride or groom to break off a betrothal even

---

41. See, e.g., Hil. 378, f. 157r (forty days of fasting); SANU 122(47), f. 15r (one year's exclusion from communion or forty days of fasting).
42. See *Sintagmat*, 191–192.
43. Peć 77, ff. 283v–284r.
44. Ancyra Canons, art. 11, in *Kormčaja*, 233; Kiev 49, f. 646r; *Sintagmat*, 104.

against his child's wishes. The church upheld the children's right to oppose a marriage when they reached the age of maturity, particularly for the purpose of taking monastic vows. Finally, in the interest of not compounding sins, the church forbade a betrothed couple to marry if the groom had slept with the bride's mother.[45]

When there was just cause, then, the betrothal might be broken, but there could be other complications, as in the case of the Cossack Vaska Klement'ev. Vaska petitioned Tsar Michael in a civil suit against the widow Anna Ivanova *žena* Zavalina and her three male friends. Vaska and Anna had been betrothed in a church ceremony. Later, Anna's friends invited her to their house, got her drunk, and persuaded her not to go through with the wedding. She apparently took up residence with them. Under the circumstances, Vaska doubtless could win release from the betrothal, on the grounds of Anna's improper association with other men. In a civil complaint he sought compensation for the money he had paid in advance for the wedding feast that never took place.[46]

Byzantine civil law recognized a written contract as a binding form of marriage with or without a church ceremony. Canon law both in Byzantium and among the Slavs recognized that such prenuptial arrangements existed but withheld affirmation of them, holding that the couple was free to call off the wedding with no ecclesiastical penalty.[47] In the Slavic world, marriage contracts were virtually unattested before the sixteenth-century, and did not substitute for a church ceremony. When they appeared in sixteenth-century Russia, they closely resembled other documents dealing with the disposition of property.

Among the Russian service nobility (*dvorianstvo*) of the sixteenth and seventeenth centuries, secular engagement contracts were developed to bind families to a promise of marriage. It was the transfer of service-dependent *pomest'e* land on the occasion of marriage that was central to these documents; they did not discuss relations between the spouses outside of property matters. Usually the bride was the daughter or widow of the holder of a *pomest'e*. She had retained the estate for her sustenance pending marriage. The promise to marry was conditioned upon the tsar's willingness to grant the *pomest'e* to the prospective bridegroom; the contract contained an escape clause to this effect. It sometimes provided for a monetary penalty to be levied against either party for failure to fulfill the terms of the agreement.

This system of premarital agreements fulfilled the financial needs of

45. Hil. 466, ff. 42v.–45r, 50r, 60v; NBS 688, ff. 58v–59r, 61r.
46. No. 172 (dated to 1640), in RIB, 25:224–225.
47. *Sintagmat*, 160, 188–190.

all concerned. The state ensured that the *pomest'e* would continue to finance the governmental service of a warrior or bureaucrat rather than the unproductive life of a female dependent. The bridegroom received additional income for the support of his household from his wife's *pomest'e* estate. The woman continued to receive support from the income of the *pomest'e*, and gained supplemental support from her husband.[48]

The church approved of prenuptial agreements as an extension of parental authority over the choice of spouse. While such a contract did not constitute a binding commitment to marry, it contained a sworn oath, and violation of it constituted a breach of canon law. Thus a husband petitioned in an ecclesiastical court when his bride's guardian did not provide the dowry previously agreed upon.[49] When a marriage contract was used to perpetrate fraud, such as the substitution of a less favored daughter for the promised one, both the state and the church punished the offender. In such cases, the marriage was considered null and void.[50]

An ecclesiastical court case suggests the existence of nuptial agreements for nonpolitical purposes. In 1686 the deacon Mixail Fedotov, on behalf of his sister Anna, sued the clerk Arefa Malevinskij in the court of the archbishop of Ustjug, charging him with breach of promise. Arefa had been courting Anna, clearly without her brother's permission. Mixail presented to the court a number of Arefa's love letters to Anna, begging her to meet him privately. (It appears that she refused to do so.) When Arefa came for his planned assignation one night, Anna and her younger sister called Mixail, his wife, and the neighbors to catch the intruder. Under the hostile gaze of this company, Arefa signed a written agreement to marry Anna or pay a penalty of fifty rubles. No record survives of the court's decision, but the form of Arefa's defense suggests that such a contract would normally be considered legal. Arefa argued not that the agreement had no force of law but that he had signed it under duress. He argued that the love letters to Anna were forgeries, and

---

48. Questions arose about the disposition of the estate when the first husband also owned ancestral (*votčina*) land, when the second husband already held a *pomest'e* of his own, when the widow had minor children, and when the holder was an orphaned daughter. Patriarch Filaret, who was the father of Tsar Michael and shared the state's interests, spuriously invoked canon law to discourage inheritance of *votčina* by the widow. He preferred to permit the state to confiscate a childless man's *votčina* and turn it into *pomest'e* for redistribution. See *Zakonodatel'nye akty russkogo gosudarstva vtoroj poloviny XVI–pervoj poloviny XVII veka* (L., 1986), nos. 161, 234, 93–94, 171–174. To date there has been no comprehensive study of women's inheritance of *pomest'e* lands.

49. No. 28 (dated to 1627) in RIB, 25:29.

50. Grigorij Kotošixin provides an account of nuptial agreements; see Buslaev, 305–312.

he had signed the contract only under threat of death.[51] The former excuse is dubious; many people seem to have known of Arefa's passion for Anna. The second argument was undoubtedly true. Mixail's motive in forcing the agreement is not entirely clear. Arefa hardly seems to have been a respectable choice for a husband. Perhaps Arefa's attentions had given Anna an unsavory reputation and no better suitor could now be found. Or perhaps Mixail hoped that Arefa would choose to pay Anna the fifty rubles, thus fattening her dowry at no cost to her brother.

In case there were second thoughts or a change in circumstances, it was safer to have an unofficial engagement, which could be broken more easily. A court case illustrates the advantages—and disadvantages—of informal engagements. Mar'ica Ermolina *doč* Borteva petitioned the court of the bishop of Ustjug in 1646. She had previously been married; probably that marriage had ended in divorce, because she called herself a "former wife" rather than the more prestigious "widow." She charged that Vasilij Šestoperov promised marriage before an icon of the Virgin and in the presence of his father and brother. Mar'ica then slept with Vasilij. When he discovered that she was pregnant, he threw her out of the house, insulted her, and threatened her safety and that of her children by her previous marriage. She did not demand that the court enforce such a vague promise of marriage; apparently she knew that approach was hopeless. She had no church betrothal or written document to back up her claim, and her reputation was already tarnished. Instead, she seems to have wanted protection, compensation for dishonor, and child support.[52]

A church betrothal in advance of the wedding might be forgone for a variety of reasons. Sometimes a waiting period was not advisable, either for political considerations or because of the bride's premarital pregnancy. Even when the match was made well in advance, the parents of the bridal couple may have preferred not to commit themselves irrevocably. In other instances, the imperatives of the political situation that inspired the marital alliance in the first place might encourage both parties to make an immediate, virtually unbreakable commitment, especially if the bride- and groom-to-be were underaged and ineligible to marry immediately. The betrothal of the future Russian grand prince Ivan III illus-

51. N. P. Pankratova, "Ljubovnye pis'ma pod'jaščego Arefy Malevinskogo," *Trudy otdela drevnerusskoj literatury* 18 (1962): 364–369.

52. No. 192 in RIB, 25:249–250. In Western Europe, such promises were considered binding; in themselves they constituted an expression of the "marital affection" sufficient to a marriage. See Klassen, 264–265; Beatrice Gottlieb, "The Meaning of Clandestine Marriage," in Robert Wheaton and Tamara K. Hareven, eds., *Family and Sexuality in French History* (Philadelphia, 1980), 49–83.

trates this principle. His father, Vasilij II, arranged for Ivan's betrothal to Maria, daughter of Prince Boris Aleksandrovič of Tver, in 1447. The future groom was less than seven years old at the time; the age of the bride-to-be is not given. An alliance with the powerful house of Tver was certainly of value to Vasilij II, who was struggling against the claims of Dmitrij Šemjaka; the betrothal became an occasion for him to rally the support of Tverian nobles. The actual marriage took place five years later, in 1452, when the groom was still legally underaged.[53] Furthermore, the church preferred to try to control betrothals, as a means of eliminating common law marriage. To that end, Metropolitan Fotij of Russia recommended that betrothals, like marriages, be held not in private homes but in churches.[54]

The betrothal and wedding ceremonies contained many of the elements that still characterize traditional Orthodox nuptial rites. There were blessings for the health of the couple and the community, hopes for the birth of children, and praise for God, Jesus Christ, and the Mother of God for care and sustenance. One of the featured readings from Genesis recalled the creation of Adam and Eve, and a second, from Paul's first epistle to the Corinthians, explained the duties of husband and wife to each other. The Gospel reading, from John, recounted Jesus' miracle at Cana, the ecclesiastical justification of the institution of marriage.

Crowns were placed on the heads of bride and groom. Indeed, the crowning became the distinctive aspect of the wedding ceremony, which became known as *venčanie*, literally, "crowning." Numerous explanations of this custom have been offered to Orthodox believers over the centuries. Modern Orthodox teaching presents the crowns as symbols of honor, portraying the groom and bride as king and queen. Another, more religious explanation marks their status as members of the royal family of the Kingdom of Heaven. Medieval texts did not include these explanations, or, often, any explanation at all. According to St. John Chrysostom, the nuptial crowns symbolized victory over the flesh.[55] According to one text, the crowns symbolized martyrdom: marriage was portrayed as a voluntary sacrifice of the self for the greater glory of God.[56] It is possible that this explanation is the product of the imagination of a cleric, who recognized the paean to the martyrs among the processional hymns traditionally used at weddings. The nuptial crowns

53. Voskresenskaja chronicle, in *PSRL*, vol. 8 (SPb., 1859), 119, 125.
54. Fotij to Novgorod and Fotij to Pskov (1410–1417), both in RIB, 6:274, 283.
55. Dauvillier and Clercq, 40. These authors argue (42) that the crowning ceremony died out in Serbia in the fifteenth and sixteenth centuries, and that it was reintroduced from Russia. The manuscript tradition does not back up this assertion.
56. GIM, Sin. 598, ff. 83v–84r.

also represented a Christianized version of pagan floral wreaths, representing both honor to the bridal couple and magic to promote fertility.
The older custom survived and was adapted to Orthodox thinking: one
trebnik includes prayers for the removal and burning of the bridal
wreaths on the eighth day after the wedding.[57] Another custom of pagan
origin, that of married women wearing distinctive head coverings, similarly entered the realm of acceptable Orthodox rites.[58]

For members of the aristocracy, the wedding constituted a public
announcement of an alliance between families. Participation in the
ceremony marked support for the political ambitions that had prompted
the union. For that reason, Russian wedding announcements were extraordinarily detailed concerning the names and ranks of all the witnesses
and attendants.[59] Dynastic marriages were one of the major topics in the
Serbian chronicle.[60] Serbian tradition institutionalized the witnesses' expressions of support by naming them *kumovi* (spiritual relatives), and
thus official allies.[61]

The Choice of Spouse By parents

Both the form of the marriage and the dictates of canon law indicate
that first marriages were usually arranged by the parents. Parents had
both the right and the obligation either to arrange marriages for their
children by the time they reached the appropriate age or to arrange for
them to enter monastic life.[62] An often-repeated provision of canon law
required parental permission for marriage.[63] Numerous foreign visitors
mentioned that young people were forbidden by law and custom to
arrange their own marriages. Some brides and grooms did not even meet
before the wedding, particularly in sixteenth- and seventeenth-century
Russia, where propriety dictated that aristocratic girls remain in seclu-

---

57. Kiev 49, f. 71r. Konstantin Nikol'skij, *Posobie k izučenie ustava bogosluženija pra-voslavnoj cerkvi* (SPb., 1865), 683, discusses this custom.
58. Dečani 67, f. 203r–v.
59. See, e.g., the descriptions of aristocratic weddings in *Drevnjaja rossijskaja vivliofika*, Slavistic Printings and Reprintings, vol. 250/13 (1790; The Hague, 1970).
60. See Novaković, *Primeri književnosti i jezika*, 321–328.
61. The marriage service in Dečani 69, f. 165r, mentions the marriage *kumovi*.
62. Kotošixin reported that parents generally placed sickly or otherwise unappealing daugh-ters in convents; see Buslaev, 312.
63. This provision is very common, especially in South Slavic manuscripts, see, e.g., Hil. 300, f. 42v. On Byzantine law concerning parental permission, see Dauvillier and Clercq, 47–48. In the West, Luther and Calvin both broke with Roman Catholic canons and required parental consent for a valid marriage, deeming parents to be authorities ordained by God. See Brundage, *Law, Sex, and Christian Society*, 552–553.

sion. The parents or other relatives would visit the prospective spouse and determine his or her health, intelligence, and moral character.[64]

The medieval Orthodox Church had no objection to arranged marriages in principle or in practice. The biblical command that husbands and wives love each other was in no way viewed as incompatible with the virtual absence of individual choice in a spouse. Love between spouses reflected the spiritual love of the union between Christ and his church and between God and his children. How the marriage occurred was irrelevant. Individual choice seemed to medieval Slavs to be selfish—putting one's own desires before the welfare of the family. Obedience to parents, required both by the Fifth Commandment and by ancient tradition, had a higher priority than happiness in marriage.

Most compendia of canon law and manuals for parish priests included a rule forbidding the marriage of boys under the age of fifteen and girls under the age of twelve.[65] The frequent reiteration of this age requirement, coupled with a threat of suspension for any priest who knowingly approved a violation of it, indicates that there was a great tendency to marry children off at a very young age. In cases when the actual age of bride and groom in a first marriage were recorded, both were in their early to mid teens. A Russian decree of 1556 directed that a service-dependent *pomest'e* not be held in trust for a girl past age fifteen, an indication that a girl was expected to be married by that time.[66] Foreign visitors to Muscovy noted that girls usually married by age twelve or thirteen, and boys by age sixteen or eighteen.[67] Thus the fifteen- and twelve-year age minimums reflect the actual ages at which marriages were concluded. The age of puberty was not a consideration, because consummation was not required for a valid marriage.[68] Al-

64. See Kotošixin's account in Buslaev, 305–310; Sigismund von Herberstein, *Notes upon Russia (1517)*, *Hakluyt Society Works* 10 (London, 1851): 91–93; Giles Fletcher, *Of the Russe Commonwealth*, ed. Richard Pipes (Cambridge, Mass., 1966), 100–101; Guy Miège, *A Relation of Three Embassies from His Sacred Majestie Charles II to the Great Duke of Muscovie, the King of Sweden, and the King of Denmark* (London, 1669), 52; Collins, 35–36. Le Vasseur described (536–537) the visit of a young Cossack woman to a prospective bridegroom's family, but did not realize that this visit represented a parentally planned courtship rather than individual choice.

65. See, e.g., Metropolitan Fotij to Novgorod (1410), in RIB, 6:275; NBS I-14, f. 245r. An occasional code lists a slightly different age: Hil. 466, f. 47v, gives 14 years as the minimum for boys; Kiev 191, f. 585r, gives 13 as the age for girls. *Sintagmat*, 161, gives the minimum ages as 14 for boys and 12 for girls, in accordance with Byzantine law from the time of Leo VI.

66. *Zakonodatel'nye akty russkogo gosudarstva*, no. 14, 38.

67. Robert Best, "The Voyage Wherein Osepp Napea . . . ," *Hakluyt Society Works* 73 (1886): 355–377.

68. Peter Laslett calculated (214–230) the average age of puberty for girls to be 14 years, on the basis of census records from Belgrade, c. 1733–1734, which revealed that the average age at marriage was 14.88 years. Laslett assumed that menarche would be an essential precondition for marriage, as it was in Western Christendom, but the Orthodox Slavs had no rule to

though these ages marked legal adulthood, and for men the age of liability for military service, maturity and full responsibility were expected only at age thirty.

Although marriage was not permitted at ages below fifteen or twelve years, a betrothal could be contracted earlier. Byzantine law required that the future bride and groom be at least seven years old before betrothal, but native Slavic sources rarely repeat this rule.[69] There is some reason to suppose that the Serbian church observed this rule in the fourteenth and fifteenth centuries, when its princes adopted the Byzantine code of Matthew Blastares. The purpose of the rule could not have been to ensure the child's consent to the betrothal—a seven-year-old could not have been considered competent to make such a decision. Doubtless more practical considerations were involved: a child who lived to age seven was likely to reach adulthood, whereas a younger child's survival was much more in doubt. Because Orthodox canons recognized betrothal as binding, betrothal counted as one of the three marriages permitted by the church. Were infant betrothals permitted, with only a little bad luck three intended spouses could perish in infancy, leaving the survivor canonically unmarriageable even before adulthood. But even if the church had wanted to restrict betrothals to children who had attained the canonical age, it would not have been practical to do so, given the reality of politically motivated marriages.

Marrying children off in their early teens offered a number of advantages to the families and the society. At those ages, the children could be expected still to be tractable, willing in most cases to obey their parents' dictates. Although teenagers, particularly in modern society, are notorious for their obstinacy and rebellion, in the last analysis, most do as they are told; few have the self-confidence or the material resources to do otherwise. Ultimate acceptance of the parents' choice would be the path of least resistance. In addition, if a girl were married just before the age of puberty, the risk of premarital pregnancy could be avoided. Any sexual experimentation could be done within the confines of marriage. And the young woman's childbearing years were maximized to the phys-

---

that effect. In fact, one tradition in Roman Catholic canon law permitted marriage at age 12 for girls and 14 for boys, even if they were prepubescent, with the understanding that consummation would take place in due course; see W. Onclin, "L'Age requis pour le mariage dans la doctrine canonique mediévale," *Proceedings of the Second International Congress of Medieval Canon Law, Boston College, 12–16 August 1963*, Monumenta Iuris Canonici, ser. C: Subsidia, vol. 1 (Vatican, 1965), 237–247. Nonetheless, other evidence supports Laslett's conclusion on the average age at menarche; see Darrel W. Amundsen and Carol Jean Diers, "The Age of Menarche in Medieval Europe" and "The Age of Menopause in Medieval Europe" *Human Biology*, 45 (1973): 363–369, 605–612.

69. Hil. 466, f. 43r.

iological limit—an important consideration in an age of high infant mortality. At the same time, the extended family structure made it possible to avoid many of the drawbacks of early marriage. The young husband and wife were not left to fend for themselves; rather, they lived with one or the other set of parents, usually the groom's. The young groom did not support his wife through his own financial endeavors, but rather cooperated with his extended family to help provide for her. Thus there was no call for a young man to wait for marriage until he inherited property at his father's death. Under parental tutelage they completed their preparation for adult responsibilities. The education of the new daughter-in-law into the ways of her husband's family was particularly important for domestic stability. The young husband, for his part, might well father a son and heir before departing for extended periods of commerce, war, or princely service. Early marriage was thus in the interests of both individual families and the society as a whole.

Early marriage was not so much in the interests of the young couple. It practically eliminated personal choice in a spouse. At such a young age, the children would not be likely to have sufficient knowledge to choose for themselves a spouse who appealed to them emotionally and was also acceptable to their parents, more concerned with political and economic advantages. Furthermore, a child would have had few contacts with potential spouses; most of their contacts would have been with persons who fell into the forbidden categories of relatives by blood, marriage, and spiritual adoption. However, the youngsters would have been reared with the expectation of making an arranged marriage, without anticipating that the union would provide emotional fulfillment.

Rather than proposing a personal choice of spouse, a young boy or girl would be more likely to object to the parents' selection. Church canons acknowledged that sons and daughters theoretically had the right to reject a marriage but did little to guarantee this option to them.

When the child did not like the spouse the parents chose, the church preferred to uphold parental authority rather than the child's right of choice. The marriage ceremony itself presented the bride and groom no opportunity to voice their consent—or lack of consent—to the marriage. By their presence in the church for the *venčanie*, the couple indicated their agreement. In the seventeenth century, under the influence of Catholics in the Ukraine, Russian *trebnici* began to add a statement of consent, analogous to the established "I do" in the Anglo-Saxon tradition. The *trebnik* of Peter Mogila included such a statement of consent, as well as instructions to the priest to ascertain that the parents had not compelled acquiescence.[70] At the same time, the bride and groom also avowed that they had not been previously betrothed—a circumstance that would invalidate the marriage in progress.[71] A foreigner who visited the Ukraine in the late seventeenth century noted that stated consent was part of the wedding ritual.[72]

The church did not permit the parents to force the child into an unwanted marriage, although it did not specifically limit methods of coercion.[73] The social pressures brought to bear on a recalcitrant child could be extreme, as indicated by a provision of Serbian secular law: "If a maiden refuses to marry the young man to whom her parents promised her, she shall be considered shameless and dishonorable among her friends and before the people."[74] Medieval Serbian epics depicted a girl who refused her parents' choice of husband as condemned to burn in Hell.[75] If a child committed suicide rather than marry the parents' choice, the church condemned the parents for the child's sin.[76] The same held true if parents refused without good cause a marriage their child desired.[77]

Canon law offered the child only one option for avoiding an unwanted marriage: the monastic life. Because the church preached that monasticism was superior to life "in the world," it could not criticize a person who chose to become a monk or nun rather than marry.[78] At the same time, the church confirmed the need to respect and obey parents. The result of these two conflicting imperatives was a set of conflicting rules about youthful entry into the monastic life. While one rule required elders to inquire about parental permission before accepting a novice, another rule upheld the validity of monastic vows taken in defiance of parental orders. The sixteenth-century Novgorodian saint Marija Odoevskaja described this dilemma in her autobiography. "Now, one

---

70. Mogila, 359. The Slavs followed Byzantine tradition in the form of the marriage service and the absence of a statement of consent. Byzantine ceremonies of the fifteenth and sixteenth centuries occasionally included a declaration of agreement, inserted before the betrothal. The Slavic form clearly was derived from Uniate sources. See K. Ritzer, *Le Mariage dans les églises chrétiennes du Ier au XIe siècle* (Paris, 1962), 211–213; Dauvillier and Clercq, 43.

71. Kiev 127, pp. 171–172, dated to 1637. This *trebnik* shows considerable Roman Catholic influence; e.g., the penitential questions begin with a statement of faith in the "Catholic Apostolic Church" rather than inquiries about first sexual encounters (p. 122).

72. John Struys, *The Voyages and Travels of John Struys* (London, 1684), 142–144.

73. Hil. 466, ff. 42v, 48r, 49v. The church did not permit a son to refuse his parents' choice of spouse in order to continue an illicit relationship with a mistress.

74. Grbaljski Zakonik, art. 66, in Novaković, *Zakonski spomenici*, 110.

75. Brkić, 42–46.

76. Jaroslav's Ustav, art. 30, in *DKU*, 96.

77. Hil. 466, f. 48v; Jaroslav's Ustav, art. 47, in *DKU*, 98.

78. *Sintagmat*, 161.

must not go against the will of one's parents, except if one wants to take monastic vows, and therefore I had the strong intention to enter one of the monasteries and to beg father to let me live there, pray for my family, and preserve my virginity in the Lord." Marija took up residence in a convent and asked the abbess, Militina, to administer the vows. ". . . The abbess did not dare to do this in order not to make my father angry. . . . Then the abbess talked with my father a long time, quoting to him from the Holy Scriptures that nobody has the right to hold back either a daughter or a son who wants to live a monastic life, or to deprive them of their possessions."[79] The weight of ecclesiastical tradition, epitomized in the *vitae* of popular Slavic saints, favored the latter position over the former. Such eminent saints as Aleksandr Svirskij and Romil Vidinski fled their parents' home and the marriage they arranged to take on "angelic form."[80] But monastic life also involved a difficult decision for a young person—vows were legally irrevocable, and the monastic life, despite its spiritual rewards, was not easy.

The church refused to recognize a union contracted without parental consent and subjected the priest who solemnized it to sanctions. If a young couple married without permission but later gained it, they were still considered guilty of illicit fornication and were placed under penance for three years.[81] By banning secret marriages and requiring a public ceremony, the church made it virtually impossible for young people to marry on their own. Under canon law, elopement was considered a form of bride abduction, which the church strongly condemned. Secular law reinforced the church's requirement. A couple who married without their parents' permission could be deprived of their property and forced to pay a large fine to the prince.[82]

At first glance, a thirteenth-century Novgorodian birchbark letter seems to contradict the notion that parental permission was an absolute requirement for marriage: "From Mikita to Ulijanica. Marry me. I want you and you want me. And as witness to this Ignat. . . ."[83] Unmistaka-

79. From Isolde R. Thyret's unpublished translation of the *Zapiski* of Marija Odoevskaja. I appreciate Ms. Thyret's willingness to make her work available to me in advance of publication. For canon law prohibiting parents from barring their children from entering monastic life, see Hil. 305, f. 32r–v.

80. *Velikij Minej-Čet'i*, August, in GIM, Sin. 997, ff. 1144v–1145r; *Xristomatija po starobŭlgarskata literatura*, 384–388. Angelov discusses this issue briefly in "Man through the Middle Ages," 32–51.

81. This provision is very common, especially in South Slavic manuscripts; see Hil. 300, ff. 42v, 47v; Peć 77, f. 217r–v.; GIM, Sin. 227, f. 191; *Sintagmat*, 171, based on St. Basil's Rule, art. 38. In seventeenth-century England, the couple and the priest could be punished for a clandestine marriage without parental permission, but the marriage itself was valid and binding. See Quaife, 96; Ingram, 131–136.

82. Grbaljski Zakonik, art. 54 and 66, in Novaković, *Zakonski spomenici*, 110.

83. A. V. Arcixovskij, et al., eds., *Novgorodskie gramoty na bereste*, 7 vols. (M., 1953–1976), 6:76–77.

[handwritten annotation: Father all mothers choice]

bly, Mikita and Ulijanica were arranging their own marriage, for love rather than political advancement. The context is uncertain, however, as the note has not been preserved intact. Perhaps the two intended to seek parental approval. Or, more likely, they were older and widowed, and consequently free to arrange their own second marriages.

The church mandated that both parents grant their permission, under the assumption that husband and wife would agree on the choice of spouse for their child.[84] If a disagreement arose, however, the church backed the father's choice over the mother's.[85] A mother was empowered to arrange a marriage for either a son or a daughter if the father was away from home on business or dead.[86] A guardian served in place of the parents for an orphaned child. Byzantine law contained complex provisions on guardianship, to accommodate its distinction between legal minors and persons who had attained majority. Among Slavs, guardianship of minor children fell to the closest relatives in the extended family, so that familial control over marriage remained intact.

In the case of slaves, the master stood in loco parentis, and his consent was required for any marriage. But although the master could withhold his permission from a proposed union, he could not refuse to grant his slaves any opportunity to marry. Churchmen realized that if slaves were prohibited from marrying, illicit sex among them would be the consequence. Thus masters were admonished to arrange proper marriages for their slaves, in order to keep them from immorality. Failure to comply was punishable by excommunication.[87] The requirement of the lord's consent was also applied to other classes of dependents, such as serfs on monastic lands, who applied to the abbot for permission.[88]

Interfaith Marriages

The church required that both partners in a marriage be Orthodox Christians. The most stringent provisions of canon law withheld recognition of an interfaith marriage, and deprived of his rank any priest who celebrated one. The person married to a nonbeliever consequently was treated as a persistent fornicator, and was denied communion until he

84. St. Basil's Rule, art. 38, 40, and 42, in *Kormčaja,* 490–491.
85. NBS 688, f. 59r.
86. Hil. 466, f. 43v.
87. "Three Spiritual Instructions to Clergy and Laity," in RIB, 6:925; Hil. 378, ff. 150r, 160v. According to the "Pravilo 'Ašče dvoženec,'" art. 21, in Smirnov, *Materialy,* 68, the lord was excluded from communion for three months. Byzantine canon law recognized the validity of slave marriages only at the end of the eleventh century; see Dauvillier and Clercq, 41–42.
88. See four Russian petitions, dating from 1660 to 1684, requesting permission for widows and maidens to marry: no. 402, *Akty juridičeskie* (SPb., 1838), 424–425.

ceased illegal cohabitation.[89] The priest was usually dismissed from his post even if he had not known that the marriage was illegal; it was his responsibility to gather sufficient information from the families to find out.[90] Parents who arranged such illegal marriages for their children were placed under penance.[91] The eleventh-century Russian metropolitan Ioann II rebuked the "well-believing princes" for marrying their daughters out of the faith.[92] The presence of a similar inquiry in a seventeenth-century list of penitential questions for the tsar indicates that the practice had continued.[93]

With the exception of the twelfth-century Russian code of Jaroslav, canons on intermarriage treated men and women equally. Jaroslav's code levied a fine four times higher (fifty *grivny*—the highest fine in the text) when an Orthodox woman married a nonbeliever than when an Orthodox man did so. In the latter case, the offense was still treated more harshly than simple fornication; the twelve-*grivny* fine placed it in the same category as incest with a distant relative.[94] Perhaps the motivation was the protection of Orthodox Russian women—a strong theme of the code as a whole. The syntagma characterized sexual contact between an Orthodox man and a Jewish or Muslim woman as worse than simple fornication, because it involved "Satanic communion."[95]

Before the Union of Florence in 1439, the status of Roman Catholics was ambiguous. The thirteenth-century Bulgarian archbishop Dimitri Xomjatin ordered the excommunication of the Orthodox partner in a mixed marriage with a Roman Catholic, but only if the couple had been married by the Latin rite. In his view, the Catholic spouse was welcome to take communion in the Orthodox Church, because no Ecumenical Church council had anathematized the Roman Catholics.[96] The Syntagma of Matthew Blastares fell short of forbidding marriage to a Roman Catholic; instead, it called upon the Catholic spouse to renounce his or

89. Timothy of Alexandria, art. 11, in *Kormčaja*, 544. This provision is one of the most frequently repeated in parish service books and compendia of canon law; see, e.g., Peć 77, f. 212v. See also Troicki, 68–69. Orthodox canon law on intermarriage with heretics is discussed in Donald M. Nicol, "Mixed Marriages in Byzantium in the Thirteenth Century," in *Byzantium: Its Ecclesiastical History and Relations with the Western World* (London, 1972), 160–172; Dauvillier and Clercq, 164–165.

90. NBS 688, f. 50r, is an exception; the priest who blessed a noncanonical marriage was put under penance for two years but he was not defrocked.

91. The penance was either three years or five years, depending on the version of the provision: SANU 124(29), f. 82r; Hil. 302, f. 15r; Rila 1/20(48), f. 125r; VAT-Bor 15, f. 481r.

92. Canonical answers of Ioann II, art. 13, in RIB, 6:7. His ruling in this matter follows precedents in Orthodox canon law; see Laodichaean Canons, art. 31, in *Kormčaja*, 273.

93. Almazov, 3:174.

94. Jaroslav's Ustav, art. 20, 54, in *DKU*, 95, 98.

95. Troicki, 84.

96. Nicol, 167–168, 172.

her heresy.[97] The Code of Stefan Dušan was slightly more stringent concerning such marriages: "And if anywhere a half-believer take a Christian woman to wife, let him be baptised into Christianity: and if he will not be baptised, let his wife and children be taken from him and let a part of the house be allotted to them, but he shall be driven forth."[98] The Code of Dušan thus acknowledged the existence of interfaith marriages, and worked to persuade the Catholic partner to adopt Orthodoxy. If we may judge by Serbian *trebnici*, it was only in the sixteenth century that Roman Catholics were specifically defined as heretics for purposes of marriage.[99] The Russians seem to have begun to regard them as heretics for purposes of marriage in the mid–fifteenth century. The Code of Jaroslav included specific prohibitions on sexual and social contacts with pagans, Muslims, and Jews, but not with Catholics.[100] The absence of a specific rule might be taken to mean that marriage to Roman Catholics could be approved, depending on the time and place.

Alternative canons were more lenient in the matter of interfaith marriage. One version upheld the validity of the union, but demanded that the non-Orthodox spouse convert.[101] Other ecclesiastical authors, including the authoritative St. Basil, relying on Scriptural precedent from Paul, insisted that a marriage to an unbeliever was valid and binding.[102] The Orthodox spouse, through prayer and example, could ultimately lead the unbeliever to salvation. As long as the Orthodox spouse was not obliged to apostasize, the marriage could be permitted. The usual ban on eating and drinking with nonbelievers was relaxed for the interfaith couple. No requirement was made concerning the religion of their children.[103] The charter issued by King Stefan Uroš III to the Dečani monastery in 1330 reveals some of the problems of enforcing bans on inter-

---

97. *Sintagmat*, 181.

98. Art. 9, in Malcolm Burr, "The Code of Stephan Dušan," *Slavonic and East European Review* 28 (1949–1950):200.

99. See, e.g., NBS 688, f. 52v.

100. Jaroslav's Ustav, art. 20, 54, in *DKU*, 95, 98.

101. E.g., SANU 125(154), f. 22v.

102. St. Basil's Rule, art. 48, in *Kormčaja*, 493–494; see also *Sintagmat*, 182–183. Pope Nicholas also espoused this view in his answers to Tsar Boris, doubtless realizing that this approach would be practical in a country just beginning to adopt Christianity. See *Izvori za bŭlgarskata istorija*, 7:114–115.

103. This interpretation is given in response to the prohibition on interfaith marriages in the Laodichaean Canons, art. 31 (n. 92 above). The interpretation is contained in a Serbian *kormčaja* of the third quarter of the fifteenth century: NBS 48, f. 86v. See also SANU 124(29), f. 114r–v. The Roman Catholic authorities could take the same view, as revealed in a letter from the Venetian Senate to the Italian archbishop of Corfu (1599): " . . . it has always been and is yet our intention that he [the archbishop] not impede marriages between those of the Greek rite with others of the Latin rite." The letter requires that children belong to the denomination of their father, whether Greek or Roman: *Spisi o istoriji pravoslavne crkve u dalmatinsko-istrijskom vladičanstvu od XV do XIX vijeka*, vol. 1 (Zadar, 1899), 44–45.

marriage. It first prohibits marriages between Serbs and pagan Vlahs, and then rules that those who form such unions be classified with free peasants.[104] Thus intermarriage was discouraged, especially for the aristocracy, but was tolerated among the peasantry. Among the South Slavs, traditions of canon law permitting and forbidding intermarriage coexisted, sometimes even in the same manuscript.[105] In the eighteenth century, the Russian church reversed its sixteenth- and seventeenth-century policy, and permitted intermarriage between Orthodox and other baptized Christians. The policy on intermarriage was flexible enough to permit it when it was likely, advantageous, and difficult to prevent.

During the period of Turkish rule, Orthodox Slavs in the Balkans occasionally arranged unions between their daughters and Muslims. Because Orthodox canon law was ambiguous, an Islamic form of marriage was used. Term cohabitation (called *mut'a* in Arabic) was permissible between Muslims and adherents of the "Book" religions, Judaism and Christianity. The marriage legally took the form of a contract, based on land rental agreements, which granted to the Muslim husband the right to "lease the field of the woman." The period of the "lease" could be set in such a way that the cohabition lasted as little as a day or as much as a century (i.e., essentially for life). The woman provided the man with sexual favors and perhaps legitimate offspring. The children were considered the property of the man and were raised as Muslims. The man provided the woman with sustenance for the period of the contract, as well as substantial gifts. These gifts guaranteed her financial security in the event that the man broke the contract.[106]

Although the Orthodox Church did not sanction intermarriage between Christians and Muslims, it was not in a position to object to unions of this type. Not only would any protest be ineffective with the Turkish party, but the intermarriages often had advantages for the Christian community. The Orthodox wife was in a position to protect the church; her children, although raised as Muslims, might be sympathetic to the Orthodox viewpoint. The church was not willing, however, to tolerate the use of Islamic law by Christians as a means of circumventing Orthodox canons. Term contracts offered Orthodox couples an easy way of establishing a temporary liaison, or contracting a union forbidden for any reason under canon law. Furthermore, civil divorce was

---

104. Novaković, *Zakonski spomenici*, 651.
105. See, e.g., Hil. 300, f. 51r; NBS 688, f. 52r; Hil. 305, f. 25r; Hil. 466, f. 44r; Rila 1/20(48), f. 100r; SANU 124(29) f.114r–v. Most interesting in this regard is NBS 48, a mid-fifteenth-century Serbian *kormčaja*: in two places, ff. 83r and 117r, it forbids intermarriage, but on f. 86r, it permits it if the non-Orthodox spouse repents.
106. Musallam describes (36–37) the terms of *mut'a* marriage in Islamic law.

available to Christian couples under Turkish law. Turkish authorities were willing to hear suits between Christians when either party appealed to them, despite attempts by the church to have the Turks confirm ecclesiastical authority. Consequently, the church had to fall back on its own methods of persuasion to prevent recourse to Turkish law. Priests were instructed to impose heavy penances—even double the usual ones for illicit fornication—and, if necessary, to ban violators from communion for life and deny them Christian burial. At the same time, the bishop could authorize exceptions. The existence of the alternative of Turkish law provided the church with a means of circumventing its own rules when it was politically advantageous to do so. For example, the church could accept a civil divorce granted by the Turks much more easily than it could dissolve a marriage in an ecclesiastical court.[107]

The rules against intermarriage served religious and social purposes. By limiting marriage to others of the same religious belief, the community could preserve its integrity and identity. Outsiders with differing rules of conduct could be kept out, or be forced to adopt the dominant ethic. In the multi-ethnic society of Russia and the Balkans in the Middle Ages, such rules were essential for maintaining ethnic identity. The same multi-ethnic milieu, however, required occasional compromise.

Remarriage

Remarriage posed difficulties. One lawful marriage was in accordance with God's command, as a method of preventing sin. Subsequent marriages were perceived as a still greater concession to human weakness, which churchmen did not wish to indulge. The propriety of remarriages became a topic of debate in the Byzantine church. The dominant opinion, which was adopted by the Slavic churches in turn, discouraged but did not forbid remarriage.[108] From the earliest adoption of Orthodoxy, Slavic leaders were aware that this position on remarriage would be unpopular. In his questions to Pope Nicholas I, Tsar Boris of Bulgaria

---

107. N. J. Pantazopoulos, *Church and Law in the Balkan Peninsula during the Ottoman Rule* (Thessaloniki, 1967), 91–107; Ladislas Hadrovics, *Le Peuple serbe et son église sous la domination turque*, (Paris, 1947), 67–78.

108. On the development of Byzantine canon law on remarriage, see Guilland, 9–30; Dauvillier and Clercq, 195–200; Brundage, *Law, Sex, and Christian Society*, 68–69, 87–88, 94–98. A less satisfactory work is St. Pascu and V. Pascu, "Le Remariage chez les orthodoxes," in J. Dupaquier et al., eds., *Marriage and Remarriage in Populations of the Past* (New York, 1981), 61–66. Serial monogamy raised questions in the Roman Catholic West as well, see Stafford, 71–74. Ultimately the Western church came to the conclusion that multiple remarriages were acceptable theologically, provided each prior union had been properly dissolved.

made a point of soliciting an opinion more favorable to remarriage.[109]

Slavic authors quoted the tenth-century patriarch Sisinnios of Constantinople: "Only one helpmate has God given to man; and for a woman only one head has been established."[110] A Russian canonist agreed: "If God had commanded the taking of two or three wives, he would have created three wives for Adam."[111] Patriarch Evtimij of Bulgaria developed a theological justification for discouraging remarriage: "If there are two Christs, then there can be two husbands and two wives; if Christ is one, there is but one head of the Church, and one wife."[112] Thus any remarriage, regardless of how the first marriage was dissolved or the age or circumstances of the survivor, failed to comply fully with God's law. Although the church never adopted a doctrine that marriages continued to be binding after death, that seems to have been the underlying supposition.

Orthodox clerics were accustomed to tolerating sin, and thus were willing to accept second marriages as a compromise with human nature. Biblical examples could be called forth as justification of this policy: did not Jacob marry both Leah and Rachel in turn?[113] The fact that Jacob's unions were polygamous escaped Slavic Orthodox authors; indeed, they had no desire whatsoever to excuse polygamy, but only to find some expression in Scripture which would permit the socially necessary policy of recognizing second marriages. As the German ambassador Sigismund von Herberstein reported after his visit to Muscovy in 1517, "if any one marry a second wife, and become a bigamist, they allow it indeed, but scarcely think it a lawful marriage."[114]

Serial monogamy and contemporaneous polygamy were both termed *mnogoženstvo*. Bigamy was considered entirely inconsistent with the Christian life; concubinage was condemned as merely a form of institutionalized adultery.[115] It mattered little whether a man actually kept two wives simultaneously in the same household or left the first and took in the second. Provisions on bigamy rarely distinguished between

109. *Izvori za bŭlgarskata istorija*, 7:67–69.

110. Peć 77, f. 254v. The philosopher Athenagoras voiced this view most forcefully: "A second marriage is decent adultery. . . . Anyone who separates himself from his first wife, even if she is dead, is a secret adulterer; he transgresses the creation by God, who made only one man and one woman; he breaks the tie that links his body with another body in perfect unity" (quoted in Guilland, 9).

111. "Pravilo 'Ašče dvoženec'", art. 3, in Smirnov, *Materialy*, 64.

112. Kaluzniacki, 243. Evtimij developed this view in justifying the prohibition on *venčanie* for a second marriage.

113. NBS 654, f. 94v.

114. Herberstein, *Notes upon Russia*, 93.

115. See, e.g., the canonical answers of Metropolitan Ioann II of Russia, art. 6, in RIB, 6:4.

these two situations.[116] Sometimes no distinction was made between bigamy and a legal second marriage.[117] In a sermon condemning multiple remarriages, Metropolitan Fotij of Russia accused those who participated in such unions of "being of the heresy of the accursed Mohammad," whose religion permitted polygamy.[118] The usual resolution of a case of bigamy—whether actual or technical—was to require the husband to remain with or return to the first wife; the second, along with any children, became a ward of the church. The hierarchs who enacted this rule realized that it was not likely to be to the taste of the bigamous husband, and warned him against treating the first wife badly.[119] If the second wife had not known about the first, she was exonerated, and was permitted to marry again.[120]

In practice, the church's stand on remarriage was governed by the often-repeated formula of Gregory the Great: "The first marriage is law; the second, dispensation; the third, transgression; the fourth, dishonor: this is a swinish life."[121] Because even a second marriage violated the divine intent, a person who remarried was directed to undergo a variable period of fasting and prayer.[122] A man who married for a second time was forbidden the normal male privilege of entering the sanctuary.[123] He was also ineligible for the deaconate and the priesthood.

This official disapproval was reflected in the ceremony used to celebrate a second marriage, which differed greatly from that used for a first marriage. Prayers for the forgiveness of sin abounded, making it clear that the second marriage was permitted only because of human weakness. They included a paraphrase of Paul's message to the Corinthians (I Cor. 7:8–9): "It is better if you remain as I am [i.e., celibate]. However, if you cannot, it is better to marry than to burn." As a further mark of ecclesiastical disfavor, the crowning (*venčanie*) was prohibited. Instead, prayers over the newlyweds were recited at vespers.[124]

---

116. Here Slavic canon law follows Byzantine civil codes; see Pavlov, "'Knigi zakonnyja,'" 75. *Sintagmat*, 165, includes a provision that clearly pertains to the keeping of two wives simultaneously; another obvious reference to two simultaneous wives is found in the answers of Pope Nicholas I to Tsar Boris: *Izvori za bŭlgarskata istorija*, 7:99.

117. See "Nekotoraja zapoved'," art. 25 and 36, in Smirnov, *Materialy*, 30–31. The twelve-year penance in the first article, in comparison with the more common three-year penance in the second, makes it likely that the first pertains not to remarriage but to bigamy.

118. Fotij to Pskov (1422–1425), in RIB, 6:432–433.

119. Jaroslav's Ustav, art. 18, in *DKU*, 95; *ZSL-K*, 50.

120. Hil. 378, f. 161r.

121. See, e.g., Fotij to Pskov (1410–1417), in RIB, 6:281.

122. Laodichaean Canons, art. 1, cited in *Sintagmat*, 163.

123. BNL 251(200), f. 130v; Dečani 68, f. 280v.

124. "Questions and Answers . . . on Pastoral Practices," art. 59, in RIB, 6:867–868; Rila 1/20(48), f. 101r; Troicki, 73, 75.

Because of the popularity of the crowning (as indicated by the use of the term to mean "wedding service") and the frequency of second marriages, some service books included it for second marriages, despite the prohibition.[125] A person could wear a crown at a second wedding only if the first marriage had been ended by the death of the spouse. A divorced person was ineligible for *venčanie*.[126] A hybrid sort of service evolved for use when only one partner had previously been married. In that case, only the "virgin" spouse wore the crown, while the one entering into a second married went without, or wore the crown on a shoulder.[127] The church also imposed a penance on the couple, as a method of healing the sin involved in transgressing the first marriage by entering into a second.

The length of the penance varies considerably from manuscript to manuscript, a reflection of traditions that varied in their tolerance of remarriage. All traditions distinguished between a somewhat sinful second marriage and a decidedly suspicious third marriage, in keeping with the formula of Gregory the Great. The Slavs did not accept penances recommended by the strictest of the Orthodox Church Fathers, Nicephoros the Confessor.[128] Rules attributed to St. Basil recommended a penance of one or two years for a second marriage, and three or four for a third marriage—when they permitted such a union at all.[129] Some Slavic texts accept St. Basil's rules for second marriages; others follow the more liberal rules of St. John the Penitent, and impose a penance of only one month.[130] The penance could take the form of exclusion from communion alone among ecclesiastical rites, or a prohibition on entry into the church building.[131] The fees levied for marriage increased with each remarriage. In the Russian church in the sixteenth century, they consisted of one *altyn* for the first marriage, two *altyny* for the second, and four *altyny* for the third.[132] A hundred and thirty years later they were raised (to counteract inflation or to increase income) to four *altyny* for the first marriage, six when one spouse had previously been married, eight when both partners were previously married, and ten when either

125. NBS 51, f. 24r–v; NBS 52, f. 168v; VAT-Bor. 15, f. 480r; Kiev 49, f. 76r.
126. Tixonravov, *Pamjatniki otrečennoj russkoj literatury*, 1:296; Smirnov, *Materialy*, 92–93.
127. "Pravilo s imenem Maksima," art. 5, in Smirnov, *Materialy*, 51; Kiev 136, f. 145v. Kotošixin also reports this custom; see Buslaev, 310.
128. Pavlov, *Nomokanon pri Bol'šom Trebnike*, 171.
129. St. Basil's Rule, art. 4, 50, in *Kormčaja*, 467–468, 494; Troicki, 68; GIM, Sin. 227, f. 181r–v.
130. E.g., SANU 123(28), f. 30r, quotes both St. Basil (one year) and St. John (one month). See also Dečani 69, f. 112r (two years); and the unusual Hil. 305, which imposes one to two years in one place (f. 25r) and six months in another (f. 112r).
131. The English traveler Samuel Collins noted (11) that remarried persons stood outside the church building.
132. From *Stoglav*, chapter 48, cited in Benešević, *Sbornik pamjatnikov*, 59.

partner had been married twice before.[133] Among the South Slavs in the same period, the fee doubled on the occasion of the second marriage and quadrupled for the third.[134]

The penances often reflected the ages of the individuals who entered into a second marriage. The church usually defined "youth" as under the age of thirty; for such people sexual restraint was desirable but not realistically expected. A second marriage for "older" couples, usually defined as those over age forty, was discouraged but not prohibited. If the penance for a young couple was two years, the penance for an older couple might be three or four years.[135] A provision that appeared occasionally forbade a widow over age sixty to remarry, presumably because she could no longer bear children.[136] A Russian tale warned of the dangers of a May–December marriage. The prospective bride told her older suitor that she would make his life miserable by disobeying his instructions and taking a young lover to satisfy her physically. An old man, she said, should be thinking about his salvation, not about pleasing a wife. The old man persuaded the maiden's parents to give her in marriage, even against her will. Of course, the worst came to pass, and the author concluded blackly, "Old men should not marry young wives."[137]

Ecclesiastical writers were unsympathetic to the idea of remarrying to fulfill sexual desires. A didactic tale pointed the moral that widows and widowers should not seek a second union, especially for the purpose of obtaining semilicit physical companionship. In this story, a widower approached a widow with a proposal of marriage. She agreed, with the proviso that he not eat until she called him to her. After four days, she invited him to her home and offered him a choice: a fine dinner at her table or a place in her bed. Of course, the starving man chose the food. The widow pointed out how easily fasting could defeat evil thoughts, and recommended that they both enter monasteries instead of marrying.[138]

Russian law did not require a waiting period between the death or divorce of a first spouse and the conclusion of a second marriage. Byzan-

133. From a decree of Metropolitan Pavel of Nižegorod (1687), no. 295, in *Akty sobrannye v bibliotekax i arxivax Rossijskoj imperii*, vol. 4 (SPb., 1836), 442–443.

134. Hadrovics, 77–78.

135. "Three Spiritual Instructions to Clergy and Laity," in RIB, 6:920 (four years); Hil. 169, f. 79r (three years); Kiev 49, f. 648v (three years).

136. Hil. 378, f. 158r; GIM, Sin. 227, f. 189r.

137. "Pritča o starom muže i molodoj device," in *Pamjatniki starinnoj russkoj literatury*, 2:453–454. Dauvillier and Clercq state (159) that the Russian nomocanon prohibited marriages between persons of vastly different ages, but they provide no citation.

138. Nikolova, 271–272; "Povest' o celomudrennoj vdove," in *Pamjatniki starinnoj russkoj literatury*, 1:213–214.

tine and South Slavic laws required that a widow observe a mourning period of a year before remarrying. Thus there could be no question about the paternity of a child born of a newly widowed woman. Men were also required to observe a period of mourning.[139]

The church regarded third marriages with suspicion. Certain Church Fathers forbade third marriages altogether. Some Slavic hierarchs, especially Russians, accepted this view, labeling third and fourth marriages "a great evil," especially for women.[140] The Charter of Vsevolod, from late-thirteenth-century Russia, ruled that the children of third and fourth marriages could not receive shares of the paternal inheritance equal to those given to the children of legitimate unions.[141]

Most churchmen, however, were willing to permit third marriages, with restrictions and penances of three to seven years.[142] It is not uncommon to find collections of canon laws which reflect both views.[143] One view, espoused by Metropolitan Peter of Russia, among others, held that third marriages were appropriate only for individuals who were "young" and had no children by either prior union.[144] A twice-married man or woman who was over age forty or had children had no reason to seek a third marriage. Metropolitan Kiprian of Russia was a reluctant adherent of this view. Although he regarded third marriages as appropriate only as a dispensation for the young and weak, "so they do not perish from lust and obscenity," he permitted those twice-married persons who were living in sin and having illegitimate children to regularize their unions. He mandated a penance of two or three years. He withheld his permission only from the "old," who could justify a third marriage by neither childbearing nor youthful incontinence.[145] Kiprian's view reflected a South Slavic tradition—one that became dominant in seventeenth-century Serbia. Most manuscripts of that period recommended a penance of four years for a third marriage when a person had no children, and five years when he was under age forty and had children. Sometimes the lower penances of the tradition of St. John the

---

139. *Sintagmat*, 146; Grbaljski Zakonik, art. 52, in Novaković, *Zakonski spomenici*, 109.

140. See, e.g., "Canonical Answers of Metropolitan Ioann II," art. 17; "Instruction of Metropolitan Peter to the Clergy," 1308–1326; and encyclical letter of Archbishop of Rostov, fifteenth century, all in RIB, 6:9, 161, 876; GIM, Sin. 227, f. 192v; "Nekotoraja zapoved," art. 20, in Smirnov, *Materialy*, 29; Hil. 302, f. 78r; Kiev 191, f. 584r.

141. Art. 24, in *DKU*, 158; also in Beneševič, *Sbornik pamjatnikov*, 94–95.

142. Hil. 378, f. 153v, gives penances of three, four, and five years; Kiev 136, ff. 152r–153r, gives penances of five and seven years; "Pravilo 'Ašče dvoženec,'" art. 2, in Smirnov, *Materialy*, 63, also gives seven years.

143. E.g., Rila 1/20(48) anathematizes third marriages on f. 102r and lists penances of three and four years on ff. 95r and 102r.

144. "Poučenie Petra Mitropolita," in *Pamjatniki starinnoj russkoj literatury*, 4:186–188.

145. Metropolitan Kiprian to Abbot Afanasij (1390–1405), in RIB, 6:252–253.

Penitent were also cited: four months in the former case, one year in the latter. A person who was over age forty and had children was forbidden to marry.[146]

In Russia, a different tradition developed in regard to third marriages. They were permitted even for older persons, but with substantial penances. The actual length varied somewhat: Metropolitan Fotij of Russia recommended a penance of five years' exclusion from communion for an older person.[147] In other texts, the penance might be less—four years or as long as six to eight years.[148] Thus a person under age thirty would undergo a penance of three years; a middle-aged person, five years; and an older person (forty-five or fifty or older), seven years.[149]

If third marriages were little better than legitimized adultery, fourth marriages were scandalous. The venerable St. Basil declared that fourth marriages were a greater insult to God's law than simple fornication. The acceptability of fourth marriages, even more than third marriages, had been a matter of debate in the Byzantine church and state, and Slavic hierarchs were aware of the controversy.[150] Most Slavic writers forbade fourth marriages outright. Those who entered into fourth marriages were to be denied participation in any ecclesiastical rites until they had separated from their illicit spouses.[151]

The inclusion of fourth marriages in the formula of Gregory the Great opened the way to grudging permission. In fourteenth- and early fifteenth-century Serbian manuscripts, fourth marriages were permitted, with a penance of five years.[152] Late-fifteenth- and sixteenth-century texts raised the penance to eight years.[153] Seventeenth-century texts usually forbade fourth marriages altogether, imposing a penance of five to eight years after the illicit union was dissolved. Under the rules of St. John the Penitent, this penance might be reduced to one year.[154] The Russian tradition was less uniform in its treatment of fourth marriages.

146. SANU 122(47), ff. 14v–15r.
147. Fotij to Novgorod (1410), in RIB, 6:273.
148. "Three Spiritual Instructions to Clergy and Laity" and "Questions and Answers . . . on Pastoral Practices," art. 13, both in ibid., 920, 859.
149. VAT-Bor. 15, f. 480r; Kiev 49, f. 647v. A Serbian printed book from 1546 also picked up this tradition: NBS I-14, f. 250r.
150. *Sintagmat*, 167–168, quoting St. Basil's Rule, art. 80.
151. See, e.g, Fotij to Novgorod (1410), in RIB, 6:273. It is worth noting, however, that Metropolitan Fotij grudgingly permitted fourth marriages in a copy of the letter to Pskov. See Daniel H. Kaiser, "The Transformation of Legal Relations in Old Rus' (Thirteenth to Fifteenth Centuries)" (Ph.D. diss., University of Chicago, 1972), 422.
152. See, e.g., Dečani 69, f. 112r. Hil. 466, f. 50r, permits a fourth marriage only for a young widow or widower.
153. See, e.g., Hil. 169, f. 79r.
154. SANU 122(47), f. 15r; Hil. 170, f. 87r. Serbian epics describe fourth marriages in derogatory terms but considered them valid; see Brkić, 51–54.

Some texts permitted them, with penances of five to eight years, while others did not.[155] The sixteenth-century code Stoglav barred a person married for the fourth time from entering the church building for four years, and ordered an additional year of exclusion from communion. Later the same text forbade priests to celebrate fourth marriages.[156] This second opinion became dominant in the seventeenth century, when Metropolitan Pitrim of Novgorod issued an order regarding priests who fled from episcopal justice after performing a forbidden fourth marriage for a parishioner.[157]

The Orthodox Church had an established tradition forbidding more than four marriages, regardless of age or circumstances. The justification for this prohibition was found in John 4:16–18, where Jesus reproaches a Samaritan woman for having had five husbands.[158] With the exception of a minority opinion from Serbia, no Slavic source recognized remarriage after the dissolution of four unions.[159]

In deciding whether to authorize remarriage, Slavic Orthodox hierarchs also took into consideration the circumstances under which the previous marriage was dissolved. If, at the death of a spouse, a widow or widower made a promise not to remarry, no later union was permitted. The church regarded such oaths as binding, even if they did not take the form of monastic vows.[160] Marriages that were declared invalid because they violated canon law on minimum age or consanguinity simply did not count. The later formation of a lawful union was permitted, and this marriage counted as the first.[161] After the Slavic Orthodox churches withdrew tacit approval of common law marriages, these unions similarly did not affect remarriage. The church had every interest in encouraging believers to end sinful unions and enter into licit ones. For that reason, the church placed no bar on remarriage in such circumstances, and demanded only the usual penance for the earlier sin.

There were social as well as religious pressures against remarriage, especially for widows with children. As long as a widow did not remar-

155. E.g., VAT-Bor. 15, ff. 478r, 480v.

156. *Stoglav*, 89, 215.

157. No. 162 (dated to 1668) in *Akty sobrannye v bibliotekax i arxivax Rossijskoj imperii*, 4:215.

158. *Sintagmat*, 165, quoting St. Basil's Rule, art. 4.

159. NBS 688, f. 46v. The penance for a fourth or fifth marriage here is eight years. The existence of a provision permitting fifth marriages at all is unusual; I found it only in this manuscript. It is likely that the provision was included in the original compilation of the Serbian *zakonik*, which probably dated to the time of Stefan Dušan. It could date from the time of Milutin or his son; Milutin probably married five times, and had reason to want all of the marriages to be considered legitimate; see below.

160. Peć 77, f. 222v.

161. *Sintagmat*, 145. Some codes, however, called for a fifteen-year penance for persons previously involved in illegal marriages; see Hil. 302, f. 92r; SOCH 197, f. 60r.

ry, she held guardianship of minor children and often retained control of her late husband's estate. At the very least, she was entitled to remain in her husband's home and receive financial support from his family.[162] Men were advised, in instructions on how to write a will, to provide sufficient property for their widows to keep them from destitution. But Slavic law and custom forbade the placing of children under the the authority of a stepfather. Therefore, if a widow remarried, she usually lost guardianship of her children to her late husband's nearest male relatives. And unless her husband's will stated otherwise, she retained nothing of her first husband's property when she married for the second time.[163] For that reason, it was often not in a widow's economic interest to remarry. When a man remarried, he set up a potential rivalry between the children of the first marriage and their stepmother and half-siblings. The didactic collection *Pčela* warned of possible disaster: "A second marriage is the beginning of war and rebellion."[164] When the marriage had been arranged to advance familial interests, the parents and parents-in-law of a young widow or widower might want to discourage a second marriage, because it would break established alliances. Or conversely, they might want to use the child's widowhood as an opportunity to break one alliance and establish another.

In the problem of remarriage, the church had several practical interests. First, for the welfare of the community, the church wished to uphold a high standard of sexual morality. From the ecclesiastical viewpoint, acceptance of a chaste widowhood, perhaps confirmed by monastic vows, was the best option. A second marriage was appropriate for persons who were not capable of mature restraint and for those who had no surviving children. The church wished to prevent common law marriages and illicit sexual contacts. Second, clerics wished to make sure that widows and orphans were not left destitute, because the church had the responsibility of providing for the poor. In addition to issuing sermons about protecting widows and orphans, the church urged, under

162. In the seventeenth century a widow petitioned the episcopal court to force her father-in-law to provide for her and her daughter. He held that he was not responsible for her because she had chosen to return to her parents' home, but the court overruled him. See no. 246 (dated to 1695) in RIB, 12:1154–1162.

163. The widow's right of guardianship in Russia is discussed in Goehrke and in Eve Levin, "The Role and Status of Women in Medieval Novgorod" (Ph.D. diss., Indiana University, 1983), chap. 1. A petition by two brothers against their former sister-in-law illustrates the enforcement of this rule; see no. 20 in RIB, 25:20–21. Such cases came under the jurisdiction of secular rather than ecclesiastical authorities. I know of no study of female inheritance among the South Slavs, but the provisions of the Serbian Lekin Zakonik of the fourteenth century are very similar to those of the Russian Russkaja Pravda in the matter of guardianship; see arts. 32–33, in Novaković, *Zakonski spomenici*, 102.

164. TsGADA, F. 181, no. 370, f. 121r–v.

the auspices of the Fifth Commandment, that children provide for their aged parents. In Russia, both ecclesiastical and secular authorities ruled that a widow had the right to remain in her husband's house, regardless of the children's wishes in the matter. Third, the church had an interest in preserving the stability of the family. To this end, clerical authors warned widowers against remarrying, lest rivalry develop between the second wife and her stepchildren. But the proper operation of the household—whether urban or rural—required both an adult man and an adult woman, and both men and women needed children to guarantee their support in old age. Consequently, the church affirmed the right of a widow to decide for herself whether she wished to remarry, without the approval of her parents or in-laws.[165] Thus in any given case it might be in the interests of the church either to permit or to discourage a second marriage.

Divorce

The theological basis for permitting divorce was shaky at best. In theory, divorce was forbidden to Christians; Jesus Christ himself had forbidden it (Mark 10:2–12). But even Jesus expressed willingness to recognize a wife's adultery as justification for divorce (Matt. 5:31–32). Two issues were involved in the consideration of divorce. The first, the separation of spouses, in itself did not violate major canons. Hierarchs disapproved it primarily because of the likelihood of illicit sexual contact in its wake. The second, remarriage after the termination of a legal union, caused Orthodox clerics more difficulty, because it ultimately authorized sexual intercourse with more than one partner. If this situation created unease in the case of remarriage after the death of a spouse, it was considerably more unsettling when that spouse was still alive.

Under most circumstances, Slavic canon law did not expressly forbid the innocent party to a divorce to remarry. Indeed, it operated on the assumption that most men would contract a second union, and placed few obstacles to it other than those inherent in the rules governing second marriages.[166] A woman who abandoned her husband without cause was condemned for forcing him into sin. The remarriage of an innocent divorcee made Slavic clerics uncomfortable. Although they did not forbid remarriage in this case, the divorcee technically became an

---

165. E.g., BNL 251(200), f. 130v.

166. St. Basil's Rule, art. 37, in *Kormčaja*, 490, permits a divorced man to remarry after a year.

adulteress, even though her former husband bore the burden of her sin. They preferred to see such women remain chaste, in the hope that the guilty husband would see his error and correct it.[167] But when presented with cases of men who had married blameless divorcees, clerics agreed that they had committed no sin and were worthy of communion.[168]

The Orthodox Church obliquely outlawed remarriage for a wife guilty of adultery, specifically by denying men permission to marry an adulteress.[169] An occasional text contained a provision allowing a man to marry a woman who had left her first husband, but with a penance of four to nine years.[170] According to biblical principles, a man who married an adulteress himself became an adulterer, regardless of his own personal sexual conduct.[171] If the second husband did not know of his wife's past, however, he was exonerated.[172] A woman who married an adulterer became an adulteress by virtue of being the second wife in a bigamous relationship, because the Slavic churches generally did not recognize the husband's adultery as grounds for divorce.

Although hierarchs had difficulty establishing a theoretical justification for divorce, they recognized the social necessity of it. Byzantine canon and secular law provided a considerable number of reasons for legal termination of a marriage. The Slavs adopted many of these grounds, rejected others, and added some of their own.[173]

The first reason for a husband to divorce his wife, following the authorization of the Gospels, was adultery.[174] Canon law listed a number of suspicious activities that could be accepted as proofs of the wife's infidelity, entitling the husband to a divorce. Under Byzantine law, a wife was presumed to be unfaithful if she slept elsewhere than at the home of her husband or of her parents; attended a horse race, hunt, or dance; traveled with another man; or went to a public bath.[175] Slavic

167. GIM, Sin. 227, f. 192v; Voprosy Kirika, art. 94, in RIB, 6:48–49, quoting Slavonic versions of St. Basil's Rule.
168. "Questions and Answers . . . on Pastoral Practices," art. 63, in RIB, 6:868.
169. *Sintagmat*, 396; also Hil. 300, f. 39v; Dauvillier and Clercq, 191–192.
170. Hil. 378, f. 158r; Hil. 302, f. 21r.
171. St. Basil's Rule, art. 39, in *Kormčaja*, 491; Peć 77, ff. 217v–218r.
172. GIM, Sin. 227, f. 191r.
173. The most complete single list of Byzantine rules known among the Slavs is in *Sintagmat*, sec. 3, chap. 13, 183–187. For the development of Byzantine law on divorce, see Dauvillier and Clercq, 84–93. For Western canon law on the dissolution of marriages, see John T. Noonan, Jr., *Power to Dissolve: Lawyers and Marriages in the Courts of the Roman Curia* (Cambridge, Mass., 1972). Apparently Tsar Boris inquired about a variety of grounds for divorce in his questions for Pope Nicholas; he received the response that all sins except adultery had to be tolerated. See *Izvori za bŭlgarskata istorija*, 7:120.
174. See, e.g., Voprosy Kirika, art. 92, in RIB, 6:48. The method of proving adultery and the ecclesiastical penalties for it are discussed in chap.. 4.
175. Procheiron, art. 7–9, in Pavlov, "'Knigi zakonnyja,'" 81. In seventeenth-century England, suspicious circumstances consisted of riding a horse together or sharing a house. Adul-

clerics accepted the Byzantine notion that certain activities denoted infidelity but altered them to fit Slavic notions of propriety. Among Slavs,
leaving the husband's home, especially with his property, sufficed as
proof of adultery.[176] The Slavs did not have hippodromes, with their
public spectacles and racy underlife; for them, horse races were not
particularly risqué. Baths similarly had a different connotation in the
Slavic world (as we shall see), in particular among the Russians. Among
Slavs, certain sorts of bacchanalia, survivals of pagan festivals marked
by drinking, dancing, and ritual sex, had similar connotations of sexual
license. Consequently, under Slavic canon law, a wife could be divorced
if she attended such a gathering without her husband's knowledge.

A husband could divorce his wife for some offenses other than adultery, proved or presumed. First, following Byzantine law, a husband
could divorce his wife if she knew of treason against the emperor and
failed to report it to her husband. The Slavs changed the word "emperor" to "prince" (during periods when the Slavic rulers did not claim
the imperial title) but otherwise left the provision intact. The Slavs similarly left intact the Byzantine rule permitting a husband to divorce his
wife if she attempted to murder him. In case of attempted murder, civil
law came into play also.[177]

Slavic sources were not consistent on the issue of the wife's theft from
her husband and his family. Otherwise identical versions of the Code of
Jaroslav gave contradictory information on this point. One article mandated divorce if a wife stole from her husband; another forbade divorce
but permitted the husband to punish the wife as he saw fit.[178] In two
court cases concerning a wife's theft from her father-in-law, the victims
asked not for divorce but only that the wives be forced to repay the value
of the stolen goods.[179]

Although the Gospels never attributed to Jesus any permission for a

---

tery could also be inferred from the man's presence close to the woman's house after dark, or
from the woman's association with soldiers from outside the village. See Quaife, 48–49.

176. According to the Grbaljski Zakonik, a wife was punished the same for fleeing her
husband's home with her property as for overt infidelity. See arts. 110, 14, in Novaković,
Zakonski spomenici, 106, 114.

177. Procheiron, art. 6, in Pavlov, "'Knigi zakonnyja,'" 81. And see, e.g., a case from 1629,
no. 68, in RIB, 25:79–81. A certain Nefedko Sidorov petitioned both Tsar Michael and the
archbishop of Ustjug, accusing his wife, Ontonidka, of trying to murder him in his sleep on the
night of April 8. He averred that her parents and relatives incited her to harm him. In order to
strengthen his case, he accused her of drunkenness, absence from the home, and theft as well.
Nefedko did not ask specifically for a divorce, but the accumulation of charges indicates his
intention. The verdict is not recorded. This case rebuts Brkić's dubious argument (130–131)
that the scenes of wives killing husbands in Serbian epics were purely imaginary and beyond
popular comprehension. In a patriarchal society, he opined, all wives would be too loyal to
their husbands to conceive of murdering them.

178. Jaroslav's Ustav, arts. 37, 56; "Stat'i o razvodax," art. 6, both in *DKU*, 97, 99, 207.

179. Nos. 5 (dated to 1626) and 109 (dated to 1632) in RIB, 25:6–7, 135–136. In no. 5, the
daughter-in-law had also run away, but even so, there was no request for a divorce.

wife to divorce her husband, Orthodox canon law recognized several appropriate circumstances. The husband's adultery was not among them. The inequity of the situation was not lost on the most astute of the Church Fathers, but they were able to rationalize it away. In particular, they quoted St. Paul, saying that a wife should gain her salvation through her husband, and they urged her to be patient with her erring mate.[180] In fact, Orthodox canon law tended to define adultery as illicit sex with a married woman; the man's marital state was not an issue. For that reason, a husband who had an extramarital affair with an unmarried woman was guilty of no more than illicit fornication, which did not justify divorce. Slave mistresses also did not count; other methods were used to end the husband's infidelity in this case (as we shall see in due course). Once the husband's infidelity was stopped, the wife had no further grounds for divorce. Even the most extreme forms of infidelity, such as the husband's incest with his wife's mother, did not justify divorce.[181]

In cases of persistent and blatant adultery, however, the church might relent. Byzantine law permitted a wife to divorce her husband only if he kept his mistress in the same household or the same town as his wife, and did not desist after two warnings from his wife's relatives.[182] One version of Slavic law permitted a woman to seek divorce if her husband committed adultery (presumably with a married woman) and then lied about it.[183] Another permitted divorce for adultery if the husband also beat his wife.[184] Physical abuse alone did not suffice as justification for divorce under canon law, although a number of seventeenth-century Russian court cases suggest otherwise.

A wife might be granted a divorce if her husband committed treason against the emperor (or prince) or if he tried to murder her.[185] Furthermore, she could divorce him if he deliberately damaged her sexual chastity or reputation. A husband who forced his wife into prostitution could be divorced, under both Byzantine and Slavic canon law, but only if she had previously been chaste.[186] According to some Orthodox canonists, she was also entitled to a divorce if her husband raped her, or if he falsely accused her of infidelity or expelled her from the home.[187] Other

180. *Sintagmat*, sec. 3, chap. 16, 195–196; Hil. 378, ff. 155–157r.
181. Hil. 628, f. 18r–v.
182. Procheiron, art. 16, in Pavlov, "'Knigi zakonnyja,'" 83–84.
183. Hil. 300, ff. 52v–53r.
184. Smirnov, *Materialy*, 70.
185. Procheiron, arts. 12–13, in Pavlov, "'Knigi zakonnyja,'" 82.
186. Hil. 466, f. 70r. Byzantine civil law orders flogging, exile, and mutilation for both the husband and the customer in this case, but does not mention the possibility of divorce. See Pavlov, "'Knigi zakonnyja,'" 73, 82.
187. Voprosy Kirika, art. 93 and 94, in RIB, 6:48–49; Procheiron, arts. 10 and 15, in Pavlov, "'Knigi zakonnyja,'" 81–83.

authors called for the offending husband's excommunication in such cases but did not authorize a divorce.[188]

Byzantine law permitted a divorce on the grounds of the husband's impotence, but the Slavs did not adopt this provision, in keeping with their refusal to make consummation a requirement of marriage.[189] Instead, the Slavs instituted a vague provision, permitting divorce if "a husband cannot tolerate his wife or a wife her husband."[190] Impotence could be a cause for divorce under this provision, but so could what we now call "irreconcilable differences." Byzantine civil law permitted a woman to sue for divorce on grounds of desertion, but the Slavs more frequently repeated Byzantine canon law, which prohibited remarriage after a husband's disappearance.[191]

A wife could also divorce her husband if he sold himself into slavery, lest she become a slave also.[192] In Russia, a woman who married a slave in practice remained free.[193] In contrast, a man who married a slave, according to Russkaja Pravda, became a slave himself, unless he had made a prior agreement with the woman's owner.[194] The Slavic Orthodox Church did not disapprove of slavery as an institution and was not troubled by the woman's loss of freedom per se. To the church, the issue was moral: slave women were not able to maintain their sexual purity; they were bound to obey their masters, even in committing a sin. The church did not approve of the sexual exploitation of women slaves, but recognized that it was bound to occur. Rather than have a wife forced into adultery when her husband sold the family into servitude, the church was willing to permit her to leave her husband. Perhaps concern for the maintenance of the family unit lay behind the provision in the code of Stefan Dušan prohibiting a lord from including slaves in his daughters' dowries: when the daughter left for her husband's home, a slave family might be broken.[195]

Russian canons also permitted a wife to divorce her husband if he severely damaged her economic standing. No South Slavic equivalent rules have survived. According to the twelfth-century Kirik's question-

---

188. Apostles' Rule, art. 48, in *Kormčaja*, 72.

189. See Pavlov, "'Knigi zakonnyja,'" 79; *Sintagmat*, 186. Impotence was defined as the inability to complete coition for a period of three years. Dauvillier and Clercq assert (88, 92) that the provision on impotence also applied among the Slavs.

190. Voprosy Kirika, art. 92, in RIB, 6:48.

191. "Procheiron," art. 4, in Pavlov, "'Knigi zakonnyja,'" 79–80.

192. "Stat'i o razvodax," in *DKU*, 207. Justinianic law provided a precedent for this law; see Dauvillier and Clercq, 89, 183.

193. N. L. Puškareva and Eve Levin, "Ženščina v srednevekovom Novgorode XI–XV vv.," *Vestnik Moskovskogo Universiteta, Serija Istorija*, 1983, no. 3: 80.

194. Art. 110, in *PRP*, 1:119.

195. Art. 44, in Burr, 207.

naire, a wife was entitled to a divorce (with a moderate three-year penance) if her husband was a perpetual drunkard, if he took her private belongings, or if he built up massive debts.[196]

Two court cases illustrate implementation of this provision. Lukerija, the wife of Vaska Ivanov *syn* Skornjakov, had her dissolute husband sent to debtors' prison. She went to live with her brother Andrij, with his help bought up Vaska's IOUs, and began preparations to terminate the marriage and take monastic vows. As Andrij was a priest, it is likely that Lukerija was acting in accordance with established canons.[197] Similarly, Annica Semenova *doč'* appealed to the court for assistance because of her husband's failure to support her. Her husband, Klementij Isakov *syn* Osokin, had appropriated her property, sold their home, and given the proceeds to the Arxangelskij monastery, where he had taken up residence. She had sold her bast shoes (*lapy*) to buy food, but Klementij took even that pittance. For good measure, she accused her husband of getting drunk, threatening her life, and beating her during Lent. Although Annica did not specifically ask for a divorce, that was clearly her intent; attempted murder, persistent drunkenness, and severe financial exploitation all were legitimate grounds.[198]

Slavic canon law was contradictory on the legality of divorcing a wife because of her protracted illness. The Zakon Sudnyj Ljudem, drawn from Byzantine inspiration and used in Bulgaria, permitted a divorce in this situation, and dictated a procedure involving public testimony in order to prevent misuse of this statute.[199] The Russian Pravosud'e mitropolič'e concurred, and included insanity and blindness.[200] The Code of Jaroslav, however, precluded divorce of a wife or a husband who became seriously ill or blind.[201]

Slavic canon law did not accept Byzantine authorization for divorce on the grounds of the spouse's crime. Byzantine emperors had issued laws permitting a wife to divorce a husband who was a murderer, poisoner, brigand, church robber, or cattle thief. A husband could divorce

---

196. Voprosy Kirika, art. 92, in RIB, 6:48. Western canon law also occasionally permitted a wife to obtain a legal separation because of drunkenness, cruelty, death threats, and fiscal irresponsibility. Separate residence, however, did not necessarily imply a termination of conjugal obligations. See Brundage, *Law, Sex, and Christian Society*, 511.

197. No. 46 (dated to 1627) in RIB, 25:48–50. The source is a petition by Vaska, who was clearly biased against his brother-in-law. He accused Andrij of plotting to harm him and said that he feared for the safety of Lukerija and their children. Vaska's own testimony acquits Andrij of any wrongdoing; it is apparent that Andrij acted in his sister's interest and with her full consent.

198. No. 225 (dated to 1659) in RIB, 25:305–306.

199. ZSL-K, 46.

200. Art. 8, in DKU, 209.

201. Jaroslav's Ustav, arts. 12–13, in DKU, 95.

his wife for these or other major crimes. Byzantine law also permitted divorce for a range of sexual offenses under provisions not integrated into Slavic canons. Under some Byzantine laws, a husband was permitted to divorce his wife for running a prostitution ring or having an abortion. A wife could divorce her husband for defiling virgins, having an affair with a married woman (i.e., committing adultery), meeting prostitutes publicly, or engaging in "sodomy." Byzantine law also permitted divorce if the groom discovered that his bride was not a virgin, or had some physical defect.[202] The Slavs allowed divorce in the case of a nonvirginal bride only for priests, and prohibited remarriage.[203] Thus the Slavs narrowed the reasons for divorce, particularly in the areas of criminal activity, nonfullfillment of conjugal relations, and the husband's sexual misconduct. They expanded the grounds for divorce when the woman's physical or economic well-being was at stake.

In most instances, it would not be in a wife's interest to divorce her husband, even if she had legal grounds to do so. Given the church's attitude toward adultery, remarriage was not a likely option for a divorcee. And life as a single woman would be difficult, unless her natal family were prepared to support her into old age. Even an innocent divorcee did not get custody of her children; they remained with her husband and his family. Unless the divorcee was prepared to enter a convent, she was better off remaining married, no matter how unsatisfactory her husband. It is likely that only life-threatening abuse could impel most women to seek a divorce.

Canon law allowed dissolution of a marriage for one additional reason—the taking of monastic vows. Because monastic life was considered superior to marriage, the church was willing to grant a "no-fault" divorce in this case.[204] The proper procedure was very important, because, while the church agreed that a desire for celibacy was commendable, it also anathematized women who left their husbands of their own volition because they disliked sex.[205] In theory, the church demanded that both husband and wife agree wholeheartedly, "giving consent and the scissors"; otherwise, the monastery was forbidden to accept the postulant.[206] Ideally, both parties would take monastic vows, but canon law did not make this demand; it was sufficient if either husband

---

202. Dauvillier and Clercq, 86–92.

203. The French traveler Le Vasseur observed (538) that Ukrainian Cossacks permitted a dissatisfied groom to send his sullied bride back to her parents in disgrace. Canon law makes no provision for this action.

204. M. N. Tixomirov, ed., *Merilo pravednoe po rukopisi XIV veka* (M., 1961), 329–331, based on Justinianic law. See also Dauvillier and Clercq, 171–179.

205. Grangre Canons, art. 14, in *Kormčaja*, 247; *Sintagmat*, 147–148.

206. Fotij to Pskov (1422–1425), in RIB, 6:430–431.

or wife took vows. The spouse left in the lay community, however, was not supposed to remarry; permission to end the marital bond was to be denied if the nonmonastic spouse did not feel capable of remaining chaste.[207] In the event that a wife nonetheless remarried after her husband left her to take monastic vows, he was not considered responsible for her sin of adultery.[208] Although entry into the religious life was usually irreversible, some hierarchs were willing to make an exception for married couples. They recognized that a married person might be unable to keep a vow of celibacy. In particular, clerics were sensitive to the case of deathbed monastic vows, a widespread custom among the Slavs. If the patient recovered, he might find a monk's life intolerable. If a couple had to violate a self-imposed vow to shun conjugal relations, their confessor could permit them to do so, imposing only a year's penance.[209]

In fact, the church allowed the provision for the dissolution of a marriage upon the taking of monastic vows to be used in quite a different way. Canon law did not permit divorce because of a wife's barrenness. In defense of this position, churchmen could point to Scriptural and patristic examples of previously childless women who had borne a saintly child. In the real world, however, men who had no heirs (or who wanted more sons) were not likely to rely solely on divine providence; they wanted younger and, they hoped, more fertile wives. Or they might want a politically or economically more valuable alliance. The church responded to this societal need by stretching the rule on ending a marriage for reasons of piety. The wife's "desire for the religious life" became the favorite excuse offered by men who wanted to end one marriage and enter into another. The wife could be persuaded or forced to retire to a convent, leaving her husband free to select a successor.

The use of this subterfuge is well documented. In the ninth century, Tsar Boris asked Pope Nicholas I whether a forced monastic vow was binding. The response was negative.[210] Adam Olearius believed that the Russian church of the seventeenth century authorized the divorce of barren wives. He noted that a husband was permitted to marry six weeks after the divorce, indicating that only a minimal penance was imposed.[211] In some cases, the first wife might be willing to accede to her husband's desire for remarriage, realizing that she was no longer

207. GIM, Sin. 227, ff. 210v–211v.
208. "Canonical Answers of Metropolitan Ioann II of Russia," art. 12, in RIB, 6:6–7.
209. "Questions and Answers . . . on Pastoral Practice," art. 25, in ibid., 861.
210. *Izvori za bŭlgarskata istorija*, 7:116–117.
211. Adam Olearius, *The Travels of Olearius in Seventeenth-Century Russia*, ed. Samuel H. Baron (Stanford, 1967), 171. Miège also made this observation (77). Collins also noticed (11) that men put their wives in convents when they wished to remarry.

welcome in his home. A petition by a seventeenth-century Russian peasant woman, Paraskov'ja Kostentinova, explained that she wished to
dissolve her marriage of eight years and take vows as a nun. She gave as
her reasons first her ill health and then her husband's desire to make a
"legal marriage to another woman." Melanija Antonova *doč'* Volkova,
another woman who took vows because of sickness, stated specifically
in her petition that her husband, Ivan Zenjakin, had not forced her in
this matter.[212]

Other wives did not enter a convent voluntarily. A man from Nižnyj
Novgorod, Gavrilko Oleksandrov *syn* Putilov, was accused by the patriarch's court of abusing his wife, Tat'janica, and forcing her, while
pregnant, to enter a convent. Gavrilko then remarried. Tat'janica and
her father petitioned—not for the dissolution of Gavrilko's second marriage (as was their right) but for the return of Tat'janica's dowry and her
provisioning in the convent. The court ruled in her favor.[213] When an
illegally divorced wife did not wish to remain in the monastery to which
her husband sent her, she could demand to be discharged. Feklica, the
wife of the boyar Ivan Anikiev, petitioned the archbishop of Ustjug after
her husband divorced her. The archbishop ordered that she not be
forced to take vows; her release from the convent was imminent.[214]

Occasionally churchmen objected to the abuse of the provision for
divorce to enter the religious life. In 1681, Patriarch Ioakim of Moscow
and several of his colleagues issued a joint decree prohibiting abbots to
accept monastic vows from married persons when the purpose was to
permit the remaining spouse to remarry. Men and women who violated
this order were to be placed under penance and excluded from the
sacraments.[215] Such attempts to close the loophole in canon law were
rare. Hierarchs were realistic enough to know that powerful persons
would sometimes seek to dissolve marriages, citing raisons d'état. It
behooved the church to be flexible.

Earlier Byzantine canon law did not consider marriages to be dissolved when spouses had disappeared and their whereabouts were not
known. The husband of a missing wife could apply for a legal divorce on
the presumption of adultery; the wife was sleeping away from home and
presumably had traveled in the company of other men.[216] A husband
who had vanished presented a more difficult case; if his wife remarried

---

212. No. 404, I–II, (dated to 1697 and 1675, respectively), in *Akty juridičeskie*, 425–426.
Because Paraskov'ja was a serf, she addressed the petition to her master, Prince Dmitrij
Myšetckij.
213. No. 206 (dated to 1642) in RIB, 2:946–949.
214. No. 190 in RIB, 12:911–913.
215. No. 247 in *Akty sobrannye v bibliotekax i arxivax Rossijskoj imperii*, 4:343.
216. Hil. 378, f. 159v.

while he was still alive, she was technically guilty of adultery. In general, Slavic codes adopted the Byzantine rule requiring that a husband or wife wait until the death of a missing spouse was confirmed before entering into a second marriage.[217]

An alternative but weaker tradition was more lenient on a woman whose spouse had been taken captive and not been heard from, and who then remarried: the Slavic translation of the syntagma included a provision attributed to St. Basil urging mercy for the "bigamous" wife. Another article permitted remarriage after five years for men and women whose spouses had disappeared but were not known to be dead.[218] The native Serbian Lekin Zakonik of the fourteenth century attempted to distinguish between husbands who had left for just cause and those whose absence was unexplained. The only restriction concerned the wife of a soldier, who had to wait until she learned of his fate.[219] According to a Russian penitential text, a woman who remarried before she received proof of her widowed status was placed under penance for a year.[220]

Desertion was dealt with in a variety of ways. A seventeenth-century Russian, Ivaško Tarasov *syn* Pinegin, returned home after a lengthy absence to discover that his wife, Zinov'ja, had taken a live-in lover, Vasilij Kiselev Krasilnikov. Ivaško did not ask the episcopal court to grant him a divorce, though he clearly had no intention of resuming cohabitation with his wife. Instead, he asked the archbishop to force Vasilij to turn over twenty rubles, representing the proceeds from the sale of a piece of Ivaško's land. Ivaško regarded Zinov'ja's conduct as inappropriate—he called her relationship with Vasilij "lawless"—but he did not feel secure enough to petition the court to punish her and her lover for adultery, inasmuch as he could be considered at fault also.[221]

Ignatko Ivanov *syn* Logdin complained to Metropolitan Varlaam of Ustjug, Rostov, and Jaroslavl' that his daughter-in-law, Ustin'ja, refused "to live according to the teachings and the writings of the Holy Fathers." Her husband, Vaska, had been gone for over a year on a trip to Siberia. Ustin'ja grew tired of waiting for his return and left Ignatko's house. By asking the prelate to excuse Vaska from a fine for noncohabitation, Ignatko was asking him to declare Ustin'ja at fault rather than

217. St. Basil's Rule, art. 36, in *Kormčaja*, 490; *Sintagmat*, 169–170; Dečani 68, f. 282v; "A ce grexi," art. 50, in Smirnov, *Materialy*, 47; Troicki, 74.
218. *Sintagmat*, 169, 186.
219. Lekin Zakonik, art. 30, in Novaković, *Zakonski spomenici*, 101.
220. Almazov, 3:283.
221. No. 1 (dated to 1621–1622) in RIB, 25:1–2.

his son.[222] Apparently Vaska's absence did not constitute abandonment, and Ustin'ja was not entitled to consider herself free of marital obligations. Ustin'ja's own absence, however, implied adultery.

To avoid condemnation, Ustin'ja would have had to act in the same manner as Matrenka Kostjantinova *doč*, another woman whose husband went on an open-ended trip to Siberia. Matrenka petitioned the court for permission to live with "good people" and earn her own living. Her husband, Ivan Pankratov Zavalovskij, had left Matrenka in the care of his mother, Marfa, and the two did not get along. Marfa eventually threw Matrenka out of the house, keeping her dowry, the contents of which were listed in the petition.[223] By requesting episcopal approval for residence outside her husband's home and promising suitable housemates, Matrenka protected her reputation.

The Slavic churches were greatly concerned about irregular divorces and remarriages, which constituted a perennial problem. For a divorce to be legal, it had to be approved by the bishop if not the patriarch. The Russian Code of Jaroslav imposed a substantial fine of twelve *grivny* on a couple who divorced by mutual consent.[224] In his charter to the Žiča monastery (1222–1228), King Stefan the First-Crowned of Serbia addressed the problem of improper divorces. A man who repudiated his wife was required to pay a fine, varying with social class, to the king, and to take his wife back. His compliance could be enforced by a threat of excommunication and revenge by the wife's family. Furthermore, any man who dared to offer his daughter as a second wife to a husband who had illegally cast out his first wife was subject to the same penalties as the husband. When it was the wife's parents who initiated the divorce, they were similarly punished. If a wife left her husband of her own volition, her dowry was confiscated. When the offending wife had no dowry, she was returned to her husband to be punished as he saw fit. He could even sell her into slavery if he did not wish to keep her.[225]

The dividing line between a self-made divorce and abandonment was

222. No. 61 (dated to 1628) in ibid., 70–71. A similar case was brought by Griška Kondratiev *syn* Korev, who petitioned Metropolitan Varlaam on behalf of his son Leontij. Leontij's wife, Domna, had been so unhappy in the marriage that she threatened suicide and ran away several times. Griška and Leontij expressed no wish for the court to locate Domna and return her to them. Instead, they asked for an exemption from the fine levied against married couples who refused to resume cohabitation: no. 26 (dated to 1626) in ibid., 25:27–28.

223. No. 159 in ibid., 207–208.

224. *DKU*, 95. The fine was halved for couples who had been married only under common law.

225. Fr. Miklosich, *Monumenta Serbica spectantia historiam Serbiae Bosnae Ragusii* (Vienna, 1858), 14–15, discussed in Krstić, 226–227. In this early period of Christianization in Serbia, the secular and ecclesiastical authorities were not clearly divided. Stefan Prvovenčani was a strong promoter of Orthodoxy; his brother, St. Sava, was archbishop.

not always clear, as two ecclesiastical court cases indicate. In 1661 Oksin'ica Ostaf'eva *doč'* filed a petition with the archbishop of Ustjug, complaining that her husband, Vasilij Jakovlev *syn* Zatykinskij, had divorced her illegally. She blamed the Devil and the nefarious influence of a certain Ogrofena Grigor'eva *doč'* Goldixa, with whom he had taken up residence and conjugal life. Oksin'ica described herself as a homeless and destitute abandoned wife. Vasilij, however, explained that the supposed "abandonment" had taken place seven years earlier, and Oksin'ica had not protested it at the time. There is every indication that she had agreed to it, voluntarily taking up the life of an itinerant "fool in Christ" (*skitajusja xristovym" imjanem"*). She formulated her grievance only when she tired of the life of the wandering eremite. Vasilij evidently believed that he was in the right. When Oksin'ica first returned and called upon him to provide financial support, he threatened to call in the civil authorities. The archiepiscopal court had three options. If it believed Oksin'ica's story, it could order Vasilij to return to her, giving up Ogrofena and his new family. Or the court could decide that Oksin'ica had either voluntarily taken monastic vows or abandoned her husband, so that their marriage was dissolved. Vasilij would then be guilty of only a technicality: marrying Ogrofena without awaiting an official divorce decree. Finally, the court could charge Oksin'ica and Vasilij with arranging their own divorce and fine them both. The court's actual decision is not recorded.[226]

In a second case, the court's decision has survived. Ivan Zinoviev petitioned for a divorce from Irina Vasil'eva *doč'* so that he could remarry legally. Irina had run away from him seven years earlier and had not been heard from since. The archbishop ordered an investigation. The neighbors testified to Irina's long absence, and also that Ivan had not expelled her from their home; had he done so, the action would have been a legal impediment to his remarriage. The court ultimately granted the divorce and permitted Ivan's second marriage, ruling that he was not at fault.[227]

The church objected to informal divorces chiefly because of the adulterous second unions that followed. One hierarch after another condemned people who remarried without first seeking an ecclesiastical dissolution of the prior marriage. The fifteenth-century metropolitan Fotij of Russia ordered the guilty parties excluded from communion until they gave up the illicit second marriage.[228] Seventeenth-century

226. No. 232 in RIB, 25:316–317.
227. *Sbornik starinnyx bumag xranjaščixsja v muzee P. I. Ščukina*, pt. 4 (M., 1898), 53–55 (dated to 1704).
228. "Canonical Answers of Ioann II," art. 21, in RIB, 6:10; Voprosy Kirika, art. 92, in

trebnici imposed a nine-year penance and observance of a dry fast three days a week.[229] Priests who blessed later marriages after unapproved divorces could be defrocked.[230]

Unauthorized divorces and illegitimate remarriages occurred despite the rules against them, because neither the average believer nor his priest felt that episcopal confirmation of just grounds was essential. Metropolitan Fotij of Russia complained of frequent violations committed with the knowledge and acquiescence of parish priests:

> And what do you write me, that certain men, having driven out the first wife or the second, take a third, or fourth, and the priests bless them! Those priests, according to the rule, are without rank. . . . What do you write me, that many among you have fifth marriages and more! Nowhere is this ever heard of in Orthodox Christendom, and God knows how much anguish this has caused me. Like great adulterers, infidels in God's flock and chosen, there is lawlessness for the sake of the perishable, mortal body.[231]

Other clerics reported as many as ten marriages, contracted with the blessing of ignorant or lazy priests.[232] Even prelates could be guilty of permitting illegal divorces, as a seventeenth-century penitential questionnaire for patriarchs reveals.[233]

Violations of Canons on Marriage

As a whole, the medieval Slavic Orthodox regulations on marriage seem unrealistic, and the numerous complaints over the centuries about violations indicate that they were not always observed. Even the people most likely to feel obliged to obey the church's rules—the aristocracy and the clergy—were likely to transgress, knowingly or unknowingly. The pages of history reveal a sizable number of violations by the ruling class.

In Russia, the Kievan princess Verxuslava Vsevolodovna married when she was only eight years old, despite the canons prohibiting the marriage of underaged children.[234] Prince Roman Rostislavič repudi-

---

ibid., 48. Metropolitan Fotij ordered offenders excluded from communion for twenty years or until the hour of death; see "Instruction of Metropolitan Fotij . . . on the Responsibilities of Clergymen" (c. 1431), in ibid., 6:512.

229. Kiev 49, f. 669r–669v; Hil. 302, f. 21r.
230. Fotij to Pskov (1422–1425), in RIB, 6:433.
231. Ibid., 432–433.
232. Metropolitan Iona to Vjatka (c. 1456), in RIB, 6:605–606.
233. Almazov, 3:186.
234. Puškareva, "Ni svjaščennika čtjut," 16.

ated his wife, apparently without any protest from the church, when his alliance with her father, Prince Rjurik, failed.[235] Ivan III arranged to marry his daughter Elena to Grand Prince Alexander of Lithuania, despite the prince's Roman Catholicism. The church agreed to the marriage, with the proviso that she be permitted to observe the Orthodox rites. The bride was instructed not to visit Roman churches or monasteries, except "once or twice" to take a look. She was permitted to enter the choir loft of a Roman church, to keep her mother-in-law company.[236]

Grand Prince Vasilij III, concerned over the lack of an heir, divorced Solomonia, his wife of seventeen years, and had her forcibly confined in the Pokrovskij convent in Suzdal. He was remarried the next year, in 1524, to Elena Glinskaja. The divorce and remarriage caused controversy. Supporters of Vasilij's actions were careful to establish the legitimacy of his conduct. They argued that Solomonia had in fact entered the convent voluntarily, despite Vasilij's reluctance to dissolve the marriage. He remarried only for the good of his people, in order to provide an heir to the throne and forestall a civil war among his brothers. Both Metropolitan Danilo and Archbishop Makarij of Novgorod supported the divorce and remarriage, reciting prayers for the new couple's fertility. There were dissenting voices, however. The four ecumenical patriarchs—of Jerusalem, Alexandria, Antioch, and Constantinople—all refused their blessings. The churchman Vas'jan Kosoj accused Vasilij of planning adultery, and warned that such misconduct by the tsar could lead to barbarian invasions. The answer from Mount Athos was more guarded. The monks recognized that Vasilij had been instrumental in protecting the interests of the Holy Mount against incursions by the Turks. They recognized the benefits of his having an heir, who might continue his policies. At the same time, canon law did not authorize divorce and remarriage under such circumstances.[237] Writers on both sides of the issue acknowledged that Vasilij's divorce and remarriage technically violated canon law. They disagreed on whether the potential benefits would outweigh the dangers of the sin.[238]

A number of Serbian and Bulgarian rulers contracted marriage al-

235. Novgorod V chronicle, under the year 6712 (= 1204), in *PSRL*, 4:180.

236. *Drevnjaja rossijskaja vivliofika*, 14:1–21.

237. Ju. K. Begunov, "Povest' o vtorom brake Vasilija III," *Trudy otdela drevnerusskoj literatury* 25 (1970): 105–118; A. A. Zimin, "Vypis' o vtorom brake Vasilija III," *Trudy otdela drevnerusskoj literatury* 30 (1976): 132–148. The chronicle account reflects both points of view about the legitimacy of the divorce and remarriage in different manuscripts, see Pskovskaja I chronicle, in *PSRL*, 4:295–296.

238. The choice of Elena Glinskaja was doubtless politically motivated, but the issues have not been studied. Elena's mother was Serbian, of the Jaksić dynasty; through them she was related to other powerful Balkan families, including the Brankovići.

liances with Turkish leaders in an attempt to forestall conquest. Such unions violated canons against intermarriage with non-Orthodox. The Serbian prince Stefan Lazarević, for example, married his sister to the sultan Bajazid in 1390. Despite the religious difference, the church and the nobility approved the union. Stefan Lazarević was canonized, and the author of his *vita* praised him for arranging the marriage "in order to save the Christ-loving flock from the wolves."[239] The Bulgarian princess Tamara was married to the Turkish sultan Murat I in 1375, and the Serbian princess Mara Branković to Murat II in 1435. Far from condemning these marriages, Serbian and Bulgarian sources, including those of the church, praised the positive influence each of these women had at the Turkish court. Mara, for example, was credited with facilitating the transfer of the relics of St. Ivan Rilski from Trnovo to Rila.[240] The Orthodox brides' refusal to apostasize to Islam certainly made these marriages more palatable to the church.

The Bulgarian church apparently did not protest the noncanonical marriages arranged by Tsar Ivan Alexander IV in the fourteenth century. He concluded two marital alliances with Byzantium between 1331 and 1352; the second involved his four-year-old daughter Keraca-Maria and the future Andronikos IV, grandson of Andronikos III. This union certainly violated Byzantine canon law, which forbade the betrothal of a child under the age of seven. Furthermore, the previous marriage alliance made the union incestuous. The circumstances of Ivan Alexander's own two marriages remain murky. His first wife, Teodora, was the daughter of a Vlah *voevoda*; the marriage had been contracted before Ivan Alexander took the Bulgarian throne in 1331. Sometime between 1337 and 1345 he forced her to take the veil. She had produced several sons; Ivan did not have the excuse of childlessness to justify divorce. Nor was there an obvious political motivation; the Vlah alliance was solid. The second wife, also named Teodora, offered no political advantage. She was of an unknown Bulgarian Jewish family. Teodora II cleverly forestalled any objection from the church by converting to Christianity and becoming a patron of ecclesiastical institutions and religious learning. Ivan Alexander clearly favored the children of the second marriage, naming Ivan Šišman as heir in preference to his older half-brothers.[241]

239. J. Šafařík, "Život despota Stefana Lazarevića, velikog kneza srpskog," *Glasnik srpskog učenog društva* 28 (1870): 386; *Xristomatija po starobŭlgarskata literatura*, 452.
240. Ivan Božilov, *Familijata na Asenevci: Genealogija i prosopografija* (Sofia, 1985), 214–218; Ivanov, *Starobŭlgarski razkazi*, 230.
241. Following the reconstruction of the genealogy in Božilov, 149–178 and chart 1; Aleksa Ivić, *Rodoslovne tablice srpskih dinastija i vlastele* (Novi Sad, 1928), chart 2. *Cambridge Medieval History: The Byzantine Empire*, vol. 4, pt. 1 (Cambridge, Eng., 1966), omits the marriage to Michael Asen and lists Maria as Ivan Alexander's granddaughter (chart 9).

The Serbian church seems not to have objected to the divorce of Stefan the First-Crowned from his wife, Eùdocia, in 1200 or 1201. She was the daughter of the Byzantine emperor, but the attractiveness of that alliance had faded. Stefan gave adultery as the official grounds for divorce. In keeping with both Byzantine and Serbian law governing the wife's infidelity, Stefan drove Eudocia from his home and from the city. As the "innocent" party, Stefan was free to remarry, and he did, twice. The Byzantine church considered Eudocia to be the victim of an illegal divorce and permitted her to remarry as well.[242]

The church did not automatically give its blessing to noncanonical unions by princes, no matter how powerful. Metropolitan Filipp expressed reservations about the marriage between Ivan III and Sophia Paleologina when the bridal party approached the city carrying Roman Catholic symbols. Ivan ordered them removed, and the metropolitan then gave his blessing to the marriage, confirming Sophia in the Orthodox faith. The marriage was prestigious enough—and valuable enough politically—for the Russian church to wish to accept it.[243] The Russian church sanctioned Ivan IV's third marriage in 1571, despite the fact that he had surpassed the age limit of forty years. The third wife having died a month after the wedding, the church also permitted his fourth marriage the next year. Perhaps hierarchs were wary of challenging Ivan; he had removed Metropolitan Filipp from his post in 1569 and probably ordered his murder. But a fifth marriage the church could not countenance; Ivan was denied permission to enter into the church building— the normal procedure for unrepentant sinners. So Ivan made use of an innovation in church architecture, the outside porch, which first appeared in the rebuilt Cathedral of the Annunciation in the Kremlin during his reign.[244]

The church could object to a marriage on purely political grounds. The Novgorod chronicle under the year 1136 records the wedding of Prince Svjatoslav Olgovič of Černigov to a daughter of the Novgorodian aristocracy. Bishop Nifont refused to perform the ceremony, claiming it to be "unworthy"; Prince Svjatoslav had to call upon his own priests. The account gives no explanation for Nifont's objection. Possibly there was some violation of canon law: Svjatoslav had been married almost thirty years earlier to a Polovtsian princess. Her fate is not known. Perhaps she had died earlier; almost certainly she had not borne her husband children. In either case, any but the most inflexible hierarch

---

242. Guilland, 29; John V. A. Fine, *The Late Medieval Balkans* (Ann Arbor, 1987), 46 and *passim*.

243. Voskresenskaja chronicle, in *PSRL*, 8:175–176.

244. On the architecture of this cathedral, see Arthur Voyce, *The Art and Architecture of Medieval Russia* (Norman, Okla., 1967), 162–163 and plate 67.

would have permitted a second marriage, had it been desirable from the church's perspective. This particular match was not in the interests of the Novgorodian church, however: it gave Svjatoslav a strong local base in the city. Despite this marriage, Svjatoslav acquired only limited support among the local population, and he was ousted a few years later.[245]

King Milutin of Serbia represents the best example of royal violations of marriage law. Many details of his marriages are uncertain, including the names of some of the brides and the length of time each marriage was in force. It is also uncertain which of his children were born to which mother, but all were treated as legitimate. Five unions are known. There is little information about the first marriage, with a Serbian noblewoman, which was arranged while Milutin was in his teens. It is likely but not certain that his heir, Stefan Dečanski, was born of this union. Milutin's father, Stefan Uroš I, negotiated a marriage between Milutin and the daughter of the Byzantine emperor Michael VIII Paleologus, but changing political circumstances made it unattractive. Probably a formal betrothal had taken place. Milutin married instead the daughter of Sebastocrator John of Thessaly, around 1273, the previous marriage and betrothal notwithstanding. A decade later Milutin married yet again. This marriage, to the Hungarian princess Elizabeth, may well have been at the behest of his mother, the dowager queen Elena. She was Angevin by birth and eager to bring Serbia into her natal family's alliance as well as into the Roman Catholic fold. To this end, she had engineered a marriage between her elder son, Dragutin, and the Hungarian princess Catherine. She could not count on the uneasy peace between her two sons to last. The marriage to Elizabeth was of questionable legitimacy on several counts. First, Milutin's previous marriages had not been terminated for reasons justifiable under canon law. Second, Elizabeth was a Roman Catholic, and thus a heretic. Third, she was Dragutin's sister-in-law, so the marriage was incestuous under Orthodox law (though not under Catholic law). In any case, the marriage did not last. In 1284 Milutin formed an alliance with Tsar George Terterij of Bulgaria and married his daughter, Ana. That marriage lasted some fifteen years, until George Terterij lost his throne and a new Byzantine alliance became attractive. Milutin then prevailed upon Andronicus II to send him his five-year-old daughter, Simonida. Because of Milutin's multiple previous marriages and Simonida's age, the patriarch of Constantinople refused to solemnize the marriage, and the archbishop of Ohrid had to be prevailed upon to perform the ceremony.[246]

245. Novgorod IV chronicle, in *PSRL* 4:146–147, Novgorodskaja I chronicle, Sofijskij manuscript, in *Novgorodskaja pervaja letopis'*, 18–21, 25.

246. Guilland, 28; Nicol, 164. Milutin's marriages and the political circumstances and historiographical debates surrounding them are discussed in Vladimir Mošin, "Balkanskata

Because Orthodox canon law acknowledged the possibility only of four marriages, observers and historians of Milutin's time had to discount the validity of at least one. The innovation in one Serbian manuscript tradition, admitting of the possibility of a fifth marriage, might well have originated in response to Milutin's situation. Churchmen objected to various of Milutin's marriages, but canon law seems to have been merely an excuse; the real opposition was always to the alliance the marriage confirmed. His biographer, Archbishop Danilo II, had an interest in presenting Milutin as a great Orthodox prince, and consequently mentioned only his last marriage, to Simonida.

The Social Context of Divorce and Remarriage

Clerical approval and disapproval of divorce and remarriage seems to have been governed as much by practical considerations as by conceptions of sexual morality. The church's policy on remarriages could be adjusted to fit the circumstances of time and place. Canons from the late fourteenth century on permitted third and fourth unions. One reason for the change may be found in the Black Death. Young adults were particularly susceptible to the plague; consequently, there were more twice- and thrice-married widows and widowers under the age of forty. The wars of the period added to the numbers of widows and widowers, and many other persons could no longer be sure of their marital status. To require sure proof of a spouse's death before permitting the survivor to remarry would have been both cruel and impractical. The rules against multiple remarriages, when observed, discouraged the breaking of political bonds formed between two families by the marriage of their children. These bonds remained intact even after the death of one spouse, provided no remarriage occurred. Remarriage could also serve as a necessary tool for political advancement, however, replacing unproductive or detrimental ties with more promising ones. By discouraging divorce and remarriage officially while readily permitting exceptions, the Orthodox churches encouraged use of the marital bond for familial political ends.

Furthermore, remarriage was bound to be common in medieval Slavic society. Both men and women could easily be widowed at a young age. Women might die in childbirth. Men, especially of the aristocracy, might be killed in war. For the individuals involved, the economic and social structures of medieval Slavic society made the married state advan-

diplomatija i dinastičkite brakovi na kralot Milutin," in *Spomenici za srednovekovnata i ponovata istorija na Makedonija*, vol. 2 (Skoplje, 1977), 89–213; and L. Maksimović, "Georgije Paximer," in *Vizantijski izvori za istoriju naroda Jugoslavije*, vol. 6 (Belgrade, 1986), 1–62, esp. nn. 80–90.

tageous. In the household, the basic economic unit, tasks were distributed by sex. Without a wife, a man would have to take on the "feminine" tasks of cooking, weaving, and sewing, for which he was not trained. Women's work not only contributed to the comfort of the household but was an important source of income; the products of women's labor, such as linen cloth, beer, and cheese, made up a significant part of the rents paid to landlords. For men of the aristocracy, who were likely to travel frequently on business or military service, a wife filled the role of business manager, coordinating familial interests from the home base. The other women of the extended family, burdened with responsibilities to their own husbands and children, could be at best a poor substitute for a wife. A woman left without a husband was in even more dire straits, unless her natal or marital family supported her. Peasant women relied on their husbands to till the fields and carry out much of the heavy work of farming. Women of the aristocracy, although not without rights and powers, relied on their husbands to protect them in courts of law. An adult son might serve as an adequate substitute, but a young widow or one without children might well be viewed by her husband's extended family as an unwelcome burden. Thus remarriage was a reasonable way of easing the economic burdens of widowhood. If either a man or a woman was widowed without children, remarriage became a virtual necessity. Only children guaranteed support and care in old age. Finally, if widows and widowers desired a licit sexual outlet, remarriage was the only option. Given these imperatives, it is not surprising that the hierarchy had difficulty in prohibiting remarriage. Parish priests could be pressured by their parishioners into giving their blessing to noncanonical third and fourth marriages.[247]

The regulations on betrothal, marriage, remarriage, and divorce provided a balance between the ideal and the reality in the moral realm, as well as between the interests of the family and the welfare of society. Families were free to plan marriages in the interest of political and economic advancement, but limits were imposed to prevent social disorder. To this end, official betrothals were binding, public ceremonies were required, divorce was restricted, and remarriage was discouraged. At the same time, the rules were flexible enough to permit the breaking of established ties and the formation of new ones when there was great desire to do so. And even when a desired divorce or remarriage clearly was contrary to the rules, the church would turn a blind eye to the violations when they were advantageous for the society.

247. See "Instruction of Metropolitan Peter to the Clergy," in RIB, 6:161.

The Conjugal Relationship

The rules on marriage exhibited less concern for the welfare of the individual than for the desires of the family and the stability of the society. The church had relatively little to say about the emotional relationship formed between the man and the woman who cemented the national or familial alliance. It was a given that they were to subordinate their personal wishes to the greater advantage of the family; familial interests governed the choice of spouse and, if necessary, the dissolution of the marriage.

In theory, a couple could insist on remaining together if their families and their allies wished to break the connection. In fact, however, they were unlikely to do so. The bride and groom had not chosen each other freely. The wife's relatives could make themselves thoroughly obnoxious, especially by denying the husband access to the wife's dowry or taking the wife back home. The husband's family could make an unwanted wife very unwelcome, beating her and depriving her of support, and the husband could do little to protect her. It is possible that many of the ecclesiastical court cases reporting strife between a wife or husband and the in-laws originated in a falling out between the two families. It was a sin to instigate the divorce of husband and wife, but the one-year penance would not have deterred anyone who had a great deal to gain from the dissolution of the marriage.[248]

Other than recommending that parents not force reluctant children into marriage, the church did not dictate any sort of preparation of the young couple for marital duties. Their emotional state was not an issue. Churchmen understood that the purposes of marriage in medieval Slavic society did not include the happiness of the husband and wife. Personal choice, based on either erotic attraction or romantic affection, was virtually impossible in a first marriage, which was usually arranged by the families for children who had not yet reached physical or emotional maturity. Only in a second marriage could individual desires play a role in the choice of spouse. And even then, it is likely that familial economic and political considerations outweighed purely personal elements.

Nor did spouses anticipate companionship from each other. Given the division of labor in the household, men and women would normally not work together at the same tasks. Social life was also segregated; there

---

248. Almazov, 3;150, 159. The penance places this sin in the same category as arson and perjury. Medieval Czech court records describe attempts by families to disrupt marriages in order to advance more suitable unions, as well as married couples' devotion to each other to the detriment of the interests of their natal families. See Klassen, "Marriage and Family," 259–260, and "Development of the Conjugal Bond," 161–162.

were male gatherings, which proper women did not attend, and female celebrations, from which men were excluded. This tendency to separate the male and female spheres was most developed among the sixteenth- and seventeenth-century Russian aristocracy. These women possessed their own, separate section of the house, the *terem*, and did not, as a rule, meet male visitors or attend mixed social functions outside the home.[249] Segregation of women helped to confirm familial control over the choice of marriage partners, as well as to limit the possibility of sexual contacts outside of marriage. A wife's unscheduled absence from home was sufficient to convict her of adultery only in a society in which women had few proper reasons to venture afield.

The success of the familial alliance concluded by a marriage did not depend directly on the compatibility of bride and groom. It would not be unreasonable to suppose, however, that extreme disaffection between husband and wife might damage an otherwise congenial arrangement between their two families. The church's dictum that husbands love their wives and wives honor and obey their husbands must be understood in this context. In the interest of supporting stability in a marriage and thus in the society, the church reinforced the patriarchal social order while averting the extreme abuse of power such an order might permit. The church taught, for example, that the wife should obey her husband. In an apocryphal version of the story of the Garden of Eden, God told Adam, "I created your wife so that she would be in obedience to you; why then do you obey your wife?"[250] When the provision for wifely obedience appeared in the *trebnik*, however, it was immediately followed by a question and response: "But what if the husband is a fool and the wife is wise? In that case, the wife should still obey her husband sometimes, but sometimes the husband should obey his wife."[251]

Despite the lack of attention to personal desires in the choice of spouse, there is no reason to suppose that medieval Slavic marriages were more unhappy than modern ones. The expectations of the medieval bride and groom differed from those of modern couples. The notion of romantic love was alien to Slavic society before the introduction of Western culture, as was the concept of sexual fulfillment. Medieval Slavic brides and grooms did not expect to receive emotional support from their spouses, much less from their in-laws. Men expected their strongest relationships to be with their natal family, particularly parents and brothers, and from familial connections such as *kumovi*. Women,

249. Nancy Shields Kollmann, "The Seclusion of Muscovite Women," *Russian History* 10, no. 2 (1983): 170–187.
250. Novaković, *Primeri književnosti i jezika*, 491.
251. Rila 1/20(48), f. 129r–v.; Hil. 302, f. 20v.

who were separated from their own natal families in residence, would rely for emotional fulfillment on their children—particularly on their sons, who would not be married into other families at a young age. Personal choice could enter into the balance in second marriages, where law and custom guaranteed to widows and widowers the right to choose for themselves. Society could permit such freedom, understanding that full adults would be conscious of familial responsibilities and would not usually indulge purely personal desires. The conjugal relationship was secondary to family interests.

Seems most when successful marry

CHAPTER 3

Incest

Incest endangered familial stability by introducing sexual tensions into relationships that were not defined as sexual. It also endangered social stability by blurring relationships that were supposed to be clearly defined. Societal disapproval is evident in the long penances prescribed for sexual relations among kinsmen. Penances for incest are equaled in length only by those for murder, adultery by a married woman, and some forms of male homosexuality—that is, by other activities extremely disruptive to family and social order. Given the seriousness of the offense, it is not surprising that penitential literature devoted a substantial amount of space to the problem.

Slavic canon law defined broad categories of persons as relatives: individuals related by birth, by marriage (including distant affines), and by adoption (through either ecclesiastical or popular rites).[1] Any sexual relationship between kinsmen was punishable, whether overtly extramarital or confirmed through a noncanonical marriage. Canon law did not distinguish between the two. Furthermore, canon law recognized that incestuous contacts short of coitus were disruptive, and condemned them, albeit less stringently than full intercourse. Russian codes specifically forbade holding hands with a relative by blood or spiritual adoption, or dancing to the point of orgasm.[2]

The Slavs abhorred incest long before the introduction of Christianity. Authors condemned outsiders, usually unjustly, for their incestuous customs. The traditional definition of incest, however, seems to have been a

---

1. On the development of conceptions of consanguinity as impediments to marriage, see Dauvillier and Clercq, 123–154.

2. Almazov, 3:146, 274, 279. The penance was 40 days of fasting with 100 to 300 prostrations.

sexual relation between members of a family living as a unit. In-laws were included, but not more distant relatives who did not share the same household, especially through the female line. Thus Slavic notions of propriety in matters of consanguinity did not coincide in all respects with the dictates of canon law.

The Definition of Kinship

Orthodox canon law recognized four types of consanguinity: by blood, by marriage, by adoption, and by spiritual bond. Slavic hierarchs recognized restrictions on intermarriage and extramarital intercourse for all four causes. The Byzantine sources—the nomocanon, the syntagma, and secular codes—offered a wide variety of rules to chose from on consanguinity and affinity. For example, Byzantine canons prohibited marriage among distant cousins and families of in-laws, while civil law labeled as incestuous a narrow range of relations: between parents and children, stepparents and stepchildren, brothers and sisters, uncles and nieces, aunts and nephews, brothers-in-law and sisters-in-law, and first cousins.[3] The adoption of laws governing consanguinity roughly matched the dominant family structure. Sexual intercourse (and consequently marriage) was prohibited among individuals who already shared a recognized connection and some measure of communal life.

Among the South Slavs, the extended communal family (*zadruga*) was established as the basic social unit.[4] The *zadruga* commonly included the patriarch and his wife (who directed the other women in the household), his sons and their wives and children, and even those children's grandchildren. The family house could contain four generations at a time, and persons as distantly related as second or third cousins. The Slavic *zadruga* was almost exclusively patrilinear and patrilocal. Descent was traced through the father, and inheritance of land passed primarily through the male line. Sons brought their brides into the parental household, while daughters were married out into other families.

When the family became too numerous to live together comfortably,

---

3. Pavlov, "'Knigi zakonnyja,'" 74–76.

4. Robert F. Byrnes, ed., *Communal Families in the Balkans: The Zadruga* (Notre Dame, Ind., 1976), esp. the articles by Philip E. Mosely; and E. A. Hammel, "The Zadruga as Process," in Peter Laslett and Richard Wall, eds., *Household and Family in Past Time* (New York, 1972), 334–373. Most studies are based on Serbian information; evidence of family structure in medieval Bulgaria is unfortunately extremely sparse. Most scholars have accepted the contention that Bulgarian family structures recorded in the nineteenth century were of considerable antiquity. See Ivanička Georgieva, "The Bulgarian Kinship System," *Ethnologia Slavica* 3 (1971): 151–157.

or a dispute arose over shares of property, the *zadruga* would dissolve itself into nuclear families. In time, through marriage and the birth of children, each nuclear family would again become an extended *zadruga*. Usually the dissolution of the *zadruga* would be precipitated by the death of the patriarch. It was not unknown, however, for a widow to take over leadership of the communal family, or for brothers to continue to live together after their father's death. In times of disorder or high taxation (levied by household unit), most households in a community opted to remain together; in other periods, nuclear families might become the rule rather than the exception.[5] Slavic kinship terminology made no distinction between extended and nuclear families, regarding both as manifestations of the same underlying principle.

The canon law's ban on the marriage of third cousins thus coincided with the South Slavs' conception of the family unit. Relatives in the male line to four generations would be living in the same household; marriages between them would fall under the nearly universal incest taboo. Relatives in the female line, other than the mother's immediate family, might well be strangers. Thus South Slavic *trebnici* raised questions concerning marriages among *bratučedi*, literally "brother-children," but rarely mentioned the question of *sestrični*, or "sister-children." The traditions of Orthodox canon law, on the other hand, required equal observance of degrees of consanguinity in both male and female lines.

Changes in Russian versions of canon law on incest coincided with changes in family structure. The proto-Slavic *zadruga* fell into disuse as a residential system in twelfth-to-fifteenth-century Russia, although landholding continued to be communal. There the residential household usually consisted of a nuclear family, occasionally joined by an elderly parent or a young bride. The lists of peasant family units in wills of this period and the archaeology of aristocratic residences all point to the nuclear family as the dominant familial structure in this period.[6] The rules on incest in the Code of Jaroslav reflect this familial arrangement. They prescribe fines for relations between parents and children or children's spouses, brothers and sisters, and brothers-in-law and sisters-in-law. More distant relatives are not named specifically, but are subsumed under the vague category of "marriage within the clan."[7] This categorization implies that marriage was forbidden if a familial relationship was known to exist, but the exact degree of kinship was not an issue.

5. See John V. A. Fine, *The Early Medieval Balkans* (Ann Arbor, 1983), 7–8.
6. See Levin, "Role and Status of Women," chap. 3. Female inheritance rights increased in Russia in this period, at least in part because landholding did not coincide with residential units. See N. L. Puškareva, "Imuščestvennye prava ženščin na Rusi (X–XV vv.)," *Istoričeskie zapiski* 114 (1986): 180–224.
7. Jaroslav's Ustav, arts. 16, 17, 23–29, in *DKU*, 95–96. See also *ZSL-P*, 35.

More extensive rules on incest appeared toward the end of the fifteenth century. Marriages between persons more closely related than
fourth cousins were prohibited. If a union was contracted unknowingly
between third cousins, it was allowed to stand only with great reluctance.[8] This alteration may be explained in part by the influx of South
Slavic clerics who fled the Turkish takeover of the Balkans, bringing
with them the canons and outlook of their homelands. Yet the availability of an alternative set of rules on incest does not explain its acceptance. The reemergence of the extended family in late-fifteenth-century
Russia made expanded incest regulations pertinent. Land cadasters, especially from Novgorod, reveal that peasants had switched to extended
family living units akin to the South Slavic *zadruga*. The *mestničestvo*
system, in which the social rank of the aristocracy depended on generations of birth and service, required careful notice of degrees of kinship,
at least through the male line.

"Degrees" of consanguinity corresponded to the number of "births"
between the would-be bride and groom. Between father and daughter
(or mother and son) there was one "birth," that of the child; therefore,
they were related in the "first degree." Between grandfather and granddaughter were two "births," that of the granddaughter and that of her
parent. Between brother and sister there were also two "births," making
them related in the second degree. The children of two brothers (first
cousins by our reckoning) were related in the "fourth degree," the
grandchildren of two brothers (second cousins) in the "sixth degree,"
and the great-grandchildren (third cousins) in the "eighth degree." Uncle
and niece were related in the third degree because three "births" separated them: that of the uncle, that of the niece, and that of the niece's
parent, the uncle's sibling.[9] According to most ecclesiastical authors,
consanguinity up to the eighth degree precluded marriage,[10] although
some would permit a marriage between relatives in the seventh degree,
contracted unknowingly, to stand, albeit with a penance.[11] Relationships through the male and the female lines were treated identically.

This system was precise enough for the needs of the clergy, but it did
not correspond to the commonly used terminology of kinship. For that
reason, many *trebnici*, intended for parish use, substitute the more un-

---

8. Kiev 49, f. 643r.

9. The clearest exposition of the rules on consanguinity is in the *Sintagmat*, sec. 2, chap. 8,
130–146.

10. Rila 1/20(48), f. 90v. In Western Europe, early regulations similarly prohibited marriage
between individuals related more closely than the seventh degree. By the time of the Fourth
Lateran Council (1215), the Roman church found it advantageous to reduce the prohibited
degrees of consanguinity to four. See Brundage, *Law, Sex, and Christian Society*, 140–141,
192–193, 356.

11. *Sintagmat*, 132–133.

derstandable popular words, especially in penitential questions on incest. To educate the priest who was in charge of enforcing the rules, service books often include an explanation of degrees of kinship in common terms, written in the first person. Seventeenth-century books sometimes include charts. All this fuss suggests that the Slavs considered incest to be a serious matter, but specifics of ecclesiastical law on the subject were seen as obscure.

Ignorance of kinship did not constitute grounds for complete exoneration of the offending couple. Their marriage still offended God and endangered the welfare of the community. In order to prevent incestuous unions contracted out of ignorance or deceit, priests were instructed to question prospective brides and grooms carefully, and their parents as well, in order to ascertain that the marriage did not violate canon law.[12] Observance of canons on marriage probably underlay the law in the Code of Stefan Dušan requiring all Serbs to go to their own priests to be married.[13]

Blood Relatives (*Rodstvo*)

It is not surprising that the most stringent provisions against incest concerned sexual relations between family members who shared a house. The highest penances were reserved for immediate blood relatives. For father and daughter or mother and son, the penalties were always the highest on the scale employed. Penances ranged from five years of fasting to thirty years of exclusion from communion, coupled with two thousand prostrations per day.[14] The Russian Code of Jaroslav imposed a hefty fine of forty *grivny* in addition to the penance.[15] Certain South Slavic codes ordered lifelong exclusion from communion and confiscation of property.[16] Byzantine civil law, known among the Orthodox Slavs through the syntagma and other compendia, mandated execution for incest within the immediate family, but there is no evidence that the Slavs adopted this practice.[17]

Sexual intercourse between parent and child was so alien to the medieval Slavic mindset that certain authors argued that it could result only

12. For an example of such instructions, see no. 403 in *Akty juridičeskie*, 425.
13. Burr, 198.
14. E.g., Smirnov, *Materialy*, 30 (30 years and 2,000 prostrations); Almazov, 3:283 (19 years); Hil. 169, f. 76v (20 years and 366 prostrations); Peć 77, f. 111v (9 years and 150 prostrations); Almazov, 3:144 (5 years).
15. *DKU*, 96.
16. Hil. 305, f. 111r; 170, f. 86v.
17. *Sintagmat*, 176; Pavlov, "'Knigi zakonnyja,'" 74–75.

from direct instigation by the Devil. In that situation, the persons involved were victims more than perpetrators of a crime.[18] In didactic literature, sexual relations between mother and son became the worst possible sin, used to illustrate the lengths to which God would go to forgive the repentant.[19]

Incest between brother and sister was only slightly less serious than that between parent and child. Demonic operation was not proposed as an excuse; apparently it was conceivable to the medieval Slav that a man might lust after his sister, and vice versa. Almost every penitential questionnaire and code included this sin.[20] Penances ranged from a dry fast of two years to twenty years' exclusion from communion. There were numerous traditions of penances for this offense;[21] the most influential were those of St. Basil (mandating fifteen or twenty years), Matthew Blastares (mandating fifteen years), and St. John the Penitent (mandating three years and five hundred prostrations). In texts that included rules on incest with a parent or child and with a sister, the latter penance was usually somewhat less. A code that mandated twenty years for sexual relations with a daughter, for example, might require only fifteen years for a sister.[22] Similarly, a code ordering nine years for incest with a mother might impose five years for a sister.[23] In the view of other canonists, such as the author of the Code of Jaroslav, incest with a sister constituted as serious an offense as incest with a mother, carrying a fine of forty *grivny*.[24] Some South Slavic codes maintained St. Basil's distinction between incest with a full sister and with a half-sister; the latter offense was substantially less serious.[25]

Fewer codes of canon law and penitential questionnaires included questions about more distant relatives by blood, with the exception of first cousins. Instead, they included general prohibitions on "incest" and "marriage within the clan" (*v rodou*). The severity of the recommended

18. Hil. 301, f. 125r; Rila 1/20(48), f. 90r.

19. "Legenda o krovomešitele," in *Pamjatniki starinnoj russkoj literatury*, 1:415–423; BNL 740, ff. 102r–105r.

20. Because most questionnaires are written from a male perspective, usually the question asks about sisters. In the uncommon case of a questionnaire formulated especially for women (Almazov, 3:160), the penance for this offense was unusually low—only a year. It is possible that the author of this questionnaire felt that the woman was not likely to instigate the sexual relationship, and thus was less guilty than her brother.

21. E.g., Almazov, 3:277 (2 years); SANU 124(29), ff. 56r (3 years), 168v (12 years); BNL 246(103), ff. 138r (4–5 years), 156v (15 years, or 3 years and 500 prostrations); NBS 10, f. 26r (15 or 20 years); GIM, Sin. 227, f. 196r–v (12 years); Troicki, 69 (15 years, or 3 years with 300 prostrations).

22. E.g., VAT-Bor. 15, ff. 476v, 478r; Hil. 301, f. 125r.

23. Hil. 378, f. 167r.

24. *DKU*, 95.

25. E.g., SANU 122(47), f. 13r, lists 15 years or 3 years' dry fast and 250 prostrations for a full sister and 12 years or 2 years' dry fast and 150 prostrations for a half-sister.

penances indicate that close relatives were intended.[26] Although Byzantine law available in Slavic translation included provisions against sexual relations with an aunt or a niece by blood or marriage, very few native codes mention these transgressions.[27] Because the Slavic family tended to be exogamous and patrilocal, it would be unusual for an adult aunt or niece by blood to live in the same household as nephew or uncle. First cousins, however, frequently shared the same dwelling, at least as children, and their relationship was viewed as nearly as close as that between siblings or half-siblings. For that reason, analogous penances were recommended, ranging from two to sixteen years of fasting; a ten-year penance was the most common.[28]

Specific prohibitions on sexual intercourse between distant relatives by blood appeared only sporadically. Incest with cousins was more likely to be mentioned in Serbian penitential questions and *trebnik nomokanony* than in Russian or Bulgarian ones.[29] Regulations against incest between second cousins listed a penance of nine or ten years' exclusion from communion, which could be shortened under the rules of St. John the Penitent to one year and four months or two years of fasting.[30] For incest between third cousins, the basic penance was eight years, but few codes included a specific provision regarding this relationship.[31]

Russian codes earlier than the sixteenth century tended to omit specific regulations concerning illicit intercourse or marriage between second and third cousins, although descriptions of degrees of kinship forbade intermarriage between individuals so closely related.[32] Apparently Russians from the eleventh century to the fifteenth did not regard unions between cousins as incestuous. Even clerics who tended to be exacting in

26. SANU 124(29), ff. 53r, 168v (14 years); Almazov, 3:146 (9 years and 150 prostrations). Jaroslav's Ustav lists a fine of 30 or 40 *grivny* in addition to a penance: *DKU*, 95.
27. Hil. 301, f. 84v (with aunt: 12 years); Almazov, 3:104, 159, 148 (with aunt or wife's sister-in-law: 5 years); *Sintagmat*, 176–177; Pavlov, "'Knigi zakonnyja,'" 74–76.
28. E.g., Almazov, 3:146 (10 years, 250 prostrations); Smirnov, *Materialy*, 30 (16 years, 1,800 prostrations); Hil. 301, ff. 84v (10 years), 125r (12 years, 170 prostrations); SANU 124(29), ff. 7v (12 years, 170 prostrations), 46 (9 years), 56r (3 years); SANU 123(28), ff. 27r (10 years, or 2 years and 150 prostrations), 27r–v (11 years, or 2 years and 1 month and 150 prostrations).
29. The Bulgarians indicated an interest in canon law on consanguinity between distant relatives soon after the official adoption of Christianity, as evidenced by Tsar Boris's questions to the pope on this subject. See *Izvori za bŭlgarskata istorija*, 7:90.
30. Hil. 169, f. 76v (10 years, 150 prostrations); Dečani 70, f. 225r (9 years, or 1 year and 4 months and 150 prostrations); SANU 123(28), f. 27r–v (9 years, or 2 years and 150 prostrations).
31. E.g., SANU 124(29), ff. 7v–6r (8 years, 106 prostrations), 46r (3 years, 20 prostrations). The sixth and seventh folia of this manuscript were switched during rebinding.
32. For seventeenth-century Russian texts prohibiting sexual intercourse between second cousins, see Kiev 191, f. 683r, and Hil. 302, f. 76r. In both cases the penance was nine years.

regard to the letter of the law, such as the Greek-born metropolitan Ioann II, had to make concessions to native attitudes. Ioann permitted marriage between third cousins, with a penance. The terms in which he outlawed marriage between second cousins make clear that such unions took place.[33] The late-fourteenth-century explication of degrees of kinship in the Sofijskaja Kormčaja permitted marriages among blood relatives related in the sixth degree: a man could marry his first cousin's granddaughter.[34]

Cousin marriages had a practical application: reconsolidation of ancestral lands. Because the Slavs practiced partible inheritance, the ancestral lands became fragmented after a few generations. While communal ownership by the *zadruga* mitigated the effects of partible inheritance for a time, eventually holdings became subdivided. When a daughter-heir could be married to her male cousin, the ancestral estate could be reconstituted, at least in part. That might have been the motivation in an instance of marriage between cousins in fifteenth-century Novgorod. Agrafena, an heiress of the boyar class, married her second cousin, Fedor Onkifovič. Together they possessed a large portion of the entailed estate of their common ancestor, but there were still other heirs, especially Agrafena's sister's son, who kept their shares separate.[35] Incidentally, there is no evidence to suggest that the marriage was considered improper. Inheritance of landed property by daughters was a relatively unusual phenomenon among the medieval Slavs; it developed most fully in northwestern Russia in the fifteenth century. Consequently, there would not have been much community pressure on the church to reinterpret regulations on consanguinity to permit marriages between cousins.

A didactic tale warned of the dire effects of marriages arranged between blood relatives to prevent subdivision of the inheritance. The plot drew its inspiration in part from the ancient Greek legend of Oedipus. A

---

33. Canonical Answers of Ioann II, art. 23, in RIB, 6:12–13.
34. Description of the Degrees of Kinship, art. 1, in RIB, 6:143.
35. The information on the family is recorded in a land division agreement between Agrafena, with her husband and children, and her nephew Matvej. The document has been the subject of two detailed studies: V. L. Janin, *Novgorodskaja feodal'naja votčina* (M., 1981), 157–180; and N. L. Puškareva, "Rjadnaja gramota Fedora Onkifoviča s Matfeem Ivanovičem XV v. (Spornye voprosy germenevtiki pamjatnika nasledstvennogo prava)," in *Issledovanija po istočnikovedenija istorii SSSR dooktjabrskogo perioda* (M., 1982), 37–50. Janin reconstructed the genealogy of the family. He listed an Onkif in the family tree, but did not identify him as the father of Agrafena's husband. Puškareva argued persuasively that Agrafena was one of three children; her brother and a sister (Matvej's mother) predeceased her. Janin noted that Agrafena seemed to have inherited substantially more property than either of her siblings, including pieces that did not come into consideration in the agreement with Matvej. I have suggested ("Role and Status of Women," 48n) that these lands constituted Fedor Onkifovič's property rather than Agrafena's, and that the two were cousins.

prince and princess each inherited half of their father's kingdom. Rather than divide it, they decided to marry. The child conceived in such sin eventually committed great evil: he returned from long exile and unknowingly married his own mother.[36]

It was possible to contract an incestuous union unknowingly (although not between brother and sister, as in the tale), because lineage was popularly traced more through the male line than through the female. Canon law had to make provisions for the accidental incestuous marriage of third cousins before the relationship was discovered. Clerics disagreed about marriages arranged out of ignorance between persons related in the seventh or eighth degree. Some ordered such unions dissolved, and that the husband and wife undergo the penance for cousin incest (ten years); others permitted the couple to remain married, though with a penance.[37]

On rare occasion a penitential code included provisions on homosexual incest. Sexual relations between brothers carried a penance of seven to twelve years; with a son-in-law, four years.[38] These penalties were comparatively less severe than those for incest with female relatives of the same degree.

Affines (*Svatstvo*)

Canon law and custom placed a large number of relatives by marriage outside the pool of potential spouses. In calculating degrees of kinship, Orthodox Slavs counted husband and wife as one—apparently an extension of the Scriptural description of a married couple as "one body." Thus the husband's siblings became the wife's siblings, and vice versa. A man and his sister-in-law, for example, were separated by only two "births" and he was separated from her first cousin by only four "births." Canon law minimally required observance of degrees of affinity among in-laws to the fourth degree; observance of the fifth degree and further was frequently mandated.[39]

36. *Xristomatija po starobŭlgarska literatura*, 380–381.

37. Rila 1/20(48), ff. 109v–110r; Hil. 171, f. 365r. In Western Europe from the twelfth century on, the Roman Catholic Church preferred to tolerate mildly incestuous marriages rather than break up families. See Brooke, "Marriage and Society," 26. Consanguity provided an ideal excuse to end a marriage that was unhappy or that had outlived its political usefulness. The most famous such case was that of Eleanor of Aquitaine, who claimed a divorce from Louis the Pious of France on the grounds that they were third cousins once removed.

38. Rila 1/20(48), f. 185r (8 or 10 years); SANU 124(29), f. 56r (7, 8, 10, or 12 years). Almazov, 3:151, includes a penitential question dealing with homosexual incest with a nephew, but no penance was given.

39. Hil. 169, f. 74v. For Western European canons on marriage among affines, see Brundage, *Law, Sex, and Christian Society*, 193–194.

By this calculation, a sister-in-law would seem to occupy the same position in the family as a sister or a half-sister; consequently, it might be expected that the penance for incest would be the same. In fact, the range of penance for illicit sex between a man and his brother's wife was equivalent to that of a half-sister or stepsister, ranging between two and twelve years. The dominant tradition, however, mandated a penance of ten years, rather than the twelve for a half-sister or fifteen to twenty for a full sister.[40] For incest between a man and his wife's sister, the penances were again in the same range, but the dominant tradition imposed eleven years.[41]

The daughter-in-law was the most common relative by marriage in the medieval Slavic household. Even when the nuclear family was more prevalent than the extended *zadruga*, many households included the young bride of a son. She frequently was in her early teens, and her husband was not much older. Residence in the groom's household permitted easy supervision of the young couple until they gained knowledge and maturity. The daughter-in-law's position in the family was analogous to that of a daughter; the groom's father stood in loco parentis. Sexual transgression with a daughter-in-law was conceivable, but it was also considered to be an extreme abuse of authority. Consequently the penalties for incest of this sort were substantial, as much as sixteen years.[42] A few texts placed incest with a daughter-in-law in the same category as incest with a daughter. The Code of Jaroslav, for example, mandated the same forty-*grivny* fine and penance.[43] Although a considerable academic folklore has grown up about Slavic fathers-in-law who exploited their sons' young wives, the penitential literature gives no indication that this particular form of incest was more common than others.[44]

The analogous violation between mother-in-law and son-in-law was deemed less serious, because the power relationship was not the same. A mother-in-law usually did not live in the same household as her daugh-

40. E.g., Almazov, 3:277 (2 years), 144 (3 years); Hil. 628, f. 15v (10 years); NBS 654, f. 109v (10 years, or 2 years' fast and 150 prostrations); Smirnov, *Materialy*, 30 (12 years and 1,800 prostrations).

41. E.g., SANU 123(28), f. 27v (11 years, or 2 years and one month and 150 prostrations); SANU 122(47), f. 13v (2 years and 150 prostrations); Almazov, 3:148 (5 years).

42. E.g., Almazov, 3:150 (2 years); Sinai 17(17), f. 171v (4–5 years); BNL 251(103), f. 126v (11 years, or 2 years and 300 prostrations); SANU 124(29), ff. 46r (6 years, 80 prostrations), 53v (16 years), 168v (12 years); Troicki, 69 (11 years, or 2 years' dry fast and 300 prostrations).

43. *DKU*, 96. For examples of equivalent penances, see Kiev 191, f. 883r (20 years); Hil. 169, f. 75r (15 years, 160 prostrations). In this same text, incest between a young woman and her husband's grandfather carried a penance of 7 years and 29 prostrations.

44. For an example of academic credence in *snahačestvo*, see Nikola Pantelić, "Snahačestvo in Serbia and Its Origin," *Ethnologia Slavica* 3 (1971): 171–180.

ter's husband. She commanded his respect as an elder relative but had no control over his conduct or property. Regulations on incest between mother-in-law and son-in-law resembled those for stepmother and stepson.[45] Incest with a wife's grandmother came under the same rules.[46] Certain provisions of canon law suggest that the mother-in-law was likely to be the initiating party; if incest occurred, she was to be sent away, while the son-in-law remained with his wife.[47]

In contracting a second marriage, a person brought into the family a whole new group of relatives in addition to those from the first union. The kinship established by a marriage continued even after that marriage was dissolved by death or divorce. For purposes of canon law on possible marriage, a stepmother was equivalent to a natal mother, and a stepsister was akin to a sister by blood. Similarly, half-brothers and -sisters were normally treated as full siblings. However, canon law did recognize that incestuous relations between a man and his stepmother, stepsister, or stepdaughter were not such serious violations as relations with a blood relative, and mandated slightly reduced penances. Incest with a stepmother or a stepdaughter was treated analogously to the case of a half-sister, with similar penalties.[48] A stepmother or a stepsister occupied a position of close relation in the family structure even if the blood tie was not present. The ban extended to a stepparent or stepchild's relatives by marriage. A man could not contract a marriage with his stepson's wife or his late wife's stepmother.

It was considered inappropriate for a widow or widower to remarry among *svatstvo* (in-laws), especially the brother or sister of a deceased spouse.[49] A special—and very common—article in the Slavic nomocanon regulated this situation. The dominant manuscript traditions imposed a penance of either five years or eleven years for this offense.[50] Remarriage was more disruptive to the family than an illicit affair between in-laws; for that reason, the Code of Jaroslav levied a fine of twelve *grivny* for incest between brother-in-law and sister-in-law, but a

---

45. E.g., Almazov, 3:277 (2 years), 148 (5 years); SANU 124(29), ff. 5v (15 years, 160 prostrations), 46 (6 years, 8 prostrations), 96r (5 years, 200 prostrations); Hil. 305, ff. 24r (11 years), 111v (3 years).

46. E.g., SANU 125(154), f. 19r (11 years).

47. E.g., Hil. 300, ff. 87v–88r.

48. E.g., Almazov, 3:147 (2 years); VAT-Bor. 15, f. 478r (9 years, 36 prostrations); Peć 77, ff. 230v (11 years), 235 (12 years); SANU 122(47), f. 13v (12 years, or 2 years and 2 months and 200 prostrations). The Pravosudie mitropolič'e, like Jaroslav's Ustav, equates incest with a stepmother with incest with a mother or a sister: *DKU*, 211; see also GIM, Sin. 227, f. 197r.

49. GIM, Sin. 227, ff. 211r–214r contains a long discussion of the impropriety of such unions, attributed to Gregorij Presviter and Diodorus of Tarsus.

50. E.g., Kiev 49, f. 661v (5 years, 150 prostrations); Hil. 628, f. 16r (11 years); Hil. 305, ff. 24r (11 years), 111v (2 years); NBS I-14, ff. 261r (5 years, 150 prostrations), 265 (lifetime exclusion).

fine of thirty *grivny* for remarriage.[51] The charter of the Žiča monastery, issued by the Serbian king Stefan the First-Crowned, also specifically forbade remarriage between brother-in-law and sister-in-law, levying substantial fines on violators and ordering their divorce.[52] Slight leeway was permitted for an accidental violation of the rule barring remarriage to a brother-in-law or sister-in-law; the penance might be reduced by a year.[53] The Slavs' abhorrence of levirate marriage is curious, because it would seem to offer advantages in a society where marriages confirmed alliances. If a widow could marry her husband's brother, the association between the two families would not be lost. The Slavs preferred to forbid such remarriages, instead keeping the alliance alive by encouraging the widow to remain in her husband's household.

Marriage between in-laws was prohibited to the sixth or seventh degree, depending on the precise relationship.[54] No member of a husband's immediate family could marry into *svatove*, that is, his wife's immediate family. A father and son were not permitted to marry a mother and daughter; two brothers could not marry two sisters.[55] Kinship by marriage continued even after the death of a spouse. If a man were widowed, he could not marry any member of his late wife's extended family, even as distant as her second cousin. A father and son (or father-in-law and son-in-law) could not be married sequentially to the same woman.[56] The same rule held for women; a mother and daughter could not marry the same man in turn.[57] Two brothers could marry a set of second cousins, but not first cousins. Grandfather and grandson, also related in the second degree, were similarly banned from marrying a set of first cousins.[58] Marriage between two sets of first or second cousins was still permitted in Russia before the fifteenth century, but not among South Slavs.[59] Predictably, sixteenth- and seventeenth-century Russian codes adopted more extensive rules on in-law incest, and unions between cousins of spouses to the sixth degree (second cousins) were officially banned.[60] A dispensation might be granted, as in a case pre-

51. *DKU*, 96.
52. Novaković, *Zakonski spomenici*, 575.
53. VAT-Bor. 15, f. 478r (6 years if knowing, 5 years if not); also SANU 124(29), f. 6r.
54. *Sintagmat*, 134–135.
55. NBS 688, ff. 50v–51r (7 years).
56. E.g., VAT-Bor. 15, f. 478r; Hil. 301, f. 125v (6 years, 60 prostrations); SANU 124 (29), ff. 6r (6 years, 100 prostrations), 46 (12 years).
57. SANU 124(29), f. 46r (8 years, 200 prostrations). It is not clear why sequential marriages were not treated equally for men and women offenders.
58. *Sintagmat*, 135–137.
59. "Description of Degrees of Kinship," from a late-fourteenth-century Russian *kormčaja*, arts. 2 and 4, in RIB, 6:143–144; Rila 1/20 (48), f. 111r.
60. Kiev 49, f. 644r–v.

sented to the archbishop of Vologda and Beloozero in 1689. He was willing to permit the marriage of two first cousins once removed, and of two second cousins.[61]

The case of a marriage between a woman and the nephew of her aunt's husband was marginal: Matthew Blastares permitted it, on the grounds that it was not explicitly forbidden. Earlier Russian codes permitted it, while later ones did not. South Slavic codes in general prohibited such a union.[62] Some texts were more willing to permit unions between persons so distantly connected if the contracting parties remained "in place"; that is, the marriages were not cross-generational. Even if the degree of kinship was the same, the distinctions between senior and junior generations had to be maintained. A grandfather and grandson could be permitted to marry an aunt and niece, respectively, but the grandfather could not marry the niece while the grandson married the aunt; a niece should not fill the place of a grandmother to her own aunt.[63]

Canon law even banned marriages between persons connected through two marriages (termed *trirodstvo*) up to the fourth degree of kinship. A widower was not permitted to contract a second marriage with his late wife's sister-in-law. The case of two widowed brothers-in-law who married women related in the second or third degree (i.e., two sisters or aunt and niece) was debatable.[64]

Adoption

The terms for stepson and stepdaughter, *posynok* and *podščer'*, were also used to describe adopted children. Slavic canon law recognized the custom of adopting children, particularly for the purpose of providing a childless couple with an heir. Serbian secular law prohibited a man to adopt a son if he had daughters, in the interest of preserving their rights to inherit.[65] Adoption could be confirmed through a church ceremony, although it does not appear that such a ceremony was required.[66] Such children were considered legally the equals of children born to the cou-

61. *Sbornik starinnyx bumag xranjaščixsja v muzee P. I. Ščukina*, pt. 5, 51–52.
62. *Sintagmat*, 136; "Description of Degrees of Kinship," art. 3, in RIB, 6:143–144; Hil. 171, ff. 280v–281r. SOCH 197, f. 10r, permits such a union if the uncle and nephew remain "in place."
63. *Sintagmat*, 136. For other examples of distant marriages prohibited and permitted by canon law, see NBS 688, f. 37r, and Hil. 466, f. 59r.
64. *Sintagmat*, 137–141; Hil. 171, f. 282v.
65. Grbaljski Zakonik, art.· 56, in Novaković, *Zakonski spomenici*, 110. On daughters' inheritance rights, see art. 48 of the Code of Stefan Dušan, in Burr, 207.
66. See the seventeenth-century Russian ceremony in Kiev 191, ff. 520r–521r.

ple. They enjoyed full inheritance rights, and were subject to the same restrictions on intermarriage with their adoptive parents' relatives.[67] The willingness to grant full rights to adopted children permitted the enforcement of prohibitions on divorce because of barrenness and the legitimizing of natural children. Although illegitimate children did not inherit, for purposes of marriage they fell under the same restrictions of consanguinity as legitimate children.[68]

Etymologically related to *posynok* and *podščer'* are the terms for adopted brother (*pobratim*) and adopted sister (*posestrima*). These words could refer to additional children whom parents took in, but more often they signify blood brotherhood. The custom of establishing an especially binding relationship with a friend is widespread in human society. Certainly blood brotherhood predated the introduction of Christianity into the Slavic world. A few Orthodox teachers objected to adoptive brotherhood, primarily because of the pagan ceremonies involving bloodletting which confirmed the relationship. The penance for entering into such a relationship consisted of a year of fasting. The theological explanation for the prohibition was that all Christians are brothers and sisters, and it was inappropriate to distinguish special degrees among them.[69] Other clerics acquiesced in such relationships, on the grounds that since all Orthodox believers were "brothers and sisters in Christ," the granting of special recognition to this fact accorded with Christian tenets. They condemned ceremonies of pagan origin, however, and insisted on the substitution of Christian rites designed for this purpose. For the purpose of marriage, an adopted brother or sister had the same status as a sibling by blood.[70] Any sexual contact between adopted brother and sister constituted incest both in the popular mentality and under canon law.[71] Consequently questions arose concerning the validity of any existing marriages. For example, did the formation of a bond of adopted brotherhood between two brothers-in-law make one *pobratim*'s marriage to the other's sister incestuous? In general clerics responded to such ques-

67. *Sintagmat*, 141–142. The enforcement of this rule in practice can be seen in the case of Feodosija, who petitioned the Bulgarian-born Russian metropolitan Kiprian for a ruling on the claims of her adopted son, Timoška. Kiprian ruled that Timoška enjoyed all the rights of a natural-born child, but according to Russian practice, the widow was entitled to first inheritance of her intestate husband's estate: Metropolitan Kiprian to the widow Feodosija (1404), in RIB, 6:241–244.

68. *Sintagmat*, 134. On adoption law in Russia, see Marc Szeftel, "Le Statut juridique de l'enfant en Russie avant Pierre le Grand," *Recueils de la Société Jean Bodin pour l'histoire comparative des institutions* 36 (1976): 635–656.

69. SANU 123(28), f. 35v; *Sintagmat*, 131.

70. "A ce grexi," art. 54, in Smirnov, *Materialy*, 47.

71. Brkić argues (48–58), without documentation, that the institution of blood brotherhood began only in the Ottoman period. References to blood brothers are found in manuscripts dating to at least the fourteenth century.

tions in the negative, but the adding of a spiritual bond to an existing blood or marital relationship made them uncomfortable, and they advised against it.

Spiritual Relatives

The most important spiritual bond in the eyes of the church was that formed between godparent and godchild at baptism. The custom of naming a sponsor for a new Christian developed early in the history of the religion.[72] The godparent gave the appropriate responses on behalf of a child who was too young to voice his or her own rejection of the Devil and acceptance of Christ. The church also required a baptismal sponsor when an adult accepted the faith, to serve as "spiritual father" to the individual experiencing the symbolic rebirth. The sponsor became "as a parent" to the newly baptized Christian, regardless of actual age or familial relationship. Although one sponsor was required, early canons did not specifically prohibit additional ones. Consequently the custom developed, especially in Western Europe, of having two godparents, one of each sex. The dominant opinion in the Orthodox Church was that only one godparent of either sex was appropriate, but a minority opinion recommending two survived.[73] In order to prevent a temptation to incest, Russian hierarchs commanded that the sponsor be of the same sex as the godchild.[74]

No canons prohibited a person who was already related by blood or marriage from taking on the additional role of godparent. If a father stood as sponsor to his own child, however, he became a *kum* to his wife, and their marriage had to be dissolved to prevent incest.[75] Among Russians it was common to select a relative by blood or marriage as

72. For a general study of godparents with an emphasis on Western Europe, see Joseph H. Lynch, *Godparents and Kinship in Early Medieval Europe* (Princeton, 1986).

73. See "Instruction of Metropolitan Kiprian to the Novgorodian Clergy" (1395) and "Answers of Metropolitan Kiprian to Abbot Afanasij," in RIB, 6:238, 254–255. Kiprian, a Bulgarian by birth, permitted only one godparent, who could be of either sex, but noted that Russian practice differed from that of his native country. Metropolitan Fotij also ruled specifically against the practice of having two godparents; see "Instruction of Metropolitan Fotij . . . on the Responsibilities of Clergymen" (c. 1431), in ibid., 517. For the minority view, see "Questions and Answers . . . on Pastoral Practices," art. 60, in ibid., 868.

74. "Poučenie Petra mitropolita," in *Pamjatniki starinnoj russkoj literatury*, 4:187; *Dejanija moskovskix soborov*, f. 39v.

75. The penance for violating this rule was exclusion from communion for fifteen to seventeen years; see BNL 324(520), f. 4r; Hil. 627, f. 35v. Early church canons did not contain this prohibition, which developed in Byzantium in the eighth century. It was occasionally used as a way to gain permission for a divorce without proving adultery or some other major crime—an eventuality that the framers of the provision had not envisioned. See Pavlov, *Nomokanon pri Bol'šom Trebnike*, 360–375.

sponsor; the adding of a spiritual bond was thought to enhance the existing relationship. In more practical terms, the *kum* could shoulder the responsibility of providing for a child who became orphaned. The custom differed among the South Slavs. There, relatives by blood and marriage were de facto excluded from *kumstvo*, because the spiritual bond would supersede the existing natal or marital relationship. Also, *kumstvo* provided an opportunity to enlarge the family by bringing in new allies, and the occasion was best not passed up.

Because baptismal sponsorship was established in terms of parentage, canons restricted future marriages between godparent and godchild. Indeed, the spiritual relationship was considered to be superior to that established by blood, and therefore still more binding. Early rulings of ecclesiastical councils not only forbade a godfather to marry his god-daughter and a godmother to marry her godson, but also prohibited unions between the sponsor and the godchild's widowed parent.[76] The penance for intercourse between a man and his *kuma* ranged from one year and one month of fasting to twenty years of exclusion from communion.[77] Incest between a godfather and goddaughter was considered especially heinous; the penance usually matched that for incest with a daughter.[78] Relations between a man and his daughter's godmother were not quite so serious. The Code of Jaroslav mandated a fine of twelve *grivny*, thus equating intercourse between *kumovi* with incest between brother-in-law and sister-in-law.[79]

The rule on consanguinity between godparent and godchild was rapidly expanded to include the godparent's spouse and children.[80] Only an occasional medieval Slavic code permitted a marriage between a person's godchild and natural-born child; in this case, a five-year penance was imposed, similar to that in other quasi-incestuous unions, but

76. *Sintagmat*, 143, citing the canons of the Sixth Ecumenical Council, art. 56. Byzantine civil law also enacted severe penalties in these cases; see Pavlov, "'Knigi zakonnyja,'" 73.

77. SANU 122(47), f. 13v (11 years, or 2 years and one month and 150 prostrations); Kiev 191, f. 683v (11 years); Hil. 378, f. 167r–v (5 years, 150 prostrations); Dečani 70, f. 225r, lists three penances: 20 years; 4 years, 300 prostrations; and one year and one month with 150 prostrations. SANU 124(29) also lists multiple penances in different sections: ff. 46v (9 years, 300 prostrations), 53r (8 or 10 years), 73v (9 years, 150 prostrations), 168v (10 years); Smirnov, *Materialy*, 30 (15 years, 1,800 prostrations if single; 16 years if married); Hil. 169, f. 74r–v (5 years on bread and water).

78. E.g., Hil. 301, f. 84v (20 years); Kiev 49, f. 661v (12 years, 300 prostrations); Sinai 17(17), f. 171v (5 or 6 years). Penitential questionnaires for women list the penance for sex with a godfather as 5 years (Almazov, 3:160, 162, 163). In a Bulgarian apocrypha describing the Virgin's descent into Hell, she witnessed the torments of those who engaged in sex with godparents alongside those who fornicated with mothers, mothers-in-law, and sisters. See E. Karanov, "Pametnici ot Kratovo," *Sbornik za narodni umotvorenija nauka i knižnina*, 13 (1896): 269–271.

79. *DKU*, 95.

80. *Sintagmat*, 144; Procheiron, art. 17, in Pavlov, "'Knigi zakonnyja,'" 84.

the union was declared valid.[81] Most penitential codes listed penances of five or nine years for relations between children of *kumovi*, and forbade marriage.[82] In other words, in practice, penances for incest with spiritual relatives matched those for incest with close in-laws rather than blood relations. Most Slavic clerics viewed the relationship between godparent and godchild as equivalent to blood relationship, and the same rules of consanguinity applied. Thus intermarriage between godparents and godchildren was forbidden to the seventh or eighth degree of kinship, that is, to four generations.[83] This rule gained nearly universal acceptance in the Slavic Orthodox world.

Further expansions of the definition of consanguinity by spiritual relationship remained debatable. One view held that collateral relations of godparents and godchildren—that is, their brothers and sisters, along with their descendants—fell under the prohibitions against incest as well.[84] After all, marriage between blood relatives was forbidden on grounds of consanguinity, and should not the superior spiritual bond be upheld even more carefully? The reason earlier ecclesiastical authors did not prohibit these unions, it was argued spuriously, was their reluctance to talk about such obscenity![85] Byzantine permissions to the contrary were overruled by the decisions of the Bulgarian archbishop Dimitri Xomjatin.[86]

A third problem arose concerning the relationship between godchildren who shared the same sponsor. Here the weight of ecclesiastical opinion held that they had to be considered as brothers and sisters, and thus ineligible to marry.[87] As in the case of natural-born brothers, the descendants of two godbrothers were not permitted to marry for three generations (to the eighth degree of kinship).[88] Penances ranged from five to fifteen years, the same as for incest between the children of *kumovi* or between in-laws.[89] Questions arose about marriage even to a godbrother's relatives. Incest with one's spiritual brother's mother carried a penance of nine years with 150 prostrations; with his wife, six years

81. SANU 124(29), f. 74r (5 years, 36 prostrations); Hil. 169, f. 80r; Hil 302, f. 1r.
82. E.g., Smirnov, *Materialy*, 154, 242 (9 years); Hil. 169, ff. 74v–75r (5 years on bread and water).
83. SOCH 197, f. 1v. In response to a question from Tsar Boris of Bulgaria, Pope Nicholas I responded similarly concerning Roman Catholic rules on intermarriage among descendants of godparent and godchild; see *Izvori za bŭlgarskata istorija*, 7:66–67.
84. Hil. 169, f. 74v.
85. SOCH 197, f. 14r.
86. SANU 123(28), ff. 155r–170r; SOCH 197, ff. 12r–18r.
87. E.g., Hil. 627, f. 36r.
88. NBS 10, f. 59r.
89. E.g., Smirnov, *Materialy*, 66 (8 years); "Voprosy i otvety pastyrskoj praktiki," in RIB, 6:864 (15 years); Rila 1/20(48), ff. 83v–84r (7 years, 100 prostrations), 193v (5 years). For godbrothers' children, see, e.g., Kiev 49, f. 662 (5 years, 36 prostrations).

with 100 prostrations; with his daughter, five or six years with 100 prostrations; with his sister, four years with 36 to 70 prostrations.[90] Even more distant relatives by baptism were sometimes included in penitential codes, with substantial penances. Incest with a godbrother's mother-in-law or sister-in-law carried a penance of three to five years.[91] Feognost, the Russian bishop of Sarai in 1276, felt it necessary to consult the patriarch of Constantinople in order to ascertain the propriety of a marriage between a man and his godbrother's aunt or cousin. Permission was granted, on the grounds that canon law contained no specific prohibition.[92]

Other clerics regarded extensive observance of degrees of spiritual consanguinity to be unnecessary. They also ruled that entry into a baptismal relationship had no effect on the previous generations. Parents, grandparents, uncles, and aunts of *kumovi* were free to marry if they wished.[93]

The Slavic Orthodox churches, especially among the South Slavs, recognized spiritual bonds other than those of blood brothers and of godparent and godchild. A third spiritual relationship, also termed *kumstvo*, was contracted at the time of marriage. The witness to the sacrament of Christian marriage, like the witness to the sacrament of baptism, became a spiritual parent. Like other spiritual and natal parents, he and his family became forbidden as marriage partners. The custom of the marriage *kum* arose among the South Slavs in the medieval period; it was virtually unknown in Russia. Because it was not of ecclesiastical origin, not every medieval manuscript of the wedding ceremony includes mention of the *kum*. It is likely that here again the church ultimately approved and sanctified a custom of pagan origin. Finally, the witness to the first cutting of a child's hair assumed a spiritual role that precluded intermarriage. The role of the witness is not attested in medieval manuscripts, although nineteenth- and twentieth-century ethnographers remark on its prevalence. The custom of hair cutting, however, receives attention: medieval canons placed parents under penance if their child died with its hair uncut. This also was doubtless a custom of pagan origin, which the church was slow to recognize.

---

90. E.g., VAT-Bor. 15, f. 481r; Kiev 49, f. 661v–662r; Rila 1/20(48), f. 104r–104v; Hil. 169, f. 8or.

91. E.g., SANU 124(29), f. 73v (3 years, 36 prostrations); VAT-Bor. 15, f. 481r (4 years, 66 prostrations); Rila 1/20(48), f. 104v (5 years, 66 prostrations).

92. "Answers of the Patriarchal Council of Constantinople to the Questions of Feognost, Bishop of Sarai," art. 30, in RIB, 6:138.

93. Kiev 49, ff. 640v–641r; Hil. 171, ff. 277v–278r.

Violations of Canons on Incest

The actual observance of the strictures on consanguinity in canon law is difficult to estimate. Parish records of births and marriages do not survive. Other sources, such as chronicles and histories, record only the marriages of the princely families, and those intermittently and sometimes inaccurately.[94] Of course, the marriage patterns of princes were not necessarily typical of those of the society as a whole. On the one hand, rulers were in the public view, their family trees were well known, and any violation of canon law would not pass unnoticed. As the primary supporters of Orthodox Christianity in the Slavic world, the royal families would be the most knowledgeable about marital regulations and have the greatest stake in upholding the authority of the church. On the other hand, princely marriages had political implications, solidifying alliances and confirming peace treaties, which were more important to the welfare of the state than observance of canon law. Furthermore, hierarchs might well hesitate to challenge the violations of a prince who otherwise favored church institutions.

Several Rjurikid princes of Russia entered into incestuous marriages. Prince Vsevolod Davydovič of Gorodok, for example, married Agafia, daughter of Vladimir Monomax, in 1116. That the marriage held political advantages for Vsevolod cannot be doubted, but Agafia was his second cousin—they were both descendants of Jaroslav the Wise. Another union between second cousins related through Jaroslav took place about the same time: between Svjatoša, the son of Prince Davyd of Smolensk and Černigov, and Anna, daughter of Svjatopolk II, grand prince of Kiev.[95] There is no evidence that ecclesiastical officials objected to either of these matches. Vasilissa, daughter of Prince Vasilij II of Moscow, married two princes of Suzdal in succession. The first husband, Aleksandr Ivanovič, died in 1418, after barely a year of marriage. Vasilissa then married his second cousin once removed and successor, Aleksandr Daniilovič.[96] The marriage seems to have been part of an attempt by the grand prince of Moscow to control the succession to the princely seat of Suzdal. The marriage between Ivan III of Russia and

94. It might be possible to study aristocratic marriage patterns, but little such work has been done. M. E. Byčkova's *Rodoslovnye knigi XVI–XVII vv.* (M., 1975) represents a necessary first step in establishing the recension of genealogical sources for late-medieval Russia, but she does not actually reconstruct genealogies. Janin produced schematizations of several major Novgorodian families of the twelve to fifteenth centuries in *Novgorodskaja feodal'naja votčina,* but he emphasized inheritance and distribution of land rather than familial alliances.

95. Wodzimierz Dworzaczek, *Genealogia* (Warsaw, 1959), charts 21–31.

96. N. de Baumgarten, *Généalogies des branches regnantes des Rurikides du XIIIe au XVIe siècle,* Orientalia Christiana, vol. 35 (Rome, 1934), 38–43.

Sophia Paleologina was technically incestuous: Ivan's aunt Anna had previously married Sophia's uncle, Emperor John VIII Paleologus.[97] However, nobody seems to have mentioned this fact. Those who opposed the marriage did so on the more obvious grounds of religious difference; those who supported it had no desire to place additional obstacles in the way of a politically advantageous union.

Nor did the Bulgarian church protest when Tsar Boril contracted a series of overtly incestuous marriages. After the death of his uncle and predecessor, Kalojan, in 1207, Boril usurped the throne from a cousin, the minor prince Ivan Asen. Boril married his uncle's widow, a Cuman princess, in order to gain the support of the steppe empire. Boril and the Cuman princess were related in the third degree of *svatstvo*, so the marriage violated canon law. Six years later, Boril concluded an alliance with Henry, the Latin king of Constantinople, confirmed through Henry's marriage to Boril's stepdaughter (the daughter of Kalojan and the Cuman princess). Soon after, Boril divorced his Cuman wife, sacrificing that alliance, and married Henry's niece. The combination of the two unions violated canon law: father and stepdaughter were not permitted to marry niece and uncle. Not only were they related in the fourth degree of *svatstvo*, but the unions put the participants "out of place"; Henry was both son-in-law and uncle by marriage to Boril. Furthermore, Henry and his niece were Roman Catholic heretics. Later, there were more marriages of dubious legitimacy. Boril's new wife's sister married King Andrew II of Hungary; this union was legal. But then Boril's daughter by a previous marriage wedded Andrew's eldest son, Bela. The stepmothers of bride and groom were sisters, thus Bela and his bride were first cousins by adoption and forbidden to marry. After Ivan Asen came to power, he wished to preserve the Hungarian alliance, and married Andrew's daughter Maria, in violation of canons: his first cousin once removed (Boril's daughter) was his bride's sister-in-law. Thus there were four incestuous marriages in the Bulgarian royal house in the early thirteenth century. Three of them also violated rules against intermarriage with heretics. The Bulgarian church does not seem to have objected, perhaps because Boril gave the hierarchy strong support in its struggle against the Bogomils.[98]

In the fourteenth century, the Bulgarian tsar Ivan Alexander IV ar-

97. For an example of the prohibition, see Kiev 49, ff. 644r–645r.
98. For a discussion of the political circumstances surrounding these marriages, see Fine, *Late Medieval Balkans*, 91–129. Fine suggests that Boril married Kalojan's widow to enhance his legitimacy at home, but it is hard to see how this illegal union would have advanced that aim. It is more reasonable to think of the marriage in terms of the advantages of the Cuman alliance.

ranged incestuous unions for his relatives. The advantageous marriage between Ivan Alexander's sister Elena and King Stefan Dušan of Serbia was technically incestuous by some understandings of canon law: Elena's mother and Stefan Dušan's step-grandmother were second cousins. Perhaps the marriage raised no question because Milutin's marriage to the Bulgarian princess Ana had ended in divorce. The marriages with the Byzantine imperial family were more obviously in violation of canon law. Ivan Alexander betrothed his young son Michael Asen to the daughter of Andronikos III in 1331; this legal marriage was concluded in 1338 or 1339. The marital alliance with Byzantium in 1352, between his underaged daughter Keraca-Maria and the future Andronikos IV, grandson of Andronikos III, was technically incestuous: brother and sister could not marry aunt and nephew. The Bulgarian ruling family also violated other marriage canons. In 1256 Kaliman II murdered his first cousin, Michael II Asen, and married Michael's widow, daughter of the Russian prince Rostislav of Galič.[99] Such a marriage was certainly noncanonical: a widow was not permitted to marry her late husband's cousin—or his murderer.

The Serbian king Milutin, whose numerous marriages violated any number of canons, also committed incest. His marriage to the Hungarian princess Elizabeth directly violated the law prohibiting two brothers to marry two sisters. From the perspective of Milutin's mother, the dowager queen Elena, the marriage was too advantageous to be passed up. Milutin and his brother Dragutin were rivals for power; their mother wished to guarantee that her Angevin alliance would survive, no matter which of her sons ultimately triumphed. As a Roman Catholic, she saw nothing incestuous about the marriages, which were permissible under Roman canons. Supporters of the marriages and the alliance tried to evade criticism by issuing a report that the marriages had been sanctified in a double wedding. They had found a loophole in canon law. At the moment the marriages were solemnized, both were legal: neither groom was marrying his brother's wife's sister, because the brother was not yet married. In fact, the report is dubious; there is strong evidence that Dragutin married Princess Catherine of Hungary before 1282, the probable date of Milutin's marriage.

It is clear that ruling families did not permit distant kinship to stand in the way of a politically advantageous marriage. Doubtless the same held true for other social classes. When marriages were challenged, it was on religious grounds rather than because of incest. It does not appear that incest was used as an excuse to dissolve marriages had become politi-

99. See Dworzaczek; Božilov, 106–110, 113–114.

cally obsolete, although explanations for divorces are often not recorded in the sources.

A third party could use the issue of consanguinity to try to prevent a couple from marrying, as a court case in Russia in 1672 illustrates. Vasilij Babin and Ivan Akinin were both suitors for the hand of a maiden, Stefanida. Each petitioned the archiepiscopal court at the Troickij monastery to prevent the other from marrying Stefanida, on the grounds of consanguinity. Babin charged that Akinin was too closely related to Stefanida to permit them to marry: Stefanida's sister was married to a certain Ivan Lišin, whose brother, Vasilij Lišin, was married to Akinin's aunt. Akinin and Stefanida were thus in-laws of in-laws; their connection consisted of *trirodstvo* in the seventh degree. Because canon law required observance only of four degrees of *trirodstvo*, Babin added a second complaint: Akinin's aunt was married to Stefanida's great-uncle. That made Akinin and Stefanida related in the sixth degree of *svatstvo*, which constituted a marginal case. Akinin countered with an accusation that Babin's marriage to Stefanida would also be incestuous: Babin's grandfather's second wife was Stefanida's mother's first cousin. Because a stepparent counted as a blood relative for purposes of calculating consanguinity, Babin and Stefanida were technically related in the seventh degree of *rodstvo*, and that marriage was clearly forbidden. This accusation put Babin at a disadvantage in the lawsuit, and he became acrimonious, accusing Akinin of not being a true Christian. The court's decision in this lawsuit is not recorded, but the nature of the arguments reveal the extent to which consanguinity was an issue.[100] Canon law acknowledged even distant connections to be impediments to marriage; when it was convenient to do so, one could raise the issue.

The Purpose of Consanguinity Regulations

The Slavs considered incest and intermarriage within the prohibited degrees of kinship to be among the most heinous of offenses against God and the community, and punished violators with the highest fines and longest penances. Especially among the Serbs, questions about incest—broadly defined—dominated penitential questionnaires. The ecclesiastical explanation for the rules regulating the choice of marriage partner centered on matters of purity; forbidden unions were institutionalized illicit fornication (*blud*) and were an affront to God. The disruption of domestic life caused by illicit intrafamilial sexual contacts has been well

---

100. *Sbornik starinnyx bumag xranjaščixsja v muzee P. I. Ščukina*, 102–105.

documented by modern sociologists. In the medieval Slavic world, the family as a residential unit tended to be larger and more extensive; consequently, more distant relatives had to be included in the prohibition.

The extensive rules prohibiting marriages between relatives who lived apart went far beyond the universal taboo against incest or the requirements for genetic health. Many societies—including those described in the Bible—permit marriages between cousins, allow or even mandate marriages between in-laws, and do not extend restrictions on incestuous unions to fictitious kin. Had medieval Slavic societies wished to justify a narrower set of restrictions on marriage between relatives, they could easily have drawn on biblical examples to counteract the decisions of the Church Fathers. They did not; on the contrary, they expanded the inherited Byzantine canons to exclude even more distant connections. Slavic rules on familial marriages cannot be explained solely by Orthodox tradition. Rather, the restrictions must have served some social purposes not mentioned in the ecclesiastically oriented sources. Some reasonable possibilities may be suggested.

First, extensive restrictions on eligibility for marriage reinforced familial authority over the choice of spouse. Marriages had to be arranged by the families, because children in their early or mid-teens would have had little contact with anyone who was not related to the family by blood, marriage, adoption, or spiritual kinship in the broad way those terms were defined. Parents could forbid almost any union the child desired on the grounds of kinship. When these rules were combined with the other restrictions on the choice of spouse, however, they inhibited parents from grossly abusing their authority over their children while reaffirming parental power in general.

Second, this extreme form of exogamy helped to preserve peace in the community. The bride would often have to be brought from some distance—five villages away, as the Serbian proverb says. This circumstance would have advantages for both the family and the community, if not for the young bride. The groom's family would experience less interference from the bride's family over petty everyday disagreements if they were separated by some distance.

Furthermore, extensive rules on consanguinity, affinity, and adoption had the effect of dramatically increasing the number of relatives each person could claim. If the need for concerted action arose, supporters could be gathered from all over the region, through the network of family ties. In a society still heavily based in familial structures and lacking in central government—as South Slavic society remained well into the period of Turkish rule—the expansion of contacts through quasi-familial relationships signified power and security. To marry a person who was already bound to support family interests was wasteful. The advantages of using every opportunity to increase the number of allies through marriages might have been translated into canon law as a moral obligation to do so. There was an additional advantage to increasing the number of people who could be considered kinsmen. Because it was not acceptable to initiate a blood feud with any sort of relative, wide networks of kin promoted peace.[101]

Enforcement of incest restrictions among the aristocracy could serve as a tool by which the prince discouraged regional resistance to his rule. The Russian example is particularly instructive in this case: the expansion of rules prohibiting marriages between cousins occurred at precisely the time when the grand prince of Moscow was attempting to incorporate the local aristocracies of the appanages into Muscovite service. These aristocracies were very small; even in Novgorod, the largest medieval Russian city, the upper aristocracy numbered only forty or fifty families. By restricting marriages among relatives, the church forced aristocrats to seek spouses in families from other Russian principalities. The only common interest between these families would be their mutual service to the grand prince.

By establishing ecclesiastical regulations on incest, the church acquired the right to regulate and judge the formation of basic social relationships. Observance of the rules promoted social stability by reducing tensions within the family unit and by clarifying social relationships and their consequent obligations. When social stability demanded a relaxation of the rules, their violation was tolerated by church and society with a minimum of fuss.

101. Predrag Matejić suggested this interpretation to me.

CHAPTER 4

Illicit Sex

Slavic churchmen were not so naive as to believe that married persons would restrict themselves to their own lawful partners. Because most marriages were arranged without attention to the emotional or sexual compatibility of the spouses, husbands and wives were likely to seek more pleasing lovers. The rules governing the formation of marriages were so restrictive that not all persons—not even all laymen—were permitted to take a legal spouse. Consequently, while the church preached abstinence for the unwedded and restraint for the married, it prepared rules to deal with the inevitable violations.

The church sought to discourage sexual violations in part by imposing substantial penalties and in part by arguing that violations really weren't worth the trouble and sin involved. Numerous tales depict the travails of those who fell victim to the Devil's instigation, and their difficulty in regaining their lost salvation. Not only were the consequences of infidelity extremely unpleasant, but the rewards to be found in the arms of an illicit lover were few and transient.

Insofar as canon law texts explained the attention to marital and extramarital sexual behavior at all, they provided a religious justification. But the regulations for sexual conduct must have served practical purposes as well. An elite cannot successfully impose rules of personal conduct on a recalcitrant population if they contradict existing values and interfere with social stability. The acceptance and expansion of Byzantine rules on sexual conduct suggest that the classification of a wide range of sexual behaviors as illicit coincided with the native Slavic sense of propriety.

In general sexual violations by men and women were treated identically, but there were several exceptions to this rule. Female homosexuality, for example, was less serious than male homosexual activity, which involved anal intercourse. False insinuations about a woman's sexual conduct were punishable, while there was no analogous category of sexual innuendo against a man. Furthermore, while a married man was usually punished for a sexual sin in the same way as an unmarried man, a married woman was punished as an adulteress. As the provision in the nomocanon stated after a list of penances for sexual violations: "Women are given the same penances, if they do not have husbands. If they have husbands, they observe the rule for adultery, that is to say, they always observe the most years." The law specifically recognized the offended husband's jealousy of his wife's lover as a justification for imposing a more severe penance on a married woman.[1]

Marital Sex

Canon law included a large number of provisions governing the relationship between husband and wife. Although the church authorized marriage as an appropriate method of channeling sexual urges that could not be denied altogether, the married state was not a license to the couple to engage in gratification of Satanic desires. Men were discouraged from expressing immoderate attraction even to their wives. "Separate yourself from your wife, so you don't become attached to her," one didactic text advised.[2] Indeed, excessive sexual intercourse between spouses was equated with other serious violations, such as anal intercourse and association with prostitutes.[3] If a man dreamed about conjugal relations with his wife, he was considered guilty of sin, and was required to perform penitential prostrations and prayers.[4] A woman's allure, churchmen taught, endangered her husband, and women were warned that personal adornment would result in damnation.[5] Church-

1. Hil. 628, f. 16r; 301, f. 84v.
2. "Slovo i skazanie o zverex i pticax," in *Pamjatniki literatury drevnej Rusi, XIII vek*, 478. The text describes the habits of various sorts of animals and advises the reader on the lessons to be learned from their behaviors. This advice is given on the example of the turtle dove. The translation into modern Russian of this passage is faulty. In Western Europe before the mid–thirteenth century, the strength of clerical opinion held that sexual pleasure was evil and ought to be avoided, even though coition in marriage was without sin. See Brooke, "Aspects of Marriage Law," 333–344.
3. Almazov, 3:196. St. Jerome took a similar view: "Nothing is nastier than to love your own wife as if she were your mistress." See James A. Brundage, "Let Me Count the Ways: Canonists and Theologians Contemplate Coital Positions," *Journal of Medieval History* 10, no. 2 (1984): 82; and *Law, Sex, and Christian Society*, 90–91.
4. Hil. 171, f. 252r (8 prostrations); Peć 77, f. 107r (50 prostrations).
5. See, e.g., the tale of King Solomon and his beautiful and vain wife, from fifteenth-century Bulgaria, in Ivanov, *Starobŭlgarski razkazi*, 270–272; "Videnie muk grešnicy v ade," in *Pamjatniki starinnoj russkoj literatury*, 1:105–106. The idea that certain kinds of dress expressed

*Love did not
mean sex*

men regarded excessive sexual attraction between husband and wife as a distraction from higher duties to God. The church preferred to see mature restraint in the conjugal relationship, if the couple was going to consummate the marriage at all.

Canon law dictated when husband and wife could not engage in sexual intercourse and which expressions of sexuality were forbidden. Statements of appropriate marital sexual conduct were few, because churchmen did not want to encourage couples to yield to the Devil. Acceptable sexual conduct between spouses could be deduced only from the listing of inappropriate behaviors.

Medieval Orthodox Slavs did not understand the biblical commandment to husbands and wives to love each other as having any sexual content. Love in its spiritual sense—in the sense in which Christ loved the church—was antithetical to sexual expression. A truly loving husband or wife would not want to lead a spouse into demonic activity. The concept of romantic love that developed in the West in the late Middle Ages was alien to the Slavs; they did not feel that sexual intercourse was the normal and proper way for a man and a woman to express emotional bonding. The existence of emotional love in marriage was known and acknowledged, as was the existence of lust, both inside and outside of marriage. The two emotions, however, were not connected.

Even though Slavic Orthodox theologians were reluctant to admit to a direct connection between sexual intercourse and procreation, they nonetheless regarded the production of children as one of the goals of marriage. The birth of a child to a married couple served to justify the sexual intercourse that enabled it. While Roman Catholic canonists might judge the permissibility of sexual acts on the basis of procreative possibility and intent, their Orthodox counterparts judged them on the actual production of a viable and virtuous child. The parents' emotional state did not matter. Whether husband and wife enjoyed a particular act of coition was irrelevant, provided the timing and method were in accordance with canon law and a new human life resulted from it. Orthodox theologians, unlike Western ones, did not debate the rectitude of pleasure in sexual intercourse. An individual's state of mind regarding sexual expression was of concern only when it generated a pattern of sexual conduct marked by self-indulgence and the pursuit of bodily sensation, to the detriment of spiritual and familial responsibilities.

Instead of examining the attitude and purposes behind a married

women's sexual availability underlay some of the sumptuary legislation in the late-medieval West. See James A. Brundage, "Sumptuary Laws and Prostitution in Late Medieval Italy," *Journal of Medieval History* 13, no. 4 (1987): 343–355.

couple's sexual activity, Orthodox clerics regulated when and how the couple had conjugal relations. The list of prohibited activities was extensive. Ultimately, a couple escaped all censure only if they produced a child through marital relations restricted to vaginal genital contact in the "missionary" position, on a day not set aside for religious observance or bodily purification.[6]

The Timing of Marital Sex

Because spiritual matters outweighed physical ones, the demands of religious observance took precedence over sexual expression. On holy days, the faithful were supposed to turn their thoughts to God; sexual activity, which originated with the Devil, was viewed as inimical to the spiritual benefits of the holiday. For that reason, a wide range of regulations arose to prevent conjugal relations in close temporal proximity to ecclesiastical rites.

Early church canons forbade conjugal relations on Sundays and holy days.[7] Because Christians needed to prepare themselves spiritually to receive the Gifts, husbands and wives were directed to abstain from sex on Saturdays as well. In addition to weekly services, the Orthodox religious calendar contained a multitude of fast days, intended for spiritual renewal through prayer and self-discipline. The most extensive rules required sexual abstinence on Wednesdays and Fridays throughout the year, as well as during the four annual Lents: before Easter (sometimes termed the "Great Lent"), before Christmas, before the Feast of Saints Peter and Paul, and during St. Philip's Week.[8] Penitential fasts could also include an obligation to abstain from marital intercourse.[9]

All Orthodox hierarchs considered sexual abstinence on days of religious observance to be appropriate and praiseworthy. They disagreed, however, on how many days of abstinence to require and how seriously

6. For a brief consideration of the restrictions on marital sex in the medieval West, see the delightful "flow chart" in Brundage, *Law, Sex, and Christian Society*, 162, and the explanation of it, 155–163.
7. Timothy of Alexandria, art. 3, in *Kormčaja*, 545. On prohibitions on marital relations in Roman Catholic canon law, see Payer, "Early medieval regulations," 361–368, and *Sex and the Penitentials*, 23–28. In *Un Temps pour embrasser*, 6, 8–40, Flandrin notes that restrictions on the times when conjugal sex could take place were very common in the West in the early Middle Ages but became unusual after the eleventh century.
8. Smirnov, *Materialy*, 43, 67, 116, 207. There are additional single days of observance in the calendar; e.g., the Assumption of the Virgin, August 15. Pavlov pointed out (*Nomokanon pri Bol'šom Trebnike*, 166–167) that the Byzantine prototypes of these prohibitions on marital sex during Lent were not included in the Greek nomocanon, but entered the Slavic *trebnik* independently. This provenance reinforces the view that the Slavs deliberately selected the stringent prohibition on marital sex.
9. The foreign visitor Guy Miège commented on this rule (74).

to punish violations. In the view of some clerics, abstinence was essential on all days of observance. Sexual intercourse on those days constituted an indulgence of the evil inclination, and was labeled illicit fornication (*blud*).[10] Couples could be expected to abstain on holy days, one author argued, because there were many other days when marital coitus was permitted.[11] Instructions to newlyweds make sexual restraint on holy days the determining factor in salvation: "If you will remain in the law [i.e., abstinent], then the Angel of God will write your good deeds in the book. But if you remain in disobedience to the law, then the Angel of Satan will write your evil deeds in the book."[12] Not even the desire for children could justify violation of a fast day. The production of new Christian persons was less important than the improvement of those already created.[13] "Restrain yourself on holidays and fasts, because God gave you a wife in order to bear children and not for whoremongering. Listen and you will not suffer the evil of eternal torment."[14] The strong implication was that a godly child could not be conceived on an inappropriate occasion; therefore sexual activity could not be justified.

A miracle attributed to the icon of the Virgin at Hilandar illustrates a widespread but noncanonical belief in the awful results of conjugal intercourse on a holy day. The tale tells of a husband who raped his wife on Holy Saturday, when she wished to abstain out of piety. In anger, she vowed to dedicate the child then conceived to the Devil. However, the boy miraculously turned out to be pious and beautiful, despite his origins. When the Devil came to claim him, the boy called upon the power of the Virgin to rescue him from the consequences of his unfortunate mother's hasty promise.[15]

A minority liberal opinion thrived for a time in medieval Russia. While praising abstinence as a mark of piety, Bishop Nifont of Novgorod denied the necessity of refraining from marital intercourse on most days of observance. He did not believe that a child conceived through marital intercourse on a holy day would turn out to be a mur-

---

10. GIM, Sin. 227, ff. 211v–212r; *Kormčaja*, 542. The Slavs learned to be concerned about marital intercourse on holy days early; Tsar Boris inquired about it in his questions to Pope Nicholas I, who responded that it was acceptable only if passion could be avoided. See *Izvori za bŭlgarskata istorija*, 7:98–99, 105–106. Roman Catholic churchmen in the West taught that a child conceived on a day of abstinence was a bastard in God's eyes. See Brundage, *Law, Sex, and Christian Society*, 155.

11. Troicki, 79, attributed to Bishop John of Kitros.

12. Smirnov, *Materialy*, 207.

13. Noonan, *Contraception*, 84, notes this point of view among Church Fathers in their approval of abstinence, which of course constitutes a means of birth control.

14. BNL 275, f. 45v.

15. BNL 740(168), ff. 105r–106v. Compare this story with the belief in the medieval West that children conceived in defiance of requirements of abstinence would be born physically deformed: Flandrin, *Un Temps pour embrasser*, 119–120, 147–149.

derer, thief, brigand, or adulterer, and ordered that books that promoted this view be burned. In his view, other sins were more serious impediments to receiving communion; he named specifically anger against others, drunkenness, swearing, and dishonesty in business.[16] His views were not widely shared, as revealed by the debate between him and his pupil Kirik:

> I [Kirik] asked, "Is it right to give communion to someone who had intercourse with his wife during the Great Fast?"
> He [Bishop Nifont] grew angry. "How," he said, "can you teach men to abstain from their wives during Lent? The sin is yours in this!"
> I said, "Lord, it is written in the code for priests [*ustav beleč'skij*] that it is good to preserve oneself, because it is Christ's fast."
> "Feodos heard this from the Metropolitan," he said, "and wrote it down: if they cannot [abstain] completely, then [they should abstain] the first and last weeks. Also," he said, "neither the Metropolitan nor Feodos required anything except Holy Week; and during Holy Week, all days are observed as Sunday."[17]

Archbishop Ilja of Novgorod took a similar position, arguing that priests who required total abstinence were hypocrites, because they were not able to fulfill this order themselves.[18] But while Nifont was more liberal than many of his fellow hierarchs regarding abstinence during Lent, he shared the general view concerning Saturdays and Sundays. Indeed, in an unusual expansion of the rule, he directed that couples should not enter into conjugal relations until Monday evening.[19]

Nifont did not regard marital relations on a day of observance as a serious offense, especially for young couples: "if they are young, and will not be able [to abstain], there is nothing unfortunate in that; there is no sin in one's wife." He advocated giving them instructions about the propriety of abstinence on days of religious observance in lieu of a penance.[20]

Most other clerical authors were not so lenient, considering sex on holy days an "evil sin."[21] According to an anonymous late-fifteenth-century Russian author, it was the Devil who led a person into the desire for sex after communion. If a man fell ill on the same day he had slept

16. Voprosy Kirika, arts. 74, 71, in RIB, 6:44, 42.
17. Ibid., art. 57, pp. 37–38. The identity of Feodos and the metropolitan have not been established.
18. "Poučenie arxiepiskopa Ilji," art. 18, in RIB, 6:364–366.
19. Voprosy Kirika, art. 57, in RIB, 6:37–38; see also arts. 72–73, pp. 43–44; Voprosy Savy, art. 22, p. 57.
20. Voprosy Ilji, art. 21, in RIB, 6:61.
21. Almazov, 3:279.

with his wife, he could not receive communion unless he was near death. Even then, he first had to bathe and change his clothes.[22] If a priest knew that parishioners had violated rules of dietary and sexual abstinence during a fast period, he could refuse to give them communion on the holiday that concluded it.[23] The penitential fast for violation of the requirement of sexual abstinence on Sunday, holidays, and the day of communion usually ranged from six days to fifty days.[24] Engaging in conjugal relations during Lent could result in a penitential fast as long as a year.[25] Russian clerics worried especially about sexual activity on Saturdays, because of the survival of pagan rites involving ritual sex held on Saturday evenings. Although the usual penances for Saturday-night sex fell within the range of those for violations of Sundays and holy days, an occasional author recommended a more severe punishment: in one case, a fast of eighty days, and in another, eight days of a diet of bread and cabbage.[26] Abstinence on regular Wednesday and Friday fasts was considered less important than weekend and Lenten observances; most penitential questionnaires and codes of canon law did not mention this sin.[27]

The most important days of observance in the Orthodox calendar were those immediately preceding Easter. Even the liberal Bishop Nifont required abstinence at that time. However, abstinence contradicted another Orthodox teaching: that husbands and wives not deny each other sexual release except by mutual consent. The concern about marital abstinence, reflected in the writings of Paul and repeated by Slavic Orthodox hierarchs, was that by refusing a licit sexual outlet, uncooperative spouses could drive their mates into illicit relationships.[28] A Serbian tale illustrated the danger of overzealous abstinence:

On Holy Saturday evening, a priest was tormented by a demon of lust. Remembering the requirement of abstinence, his wife refused to satisfy his urges. As a result, the priest went out to the barn and sought release with a cow. The next day, during the Easter mass, flocks of birds attacked the church. The priest ordered that the doors and windows be

22. "Voprosy i otvety pastyrskoj praktiki," arts. 16, 21, 37, in RIB, 6:859–860, 864.

23. Smirnov, *Materialy*, 43, 67; SANU 124(67), f. 13v.

24. See, e.g., Almazov, 3:145 (40 days, or 6 days and 40 prostrations), 150 (30 days), 151 (8 days), 274 (6 weeks); BNL 251(200), f. 127r (8 days); Rila 1/20(48), ff. 26v, 189r (8 days and 100 prostrations); Peć 77, f. 106r (8 days); Dečani 68, f. 276r (50 days, 100 prostrations).

25. "Voprosy i otvety pastyrskoj praktiki," art. 41, in RIB, 6:865.

26. Almazov, 3:145, 148, 151, 161, 279; Smirnov, *Materialy*, 51, 65, 241.

27. For an exception, see Almazov, 3:151.

28. The Bogomils were attacked for encouraging wives to deny their husbands: Begunov, *Kozma Presviter*, 368–369. Under the Augustinian doctrine of "conjugal debt" in the Roman Catholic Church, only ill health and pregnancy justified refusal to agree to marital intercourse. See Tentler, 170–172, 213–217.

barred against the onslaught, and he tearfully confessed his sin before the congregation. The priest and the congregants then opened the door and were allowed to leave unharmed. When the priest's wife went out, however, the birds descended upon her and tore her to pieces. Clearly she was seen as responsible for her husband's sin, because she had driven him to it.[29]

In order to encourage married couples to observe the required periods of abstinence, clerical authors recommended that they sleep separately: "It is good for every Christian, both men and women, to have two beds in their house, and to sleep separately on Sundays and holidays and during Holy Week, if sometimes someone cannot restrain himself for God's sake; for on these days it is proper to exercise restraint, and not always wallow like a pig in a sty. From such lack of restraint grows an evil seed."[30] One churchman went so far as to prohibit husband and wife to take communion if they had shared a bed, even if they did not have conjugal relations.[31] Priests also were instructed to impose a fast of three weeks on couples who skipped mass in order to indulge in sexual intercourse without violating the sanctity of the sacraments.[32]

Because canon law forbade sexual intercourse during Lenten periods and on the day of communion, problems arose concerning the celebration of marriages. Canons forbade marriages during Lent; wedding parties were contrary to the solemnity of the fast, and the consummation of the marriage would violate the law.[33] To prevent temptation during Lent, weddings were sometimes prohibited during the preceding week as well. Whenever the marriage was celebrated, however, the service included communion, and in theory the bridal couple was required to abstain from sexual intercourse until the next day. The liberal bishop Nifont was willing to make an exception for a newly married couple. He argued first that bride and groom constituted "one body" and therefore could not be forbidden to each other. Second, he pointed out that church canons directed that the bridal couple be given communion but did not specifically order them to abstain from sexual intercourse. Finally, Nifont argued that marriage carried no penance, and requiring abstinence for three days on pain of denying communion constituted a penance. These arguments could be applied to all husbands and wives, not only to newlyweds, but Nifont did not do so; he continued to recommend abstinence from the day preceding communion until the evening of the fol-

29. SANU 124(29), f. 130v. The similarity to the Alfred Hitchcock film *The Birds* is striking.
30. Kiev 49, f. 671r.
31. GIM, Sin. 227, f. 210v.
32. Almazov, 3:149, 275.
33. Smirnov, *Materialy*, 54, 117, 133, 242; Hil. 171, f. 249v; Peć 77, f. 105r.

lowing day for all but newlyweds. Another anonymous cleric proposed a different solution to the problem of consummation of the marriage: he ordered the newlywed couple banned from the church and communion for forty days, as though fulfilling a penance.[34]

Canon law proscribed other ecclesiastical rites in addition to communion for couples who had engaged in conjugal relations, even at an appropriate time in the appropriate manner. Any sexual contact made a person ritually impure—a state akin to sinfulness, in the Slavic Orthodox conception. Mere entry into the church building was regarded as a transgression. A didactic tale told of a young bride who committed this offense, and was consequently possessed by a demon.[35] Ritual impurity could be washed away by a ritual of purification. A man who had slept with his wife was forbidden to kiss relics of the saints until he had washed below the waist.[36] To prevent accidental defilement of holy things through contact with sexuality, some Russian clerics required that both husbands and wives bathe after having marital relations.[37] According to an Old Believer *vita* of St. Epifanij, it was inappropriate for a person to visit a holy man after marital intercourse without bathing. A man who did so was attacked and killed by a demon.[38]

A debate arose as to the propriety of engaging in conjugal relations in the presence of icons, crosses, or other objects imbued with sanctity. Nifont espoused the liberal view, regarding marital intercourse as devoid of sin, and thus appropriate in the presence of holy objects. He cited Greek custom to back up his view.[39] The very question, however, indicated the existence of a contrary opinion: even marital sex was sinful. This view became dominant in Russia by the sixteenth century.[40] According to the report of an anonymous Dutch merchant who witnessed the brief reign of the False Dmitrij in Muscovy, popular rumor castigated the impostor for sleeping with his wife in the presence of an icon of the Virgin.[41] Sexual activity of any sort in the church building

34. Smirnov, *Materialy*, 40; 244. Similar rules were known in the West, where the bridal couple might be prohibited entry into the church for 3 to 40 days; see Flandrin, *Un Temps pour embrasser*, 113–114.

35. *Pamjatniki starinnoj russkoj literatury*, 1:210. For a discussion of Judeo-Christian ideas about the impurity of sex, see Flandrin, *Un Temps pour embrasser*, 97–100, 112–113.

36. Voprosy Kirika, art. 26, in RIB, 6:30.

37. Almazov, 3:145, 146, 148, 160, 274. The usual penance for failure to wash after sex was a three-day fast, but one text ordered a fast of 40 days with 25 prostrations a day.

38. Barskov, 229–231.

39. Voprosy Savy, art. 4, in RIB, 6:52. A later Russian code from the fourteenth century permits marital sex in front of icons, but not illicit fornication; see Smirnov, *Materialy*, 67.

40. Kaiser, "Transformation of Legal Relations," 420.

41. "The Reporte of a Bloudie and Terrible Massacre in the City of Mosco . . . ," in S. E. Howe, *The False Dmitri—A Russian Romance and Tragedy* (London, 1916), 58.

was strictly forbidden, even if the couple was married.[42] A man was forbidden to sleep with his wife for eight days after chrismation.[43]

Because canon law and popular wisdom prohibited contact between sanctified materials and manifestations of sexuality, a particular problem arose in the treatment of venereal disease. Churchmen certainly did not want sufferers to turn to semipagan healers instead of bringing their ailments to their priests for treatment, often with sanctified myrrh. Ordinarily the priest applied his unguent to the affected organ in the church, but that would not be appropriate in the case of genital infections, so the priest directed the patient to take a container of myrrh home and place it in front of the icons. He then extinguished the candles and lamps, recited his prayers, and applied it himself in complete privacy. Sexual intercourse and consumption of alcoholic beverages were forbidden for the day.[44]

Female Impurity

Orthodox canon law forbade husband and wife to sleep together when she was "unclean," that is, while she was experiencing a flow of menstrual or postpartum blood. For menstruation, the prohibition was for six to eight days—in other words, the entire length of actual blood flow—but no additional period of purification was required, as under Jewish law.[45] Orthodox clerics were aware of a tradition of a longer period of abstinence for menstruation, but did not consider it to be necessary.[46] Menstruation made a woman "unclean" not only for conjugal relations but also for participation in ecclesiastical rites. At that time a woman was forbidden to enter the church building, and most important, to take communion. The penances imposed for violation were heavy for what would seem to be a minor offense. Simply for entering the church while "unclean," the penance was one hundred prostrations. If the woman dared to take communion, a fast of one to three years was imposed.[47] Literary sources illustrated the seriousness of

---

42. Almazov, 3:92; BNL 246(103), f. 135v. According to one tale, even illicit sex in the church building was a lesser affront to God than a drunken priest. See *Pamjatniki starinnoj russkoj literatury*, 1:149.

43. "Voprosy i otvety pastyrskoj praktiki," art. 11, in RIB, 6:858.

44. "Slovo ob iscelenii boleznej mirom," in *Pamjatniki starinnoj russkoj literatury*, 4:216.

45. E.g., Rila 1/20(48), f. 134v; Kiev 191, ff. 163r, 686v.

46. Kiev 49, ff. 674v–675r.

47. E.g., Rila 1/20(48), ff. 134v–135r, 193r (3 years, 100 prostrations); Peć 77, f. 114v (1 year, 50 prostrations); Almazov, 3:160 (2 years). In response to a question from Tsar Boris, Pope Nicholas I replied that menstruating women need not be excluded from communion at all; see *Izvori za bŭlgarskata istorija*, 7:106–107. For a discussion on the debate in the West about restrictions on the participation of menstruating women in ecclesiastical rituals, see Flandrin, *Un Temps pour embrasser*, 11, 73–82.

this violation. The *vita* of the Novgorodian saints Ioann and Loggin Jarengskie told of a menstruating woman who was struck down by lightning when she accidentally transgressed the saints' unmarked grave. When she repented of her sin, she was miraculously "cured" of her period.[48] In another story, a woman who dared to receive communion every week was turned into a horse for her sin.[49] Only if the woman's death was imminent could an exception be made to this rule. If her period started while she was in church, she was to leave immediately, despite the embarrassment she might feel at advertising her condition in this manner. Failure to do so resulted in a penance of six months of fasting, with fifty prostrations per day.[50]

Slavic clerics could offer no reasonable explanation for these strictures; they simply accepted the rules as appropriate for the sake of "purity," and made no changes in biblical commandments regarding menstruation except to shorten the period of abstinence:

We are more knowledgeably experienced, and order that a couple wait until the sixth or the eighth day in order to complete purification, so there will be no defilement. For every creation of God is good, and nothing is rejected, but for the sake of greater purity we have agreed, for the sake of the Holy Church and liturgy and communion.

Because God created man and woman in the beginning in order to revive the world as their inheritance, he gave us a custom to see. For that reason, every month we see how a conception was made. It is not as some say, that the woman experiences birth from the man, and there is nothing from the woman. It is apparent that blood is taken from the woman . . . and flesh from the man. [51]

A contradiction is apparent in this explanation of menstruation and the restrictions surrounding it. If the creation and procreation are good, how can there be defilement in a normal manifestation of them? Furthermore, church hierarchs obviously considered the segregation of menstruating women from both the ecclesiastical functions and their husbands to be of considerable importance. The proof lies in the length of the penances for violations, measured in years, as compared to the days or weeks prescribed for lesser sins.

The Slavic Orthodox attitude toward menstruation might be explained in part by underlying presuppositions about the origin of sex-

48. GPB, Solov. 183/183, ff. 81v–83r.
49. N. K. Nikol'skij, *Materialy dlja istorii drevnerusskoj duxovnoj pismennosti,* Sbornik otdelenija russkago jazyka i slovesnosti imperatorskoj akademii nauk, vol. 82 (SPb., 1907), 139–140.
50. Kiev 49, ff. 674v–675r.
51. Ibid.

uality. Because Orthodox thinkers regarded childbearing as post facto justification for marital sex, the appearance of a woman's menstrual blood represented a failure to conceive—or worse, the spontaneous abortion of a child. The shedding of menstrual blood was analogous to the emission of semen outside of conjugal relations; both were wasteful, and thus deserving of penance. Just as pregnant women were held responsible for miscarriages and put under penance for the "sin," menstruating women were responsible for the loss of an opportunity to procreate. By this rationale, however, only married women would be excluded from the church during menstruation; single women were not supposed to get pregnant. In fact, all menstruating women were excluded, regardless of marital status.[52] This inconsistency is best explained not by Orthodox theology but by the survival of pre-Christian prejudices. Ancient Israelite culture was not the only one to regard the appearance of menstrual blood as defiling; such notions were widespread among premodern cultures.

The regulations surrounding the purification of women after childbirth give further support to the idea that both pagan and Orthodox attitudes were involved in the treatment of menstruation. Most canonists mandated that the new mother abstain from marital intercourse and participation in ecclesiastical rites for forty days. Unlike biblical and early Western law, Orthodox canons did not differentiate in this regard between the birth of a boy and the birth of a girl.[53] An exception could be made if the woman were dying, but even then she had to be bathed and carried into another building, so as not to defile the communion.[54] If she happened to recover, she was then required to undergo a penitential fast for needlessly transgressing the sacrament.[55] A woman criminal under a sentence of death could not be executed until forty days after giving birth, so that she could confess her sins and receive communion before she died.[56]

This period coincides with both biblical law and modern medical advice: postpartum bleeding usually continues for three to six weeks. A few Russian hierarchs, however, were more lenient on postpartum sex, if not on entry into the church. One provision recommending forty days' abstinence concluded: "but if they are impatient, then twenty days; if

52. See Almazov, 3:169, where a question about entry into the church while menstruating is directed to unmarried girls.
53. Kiev 191, f. 163r; *Sintagmat*, 109–110.
54. Voprosy Savy, art. 2, in RIB, 6:51–52.
55. "Tri svjatitel'skija poučenija," in RIB, 6:920.
56. No. 244, in *Zakonodatel'nye akty russkogo gosudarstvo* (dated to 1637), 179. The law also forbade the execution of a pregnant woman. In order to preserve the life of the child, who was innocent of its mother's offense, the state paid for a wetnurse for a year.

they are very impatient, then twelve days."[57] Bishop Nifont required only eight days; anything more was optional.[58] Few texts mention any penance for violating this period of abstinence, and when a penance was given, it was comparatively light: six days of exclusion from the church and communion.[59] While Slavic hierarchs accepted the idea that childbirth was defiling—even to the point of ordering repurification of a church if a birth took place inside it[60]—they clearly did not regard the postpartum flow of blood in the same light as menstruation. As a further indication that failure to conceive was the major issue, it should be noted that Slavic Orthodox canon law included no prohibition on marital relations during pregnancy.[61]

Coital Positions

Even sexual intercourse between husband and wife at an appropriate time and resulting in the birth of a child was not necessarily without sin. Canon law restricted the sorts of sexual contact that were permitted. The three requirements for licit sex were procreation, vaginal penetration, and the missionary position. Anything else constituted "a sacrifice of semen to the Devil without purpose," "sodomy," or illicit fornication.[62]

The "correct" position for sexual intercourse placed the woman supine and the man astride her. The term in Church Slavonic for this position was "on a horse" (*na koně*), emphasizing the male's dominant role over the female.[63] The Russians particularly opposed the reversal of the "proper" positions of husband and wife, imposing penances ranging from three to ten years. The authors of the penitentials labeled this reversed position as a "great sin."[64] In the medieval Russian perception,

57. Smirnov, *Materialy*, 59, 61, 64.
58. Voprosy Savy, art. 24, in RIB, 6:57.
59. Smirnov, *Materialy*, 59.
60. Voprosy Kirika, art. 46, in RIB, 6:34.
61. Such restrictions were known in the East through the Apostles' Rule, which originated in Syria in the third century; see Noonan, *Contraception*, 77. They also occurred in the early medieval West; see Flandrin, *Un Temps pour embrasser*, 13–15, 82–91.
62. Smirnov, *Materialy*, 144, 207; "Poslanie Esifa k detem," in Nikol'skij, *Materialy*, 139; Almazov, 3:181.
63. The term *na koně* has confused scholars (including myself) into thinking that some sort of bestiality was involved. However, in the text "Pravilo o verujuščix v gady," from a fourteenth-century Russian nomocanon (Smirnov, *Materialy*, 144), sexual intercourse *na koně* is specifically exempted from the categories of illicit sex, and bestiality was certainly illicit. The interpretation of *na koně* as the medieval Slavic vernacular for "missionary position" fits every instance of this phrase in the context of sexual regulations.
64. Almazov, 3:146 (3 years, 150 prostrations), 160 (5 years), 277 (7 years), 282 (10 years, 100 prostrations), 277. Only one text, Almazov, 3:150, lists a minor penance for this sin: 40 days with 60 prostrations a day. Certain Western canonists also believed that intercourse with the woman on top was the most sinful posture; see Tentler, 189–192; Brundage, "Let Me Count the Ways," 86–87.

it was not proper to put a woman in a position of domination, where she "defiled the image of God."[65] Man was made in the "image of God," while woman was made merely from man's rib; thus the wife should properly assume a position of subservience to her husband in all things, and particularly in sexual intercourse. Anything else constituted a violation of the divinely ordained structure of the universe. The length of penance placed this violation in the category of major sexual sins, such as adultery or incest with a close relative. There is no evidence of an opposing view.

Coitus from behind also violated canon law. Although the woman still maintained a subordinate position in dorsal sex, there were other grounds for objection. This posture was described as "cattle-like" (*skotsko*), as much a pejorative as a description.[66] In addition, Slavic hierarchs objected to rear penetration on the grounds that the woman behaved "as a man" (*mužsko*), that is, mimicking the position of the passive male in homosexual intercourse.[67] Regulations on intercourse from behind did not always distinguish between vaginal and anal penetration, but simply described rear entry as "against nature."[68] Certain provisions referred unambiguously to anal intercourse (*zadnij proxod* or *afedron*).[69] In some cases, the two were specifically equated and were given the same penance, an indication that the source of the objection lay in the configuration of male and female rather than the orifice used or the potential for conception.[70]

Texts of penitential rules and canon law record a wide range of penances for sexual intercourse from behind, from a minimum of six hundred prostrations without a fast or exclusion from communion to thirty years of exclusion from the church.[71] Provisions that seemingly pertained to vaginal penetration (*sozadi*, "from behind") tended to have lower penances, usually a fast of forty days with a limited number of prostrations per day.[72] Regulations for heterosexual anal intercourse

65. Smirnov, *Materialy*, 28.
66. Ibid.
67. E.g., Almazov, 3:104; Hil. 305, f. 24v.
68. E.g., Almazov, 3:104; Hil. 301, f. 85r; BNL 251(200), f. 127r.
69. E.g., Almazov, 3:146; BNL 246(103), f. 157r; SANU 124(29), ff. 56r, 78r, 168v.
70. Kiev 191, ff. 153v, 163r. For a discussion of heterosexual intercourse *retro* and *a tergo* in Roman Catholic canon law, see Payer, "Early Medieval Regulations," 357–358, and *Sex and the Penitentials*, 29, 118; Brundage, "Let Me Count the Ways," 81–83. Alternative coital positions seem to have disturbed Western canonists for three reasons. First, the purpose was to enhance pleasure, which was deemed suspicious. Second, it was believed that alternative positions, even with vaginal intercourse, promoted contraception. Third, alternative positions were unseemly, resembling sodomy. Later Western penitentials tended to omit details about non-preferred methods of coitus, perhaps to avoid giving parishioners sinful ideas.
71. Smirnov, *Materialy*, 154; Peć 77, f. 235v.
72. E.g., Almazov, 3:145 (40 days, 40 prostrations), 61 (40 days, 7 prostrations). Kaiser, "Transformation of Legal Relations," 420, cites a sixteenth-century manuscript listing a penance of two weeks for this sin.

usually recommended longer penances, often three or four years of fasting and a large number of prostrations daily.[73] There are exceptions to this pattern, however. Penances prescribed for intercourse from behind tended to be milder in Russian codes than in South Slavic codes.[74]

In determining penances for intercourse "from behind"—whether anal or vaginal—priests were instructed to take certain circumstances into consideration. First, couples who used rear entry only a few times received shorter penances than those who preferred it.[75] Second, leniency might be shown to a young couple, under the age of thirty, but older couples were to be excluded from communion until they desisted. Third, use of a rear approach during Lent—when all sexual activity was supposed to be curtailed—justified a lengthened period of penitential fasting.[76] Fourth, the priest was to consider whether the wife participated voluntarily in coitus from behind. For women, anal intercourse or vaginal intercourse from the rear is often less pleasurable than frontal coition, because clitoral stimulation is lessened. However, anal sex offered women the advantage of satisfying their husbands without the danger of pregnancy. If the wife voluntarily accepted intercourse from behind, she was to undergo the same penance as her husband; if she acquiesced reluctantly, her penance was lessened.[77] The priest was instructed to "give good counsel" to a woman whose husband forced her into sexual intercourse "against nature."[78] Where rear-entry intercourse was concerned, canon law did not distinguish between married couples and illicit lovers; the same penances applied in both cases.[79]

73. E.g., Almazov, 3:146 (3 years, 150 prostrations); Hil. 171, f. 374v (4 years, 150 prostrations); NBS 654, f. 110v (3 years, 200 prostrations, or 15 years' exclusion from communion); Hil. 301, f. 126r–v (4 years, 200 prostrations). Even the strictest of Slavic Orthodox penalties are mild in comparison with those imposed in Renaissance Venice. There the official penalty for marital anal intercourse (categorized as "sodomy") was death; the usual penalty in fact was exile. See Guido Ruggiero, *The Boundaries of Eros: Sex Crime and Sexuality in Renaissance Venice* (New York, 1985), 118–119.

74. See Almazov, 3:163; VAT-Bor 15, f. 477r. Cf. the Russian code in Smirnov, *Materialy*, 66; the Bulgarian BNL 251(200), f. 127r; and the Serbian Dečani 69, f. 108r. An obscene proverb from Russia reveals the casual way in which anal intercourse or penetration from the rear was viewed: "V seredu—s peredu, a v pjatnicu v zadnicu" (Wednesday in front and Friday behind); see Claude Carey, *Les Proverbes érotiques russes* (The Hague, 1972), 45. Stern reported (72) that intercourse from the rear is the preferred posture in the Soviet Union today, but he may have exaggerated.

75. See Almazov, 3:282 (1 year if occasional, 10 years and 100 prostrations if frequent); SANU 124(29), f. 56r (2 years if once or twice, 7, 8, 10, or 12 years for multiple infractions).

76. See BNL 251(200), f. 127r (2 weeks normally, 8 if during Lent); Hil. 169, f. 71r (12 weeks normally, 18 if during Lent).

77. Hil. 628, f. 16r; NBS 10, f. 26r.

78. Kiev 191, ff. 683v–684r. This provision incontrovertibly deals with marital rape (*nasil'stvuet" zol" mouž"*). It is uncertain what sort of "good counsel" the priest would give the victim-wife in this case: whether on ways to avoid anal intercourse in the future or on the possibility of divorcing her husband.

79. Hil. 301, f. 85r; Hil. 302, ff. 17, 77. Smirnov, *Materialy*, 66, does distinguish between a bachelor and a married man. If a married man engaged in anal sex with either his wife or

_handwritten_No open mouth kissing.
Tatar_

Nongenital contacts as part of marital intercourse occupied an anomalous position in Slavic Orthodox canons. They neither contributed to nor detracted from vaginal intercourse. For this reason, South Slavic sources usually ignored them. Only mutual masturbation between husband and wife was deemed sinful; it was equated with masturbation between two men. It did not matter whether this technique was used as a prelude to vaginal intercourse or a substitute for it.[80] Russian sources devoted somewhat more attention to nongenital sex, although condemnations appeared only sporadically. Open-mouthed kissing was deemed inappropriate, even as foreplay. The short penance, consisting of a dry fast of twelve days, indicates that the offense was minor.[81] One Russian penitential questionnaire termed open-mouthed kissing "Tatar," although certainly Russians were acquainted with the practice before their contact with the Mongols.[82] If a man inserted his finger, hand, or foot into his wife's vagina, he was to undergo a penance of three weeks of fasting. A similar penance was mandated if he used a piece of clothing. Fellatio and cunnilingus, which only occasional Russian codes mentioned, were more serious, calling for penances of two or three years of fasting.[83] These penances are analogous to those for major sins, such as adultery and incest with an in-law. No ecclesiastical source provides a rationale for condemning these practices so severely. In general, nongenital contacts were deemed little worse than an indulgence of the sensual, deserving of little attention and only a short penance.

Birth Control

_handwritten_No Birth cntrl
That was reason for sex_

Because only the birth of a child justified sexual intercourse between husband and wife, any attempt to prevent conception was regarded as evil. From the medieval Slavic perspective, contraception, abortion, and infanticide were similar offenses; provisions against birth control did not always distinguish among them.[84] All three represented the same

another woman, the penance was 3 years. For a bachelor, the penance was 12 weeks. This provision might be best understood as reflecting the usual leniency toward young men.

80. E.g., Hil. 627, f. 16r.

81. Almazov, 3:275. The questionnaire on p. 279 adds 60 prostrations per day to this penance. Unlike Roman Catholics, Orthodox Slavs did not regard such nongenital contacts that did not serve as a prelude to vaginal coition as worse between spouses than between unmarried individuals. For the Western view, see Tentler, 187–212; Brundage, "Carnal Delight," 372.

82. Almazov, 3:166. It is not unusual to attribute risqué sexual practices to foreigners; witness the English term "French kissing" for the same technique.

83. Almazov, 3:192, 275, 277, 279, 282–283. In the ancient world, fellatio was considered demeaning, especially for the partner who performed it. See Veyne, "Homosexuality in Ancient Rome," 30–31. Roman Catholic canon law tended to be much more stringent about oral sex; see Payer, "Early Medieval Regulations," 358. Indeed, early Western penitentials regarded oral sex as more serious than anal sex; see Brundage, *Law, Sex, and Christian Society*, 167.

84. See Eve Levin, "Infanticide in Pre-Petrine Russia, *Jahrbücher für Geschichte Osteuropas*

thing: an attempt to forestall the introduction into the world of a new soul. For that reason, all three offenses were sometimes called *du-šegub'e*, literally, "the destruction of a soul."

> It is worth asking both men and women how long they were in that state and how many children they killed . . . for what reason and in which manner. There are those who make a potion to drink so that they cannot conceive a child. This is worst of all, because they do not know how many would have been born. And by means of another potion they kill infants at each new moon. . . . If they do not stop this, they may not receive communion.[85]

Following this reasoning, some codes levied a higher penance for the use of contraceptives than for abortion.[86] Voluntarily preventing conception or aborting a pregnancy could carry a penance of three to ten years.[87] Churchmen were concerned about more than the destruction of an unborn child: they recognized that the methods then available often resulted in the death of the woman as well.[88] Even a spontaneous miscarriage was sinful, and carried a penance of a year's exclusion from communion.[89]

Some clerics reasoned that it was worse for a married woman to practice birth control than for a single woman in an illicit relationship.[90] Perhaps the underlying belief was that the offspring of an illicit relationship would doubtless come to no good, because of the parents' sin.

Most Slavic Orthodox churchmen did not consider how far the pregnancy had advanced in determining penances, but a minority opinion held that a "soul" had not perished if the fetus had not yet attained

34, no. 2 (1986): 215–224. South Slavic canon law on infanticide was virtually identical to the Russian. On infanticide in the West, see Flandrin, *Sexe et l'Occident*, 151–211. St. Augustine espoused a similar view, categorizing abandonment of an infant together with contraception and abortion, and condemning couples who engaged in any of these practices as adulterers. See Flandrin, *Un Temps pour embrasser*, 115. For a consideration of contraception in the West, the best source is Noonan, *Contraception*; see also Flandrin, *Sexe et l'Occident*, 109–126.

85. Mount Sinai 17(17), ff. 170v–171r; BNL 251(200), ff. 137v–138r. Apparently the contraceptive measure the author had in mind brought on the woman's menstrual period. Serbian epics similarly presented women who used contraceptives as burning in Hell for their failure to bear the number of children God had intended; see Brkić, 42–43.

86. Hil. 170, f. 89r, lists a penance of 5 years for consuming an abortifacient potion and 7 years for a contraceptive potion.

87. Dečani 68, f. 279v (3 years); Kiev 127, pp. 145–146 (6 years); Hil. 302, f. 22r (7 years and 200 prostrations for contraception, 8 years and 367 prostrations for abortion); SANU 124(29), f. 47r (10 years for contraception, abortion, or infanticide); Peć 77, ff. 198r–200v (10 years).

88. Peć 77, ff. 198r–200v.

89. Hil. 628, ff. 4v–5r. Recall the discussion of prayers for forgiveness for miscarriage in chap. 1.

90. NBS I-14, f. 263v.

visible form.[91] One version of a late-fifteenth-century Russian text made the penance accord with the level of the fetus's development. If the fetus could not yet be distinguished from the placenta, the penance was five years. If it had visible form, the penance was seven years. If it had quickened, the penance was fifteen years—that is, the same as for murder. Another version of this text omitted the first category of development, indicating an inability to distinguish early abortion from a hemorrhage unrelated to pregnancy.[92]

Another objection to abortion and contraception involved the methods used in the medieval Slavic world. The most frequently mentioned way of terminating an unwanted pregnancy was to consume a sort of herbal potion; penitential literature also reported the wearing of amulets and the recitation of spells. These things could be obtained from semi-pagan wise women, called in hostile ecclesiastical sources *baby bogomerzskija*, "God-insulting grannies."[93] The efficacy of these methods may be doubted, but the church could not afford to ignore them. Their use reflected the continuation of pagan beliefs and practices, which were literally anathema to Orthodox clerics.

Witches

Spells to assist conception were condemned as strongly as abortifacients. According to one version of the law, a woman who consumed a pagan medicine to help her bear a child first underwent a fast of fifty days, then was the subject of prayers of purification. Significantly, the prayers required were those for a person who had "returned from the pagans." She was excluded from communion for the following year, and was ordered to perform one hundred prostrations each day.[94] Another text recommended a penance of one year, "whether a conception occurred or not."[95] The church did not challenge the effectiveness of pagan methods, only their appropriateness for Christians. Yet sometimes the same substance was recommended both to aid and to prevent conception. It was believed, for example, that a woman who ate the placen-

91. See Peć 77, ff. 198r–200v, for a lengthy discussion of abortion.

92. "Voprosy i otvety pastyrskoj praktiki," art. 28, in RIB, 6:862; see also Pavlov, *Nomokanon pri Bol'šom Trebnike*, 184–185. The Decretists in the Roman Catholic Church also came to equate abortion with murder; see Noonan, *Contraception*, 232–237.

93. Kiev 127, pp. 145–146. See also Smirnov, "Baby bogomerzskija," 232. Bulgarian Jewish documents report questions on the propriety of a Jewish physician's performing an abortion on a gentile woman, indicating another source of help in terminating a pregnancy. The decision was that the doctor could perform an abortion only when the woman's life was endangered. See no. 37 in *Evrejski izvori za obščestveno-ikonomičeskoto razvitie na balkanskite zemi*, vol. 2 (Sofia, 1960), 99. Although Orthodox ecclesiastical sources did not mention Jewish doctors in connection with abortion, it is likely that they would consider consulting a Jew no more acceptable than consulting a pagan practitioner.

94. BNL 246(103), f. 158r. BNL 251(200), f. 127v, reduces the initial fast to 7 days and omits the prostrations.

95. Hil. 378, f. 170r–v; Dečani 68, f. 285r.

ta of a newborn would then conceive a child herself—or that she thereby prevented conception.[96] The person who supplied the magic potion also underwent a long penance—as much as nine years.[97] Similarly, canon law forbade the use of spells to discover whether a pregnant woman carried a boy or a girl, imposing the same six-year penance as for contraception or abortion.[98] No matter what the use of the pagan charm or medicine, Orthodox clergy were equally opposed; such sins were classified together. One questionnaire asks: "Did you drink any sort of beverage to conceive a child or not conceive, or did you drink something for another purpose?"[99] Penitential literature also condemned the use of aphrodisiacs, which had their origin in magical spells and herbal medicine.[100]

Although most provisions on birth control were directed toward women rather than men, churchmen recognized that the decision to try to limit family size might be made jointly by husband and wife. Questions sometimes appeared with masculine grammatical forms. When the decision was made jointly, the husband was placed under the same penance as the wife.[101]

Thus, even marital intercourse was subject to numerous restrictions. If a couple strictly observed sexual abstinence on fasts and holidays as well as during the wife's menstrual period, they refrained from marital intercourse on nearly three hundred days of the year.[102] It becomes clear that facilitation of procreation was accorded lesser priority than protection of the ritual purity of the church and the spouses. The restrictions on coital activities even when they were permitted hampered the unconstrained expression of sexual desire. A couple was not permitted free rein to experiment with methods and positions in order to increase sexual enjoyment.

96. Hil. 627, f. 17v (for conception); Kiev 191, f. 671 (for contraception). The penance varied greatly, even in different sections of the same manuscript: from 7 years to just 7 days (Hil. 169, ff. 71r, 81v).
97. Hil. 169, f. 82r.
98. Kiev 127, pp. 146–147.
99. BNL 246(103), f. 136r. The penance for this offense in SANU 124(29), f. 47v, is one year of fasting. See also SANU 125(154), ff. 2v–3r.
100. Voprosy Ilji, art. 14, in RIB, 6:60; Kiev 191, f. 163v. In Almazov, 3:287, women's cosmetics were categorized with aphrodisiacs, and their use carried a penance of 3 years of fasting and 100 prostrations per day.
101. Hil. 302, f. 19r.
102. The four annual fasts (Great Lent, Advent, Peter's Fast, and Philip's Week) add up to 101 days. The wife's menstrual periods would exclude another 84 days on the average. Wednesdays, Fridays, Saturdays, and Sundays in the remaining 25 weeks out of the year would total another 100 days. According to Flandrin, all but an average of 44 days per year would be forbidden in Western Europe before the eleventh century; see *Un Temps pour embrasser*, 41–71. He argues that this restriction on intercourse endangered the demographic balance.

Slavic Orthodox churchmen did not consider pleasure to be an important issue in marriage. Indeed, the pursuit of sexual satisfaction was denigrated as selfish at best and Satanic at worst. But it should not be assumed that the churchmen intended to lessen the satisfactions of marriage. On the contrary: churchmen had every interest in promoting the stability of marriages, in order to forestall fornication. The restrictions on the conjugal relationship may be understood as part of a plan to bolster marital contentment rather than to subvert it. Marriages, it should be remembered, were contracted not for love but for political and economic reasons. Sexual attraction between husband and wife could not be expected; performance of marital intercourse was a duty to family rather than an expression of emotional attachment. Procreation was important to the welfare of the family, so anything that prevented conception was discouraged. The maintenance of appropriate sex roles for men and women was also important to family and social stability, so coital postures that upset established lines of dominance were condemned. Nongenital techniques served no direct purpose, so churchmen declared them sinful, but imposed only short penances. Thus a husband or wife who did not enjoy them had grounds to object, while couples who liked them would not be seriously deterred. Taken as a whole, the church's regulations on marital intercourse doubtless helped to ease tensions in arranged marriages.

Extramarital Sex

Canon law forbade all sexual contacts outside of marriage, classifying them as either "adultery" (*preljubodĕistvo*) or "illicit fornication" (*blud*). To the medieval Slavic churchman, all extramarital sex was sinful; without repentance, it would lead to eternal damnation, as depicted in a vivid Bulgarian fresco (fig. 12). Anyone who died while committing one of these sins was denied Christian burial.[103] But the clerical estimation of the seriousness of violations varied considerably. In determining the stringency of the penance, the confessor took into consideration the marital status of both partners, their ages, and the nature of the sexual contact.

Adultery

Adultery was the most serious extramarital heterosexual sin. The definition of adultery in medieval Slavic canon law requires some clarifica-

103. E.g., Smirnov, *Materialy*, 149.

12. The Judgment of Fornicators and Adulterers. Notice the large breasts and loose hair. Fresco at Rila Monastery, Bulgaria (eighteenth century). Reproduced from 24 *Stenopisa ot rilskija manastir* (Sofia, 1983), no. 7, by permission of Jus Autor.

tion. Technically, *preljubodĕistvo* consisted of sexual intercourse between a married woman and a man other than her husband. In theory,
the man's marital status was unimportant; he became liable for charges
of adultery by engaging in sexual relations with a married woman. "A
man who is living with his wife and trespasses his marriage with another
free woman shall not be convicted as an adulterer, but as a fornicator
instead."[104]

The Slavic definition of adultery followed the dominant tradition in
the Eastern Orthodox Church, which was derived from earlier Jewish
conceptions. Under Jewish law, adultery consisted of sexual intercourse
between two individuals who could not legally be married. A woman
who was already married to someone else obviously fell into this category, but a married man did not, because ancient Jewish law permitted
polygamy. Although Byzantine Christian law forbade multiple wives, it
retained the Jewish distinction between the husband's and the wife's
marital infidelity. Thus a single man who had an affair with a married
woman was guilty of adultery, but a married man who had an affair
with a single woman was not.[105]

Orthodox writers were aware of the disparity in the treatment of
extramarital sex by husband and wife. St. Basil noted that New Testament teachings mandated the same treatment of men and women in
cases of illicit fornication. However, he upheld the unequal treatment
customary in his day, using Paul and the Old Testament to back up his
decision. Because, according to Paul, a wife should gain her salvation
through her husband (Eph. 5:22–24), she should not compound his sin
of infidelity by her own through divorcing him (I Cor. 7:10). St. Basil
did not advocate divorce even when the husband physically abused his
wife or deprived her of income. He was willing to consider permitting a
wife to leave her husband only if he was unfaithful to her with a married
woman, and then only on his second offense.[106] These exceptions to the
general rule forbidding a wife to divorce her erring husband were not
widely disseminated among the Slavs.

---

104. Hil. 378, f. 156v. The passage is a paraphrase of St. Basil's Rule, art. 24, NBS 48, f.
181v. See Smirnov, *Materialy*, 106, and Hil. 627, f. 2r, for another wording of the same
concept. For the purpose of defining adultery, however, a betrothed maiden counted as a
married woman; see Byzantine provisions translated in, e.g., Hil. 169, f. 77v. It should not be
assumed that the fines prescribed in the provisions of Byzantine origin were actually levied in
Slavic countries.
105. See St. Basil's Rule, art. 39, in *Kormčaja*, 491. Olearius reported (170) that a married
man was deemed guilty of adultery only if he entered into an illegal second marriage with
another man's wife; a casual affair did not constitute adultery. Canon law did not define
adultery in this way, although it is possible that in practice only that type of case was
prosecuted.
106. GIM, Sin. 227, f. 183r–v; St. Basil's Rule, arts. 9, 36, in *Sintagmat*, 195–196, 396.

Slavic texts recommended fifteen years of exclusion from communion for adultery, as directed by St. Basil, or two or three years of fasting. According to the formula of St. John the Penitent, the penance should have been a fast of three years, with 250 prostrations a day. In fact, the dominant textual traditions mandated either a three-year fast without prostrations or a two-year fast with 200 prostrations.[107] The decision of Gregory of Nyssa, mandating eighteen years of penance, appeared occasionally in codes, but never exclusively.[108] An independent Russian tradition, attributed apocryphally to Christ personally, ordered eight or ten years of stringent fasting, with 1,000 prostrations a day.[109] In determining the penance for any sort of sexual misconduct, the priest was directed to inquire about the marital status of the woman involved and to set the penance accordingly.[110]

Adultery by a wife constituted misconduct of the worst sort. Illicit sex defiled a married woman, so that her husband became an adulterer through her. An adulterous wife was disloyal and disobedient, leaving her husband open to public ridicule. In more practical terms, she might present her husband's family with an unwelcome bastard child, or run off with her lover, depriving the family of her labor and the use of her dowry.[111] Adultery was potentially the most disruptive sexual deviation.

No circumstance justified a married woman's voluntary infidelity. This was the moral of a didactic tale. A wealthy but unscrupulous man approached the wife of a man imprisoned for debt, and offered to settle with all of the husband's creditors and get him released. His price, of course, was a night with her. Quoting Paul's first epistle to the Corinthians (7:4), she replied that she did not control her own body, and would have to ask her husband. A brigand sharing the husband's cell was so impressed by her devotion and righteousness that he revealed to her where he had stashed his loot. Thus the wife gained her husband's freedom without sacrificing her virtue.[112]

The church both permitted and encouraged a husband to divorce his errant wife. A man who lived with an adulteress, clerical writings warned, was himself an adulterer. A set of didactic riddles included the question: "If a married woman sins with another man, is there any sin for her husband?" The response was cryptic: "As Eve led Adam from Para-

---

107. E.g., BNL 251(200), f. 126r; Hil. 627, ff. 6v, 12r; Kiev 191, f. 670r; Hil. 171, f. 248r.
108. Troicki, 68.
109. Smirnov, *Materialy*, 152. This passage equates bestiality with adultery.
110. Hil. 627, f. 14r.
111. Considerations of finances and honor seem to have been dominant in regulations concerning married women's adultery in Renaissance Venice; see Ruggiero, 51.
112. Nikolova, 177–178.

dise," but the implication was that an evil woman could lead her husband astray, regardless of his own personal conduct.[113]

If a man knew about his wife's sin and condoned it by remaining married to her, he was guilty also. Byzantine civil law considered a man who kept an adulterous wife to be a pimp. At the very least, he was supposed to send her to a convent for two years for punishment; after that period, he could reclaim her if he wanted.[114] The Code of Jaroslav contained a similar provision: a man could send an adulterous wife for confinement in a convent "until her clan redeems her."[115] Although the husband could legally divorce his wife for adultery—and might have been under considerable pressure from the church and the community to do so—he was not obliged to follow this course.

If the husband did not know about his wife's adultery, he was innocent of wrongdoing. Although clerics readily supported the expulsion of a guilty wife when the husband knew of her offense, they did not advocate bringing the wife's misconduct to her husband's attention if he did not know of it already. When a priest heard a wife's confession of secret adultery, he was not to accuse her publicly, but was to impose only a penance that would not attract attention, such as exclusion from communion. The reason for this leniency was concern for the fate of the woman who had just come into repentance; the outraged husband might kill her before she had completed the healing penance.[116]

Clerical opinion diverged on the proof necessary in adultery cases. A minority view held that only eyewitnesses—preferably the husband himself—could prove adultery; otherwise, the wife had to be considered innocent.[117] The majority view, as we have seen, regarded any sugges-

113. BNL 309, f. 154v. In ancient Greece, a man was required to divorce a wife found guilty of adultery. See Keuls, 208–209. The Roman Catholic canonist Gratian permitted divorce in the case of adultery but forbade remarriage, even for the innocent party. See Brundage, *Law, Sex, and Christian Society*, 244.

114. *Sintagmat*, 397. Roman law demanded that the husband repudiate the adulterous wife; see Brundage, *Law, Sex, and Christian Society*, 45–46.

115. Jaroslav's Ustav, in *DKU*, 94; Tixomirov, *Merilo pravednoe*, 264.

116. NBS 48, f. 184r, in the commentary to St. Basil's Rule, art. 34. See also *Sintagmat*, 396, for a Slavic translation of St. Basil's Rule, and GIM, Sin. 227, ff. 190v–191r. Hierarchs advocated the same sort of discretion in the case of men who privately and voluntarily confessed homosexuality or bestiality; see Troicki, 77. The medieval Orthodox Church did not have an elaborately articulated theory of the confidentiality of the confessional of the sort that emerged in the Roman Catholic Church. It was understood that the priest should not disclose what he heard in confession, but priests might erroneously believe that it was more important to remove a grievous sinner from the community than to keep private confession secret. Peter the Great used this belief to advantage when he required priests to disclose treason they learned about through confessions.

117. Byzantine civil law required three witnesses to a wife's adultery; see Pavlov, "'Knigi zakonnyja,'" 68–69.

tive activity as grounds for divorce. In practice, the husband could act on his own volition, expelling his wife from the home on the merest rumor. In a birchbark document from twelfth-century Novgorod, a woman named Ana appealed to her brother for assistance after her husband, Fedor, threw her out. Fedor believed the accusations made by one of Ana's debtors, who called her a "cow" and her daughter a "whore."[118] Churchmen were aware that an honorable woman ran the risk of false accusations, and discouraged them with heavy fines and stern lessons. A didactic tale taught that rumors of sexual misconduct should not be believed, no matter how things might appear. The hero was a pious monk, Father Daniil. At the request of a young husband, he prayed for relief of the wife's barrenness. When the wife later bore a child, the community gossiped about the nature of Father Daniil's assistance. The virtuous monk called upon the child to name his father, and the monk and the wife were exonerated.[119]

Byzantine civil law permitted the cuckolded husband to kill his wife and her lover if he caught them in flagrante delicto,[120] but church hierarchs were divided on this issue. One author permitted and even encouraged the injured husband to take personal vengeance; by punishing his adulterous wife and her lover for their sins with death, he was enabling the salvation of their souls. Another author took the opposite view: a husband who killed his adulterous wife, even if he caught her in the act, showed a lack of Christian charity. Slavic churchmen recorded both sides of this debate.[121] Among Slavs the preferred treatment of an erring wife seems to have been divorce, but personal revenge was not unknown. Serbian law permitted the victimized husband to cut off his wife's nose and ear before expelling her from the house.[122]

The marital status of a wife's lover was not a matter of concern in determining the degree of her offense. The lover's social status, however, did come into play in Byzantine laws that were adopted in medieval Serbia. The Code of Stefan Dušan ordered a special penalty when a noblewoman took her servant as her lover: both were to lose their hands and their noses.[123] A wife who turned to a man of a lower class for

118. No. 531 in Arcixovskij et al., 7:130–134.

119. Demina, 235.

120. Pavlov, "'Knigi zakonnyja,'" art. 26, 68–69;

121. Rila 1/20(48), f. 93r; Kiev 49, f. 672v; *Sintagmat*, sec. 40, chap. 14, 394–399.

122. Grbaljski Zakonik, art. 14, in Novaković, *Zakonski spomenici*, 106. The dating of this code is problematical, because there is no extant manuscript. Novaković copied it from an earlier publication of an early-fifteenth-century manuscript, and argues that a prototype existed in the twelfth century. The influence of Byzantine secular law is very obvious in marital provisions.

123. Burr, 208. The Byzantine provision was available in Slavonic translation in the "Zakon o kaznex"; see Pavlov, "'Knigi zakonnyja,'" 69. The punishment was different: the wife

sexual companionship not only injured her husband's honor but insulted his dignity.

Both ecclesiastical and secular authorities could punish an unfaithful husband, but divorce and confinement in a monastery were not mandated.[124] It was unusual for the penance for an erring husband to be set as high as the fifteen years mandated by St. Basil for adulterous wives.[125] More commonly, the husband underwent the usual penance for illicit fornication: seven years according to St. Basil, or one to three years according to St. John the Penitent.[126] One Russian text went so far as to recommend a penance of only six weeks for an erring husband, if his extramarital intercourse had not been premeditated.[127] St. Basil further made allowance for a married man who was not living with his wife, excusing him from all penances. The "demands of nature," he reasoned, made it difficult for a man to abstain completely when he had no lawful sexual outlet.[128] And of course, a husband normally could not be divorced for extramarital sex alone. Even if the husband left his home and his wife to pursue an extramarital affair, she had to take him back when he wished to return, and accept renewed conjugal relations.[129]

Alternative traditions in Orthodox canon law could have provided a means of treating infidelity by husband and wife equally. Article 20 of the decisions of the Ancyra Council reduced the penance for adultery from fifteen years to seven, the same way as for fornication. Thus an erring wife would undergo the same penance as her husband. While numerous penitential codes referred to the Ancyra article, none substituted it for the dominant codes of St. Basil and John the Penitent, or gave any indication that it was to be preferred.[130] Despite the inequalities inherent in the definition of adultery, native Slavic provisions might recommend the same penances for extramarital sex for both husband and wife. The pattern is most noticeable in one tradition of Russian canon law, where the equivalency of the husband's and the wife's

---

suffered beating, mutilation of her nose, exile, and confiscation of property; the slave was executed.

124. Jaroslav's Ustav, in *DKU*, 95, 100; Grbaljski Zakonik, in Novaković, *Zakonski spomenici*, 106.

125. "Voprosy i otvety pastyrskoj praktiki," art. 29, in RIB, 6:862, recommended 15 or 20 years, but it seems to have been unique.

126. GIM, Sin. 227, f. 196v, refers to a husband's extramarital affair as "adultery," but clearly the rule applied only to cases in which the husband abandoned his lawful wife for a long-term liaison with another woman. The penance consisted of the usual 7 years mandated by St. Basil.

127. Kaiser, "Transformation of Legal Relations," 425.

128. *Sintagmat*, 196, citing St. Basil's Rule, art. 21.

129. GIM, Sin. 227, f. 188r–v.

130. E.g., SANU 125(154), f. 19r; Hil. 628, f. 15r; Hil. 302, f. 76r.

sin was made explicit. One code prescribed a penance of three years for either an adulterous husband or an adulterous wife; others, two years or eight years. An occasional South Slavic text followed the same pattern.[131]

Because adultery (*preljubodĕistvo*) was considered more serious than fornication (*blud*), there was a tendency to use the former term as a pejorative label for sexual violations that technically were not adulterous. For that reason illegal marriages and concubinage were labeled "adultery" even when such unions did not involve a woman already married to another.[132] Sexual relations or a pseudomarriage between a monk and a nun, especially those who adopted the most ascetic rule (*sxima*), was sometimes called "adultery." Sex between a monk and a nun of lesser rank was merely "illicit fornication."[133] The seriousness of a sin rather than its nature seemed to determine the category: rape and the defilement of a virgin were also "adultery."[134]

Premarital Sex

Premarital sex fell into the category of illicit fornication. Although *blud* was less serious than adultery, it could not be viewed with equanimity. The early age of marriage helped somewhat to cut down on illicit sexual activity. By encouraging marriages for boys and girls in their early to mid teens, Slavic clerics could hope to restrict most sexual experimentation to the marriage bed. But even so, there were still problems with premarital sex.

Betrothed couples were discouraged from sleeping together before the wedding through a penance of a year of exclusion from communion. An occasional text permitted the shortening of this penance to a fast of forty days with fifty prostrations a day.[135] Premarital sex between fiancés was not socially disruptive in the way that adultery was; it did not endanger the stability of the marriage. Yet it was an offense to God for a couple to "steal the marriage" by engaging in sex before they were authorized to do so. Furthermore, the family could be embarrassed if the proofs of virginity were not forthcoming the morning after the wedding.

Churchmen relied on parents to prevent their sons and daughters

131. Smirnov, *Materialy*, 62, 65, 242; SANU 124(29), f. 46v (12 years, 80 prostrations). An additional article in the syntagma noted that a married man deserved a greater penance for *blud* than an unmarried man, but did not recommend a specific sentence; see Troicki, 67.

132. NBS 688, f. 92r.

133. In a similar vein, relations between a monk and a nun might also be termed "incest."

134. Rila 1/20(48), f. 89v; Hil. 169, f. 75r–v.

135. E.g., Kiev 191, f. 685v; Dečani 70, f. 227r. GIM, Sin. 227, f. 189r, placed more blame on the groom than on the bride.

from engaging in premarital sex. Parents bore the responsibility of educating their children to avoid sin. Those who failed in this duty were doomed: "At the Court of Judgment they will receive the inheritance of eternal fire, together with their children, whom they bore and reared wickedly."[136] Failure to preserve a daughter's virginity, the sixteenth-century Russian advice book *Domostroj* warned parents, would "make you a laughingstock to your acquaintances and shame you before the multitudes."[137] To prevent sin and public disgrace, parents were directed to arrange marriages for their children as soon as they reached the age of majority:

> Every parent ought to arrange a marriage for his son when he has grown up, at fifteen years, and for his daughter at twelve. This is the true law. If, by the parent's inattention, either a son or a daughter who is of legal age happens to engage in sexual intercourse, this is the parents' sin. If either a daughter under age twelve or a son under age fifteen engages in sexual intercourse, it is the sin of the one who did it, and he will receive God's anger.[138]

Serbian secular law directed that the families punish children who engage in premarital sex.[139] Parents were urged to provide a good example to their children, by themselves avoiding obscene and blasphemous speech, homosexuality, bestiality, and masturbation.[140] Similarly, masters were responsible for teaching their slaves to observe Christian marital forms and sexual morality. If slaves engaged in illicit sex because their masters failed to arrange marriages for them, the masters could be excommunicated.[141]

As a further indication of societal hostility to the sexual exploitation of children, few churchmen reduced the penance for this transgression.[142] An adult who had sexual relations with an underage girl (that is, younger than twelve years) was subjected to a penance of twelve years.[143] Homosexual abuse of an underaged boy was equated with rape of a three-year-old girl.[144] But sexual activity short of intercourse,

136. Rila 1/20(48), f. 98r–v.
137. *Domostroi*, 60–61.
138. Kiev 49, f. 646v; Rila 1/20(48), f. 99r–v. In SANU 124(29), f. 91v, the parents are made responsible for a daughter's conduct after age 15.
139. Grbaljski Zakonik, in Novaković, *Zakonski spomenici*, 106.
140. *Stoglav*, 117.
141. Hil. 378, ff. 149v–150r; "Tri svjatitel'skija poučenija," in RIB, 6:925.
142. E.g., Hil. 628, f. 16r; Kiev 191, f. 683v. SANU 123(28), f. 28r includes an alternative penance of 2 years and 2 months of fasting 5 days a week, along with 200 prostrations a day.
143. E.g., Kiev 191, f. 683v; Hil. 305, f. 24r.
144. Hil. 301, f. 126r–v.

especially among the children themselves, did not arouse nearly the same opposition; it was assumed that they did not understand what they were doing. In response to a question about the propriety of masturbation by children, Bishop Nifont replied that there was no reason to be concerned about boys under the age of ten. He was more concerned about girls' masturbation, perhaps because they could puncture the hymen and destroy the physical sign of virginity.[145]

Slavic Orthodox clerics were generally forgiving of <u>young bachelors'</u> sexual adventures, provided they restricted themselves to suitable partners. One author imposed only half of the usual penance for violating a maiden when the penitent was young and unmarried.[146] Bishop Nifont did not expect complete abstinence from youths, whom he divided into three categories: those who restrained themselves completely from fornication, those who restrained themselves somewhat, and those who hardly restrained themselves at all. All three groups, he ordered, should be permitted to participate in ecclesiastical rites and receive communion.[147] A bachelor did not need to vow to abstain in the future in order to receive the sacraments of penance and communion. It was sufficient for him to admit his weakness and listen to instructions from the priest on how to desist from sin.[148] Nifont assumed that unmarried young men would not abstain from sex, even during periods of religious observance. "Bachelors should be given communion on Easter," he wrote "if they preserved their purity during the Great Fast. If they sinned sometimes, examine them to see that it was not with a married woman, or some other great evil, but that they held themselves to good."[149] Other authors were less lenient, and required bachelors to abstain from fornication, at least during Lent, if they wished to receive communion at Easter.[150] Because it was assumed that young men regularly engaged in fornication, clerics found it necessary to specify a period of abstention before they married—usually forty days, although as much as fifty or even eighty days were considered appropriate.[151]

Churchmen varied the penance for a single man, depending on the marital status and sexual experience of his female partner. A married woman or a nun was the least appropriate choice as a mistress. In theory, the penance for an affair with a married woman should have

145. Voprosy Kirika, art. 49, in RIB, 6:35. See also Smirnov, *Materialy*, 68.
146. "Tri svjatitel'skija poučenija," in RIB, 6:923–924. The penance is 4 years for mature men and 2 years for youths.
147. Voprosy Kirika, art. 67, in RIB, 6:41.
148. Voprosy Ilji, art. 13, in RIB, 6:59–60.
149. Voprosy Kirika, art. 30, in RIB, 6:31.
150. Smirnov, *Materialy*, 66–67, 106.
151. Voprosy Savy, art. 22, in RIB, 6:57.

been fifteen years, according to St. Basil's Rule. In fact, most Slavic provisions specific to this situation listed a lower penance. The highest penance consisted of nine years with one hundred prostrations a day, and was intended only when the bachelor got another man's wife pregnant.[152] Otherwise, the penance ranged from six years and five hundred prostrations at the highest to a low of two weeks (extended to eight weeks if the sin occurred during Lent).[153] Several authors raised the penance considerably if the bachelor had sinned with many married women, rather than restricting himself to one or two.[154] Another author was unforgiving of a single lapse with a married woman, equating it with murder.[155]

An unmarried maiden, in the view of some clerics, was not appreciably better: defiling a virgin was tantamount to rape, even if she consented, and the penance was as high as nine years.[156] Other churchmen did not share this concern over violation of a maiden's purity. St. Basil's Rule listed a penance of seven years of exclusion from communion for *blud*. Slavic authors preferred the shorter but more intense penance, based on the rule of St. John the Penitent. The reduced penance ranged between one and three years of fasting, accompanied by one hundred to two hundred prostrations a day.[157] One author envisioned a substantial show of contrition, at least at the beginning of the sentence: only one meal a day and abstinence from meat, milk, fish, nuts, and alcohol three days a week for the first forty days.[158] If both the man and the woman were unmarried, the penance was shorter: as little as six weeks or as much as three years, depending on the number of violations.[159] The full seven years were mandated only if a parishioner was recalcitrant, or if illicit fornication was but one of numerous sins.[160]

In defining illicit fornication, clerics categorized widows with maidens

---

152. SANU 124(29), f. 46v.

153. E.g., Kiev 49, f. 649v (6 years, 500 prostrations); Almazov, 3:277 (5 years), 149 (1 or 2 years); Dečani 69, f. 108r (12 weeks, or 18 weeks during Lent); BNL 251(200), f. 127r (2 weeks, or 8 weeks during Lent).

154. Almazov, 3:145 (3 years for one or two women; 5 years if with many), 285 (5 years with one woman, 7 years with two or three).

155. Peć 77, f. 122v.

156. E.g., Hil. 169, f. 79v; 302, f. 17r.

157. E.g., VAT-Bor. 15, f. 476v (6 years or 1 year and 100 prostrations); Hil. 627, f. 13v (7 years, or 1-1/2 years and 150 prostrations); Hil. 300, ff. 101v–102r (7 years, or 2 years and 250 prostrations); Hil 169, f. 69v (6 years, or 1 year and 150 prostrations). The oldest manuscript, Sinai 37, prescribes the longest penance (3 years).

158. SANU 123(28), ff. 7v–8v.

159. Smirnov, *Materialy*, 70 (6 weeks for one maiden, 2 years for many), 152 (1 year), 243 (3 years).

160. Peć 77, ff. 104v, 221v, 261v–262r; Troicki, 67. One Russian text mandated a penance of 8 years for a man who was not able to abstain: Smirnov, *Materialy*, 151.

and imposed similar penances.[161] There were advantages to having an affair with a widow rather than a maiden. A man could not be accused of "defiling" a widow, because she was no longer a virgin, and her parents could not pressure him to marry her, as she was free to make her own choices concerning remarriage. Furthermore, the widow herself might very well be reluctant to enter into a second marriage; if she did, she lost both her first husband's property and guardianship of her children. The seventeenth-century metropolitan Pavel of Nižegorod was only one in a long line of prelates who condemned widows who lived with men out of wedlock. To discourage the practice, he levied a fine of two rubles on offenders—that is, twice the fee for a second marriage.[162]

Divorcees represented a different case. Technically, they were still married, and therefore men who had sex with them became adulterers. While churchmen objected to marriage with a divorcee, they remained silent on the sin of sleeping with her without benefit of clergy. By implication, a divorcee made no worse a casual sex partner than any other nonvirgin single woman. Furthermore, her sexual activity might be expected; after all, the usual justification for divorce was infidelity. And once a woman had been cast out, she had few ways of supporting herself other than ecclesiastical charity and prostitution.

A prostitute might be considered a better choice than any other free and unmarried woman. In general, Slavic ecclesiastical literature did not distinguish between a prostitute and a woman who slept with a man other than her husband voluntarily, without financial gain. The Church Slavonic word for both was *bludnica*, and the penance was the same whether or not money changed hands. Only the context distinguished one type of *bludnica* from another. Few canons referred to prostitution. The section of the syntagma that dealt with whoremongering (*o bloudnicopaščex*) occupied less than a page. The excerpts from Byzantine civil law included under this title referred to adultery, concubinage, and the status of illegitimate children rather than prostitution per se. Of the provisions included under this title, only one, Article 86 of the Sixth Ecumenical Council, actually referred to prostitution, and then obliquely: priests and laymen were forbidden to keep houses of ill repute.[163]

---

161. Almazov, 3:144 (1 year); Smirnov, *Materialy*, 243 (3 years), 70 (3 years also, but only if she conceived and killed an illegitimate child). Almazov, 3:277, lists a penance of 5 years, equating illicit fornication with a widow with the same sin involving a virgin or a married woman.

162. No. 295 in *Akty sobrannye v bibliotekax i arxivax Rossijskoj imperii*, 4:442–443.

163. *Sintagmat*, sec. 80, chap. 17, p. 465. The Roman Catholic canonist Gratian similarly defined a prostitute as a woman who took many lovers, with the mercenary nature of the transaction secondary; see Brundage, *Law, Sex, and Christian Society*, 248.

Regulation of prostitution consequently became a matter for secular law, as a matter of public order and decency.[164]

Byzantine ecclesiastical literature evinced some recognition that a woman might become a prostitute only because of destitution,[165] but more commonly prostitutes were condemned for their love of bodily pleasure. Even so, the redemption of prostitutes from their sin was a favorite theme in Orthodox ecclesiastical literature, and this sympathy for the sinning woman was carried over into canon law. "If a prostitute leaves her evil path and confesses and promises not to follow that defiled path again, but to be humble and enter into chastity [*celomudrije*] so as to purify herself, the spiritual father should impose a smaller penance in benevolence, and give her communion with true Christians, that she may be received as Christ received another prostitute."[166] Yet clerics were wary of prostitutes who approached them for acceptance into the community of believers. If the prostitutes did not promise to give up their trade, they were to be rejected.[167]

The attitude of Slavic Orthodox clerics toward prostitution was not so negative as their general antisexual orientation might imply. After all, if men were going to have premarital sexual relations, it was less disruptive to the society if they selected partners who were not married and were not likely to marry. Consequently, some penitential canons listed only short penances for an unmarried man who consorted with prostitutes: twelve days or twelve weeks of fasting.[168] Other canons treated illicit fornication with a prostitute in the same manner as with any other unmarried woman, such as a widow or a slave.[169] Clerics were more stringent when a man was married, imposing a penance as high as sixteen years of exclusion from communion. They also would not countenance a long-standing relationship with a prostitute. A man who kept a prostitute in his home despite warnings could be excommunicated. Canons on prostitution levied penalties only against the individuals directly involved—the prostitute and her customer.[170]

Another more or less acceptable sexual outlet for a bachelor was a

164. Uloženie of 1649, chap. 22, art. 45, in *PRP*, 6:434.

165. A tale is told of a generous girl who became a prostitute because she gave away all her wealth to an unfortunate youth: Nikolova, 289–291; TsGADA, F. 381, no. 173, ff. 46v–47v.

166. Rila 1/20(48), f. 132r.

167. Hil. 378, f. 151r.

168. Almazov, 3:148, 275, 279.

169. Ibid., 145 (12 days for a widow), 146 (1 year, 70 prostrations;), 149 (2 years), 286 (7 years).

170. SANU 124(29), f. 168r; Hil. 378, f. 150r; NBS 48, f. 163r. Kiev 191, f. 153r, lists the keeping of a tavern or whorehouse as a sin, but the objection was probably as much to the selling of alcohol—which was a punishable offense under Muscovite secular law—as to pimping.

slave woman. Penances for fornication with a slave woman were often mere tokens, indicating societal acceptance of slave mistresses, at least for unmarried men. In theory, a Christian man was not supposed to keep a slave concubine; under canon law, he was either to marry her according to Orthodox canons or free her. Failure to do so could result in exclusion from the sacraments. In fact, the usual penance for a bachelor who slept with his slave was a mere forty days of fasting.[171] Kirik asked Bishop Nifont which of two options was better for a bachelor: keeping a single concubine or many slave mistresses. The bishop, naturally, replied that neither choice was good, but stopped short of condemning semipermanent nonmarital sexual relationships for bachelors. Indeed, he conceded the wisdom of the advice one contemporary priest gave his parishioners: "If you cannot restrain yourself, do it with one woman."[172] Other clerics disagreed; maintaining a concubine merely intensified an already illicit relationship and discouraged the bachelor from taking a legitimate wife. Consequently, they recommended a higher penance (two years) for keeping a concubine than for a brief sexual encounter with a single woman. Orthodox canon law officially did not recognize concubinage as anything other than illicit fornication, yet Orthodox writers did realize that the prohibition of concubinage was of relatively recent date. Slavic canon law thus contains some remnants of Byzantine rules pertaining to concubines which recognized that that sort of permanent and exclusive sexual union was not lawless in the same way as adultery or illicit fornication. For example, canon law forbade a man to engage in sex with his father's concubine in the same terms it used to forbid incest with a stepmother.[173]

Although Slavic churchmen might accept the prevailing idea that it was acceptable for a bachelor to seek sexual release with a slave woman, they could not extend this leniency to married men. The Zakon Sudnyj Ljudem, based on Byzantine principles, called for harsh treatment of a man who violated his marriage vows with his slave: he could be subjected to corporal punishment, and the slave was sold abroad so as not to tempt him further.[174] Later Slavic sources imposed different penalties. Corporal punishment was not the rule for ecclesiastical offenses, so penances and fines became the preferred punishments. Furthermore, later regulations concerning slave women revealed considerable sympa-

171. Hil. 378, f. 150v–151r; Almazov, 3:40. SANU 124(29), f. 46v, recommends a penance of 3 years with 40 prostrations a day, but it is not clear that the provision refers to a bachelor rather than a married man.

172. Voprosy Kirika, art. 69, and Voprosy Ilji, art. 7, in RIB, 6:41–42; 58–59.

173. Rila 1/20(48), f. 113r.

174. E.g., ZSL-K, 36; ZSL-P, 140; Pavlov, "'Knigi zakonnyja,'" 72–73; Peć 77, f. 115v.

thy for their plight. Still, all Slavic canons regulating a married man's adultery with his slave woman mandated a substantial penance, usually four years with fifty prostrations a day.[175] Lower penances of the type recommended by the code of St. John the Penitent were never listed for this offense.

The church recognized that a slave woman was not in a position to resist her master's sexual advances. Consequently, canon law directed the priest to establish whether the slave woman had willingly come to her master's bed before imposing any penance.[176]

Slavic churchmen were less willing to allow premarital sexual activity for young women than for young men. A maiden was expected to remain a virgin until her wedding night; otherwise, she was subject to a penance of one to four years, because of the insult to her husband and to God.[177] Most of the responsibility for violation of virginity, however, was laid upon the girl's lover. Medieval Slavic law could deal very harshly with a man who defiled a maiden; even if she had been willing and eager, he might well be charged with rape.

Though the man would incur greater blame, a single young woman was hardly free to seek pleasure without fear of consequences. The threat of premarital pregnancy might well have deterred some girls. A woman who bore an illegitimate child could be confined in a convent, or to be placed under a ten-year penance, including a year on bread and water; or she could be fined.[178] Her family could refuse her a dowry and a share of the parental inheritance.[179] At the very least, she became a poor choice as a marriage partner. The community watched for signs of illicit pregnancy, as a court petition in seventeenth-century Russia indicates. A village widow told the local priest that she suspected a girl of conceiving out of wedlock. The priest told the archbishop, who in turn ordered a physical examination. As it turned out, it was a false alarm.[180]

A girl who agreed to premarital sex could not expect to be rescued from an unexpected pregnancy by marriage. Unlike Western Europe, the Slavic Orthodox world did not view consensual intercourse as an irregu-

---

175. E.g., Rila 1/20(48), f. 193v.

176. SANU 123(28), f. 34v.

177. Smirnov, *Materialy*, 68 (1 year); Almazov, 3:160 (3 years), 163 (2 years); "Tri svjatitel'skija poučenija," in RIB, 6:923–924 (2–4 years).

178. Jaroslav's Ustav, in *DKU*, 94; BNL 246(103), f. 158v. A decree of Metropolitan Pavel of Nižegorod, in 1687, ordered a fine of two rubles (the same as for a widow living in sin), as well as a court investigation to determine paternity. See no. 295, in *Akty sobrannye v bibliotekax i arxivax Rossijskoj imperii*, 4:442–443.

179. Vsevolod's Ustav, in *DKU*, 158.

180. No. 256, dated to 1696, in RIB, 12:1229. Community observation functioned similarly in England in the same period; see Quaife, 90.

lar but binding form of marriage.[181] If a young woman bore an illegitimate child and could prove its paternity to the satisfaction of the ecclesiastical court, her lover might be ordered to marry her, but her success
was not assured. In one surviving court case, the putative father of an
illegitimate child challenged the veracity of the girl's witnesses, albeit
unsuccessfully.[182] In any case, the girl who brought her case to court
was subject to fines and penances for her offense. Furthermore, parental
consent was still mandatory.[183]

Slavic churchmen did not limit their condemnation of extramarital
sex to coital relationships. Any sort of contact with sexual intent or
connotation between individuals not married to each other was condemned. Even private thoughts were not sacrosanct: if a man lusted
after a woman other than his wife, he was considered guilty of a sin and
was placed under penance. Most clerics recommended mild penances for
"adultery in the heart," such as forty prostrations or a dry fast of three
days, but the oldest surviving Slavic nomocanon authorized penances of
up to three years on bread and water.[184] Analogous thoughts by a
woman for a man were also sinful, but the absence of biblical recognition of the problem made references to it less frequent.[185]

Russian penitential codes, in consonance with their concern about
noncoital aspects of marital intercourse, labeled as sinful any word or
touch intended to convey illicit sexual interest, even if the relationship
went no further. South Slavs did not share this concern with noncoital
relations between unmarried men and women. Russian women were
warned against winking at a man to attract his attention; the penance
for this offense consisted of a three-day fast with thirty-six prostrations
a day. Men were cautioned against saying obscene words to a woman or
a boy in the hope of encouraging compliance in sexual activity. It was a
sin—to some clerical authors a fairly serious one—to expose one's geni-
talia in order to spark sexual desire. It was also a sin to look. Nudging
someone's foot to indicate sexual interest carried a similar penance of
six to twelve days. Holding hands or kissing in a sensual manner was

181. On premarital sex as a means of common law marriage in the medieval and early
modern West, see Quaife, 179–180; Brundage, *Law, Sex, and Christian Society*, 136–137,
188–189, 235–242, 260–267, 331–336.

182. No. 38, dated to 1680, in *Istoričeskie i juridičeskie akty XVII–XVIII stoletij*, Čtenija
obščestva istorii i drevnostei rossijskix (M., 1869), no. 4, pp. 40–41.

183. E.g., Hil. 302, f. 17r.

184. E.g., Almazov, 3:145 (70 prostrations), 145–146 (3 days, 25 prostrations), 274 (3
days), 279 (3 days, 100 prostrations), 283 (40 prostrations); BNL 246(103), f. 162r (40
prostrations); Sinai 37, f. 102r (1–3 years on bread and water; but the lesser penance of 40
prostrations appears on f. 103v). The author of another code (Almazov, 3:285) was either very
strict or made a copying mistake when he compiled his list: he mandated a penance of 3 weeks
with 50 prostrations.

185. Almazov, 3:169.

worse, meriting a penance of three weeks. Even more risqué was touching or biting a woman's breast.[186]

It was also forbidden for unmarried men and women to engage in suspicious activities, such as those that sufficed as grounds for divorce for a married woman. An unmarried Russian must not visit a tavern. Clerical authors recommended vastly different penances for this sin, depending on what they believed might be happening. According to one textual variant, the penance for going to a tavern with a widow was a fast of only twelve days, an indication that the author considered the action disreputable, but no worse. To another author, visiting a tavern implied illicit sexual activity; he imposed a seven-year fast. Still others took a middle road, with penances of twelve weeks or a year. Dancing at a tavern or a private party was also forbidden. This prohibition is not surprising; churchmen disapproved of dancing at any time or place because of its connection with pagan ritual. Cross-dressing similarly bore pagan connotations and was forbidden.[187]

The Church Fathers had strongly forbidden mixed bathing, because of the sensual atmosphere of Middle Eastern bathhouses. The South Slavs may have shared the Byzantine attitude toward public baths; there is no evidence either way. To Russians, however, bathing was not obscene in and of itself. Bathhouses were centers for community interaction, for women as well as men. Mixed-sex bathing was the rule, although there might be separate but connected rooms for men and women. Such Western visitors as Adam Olearius were aghast at what appeared to them to be open licentiousness.[188] To Russians, however, nudity had no erotic implications in the bathhouse setting. A sixteenth-century Russian miniature (fig. 13) confirms the nonsexual nature of bathhouses. The female figure lacks the large breasts and loose hair that convey the message of illicit sexuality. Only the slight rounding of her features and her lack of a beard distinguish her from the male bathers. The conflict between native custom and imported canon law did not pass unnoted. A few penitential codes imposed penances on those who engaged in mixed-sex bathing, but only when an illegitimate child was conceived.[189] The Stoglav Coun-

186. Ibid.: winking, 162; lewd words, self-exposure, 162 (20 weeks, 24 prostrations), 274 (6 days' dry fast), 275 (40 days), 279 (6 days, 12 prostrations); looking, 152, 280 (8 days, 100 prostrations); nudging a foot, 145 (6 days), 146 (1 week, 25 prostrations), 280 (12 days, 30 prostrations); holding hands, kissing, 169, 285 (3 weeks, 50 prostrations); touching a breast 145 (6 days), 146 (40 days), 148, 274 (60 days).

187. Ibid.: visiting tavern, 145, 279 (12-day fast), 286 (7-year fast), 146, 148, 275 (12–52-week fast); dancing, 281 (15 days, 60 prostrations), 162 (40 days, 150 prostrations), 152; cross-dressing, 283 (7 weeks, 150 prostrations). Rybakov, *Jazyčestvo drevnej Rusi*, 139–140, 693–696, discusses dancing as part of pagan festivals.

188. Olearius, 142, 161–163.

189. Smirnov, *Materialy*, 28, 49, 154, 242.

13. A Bathhouse. The woman at the upper left is portrayed in an asexual manner. Miniature, Russian (sixteenth century), from *Drevnerusskaja knižnaja miniatjura iz sobranija gosudarstvennoj publičnoj biblioteki imeni M. E. Saltykova-Ščedrina* (Leningrad, 1980), by permission of Aurora Publishers.

cil confirmed the correctness of canon law, but the vituperative condemnations that always accompanied reports of sexual misconduct were conspicuously lacking.[190] The Moscow Synod of 1667 also protested against mixed-sex bathing, arguing that it was against Christian custom and "natural law" for men and women to see each other naked without embarrassment. The synod made no mention of sexual misconduct in the context of the bathhouse.[191]

Any sort of sexual intercourse forbidden to married couples was also forbidden in nonmarital relationships. In judging these sorts of violations, Slavic churchmen paid more attention to the offensive action than to the choice of partner. Thus anal sex with one's wife was as serious as an adulterous relationship with another woman—or, for that matter, a man.[192] Provisions on mutual masturbation between men and women did not distinguish between married and unmarried couples.[193]

[handwritten marginal note: Men & women / Rear approach]

"Unnatural" Sex

The Definition of Sodomy

Canon law and penitential literature had several pejorative epithets for intercourse from behind: "sodomy," "against nature," "deformed" (*bezobrazny*), "unnatural." The same terms were applied occasionally to other forms of sexual intercourse. Anal intercourse between men was also "against nature," although other forms of homosexual relations escaped this label. As we have seen, vaginal intercourse between husband and wife earned condemnation as "sodomy" if a rear approach was used or if the woman assumed the dominant position. Incest between close relatives (including in-laws) was labeled "unnatural" as well.[194] There seems to be no pattern differentiating "sodomy" from a sin "against nature." Because a wide variety of behaviors could be described by these terms, in the absence of clarifying descriptors it is not clear what sin is intended. Neither do the penances in these vague pro-

---

190. *Stoglav*, chap. 41, art. 18, p. 137. Surviving Russian Old Believer communities transplanted to the United States regard the bathhouse as ritually purifying rather than defiling. See A. Michael Colfer, *Morality, Kindred and Ethnic Boundary: A Study of the Oregon Old Believers* (New York, 1985), 44.

191. *Dejanija moskovskix soborov*, 13v–14r.

192. E.g., Smirnov, *Materialy*, 66; Hil. 301, f. 85r.

193. E.g., Hil. 627, f. 16r. Flandrin suggested ("Repression and Change," 32–35) that unmarried couples frequently used mutual masturbation to release sexual tensions during long courtship in medieval and early modern France. There is no comparable evidence for the medieval Slavic world, and the preference for early marriage made that sexual alternative less necessary.

194. BAN-S 48, n.p.; Mount Sinai 17 (17), f. 171v.

visions give any clue: they range from three days of fasting to four years.[195]

The medieval Orthodox Slavic understanding of conduct "against nature" seems to be unrelated to the modern use of the term. The term "sodomy" originated in the biblical story of the sinful cities of Sodom and Gomorrah (Gen. 18:20–19:29). This account did not specify the nature of the sins that led to the cities' destruction, so scholars through the ages have had to speculate. Jewish and Christian premodern interpretive traditions agreed that male homosexuality headed the list. Among clerical scholars in the medieval West, the sin of Sodom was associated with the terms "unnatural" and "against nature," which were derived from Aristotelean philosophy. "Unnatural sex" was any sexual conduct that, according to medieval science, did not occur in the animal kingdom, including male homosexual relations (regardless of technique), heterosexual anal intercourse, and nonprocreative sex. Medieval thinkers found the example of nature to be flawed for humans, however: animals do not use the missionary position or refrain from incest. Western canonists, including the eminent St. Thomas Aquinas, developed an alternative definition of "unnatural" sex which did not depend solely on either the Bible or Aristotle. The sin "against nature," they argued, consisted of the practice of sexual intercourse in a manner that precluded conception. Thus heterosexual vaginal intercourse "from behind" would be classified as "natural," as would incest; in both cases, conception could occur. "Unnatural" sex would range from masturbation to heterosexual anal penetration to any form of homosexuality. Because "unnatural" sex was deemed worse than any type of "natural" intercourse, masturbation, perhaps the most common of sexual violations, became a more serious offense than incest with a parent. Logical consistency had yielded a practical absurdity, at least from the penitential and legal perspective. But the definition of "unnatural" sex or "sodomy" as nonprocreative sex, usually involving anal or oral-genital contact, endured to become part of modern vocabulary and secular law.[196]

195. Almazov, 3:145 (3 days), 148 (3 years), 276 (3 years); VAT-Bor. 15 (4 years), f. 478r; BNL 251(200), f. 127r (2 weeks); SANU 124(29), f. 95r (1 year); Dečani 69, f. 108r (12 weeks).

196. On the development of the definition of sodomy and "unnatural" sex in the Western tradition, see Goodich, ix, 29–34; Vern L. Bullough, "The Sin against Nature and Homosexuality," in Bullough and Brundage, 55–71; and Brundage, *Law, Sex, and Christian Society*, 212–214. The hierarchy of sexual sins developed in the Roman Catholic West differed considerably from that in the Orthodox Slavic East. Tentler listed (141–142) the rank ordering of sexual sins from confession manuals before the Reformation: (1) unchaste kiss, (2) unchaste touch, (3) fornication, (4) debauchery (= seduction of a virgin), (5) simple adultery (= one partner married, one single), (6) double adultery (= both partners married), (7) voluntary sacrilege (= one partner under religious vows), (8) rape or abduction of virgin, (9) rape or abduction of wife, (10) rape or abduction of nun, (11) incest, (12) masturbation, (13) improper position (even between spouses), (14) improper orifice (most heinous between spouses), (15) sodomy (= homosexuality), (16) bestiality. See also Bullough, *Sexual Variance*, 380–382.

None of these definitions of "sodomy" and "unnatural" sex fit the usage in medieval Slavic sources. Slavic authors understood the destruction of Sodom and Gomorrah as a response to all sexual sins rather than a specific class of sins: "Fornication [*blud*] is worse than all other evil deeds. Other sins are outside the body, but fornicating defiles the body. Defiled people multiplied in Sodom and Gomorrah, and they could not tolerate the brightness of the Lord, but were burned by fire and burning stone."[197] It is tempting to see the terms merely as pejoratives, used to denigrate any heinous sexual offense. Didactic texts warned against "sodomy" in the most dire terms, attributing it to foreign, non-Christian influences.[198] Violations that were labeled "sodomy" or "against nature" tended to carry heavy penances and fines. However, other serious violations, such as rape, adultery, and fourth marriages, never carried those epithets. Indeed, according to the listing of penances, these sins exceeded the villany of those of Sodom.[199]

Upon close examination, a pattern in the depiction of certain sex acts as "against nature" emerges. "Unnatural" intercourse violates the proper order of the universe and society. Men ought not to submit to each other sexually; an adult male does not belong in a passive sexual role, nor should he seek to put another man in such a role. Neither should a man satisfy his lust with an animal; social interactions must be among human beings. It is inimical to the divinely ordained social order for a person to engage in sex with a member of his own family; therefore incest is "unnatural." It is not right for a woman to dominate a man, whom God ordained to be her master; therefore, intercourse with the female on top is "sodomy." Nor is it proper to use a woman sexually "as a man" (*mužsko*) through rear or anal penetration; women should perform only the female sexual role. In sum, "unnatural" sex inverted accepted social relationships, and for that reason constituted a serious offense.[200]

Homosexuality

Medieval Slavic canon law on homosexuality was rooted in the teachings of the Church Fathers. They in turn were heavily influenced by the established interpretations of biblical passages on sexual expression as well as the attitudes of pre-Christian Greece. The two traditions were not compatible. The attitudes of ancient Semitic society toward male

197. "Pravilo 'ašče dvoženec,'" in Smirnov, *Materialy*, 64. Cf. Almazov, 3:18.
198. *Stoglav*, chap. 33, p. 109.
199. See an excerpt from Russian manuscripts of the Izmaragd, *Pamjatniki drevnerusskoj cerkovno-učitel'noj literatury*, vyp. 3, pp. 38–39.
200. The stern prohibitions on sodomy in Renaissance Venice were similarly rooted in concern for the threat to established relationships; see Ruggiero, 109.

homosexuality were reflected in Mosaic law and interpretations of the tale of Sodom and Gomorrah. Mosaic law placed homosexuality among major crimes, punished by stoning. The apostolic preference for celibacy included discouragement of in any sort of sexual activity, whether heterosexual or homosexual, but homosexuality was specifically condemned. Neoplatonic philosophy advocated limitation of the sensual indulgence of sex, particularly when it served no procreative purpose.

Hellenic culture had nonascetic strands also, and male homosexuality was accepted if not promoted. Not all homosexual contacts, however, were equally favored. Anal intercourse was considered demeaning, at least for the passive partner, because he placed himself in a subordinate, "female" position.[201] Athenians in the Golden Age idealized a different form of homosexual relations, which occurred between older and younger men of the same elite social class. The relationship was supposed to be primarily spiritual, based on mutual respect: the youth revered his adult lover's status and achievements, while the older man admired the adolescent's physical beauty and potential. When their union was consummated physically, they practiced mutual masturbation and intercrural intercourse rather than anal penetration. Thus the milieu of early Christianity distinguished between two forms of male homosexuality: a despised variety involving anal penetration and a more respectable variety involving mutual stimulation with the hands and thighs. Although Christian writers could not acquiesce any sort of nonmarital sexual expression, they accepted the dominant premise of their society, that the one form of homosexuality was far more heinous than the other.

Thus Slavic Orthodox churchmen inherited a system of Byzantine canon law which distinguished between male homosexuals who engaged in anal intercourse and those who engaged in mutual masturbation, as well as between passive and active partners. Homosexual intercourse involving anal penetration (termed *mužebludie* or *muželožstvo*) was deemed to be as serious as heterosexual adultery. According to St. Basil, this offense carried a penance of fifteen years, as did adultery. Slavic canonists preferred the reduced penances of two or three years of fasting and prayer prescribed by St. John the Penitent.[202] Divergence from this norm, in the direction of either greater leniency or greater severity, was rare. An occasional code mandated a penance of one year, five years, or seven years—all within the range of penalties for heterosexual sins.[203]

---

201. Dover; Boswell, 74 and passim; Buffière, 19–22, 195–198. This view held in ancient Rome also; see Veyne, 30–31.

202. E.g., SANU 123(28), f. 25v (15 years, or 3 years' fast and 200 prostrations); GIM, Sin. 227, f. 195r; VAT-Bor. 15, f. 476v (15 years, or 2 years, 200 prostrations); Hil. 378, f. 167v (3 years, 500 prostrations); Troicki, 69–70.

203. E.g., Smirnov, *Materialy*, 134 (1 year), 143 (5 years); Almazov, 3:286 (7 years, 100 prostrations); Hil. 301, f. 126r (5 years, 300 prostrations).

Only rarely was an extraordinarily severe penance listed, and then only in texts that included more moderate recommendations as well.[204]

In assigning penances for homosexual relations, priests were advised to determine the age of the offender, the number of times he participated in intercourse, his marital status, his willingness, and the role he played.[205] The usual leniency for young people under thirty held for homosexual relations. One code recommended a two-year penance for a young man, three years for an older man.[206] Byzantine civil law known in Slavic translation and native Slavic rulings exonerated boys under the age of twelve of conscious wrongdoing. According to one penitential questionnaire, if a boy under age five was used sexually, his abuser bore the burden of sin; if he were over age five but not yet legally adult, it was his parents' responsibility for not teaching him to avoid sin.[207] Two or three youthful homosexual experiments were viewed as a minor violation.[208] In homosexual relations as in heterosexual fornication, bachelors were permitted greater leeway; a married man was supposed to satisfy his sexual urges with his lawful wife rather than turn to another person of either sex.[209] A youth who was coerced or forced into the passive role in homosexual anal intercourse was considered less guilty than a willing participant. At least one author exonerated the youthful victim of homosexual rape entirely.[210]

Some hierarchs viewed the passive role in homosexual relations as less sinful than the active role. This view reversed the ancient Greek perception, in which the recipient of anal penetration became déclassé, while the perpetrator retained his status. But from the perspective of Orthodox churchmen, the initiator of the sin deserved greater condemnation than the one who merely acquiesced in it. In this view, the worst possible case involved two homosexual partners alternating active and passive roles, so that both parties were equally guilty.[211] Other Slavic authors disagreed, regarding the active and passive roles as equally deserving of condemnation.[212]

In accordance with the ancient Greek distinction between anal and

204. NBS 688, ff. 25r, 93v, 110r lists a wide range of penances for homosexual anal intercourse: 2 years with 200 prostrations, 15 years, 18 years (attributed to Gregory of Nyssa), and a phenomenal 80 years. Rila 1/20(48), ff. 94v, 102r, 185r–186r, 188, lists penances of 2 years, 3 years, 5 years, 15 years and 30 years; GIM, Sin. 227, ff. 181v–182r.
205. E.g., SANU 124(29), ff. 8v, 16r; Peć 77, ff. 23v–24r.
206. Rila 1/20(48), f. 186r.
207. NBS 688, f. 25v; Almazov, 3:149.
208. Peć 77, ff. 23v–24r.
209. Kiev 191, f. 154r.
210. Rila 1/20(48), f. 21r; Hil. 301, f. 126r.
211. E.g., Peć 77, ff. 23v–24r.
212. Almazov, 3:149. In Venice the active homosexual partner was considered more culpable and abnormal than the passive partner; see Ruggiero, 121.

intercrural homosexual intercourse, Slavic churchmen usually regarded the latter as only a minor offense. While anal intercourse was categorized with such major sins as adultery and bestiality, intercrural intercourse fell under the designation of masturbation (*malakia* or *rukobludie*). The usual penance consisted of a fast of eighty days with fifty prostrations a day, that is, twice the penance for masturbation alone. An alternative penance consisting of exclusion from communion for two years without fasting appeared occasionally.[213] When a three-year penance was recommended, it clearly was made by analogy with canons on masturbation rather than those on anal homosexual relations.[214] Slavic clerics considered use of the hands in mutual masturbation to be more sinful than use of the thighs, "although both are evil and wicked."[215] Intercrural intercourse was not considered a "full fall" into sin, in the way anal intercourse was; those who engaged in it were not forbidden entry into the priesthood.[216]

Other sorts of homosexual activity were still less serious. Kissing another man with lust carried a penance of forty days with a hundred prostrations, only a little more than for kissing a woman. Trying to attract a man's attention for the purpose of initiating a homosexual encounter was no more serious than trying to interest a woman in illicit sex.[217]

It was much more serious for a man to "make himself resemble a woman" by shaving his beard; for this offense he could be anathematized. Archpriest Avvakum, the Old Believer leader, refused his blessing to the clean-shaven sons of one of his supporters on the grounds that they must be heretics. Orthodox believers recognized that they, as men, were made in the image of God, and therefore they should not seek to alter their appearance to that of women.[218]

Although Slavic Orthodox canons regarding male homosexuality

---

213. E.g., Dečani 70, f. 227r; Hil. 627, f. 15v; Kiev. 191, f. 686r; Troicki, 67. Two manuscripts include a penance of 12 years in one place but the usual 80-day penance in another: Peć 77, ff. 236v, 261v; SANU 124(29), f. 54r–v.

214. E.g., Almazov, 3:276; SANU 124(29), ff. 72r, 77r–v; NBS I-14, ff. 259r, 264v. In Renaissance Venice, intercrural homosexual intercourse was deemed as reprehensible as anal sex between men, and the initiating partner was subjected to the death penalty. See Ruggiero, 110–111, 115–116.

215. Rila 1/20(48), f. 127v. Oral sex for homosexuals was almost unknown among the medieval Slavs; only one penitential questionnaire of those 9 examined included it; see Almazov, 3:152.

216. E.g., Hil. 628, f. 38v.

217. Almazov, 3:275, 280.

218. "Poslanie rostovskago arxiepiskopa," in RIB, 6:880. Gudzij, 493. A court case from 1687 reveals enforcement of the canons against shaving, although with no implication of homosexual tendencies against the accused. He pleaded ignorance and threw himself on the mercy of the court. See no. 182 in RIB, 12:864–866.

seem to have been derived from Hellenistic and early Christian ideas, their uniform adoption by the medieval Slavic churches suggests that they satisfied societal needs and native attitudes. The objection to homosexuality was not based in the idea that it was "unnatural" for men to be attracted sexually to other men; rather Slavic clerics felt it was important for men and women to retain their designated gender roles. These roles precluded a man's submission to penile penetration by another man. Causing the "feminization" of another man by placing him in a female role was even worse. When men engaged in mutual masturbation, however, neither took the place of a woman, so proper gender roles were maintained. Consequently, Slavic churchmen could be much more sanguine about that type of homosexual activity. In any case, Slavic hierarchs—and particularly the Russians—exhibited less hostility to homosexual activity than their Western European counterparts, regarding it as the equivalent of heterosexual adultery, at worst. The code of neither Jaroslav nor Stefan Dušan considered homosexuality worth mentioning. It is possible that most homosexual activity in that period was confined to monasteries; monastic rules did contain provisions for homosexual practices. By the late fifteenth century, however, homosexuality was visible in the lay community as well, although it still did not attract particular vituperation. Samuel Collins, an Englishman who visited Russia in the seventeenth century, remarked that homosexual behavior was more open and more tolerated in Russia than at home.[219] The separation of Muscovite society into distinct male and female spheres heightened the opportunities for homosexual contacts by restricting heterosexual options.

Lesbian activity was not deemed to be a serious violation. Sexual intercourse between adult women was usually categorized as a type of masturbation (*malakia*). The recommended penance was a year of exclusion from communion.[220] This penance, greater than that recommended for mutual masturbation by males, indicated a perception of greater sin, although not of the magnitude of male homosexual anal intercourse. Article 59 of the Zakon Sudnyj Ljudem mandated flogging for women who engaged in homosexual relations with one woman sit-

---

219. To the critical modern reader, Collins' comment that Russians were "naturally inclined" to "Sodomy and Buggery" (106) suggests greater openness rather than a preference for homosexuality. He also expressed surprise that homosexuality was not punished by death, as it was in England at the time. Olearius made similar comments (142).

220. E.g., Almazov, 3:161; Smirnov, *Materialy*, 143; SANU 124(29), f. 77r–v; NBS I-14, f. 264v. One text equates mutual masturbation by women with masturbation alone, and prescribes a penance of 40 days' fast; see Almazov, 3:163. The same two texts that mandated 12–year penances for male mutual masturbation also mandate it for women: Rila 1/20(48), f. 185v; SANU 124(29), f. 54r.

ting astride the other.[221] It was not appropriate for a woman to take on a male role in sexual relations, even with another woman. At the same time, if a woman stepped out of her proper place in regard to other women, it was less of a threat to the social order than a usurpation of authority in a male milieu.

Churchmen had another concern about lesbianism: a connection between female homosexuality and pagan rites. Women who participated in lesbian activities were called "God-insulting grannies" (*baby bogomerzskie*), a frequent derisive term for female pagan leaders. They were also accused of "praying to *vily*" (female sprites) in their homosexual contacts.[222] Thus female homosexuality had a dangerous anti-Christian component that male mutual masturbation lacked.

Bishop Nifont ruled that sex between two adolescent girls merited a lighter penance than premarital heterosexual fornication, especially if the hymen remained intact.[223] Lesbian games between unmarried girls apparently were common in seventeenth-century Russia. A secular tale tells of Frol Skobeev, who wanted to marry the heiress Annuška, despite her father's objections. To this end he bribed her nursemaid and attended a party for Annuška's friends in the guise of a girl. The nursemaid, at his instigation, proposed a game of "wedding," selecting Annuška as the "bride" and Frol, in double disguise, as the "groom." In the course of the game, the young people staged the ceremony and feast and put the "bridal couple" to bed. Frol used this opportunity to rape Annuška and recruit her to his cause.[224] The anonymous author of the tale did not invent the game of "wedding" to advance his plot; penitential questions to young girls testify to its existence.[225] It could be tolerated openly, with only mild discouragement, because it prepared sheltered maidens for married life without exposing them to the risks of lost virginity and premarital pregnancy. Lesbianism between young girls reinforced appropriate behavior.

221. Dewey and Kleimola, *Zakon Sudnyj Ljudem*, 42–43. The translation is not quite accurate here, owing to the improper rendering of *na kon'*. The Roman author Seneca disparaged a woman who behaved like a man in lesbian intercourse and mounted another woman, describing her as a violator of the natural order. See Veyne, 33.

222. Kiev 191, f. 162r; Almazov, 3:161.

223. Voprosy Ilji, arts. 23 and 24, in RIB, 6:62.

224. Gudzij, 417–418. Some recent scholars have redated the "Tale of Frol Skobeev" to the 1720s; see Gitta Hammarberg, "Eighteenth-Century Narrative Variations of 'Frol Skobeev,'" *Slavic Review* 46 (1987): 529–539. The story was reworked in the eighteenth century, but the original certainly reflects the mores of late-seventeenth-century society.

225. Almazov, 3:169. Lesbian activity was similarly tolerated among young girls in Renaissance Italy as a prelude to marriage. While the Roman Catholic Church generally regarded female homosexuality as a lesser offense than male homosexuality, some earlier codes mandated the death penalty. See Judith C. Brown, *Immodest Acts: The Life of a Lesbian Nun in Renaissance Italy* (New York, 1986), 11–13.

Bestiality

Animals presented another alternative for sexual release in the agricultural medieval Slavic world. Bestiality was considered a serious sin by most Slavic churchmen (see fig. 14). Canons include descriptions of sexual use of a variety of animals, most commonly cows, but also pigs, dogs, birds, and reptiles.[226] A few canons refer to the sexual use of male animals as well as females.[227] Offenders could be of either sex, although regulations concerning men are far more numerous. Women underwent the same penances as men for this sin.[228] The usual penance of fifteen years (according to St. Basil) or two or three years of fasting with accompanying prostrations (according to John the Penitent) placed bestiality in the same category as adultery and male homosexual anal intercourse. Occasionally penitential codes distinguished between bestiality with a mammal and with a chicken or other bird. The latter carried a lower penance, doubtless because fowl were less costly to replace than other farm animals.[229] The severe condemnation of bestiality by the Ancyra Council, mandating a penance of twenty years for a young man and fifty-five years for an older married man, did not find acceptance in Slavic codes of canon law or penitential questionnaires.[230] The distinction between young, bachelor offenders and older, married ones did enter into the mainstream of Slavic canon law. For a youth, the penance could be reduced to a single year of fasting.[231] As with other sexual sins, the frequency of the violation was taken into consideration, and some Slavic codes retained the Old Testament distinction of whether the offender later consumed the meat of the animal he had used. In this case, clerics often recommended the longer penances of St. Basil.[232] From the medieval Slavic perspective, sexual contacts with animals were no more disruptive to society than other nonauthorized sexual alternatives, and thus did not merit more severe punishment. Indeed, some Russian clerics

226. E.g., Almazov, 3:277; Hil. 305, f. 11v.
227. E.g., Rila 1/20(48), f. 186r.
228. For women's bestiality, see, e.g., BNL 684, f. 157r.
229. E.g., SANU 122(47), f. 11v (15 years, or 3 years, 200 prostrations); Dečani 69, f. 107v (15 years, or 2 years, 200 prostrations); Almazov, 3:283 (3 years, 150 prostrations); VAT-Bor 15, f. 478r (15 years for a mammal, 9 years for a bird).
230. It is found only in the *Sintagmat*, 81–83, and NBS 48, f. 65r–v, among many other rulings on the subject. Canon law on bestiality in Western Europe imposed a heavy penance; e.g., Thomas of Chobh (early thirteenth century) ordered that the offender be permanently barred from entering church, and required him to go barefoot and abstain from meat, fish, and alcohol for the rest of his life. In keeping with Old Testament law, the animal was to be destroyed and its carcass buried or burned because it was unfit for human consumption. See Brundage, *Law, Sex, and Christian Society*, 400.
231. E.g., BNL 246(103), f. 158r.
232. E.g., Hil. 302, f. 17r; VAT-Bor. 15, f. 478v.

14. The Judgment of Men Who Fornicate with Animals. Men who engage in bestiality become bestial themselves. Miniature, Russian, from an Old Believer collection (seventeenth–eighteenth century), courtesy of Hilandar Research Library, Ohio State University, and Uppsala University Library (Uppsala Slav-71).

considered bestiality to be considerably less serious than many other sexual sins, and reduced the penance to a mere forty days. The Code of Jaroslav imposed a fine of twelve *grivny*, equating bestiality with incest with a sister-in-law or noncanonical divorce.[233]

Call Dud

Masturbation

Because sexual desire was evil, believers were forbidden to incite it in themselves. To masturbate and entertain lustful thoughts was deliberately to summon the Devil. In a tale that circulated in Russia in the seventeenth century, a youth who regularly committed *rukobludie* discovered that his penis had turned into a serpent.[234] But because sexual activity by an individual alone did not interfere with the social order, most clerics did not advocate stringent punishment. The usual penance for masturbation, called by the Greek term *malakia* or the Slavonic *rukobludie* or *v sja blud*, was a fast of forty or sixty days, with 8 to 150 prostrations a day.[235] An alternate tradition regarded masturbation as much more serious, recommending a penance of three years. As the two traditions coexisted in the same manuscripts, the priest had to determine the penance in each case.[236] It is likely that the longer penance was intended for persons who frequently engaged in masturbation and refused to desist, as indicated by one manuscript that included both penances.[237]

Masturbation by men and by women was usually handled identically under Slavic canon law.[238] One code, however, recommended a penance of only twelve days with sixty prostrations for a woman who masturbated.[239] Masturbation could have more serious repercussions for a man if the confessor decided to interpret it as "emitting semen for evil"

---

233. Almazov, 3:144, 147; *DKU*, 96.
234. Deržavina, 320–321.
235. E.g., Almazov, 3:286 (40 days, 8 prostrations); Hil. 628, ff. 18v–19r (40 days' fast, 100 prostrations, or a year's exclusion from communion and 50 prostrations); Hil. 171, f. 265r (60 days, 150 prostrations); Troicki, 66 (40 days, 100 prostrations). The term *v sja blud* has puzzled many researchers. Suvorov (390) read the phrase as two words instead of three (*vsja blud*), seeing it as a shortened version of *vsja tvorimyj blud*, "the lust committed by everyone." He suggested that it was calqued on a Greek idiom, which he did not cite. However, *vsja* is a feminine singular nominative form; it could not modify the masculine noun *blud* or the instrumental object of an implied verb. Reading *v sja blud*, literally "lust in oneself," makes both grammatical and semantic sense.
236. Almazov, 3:276, Kiev 49, ff. 648v, 666v; Hil. 171, f. 374v. Both traditions seem to have been offshoots of the earliest, eleventh-century penance, which was one year; see Sinai 37, f. 102r.
237. Peć 77, f. 236r–v.
238. Hil. 167, f. 229v; Hil. 627, f. 16r; Almazov, 3:275.
239. Almazov, 3:279.

(doubtless analogous to the "sacrifice of semen to the Devil" involved in illicit fornication). This sin constituted the "destruction of a soul" (*dušegubie*)—a serious spiritual offense.[240] The usual method of masturbating, as the Slavonic terms suggest, was with the hands. Autofellation earned but one mention, perhaps because few men had the agility to do it.[241] Use of an autoerotic device, such as a "vessel of wax or glass," either by a woman vaginally or by a man anally, did not make the sin worse.[242] Masturbating by lying on the ground, simulating sexual intercourse with Mother Earth, might have been expected to cause more serious concern among clerics because of its pagan overtones. In fact, the penance was less than usual, twelve or fifteen days, for both men and women offenders.[243]

Involuntary nocturnal erections and emissions of semen were understood in this context of Satanic instigation. It was a visitation by the Devil that caused the nocturnal emission. Consequently, the man who experienced one was instructed to examine his conscience in order to determine whether Satan was taking advantage of spiritual weakness. If he had been masturbating, or dreaming about women (or boys), then he bore responsibility for the Devil's visitation. In this case, a layman was forbidden to take communion that day and a priest was prohibited from serving in the church. If a man's thoughts and actions had been chaste, the nocturnal emission meant that Satan had been probing for weakness in an effort to lead him astray. If a man experienced an accidental visitation on the night before he was to receive communion, Satan may have been attempting to withhold the life-giving sacraments from him. Then it was better to defeat Satan's evil intentions by permitting communion despite the pollution.[244] According to other authors, even if the man had not instigated the "temptation," he was forbidden to enter the church, kiss the cross or icons, or receive the Virgin's bread until he had bathed.[245] One code imposed a three-day fast with 150 prostrations a day for "involuntary fornication."[246] Bishop Nifont permitted the baptism of a "great man" despite a "temptation" during sleep within the past eight days.[247] A priest who experienced an unexpected "tempta-

240. Smirnov, *Materialy*, 28, 48.
241. Almazov, 3:155.
242. E.g., Almazov, 3:159, 161; Kiev 191, f. 154v.
243. Almazov, 3:151, 275, 279.
244. GIM, Sin. 227, f. 211v; "Zapoved' ko ispovedajuščimsja synom i dščerem," in Smirnov, *Materialy*, 129; NBS 48, ff. 201v, 208r, quoting Dionysius of Alexandria 4 and Timothy of Alexandria 12.
245. "Voprosy i otvety pastyrskoj praktiki," art. 58, in RIB, 6:867; BNL 684, f. 173v. Some Roman Catholic writers placed similar restrictions on access to the sacred after a nocturnal emission, but few regarded the experience as a sin; see Tentler, 228; Goodich, 64–65.
246. Almazov, 3:146.
247. Voprosy Kirika, art. 50, in RIB, 6:35–36. The phrase "great man" suggests that this permission might have been an exception made for a convert of importance.

tion" was allowed to read the liturgy if no other priest could take his place.

In any case, a nocturnal emission, whether accidental or the result of sexual arousal, required substantial prayers for forgiveness of sin and fortification against temptation. Such prayers stretched to more than thirty pages in one manuscript. The basic prayers after a nocturnal emission were the penitential Psalm 50 (corresponding to Psalm 51 in the King James Version) and "Lord, have mercy," repeated a hundred times and accompanied by fifty prostrations.[248] If the involuntary emission of semen occurred while the man was awake, he underwent a penance of seven days of fasting with forty-nine prostrations a day.[249] Because a nocturnal emission was evidence of a serious threat to a man's salvation, prayers were developed to avoid it. One such prayer was preceded by the following admonition: "If anyone is tormented by a flesh-loving demon of lust, he should sing this troparion, which is always effective."[250] Lest men think to rid themselves of the capacity to experience a "temptation from the Devil," Orthodox churchmen strongly condemned self-castration. The usual penance was three years of fasting on bread and water.[251]

Explanations that did not identify nocturnal emissions as evidence of sin or potential sin were available. Byzantine ecclesiastical literature embraced the physiological viewpoint. Four eminent Church Fathers—Dionysius, Athanasius, Basil the Great, and John the Penitent—all wrote that the emission of semen in itself was not sinful, but natural. Athanasius compared it with other natural functions, similar to the growth of hair or the production of saliva. Impurity lay only in the evil thoughts and desires that might underlie a given incident of the expulsion of semen.[252] This alternative view became known in the Slavic world through translations of the syntagma, but it never found its way into the Slavic *trebnik*. The Slavs' belief in the Satanic origin of sexual desire made it impossible for them to adopt a physiological explanation of nocturnal emissions.

The supposition that sexuality was dangerous to the individual soul and the welfare of the community underlay the regulations of the medieval Slavic churches on illicit sex. Given the Devil's strength and mortals' weakness, even the concession of marriage would not suffice to prevent inappropriate sexual behavior. In establishing rules to govern

---

248. SANU 124(29), ff. 54r, 95v; similar: BNL 251(200), f. 129r; Smirnov, *Materialy*, 44.
249. Kiev 49, ff. 550–566r; Peć 77, f. 261v.
250. Hil. 171, ff. 395v–396r.
251. E.g., BNL 251(200), f. 120v; Hil. 171, f. 249; Smirnov, *Materialy*, 30.
252. *Sintagmat*, 356–358.

sexual violations, churchmen most often cited the need to heal sinful souls. Any taint of sin, no matter how minor, required repentance. Social realities were not far from their minds, however, as they considered the relative seriousness of sexual sins. Because the family was the basic economic and political unit, any sexual activity that interfered with its stability constituted a danger to society. It is not accidental that the most serious offenses were those most likely to cause social disorder.[253]

The most serious sexual threat to family stability lay in incest, which disrupted the hierarchical order and structure of the family unit. Infidelity by the wife raised questions about loyalty to her familial objectives, subservience to her husband, and the legitimacy of her children. Any sexual activity that suggested changes in traditionally established male and female roles—primarily the use of alternative coital positions and homosexual relations involving impregnation—threatened the gender-based distribution of authority in the family and in the community. Excessive sexual passion by husband or wife would make their relationship too volatile; it was better for them to be restrained and limit their sexual contacts to the essentials. A marriage based on duty was likely to be calmer than one based on emotion. Sexual activity by single persons could also disrupt the community and the family. A maiden who slept with men before marriage became undesirable for marriage, to the detriment of her family. A bachelor could entangle himself and his family in dishonorable and expensive situations if he chose to satisfy his sexual urges with inappropriate women.

When social disruption from sexual expression would be minimal, Slavic churchmen were willing to reprove violators mildly. A bachelor who restricted himself to prostitutes and slaves did not disturb his family or the community. It was more important to social stability to require obedience from slaves than to affirm slave women's need for chastity. A little additional marital sex at a proscribed time did not seriously disquiet clerics, provided it was a sign only of youthful energy rather than self-indulgence or disrespect for religious values. Similarly, masturbation

---

253. Scholars of sexuality in the medieval West have also concluded that the primary reason for restrictions on sexual behavior was preservation of social stability. See, Brundage, *Law, Sex, and Christian Society*, 152: "Early medieval moralists believed that passion, especially sexual passion, posed a threat to the welfare of the individual and society. Since sexual passion impelled men and women to seek carnal satisfaction with almost anyone, at any time, in any way that they could contrive, Christian moralists and lawgivers, like their pagan counterparts, saw sex as a disruptive force in social life. Sexual urges, they believed, must be curbed and controlled; otherwise they were sure to result in irrational and frenzied couplings that would disrupt the orderly creation of families and the management of household resources." Ruggiero, 9, attributes similar concerns to the secular government of Venice.

alone, between husband and wife, or in same-sex couples was worrisome because of the sensuality it reflected, but it did not in itself seriously threaten social structures.

Certainly violations of the church's regulations on illicit sex occurred. The existence of laws and penitential questions testify that they were broken. But the value of the rules and their appropriateness to medieval Slavic society was doubtless evident to virtually everyone in the community. Thus the church could rely primarily on the individuals themselves to oversee their own sexual behavior. A system of regulation of conduct based on confession is possible only when people have substantially internalized the standard. A secondary enforcement of the more important rules could come from family and community, who would report to the parish priest any doings that disrupted their peace. The priest served as teacher and judge, educating his parishioners on morality and propriety, as well as correcting their errors. Only on rare occasion did the church need to call upon secular authorities to force compliance in sexual matters: in cases of great recalcitrance, and when the sexual violation was accompanied by crimes that did not come under the church's jurisdiction. Rape represented such a situation.

CHAPTER 5

Rape

Modern sociologists regard rape primarily as an act of aggression against women rather than behavior stemming from sexual desire.[1] The medieval Slavs arrived at the same conclusion, but from a different set of suppositions. Rape could not be the result of benign but overly enthusiastic romantic love; there was no such thing. If a man revealed true love for a woman by helping her avoid sex, he manifested hatred by forcing her into it. The Devil, hating humankind, tormented men with lust; men who hated women used sex as their weapon. Thus the medieval Slavs' conception of sexuality as evil prompted them to understand forced sex as a crime of violence.

Canon law frequently placed rules regarding rape among those for sexual offenses. At the same time, other aspects of rape legislation indicated a recognition that it constituted assault rather than a sexual aberration. In recognition of the fact that rape constituted both assault and sexual misconduct, the secular and ecclesiastical authorities explicitly shared jurisdiction.[2]

1. The modern classic on rape is Susan Brownmiller's *Against Our Will* (New York, 1975). Brownmiller argues that rape is motivated by a man's desire to demonstrate power over women in a violent manner, and as such serves as a vehicle for the subjugation of all women. Women were economically powerless, she argues, and consequently they were treated as the property of husbands and fathers. Rape law, as it evolved in the Western world, reflects men's desire to preserve the value of their female property, which was cheapened by sexual assault. Brownmiller's reasoning cannot be applied directly to the medieval Slavic world, because women there enjoyed a high degree of economic independence. In Western Europe, the concept of rape arose only in the twelfth century; previously, *raptus* meant kidnapping, without reference to sexual imposition. Rape in its modern sense fell under prohibitions against assault or illicit sex in early medieval codes. See Payer, *Sex and the Penitentials*, 117. Legal questions about whether rape was a crime of fornication or of violence arose in Renaissance Venice; see Ruggiero, 88–108.

2. E.g., Beneševič, *Sbornik pamjatnikov po istorii cerkovnago prava*, 89, 92–93.

The Church Slavonic term for rape, *nasilie* or *nasil'stvo*, carried the broader meaning of "oppression," "constraint," or "violence" when it was used in other contexts. The Russian chronicles, for example, used these terms to describe the conditions of Mongol rule. *Nasilie* also could mean specifically sexual oppression, with emphasis on the use of force. It is in this sense that a prayer on the occasion of a second marriage entreated, "Rescue us from the oppression of the Devil," the source of uncontrollable sexual desires.[3] Men's nocturnal emission also constituted "demonic rape."[4]

The Literary Image of Rape

Ecclesiastical writers promoted the view that sex always had a dangerous, Satanic component. In pious literature, only persons in the Devil's clutches indulged in sex. Rapists, then, were men who had given themselves over to Satan. This state of sinfulness could be temporary, however. Ecclesiastical literature presented two models of the repentant defiler of women. The first was an infidel man who had not yet come into salvation. The second was a pious and good man, such as a monk, temporarily driven to evil by a demon of lust.

Both ecclesiastical and secular models of the raping infidel existed. The early Russian chronicle account of Grand Prince Vladimir described his sexual exploits, including the kidnapping and rape of his half-brother's bride and the forced concubinage of a Greek nun. The Slavic version of the Greek epic poem *Digenes Akrites* retained the accounts of the Muslim hero's kidnapping and rape of Christian maidens.[5] The genealogy in the *vita* of St. Pafnutij of Borovsk recounted how the saint's grandfather, a Mongol *baskak* (official), raped a Christian girl. The *baskak* subsquently converted to Orthodoxy and married his victim, thus saving both his life and his soul.[6] The non-Christian rapist was ultimately excused for his crime of rape when all his sins were forgiven through baptism.

When a pious Christian was cast as the prospective rapist in an ecclesiastical tale, both he and his equally pious victim somehow had to escape from the Devil's machinations. Usually the woman herself deflected the rapist from sin. One popular story in its fourteenth-century version told of a monk who, incited by the Devil, planned to force his

---

3. Mogila, 435.
4. Kiev 49, f. 651v.
5. *Pamjatniki literatury drevnej Rusi—XIII v.*, 32, 36, 50.
6. Halperin, *Russia and the Golden Horde*, 36.

benefactor's daughter. The virtuous maiden tried several ecclesiastical arguments on the wages of sexual sin, without effect. Finally she argued that if he raped her, she would have to kill herself, and the monk would then bear responsibility for her suicide. The monk was convinced, and repented of his evil intent. A sixteenth-century version of the story showed the maiden succeeding with another argument: she said that she was menstruating, and the monk would be defiled if he had intercourse with her.[7]

In the rarefied world of ecclesiastical literature, "good" women could not be tainted by "evil" lust, and consequently could not be raped. The lives of women saints presented numerous examples of rescues from unwanted sexual activity. In one common motif, the saint was remanded to a whorehouse as part of her tortures.[8] Other saints were threatened with violent rape. St. Gaiana avoided this fate by feigning death, upon an inspiration from Christ. Saints Cyriana and Juliana were led naked through the streets as part of their tortures, but they were clothed in divine garments to protect them from dishonor.[9] In every case, divine intervention rescued the saint from rape, although sometimes the escape came only through martyrdom.[10] St. Pelagia of Antioch, a favorite among the medieval Slavs, escaped defilement at the hands of an invading army only by praying for death.[11] That death was preferable to rape was the moral of the "Tale of the Maiden and How She Was Faithful to God." A pious Christian girl attracted the lustful intentions of her infidel captor. She persuaded him not to harm her by promising to cast a spell of invincibility over him. Only a virgin, she said, could work the incantation. When the captor demanded proof of the spell's efficacity, she urged him to try his sword on her. Of course, the "spell" was only a ruse; the maiden died at her captor's hands with her virtue still intact.[12] A tale

7. Nikolova, 176–177; TsGADA, F. 381, no. 163, ff. 193v–194r; BNL 684, ff. 187v–190r; GPB, SPbDA, no. 280, ff. 95v–97r; BNL 684, ff. 187v–190r.
8. These saints are Lucia (Dec. 13), TsGADA, F. 381, no. 163, ff. 96v–97r; Irene (Apr. 3), TsGADA, F. 381, no. 173, f. 39v; Theodora (May 27), TsGADA, F. 381, no. 173, f. 108r; Antonina (Mar. 1 and June 9), TsGADA, F. 381, no. 173, ff. 2, 122v–123r; Golinducha (July 12), TsGADA, F. 381, no. 173, ff. 158v–159v. Unnamed saintly maidens are the heroines in two similar tales; see Hil. 278, ff. 140v–142v. It is perhaps indicative of the medieval Slavic admiration of virginity and sexual chastity that only Golinducha, the least popular of these saints, was married.
9. St. Gaiana is celebrated on Sept. 30; TsGADA, F. 381, no. 162, f. 46r–v. Saints Cyriana and Juliana are celebrated on Nov. 1, TsGADA, F. 381, no. 163, f. 61r–v.
10. St. Euphrasia is possibly an exception. In the fourteenth-century version of her life, she was a slave, and it is not clear whether she escaped rape. In the seventeenth-century version, she is a free woman who escaped sex with a barbarian husband by tricking him into killing her before the marriage could be consummated. See TsGADA, F. 381, no. 163, f. 143r–v; Kiev 54, f. 521v, under Jan. 19.
11. St. Pelagia is remembered on Oct. 8, TsGADA, F. 381, no. 163, f. 39r.
12. Nikolova, 178–179; BNL 684, ff. 191r–193r.

with a similar plot concerned a man who tried to rape his daughter-in-law. She goaded him into killing her to prevent the double dishonor of rape and incest, and thus earned the honor of being buried at a monastery.[13]

Other saintly heroines mutilated themselves to become repulsive to the men who desired them. One young nun plucked out her eyes and another maiden cut off her nose and lips. The Virgin appeared at the end of the tale to restore the maidens' beauty for their heavenly bridegroom.[14] Even overt suicide was permissible, according to didactic tales, to avoid the defilement of rape.[15] This motif entered into secular literature also. Serbian epic poetry depicted honorable wives choosing death over surrender to the Turks.[16]

The life of St. Julianija of Toržok is perhaps the best example of the principle that good women could not be depicted as sexual victims. According to the chronicle, Princess Julianija's husband was murdered by Prince Jurij, his rival for the throne of Toržok. Prince Jurij then took Julianija to his bed by force. When she stabbed him in the back (literally), he had her executed, but then had to flee popular outrage. In Princess Julianija's *vita* as a saint, however, the rape incident is entirely omitted.[17] In the idealized world of ecclesiastical literature, a virtuous woman was never raped. Either through divine intervention or through her own pious wisdom, the saintly woman escaped sexual imposition.[18]

Rape Law

The rape of a good woman in the real world was evidence of an unfortunate disruption of the proper order of the universe. Thus under canon law, rape was a grave offense. Byzantine ecclesiastical and civil law provided examples for the Orthodox Slavs.[19] Though Byzantine

13. Nikolova, 359–361; Hil. 458, ff. 73v–76r. Another version of this tale is found on f. 388r–v.

14. BNL 740, ff. 35v–42v. The Bulgarian *paterikon* contains a tale on the same theme, minus the miraculous cure at the end; see Nikolova, 340–341.

15. See the tale of the martyr Magnentina, Hil. 278, f. 142v; also Deržavina, 205–207.

16. Brkić, 103.

17. Novgorod IV chronicle, *PSRL*, 4, pt. 1, p. 404; Sofijskaja II chronicle, *PSRL*, 5, pt. 1, pp. 133–134; I. Buxarev, *Žitija vsex svjatyx prazdnuemyx pravoslavnoju greko-rossijskoju cerkoviju* (M., 1896), 709. Buxarev's *vita* redates Juliania to the eleventh century because of a transposition of the chronicle date, 1406, to 1046. Clearly this is a late corruption, possible only after the Russian church adopted the Western calendar.

18. Didactic tales imported from the West do not follow the earlier pattern. See, e.g., Deržavina 205, which tells of a pious woman who was raped by a Goth. She later persuaded him to repent of his sin and restore her honor by paying compensation to the church.

19. For a brief discussion of Justinianic law on rape, see Brundage, *Law, Sex, and Christian Society*, 119–120.

provisions were duly recopied, laws of native origin differed significantly from the Greek models. Slavic law resembled the Byzantine in that it treated rape as a major crime in most cases.[20] Byzantine secular and canon law, known among the Slavs in translation, contained extensive provisions on rape, kidnapping, and the seduction of women. In determining the treatment of the rapist and his victim, Byzantine law took into account the woman's past sexual history and the location of the attack. South Slavic canon law tended to follow the Byzantine model rather than native secular law in its treatment of rape. The Russian tradition of canon law drew primarily on native concepts, with the canon law of Byzantine origin forming a secondary tradition.

Following the Byzantine model, South Slavic hierarchs distinguished between virgin victims of rape and married women. A man who raped a married woman in effect committed adultery, because he had sex with another man's wife. For that reason, the rapist of a married woman received the same penance as the adulterer.[21] True, the penances for adultery were among the highest in the *corpus juris*, but no additional penance was added to punish the offender for assault.

South Slavic canon law devoted more space to the rape of a virgin than to the rape of a married woman. According to some texts, the rape of a virgin constituted adultery rather than illicit fornication (*blud*), because adultery was the more serious offense. In this case, married women and unmarried women were treated equally.[22] A few texts mandated a longer penance for a man who raped a virgin than for one who raped a married woman.[23] The usual penance consisted of three years of fasting with 150 prostrations a day—similar to the penance for adultery, according to Slavic versions of the Code of St. John the Penitent.[24] As in the case of a married woman, it was the act of illicit sex that was of concern, rather than the violence of the method. Whether violence or seduction was used, the crime was the same: *rastlenie*, "defilement"; the willingness or unwillingness of the woman did not alter the ecclesiastical

---

20. Compare this view of rape with that in Renaissance Italy: " . . . penalties reveal rape was a minor crime in the eyes of the Forty throughout our period. If anything, it seems safe to assert that the demotion of 'regular' rape prosecution to lesser councils confirmed a trend already visible in the mild penalties and minimal rhetoric of the fourteenth century, which judged rape a minor crime of little importance to government or society. The victimization of women was just not significant enough to warrant serious concern": Ruggiero, 95–96.

21. Rila 1/20(48), f. 89v; Hil. 169, f. 75v. SANU 124(29) mandates a penance of 5 years with 24 prostrations a day for this offense.

22. E.g., Rila 1/20(48), f. 89v.

23. SANU 124(29), f. 7r, orders a penance of five years for raping a married woman and six years for a virgin.

24. E.g., BNL 246(103), f. 162r; Hil. 171, f. 262v.

penalty. All nonsanctioned intercourse with a maiden constituted statutory rape, because she was deemed incompentent to give consent.

While the South Slavs preserved Byzantine ecclesiastical penalties for rape more or less intact, they altered the civil penalties. According to Byzantine civil law, the man who deflowered a maiden could be subjected to a heavy fine. If he could not pay that much, half of his property was confiscated and paid to the woman as an indemnity. He also could be punished by mutilation.[25] Canon law, however, gave the rapist another option: he could marry his victim, if she was not betrothed to another man and if her family agreed.[26] The Slavic translation of the syntagma reflected recognition that the civil and ecclesiastical penalties served contradictory ends—punishing the rapist by mutilation and fines would not make him a better husband to his victim.[27]

Slavic law presented a rational solution to the conflicting Byzantine traditions. According to the fourteenth-century Serbian Lekin Zakonik, when a man "defamed" (*obeščasti*) a girl by force, he had the option, with her family's permission, of marrying her. She and her family were not obliged to accept an offer of marriage, but could instead demand that the rapist be legally turned over to them for vengeance. If the family were agreeable to marriage but the offender chose not to offer it, he had to pay the same compensation to her family "as though he had committed murder or some other awful thing."[28] Other variations in South Slavic texts even went so far as to order such a marriage, whether the attacker wished it or not, and "even if she is poor."[29] For an aristocrat, perhaps being saddled with a bride of low social standing might have seemed punishment enough. Once the girl's family was satisfied, the church's only remaining complaint concerned the occurrence of premarital sex. For that reason, the man underwent the penance of one year imposed upon a man who had slept with his fiancée (with her consent) before the wedding.[30] Thus South Slavic canon law gave priority to ensuring that a girl who had lost her virginity, whether through violence

---

25. Pavlov, " 'Knigi zakonnyja,' " 73–74; Hil. 378, f. 148r–v; *Sintagmat*, 210–211.

26. *Sintagmat*, 104; Pavlov, " 'Knigi zakonnyja,' " 74. Here the fine is one-third of the man's property. The Zakon Sudnyj Ljudem gives the fine as 72 gold pieces or half of the offender's estate, if he cannot afford that amount; see art. 10, *ZSL-K*, 106; art. 11, *ZSL-P*, 141. Ancient Greek custom also held that the offense of rape was nullified by subsequent marriage; see Keuls, 344.

27. Vladimir Mošin, "Vlastareva sintagma i Dušanev zakonik u Studeničkom " 'Otečniku,' " *Starine*, 42 (1949): 46.

28. "*Kao da je učinio ubistvo ili ma kakvo opasno dělo*": Lekin Zakonik, arts. 13, 36–39, in Novaković, *Zakonski spomenici*, 100–102.

29. E.g., Hil. 378, f. 148r–v, 167v.

30. E.g., Hil 305, f. 112r.

or because of her own gullibility, was provided with a husband and consequently a secure place in society.

When the woman was already married, the rapist suffered the usual penance for adultery as well as civil penalties. According to the Lekin Zakonik, the rapist paid the indemnity for murder (*krv*) to the victim and her husband.[31] Under the Code of Stefan Dušan, the punishment of the rapist varied with his social class and that of his victim. Rape between social equals was punished by mutilation. A peasant who raped an aristocrat was executed.[32]

Canon law was not consistent in its treatment of kidnapping. Some provisions forbade marriage between rapist and victim. Byzantine civil law ordered the execution of the kidnapper by means of the weapon he had used to abduct the maiden.[33] Other codes treated abduction the same as other cases of rape.[34] A set of special provisions concerned the abduction of a betrothed maiden by her fiancé. The church strongly castigated those who assisted in a marriage by abduction, considering this to be an inappropriate method for Christians to wed. For this reason, the parents of the bride were allowed to reconsider their commitment to the marriage if the groom carried her off without benefit of clergy. As a further mark of ecclesiastical disfavor, a penance of four years was imposed.[35] In determining the punishment for the male offender, the church gave major consideration to the illicit sexual contact rather than the force used to constrain the female victim.

The woman's consent became an issue only in the determination of *her* penance. Prominent Church Fathers, such as St. Basil and Gregory the Miracle Worker, ruled that a woman who was raped should not be considered guilty and did not need to undergo a healing penance.[36] Although an occasional South Slavic author adopted this view,[37] most advocated a penance for the victim. The recommended penance for a raped virgin was a fast of forty days or exclusion from communion for a year.[38] For a married woman, a shorter penance was indicated; she, at least, had not lost her virginity as a result of the rape.[39] The woman's

---

31. Lekin Zakonik, art. 41, in Novaković, *Zakonski spomenici*, 102. The thirteenth-century Croatian Vindolski Zakon also levies a fine for the rape of a married woman, with an equivalent amount given to the prince for the violation of public order; see art. 56, in Butler, 88–89.
32. *Zakonik cara Stefana Dušana*, art. 52, 176; Burr, 208.
33. *Sintagmat*, 105–107; Pavlov, "'Knigi zakonnyja,'" 67; NBS 688, f. 23r–v.
34. Hil. 171, f. 372v; SANU 124(29), f. 128v.
35. Hil. 378, f. 157r.
36. *Sintagmat*, 459–460.
37. NBS 688, f. 93v; Peć 77, f. 219r.
38. E.g., Hil. 301, ff. 86v–87r.
39. Rila 1/20(48), f. 103r; NBS I-14, f. 259v.

prior sexual conduct determined the severity of her penance. A woman of ill repute was believed to be willing to engage in sex under any circumstances. Even if she claimed that she had been forced, she underwent the penance for illicit fornication.[40] The location of the attack also influenced the penance imposed on the victim. In accordance with biblical precepts, if a woman was raped in an isolated location, where nobody could rescue her, she was excused; if the attack occurred in a populated locale, she could claim innocence only if she cried out for help. In the former case, South Slavic clerics recommended only a minor penance; in the latter, half the penance for illicit fornication.[41]

The question of whether a woman became unchaste as a result of rape was of particular importance for the wives of priests. These women had to be virgin at marriage. If any unchastity were discovered, the priest was required to divorce her. A question to the eleventh-century metropolitan Ioann II of Russia brought up the case of the priest's wife who had been returned to her husband after capture by the infidels. The priest knew that she had engaged in sex as a captive, but could not be sure if she had been raped. The wife, wisely, kept silent on this point. The metropolitan finally ruled that the priest should keep her; it was a greater sin to repudiate an innocent wife than to live with an adulteress.[42]

The Russian church developed an autonomous tradition of canon law to deal with rape. Evidently it adopted principles from native common law; there are striking resemblances between Russian ecclesiastical provisions and South Slavic secular law, as preserved in the Serbian Lekin Zakonik and the Croatian Vindolski Zakonik. Instead of considering rape as a variety of adultery or illicit fornication, Russian hierarchs regarded it as a form of dishonor (*bezčest'e*). By forcing a woman into unchastity, a man insulted her in the worst possible way. Dishonor was a secular offense in medieval Russia, but matters of interpersonal relations concerning women usually fell under the authority of the church. For that reason, the Code of Jaroslav provided for joint jurisdiction by the bishop and the prince in cases of rape. The bishop levied a fine on the rapist, and the prince was empowered to punish him as he saw fit.[43]

Unlike Byzantine and South Slavic canons, Russian rape statutes generally did not distinguish between married and unmarried women. The

40. E.g., Hil. 627, f. 29r. See Pavlov's discussion of the Greek version of this provision in *Nomokanon pri Bol'šom Trebnike*, 190.
41. Rila 1/20(48), f. 103r; ZSL-K, 75, 94; Zaozerskij and Xaxanov, 871.
42. "Kanoničeskie otvety Ioanna II," art. 26, in RIB, 6:14–15.
43. Jaroslav's Ustav, arts. 2–4, 7, in DKU, 94.

victim's punishment varied not with her marital status but with her social rank. The relative rank of the rapist was not a consideration. An insult to the wife or daughter of a great boyar constituted a greater dishonor than the same insult to a peasant woman. One article of Jaroslav's code required a man who raped a high-ranking boyarina to pay her five gold *grivny*; the same crime against a lady of the lesser nobility carried a penalty of one gold *grivna*. If the victim belonged to the well-to-do but nonnoble urban class, the fine was further reduced to two silver *grivny* or rubles. For raping a woman of the lower class, the fine was only one silver *grivna* or twelve *grivny kun*. An equal amount was paid to the bishop as a fine for the offense against public morality and an additional fine was payable by each accomplice.[44] Because of complexities in the medieval Russian monetary system, it is difficult to determine exactly the relative severity of these fines. It is clear, however, that five gold *grivny*—worth approximately four times their weight in the more common silver—constituted a substantial penalty, marking rape of a noblewoman as a major crime, while a fine of twelve *grivny kun* placed rape of a peasant woman among lesser offenses.[45] The only exception to this pattern of designating fines by social class concerned seduction and gang rape. In this case, the ringleader was fined a silver *grivna* and his accomplices paid the usual sixty *nogata*.[46]

Conspicuously absent from the Russian treatment of rape was any provision for the attacker to "right" the crime by marrying his victim. A provision offering the option of legal union appeared only in the Zakon Sudnyj Ljudem, which was of foreign origin.[47] Russian copyists often altered the articles on rape which they took from South Slavic sources. The Russian editor of a thirteenth-century version of the Kormčaja, for example, altered the wording to read that a rapist must undergo the

[margin handwritten note: Could not marry was to make it Right]

44. Ibid. In art. 4, the fine for offense against a high-ranking boyarina is listed as 300 *grivny*, represented by the letter *T*. Such a fine is impossibly high and must be a scribal error, even though it is present in most manuscripts. One incredulous scribe changed the *T* to a *G*, meaning 3; see the Belozerskij version in *DKU*, 122. Willian Veder suggested that the *T* version might have resulted from a misreading of a stylized *E*, meaning 5, in an early copy of the code. Though articles and manuscript traditions vary in the exact amounts of the fines, the proportions seem to remain consistent.

45. For discussions of the monetary system of medieval Russia, see V. L. Janin, *Denežno-vesovye sistemy russkogo srednevekovija* (M., 1956), and "Berestjanye gramoty i problema proizxoždenija novgorodskoj denežnoj sistemy XV v.," *Vspomogatel'nye istoričeskie discipliny* 3 (1970): 150–179.

46. Jaroslav's Ustav, art. 8, in *DKU*, 95. I concur with N. L. Puškareva's interpretation of *tolok* as gang rape; see "Pravovoe položenie ženščiny v srednevekovoj Rusi: Voprosy prestuplenija i nakazanija," *Sovetskoe gosudarstvo i pravo* 1985, no. 4: 121–126. Although the provision in Jaroslav's Ustav concerns only a victimized maiden, a penitential questionnaire asks about *tolok* of a widow, slave, or sister-in-law: Almazov, 3:150.

47. ZSL-K, 37; ZSL-P, 141.

established penance *even if* he married the victim.[48] A Russian *trebnik* copied the three-year penance for a rapist so prevalent in contemporary Serbian literature, but omitted the proviso offering marriage to the victim as an alternative.[49] From the Russian perspective, a man who dishonored a woman was not a suitable choice as son-in-law. By providing the injured maiden with a substantial sum of money for her dowry, Russian law made her once again an attractive marriage partner.

In determining the compensation for rape, Russian law considered not only the woman's rank by birth and marriage but also her reputation. According to a trade treaty between Smolensk and Riga, the compensation to a free woman who was raped by a Hanseatic merchant (five *grivny*) was paid only "if until then nothing lewd was heard about her"; if she had a bad reputation, she received the same amount as a slave woman.[50] Still, it must be noted that even a slave or a known prostitute was not considered fair game; she was in no position to be ruined, but she could be "shamed." Because the woman suffered "shame" through rape, some seventeenth-century Russian penitential texts adopted the South Slavic regulations recommending penances for raped women. A woman whose "earlier life was obscene" was considered a "prostitute" (*bludnica*) after rape, and underwent an appropriate penance. Otherwise, her penance was forty days.[51]

Russian churchmen did not usually consider the location of a rape in determining the severity of a penance. Only an occasional seventeenth-century Russian text included the South Slavic provision condemning as an adulteress a woman who did not cry for help when she was raped in a public place.[52] The Russians' concern for insult made assault in a public place more shaming than a private attack. Thus the revised version of the Zakon Sudnyj Ljudem altered the provision on the location of the assault, making a rape in public worse than one in private, on the grounds that the attack on her would then become known, and that knowledge would add to her shame.[53] As a rule under Russian law, the woman did not have to prove that she had resisted or had sought assistance in repelling the attack, and she did not have to produce eyewitnesses.[54] Unlike Western Europeans, the Slavs did not consider concep-

---

48. Smirnov, *Materialy*, 134.
49. VAT-Bor. 15, f. 478r.
50. "*A dotolě ne slyšati bylo bljadne ee*": PRP, 2:62, 126.
51. *Izperva žitie eja bjaše skverno*: Hil. 302, f. 8ov. Kiev 191, f. 687r, reduced the penance to 14 days.
52. Kiev 49, f. 66or–v; Hil. 302, f. 17v.
53. ZSL-P, 60, 91.
54. The Croatian Vindolski Zakonik includes a lengthy consideration of the type of witnesses necessary for proof of rape: "And if the said rape should have not witnesses, she [the

tion after rape to be proof that the woman had in fact consented to intercourse.[55]

Slavic codes also condemned physical attacks on women short of vaginal penetration. The Grbaljski Zakonik levied a fine of four barrels of wine on anyone who badgered a woman or girl "either seriously or in fun."[56] According to the Code of Jaroslav, if any man other than a woman's father or husband attacked her, she was due compensation for the insult, and the bishop received a fine of six *grivny* for the violation of public morality.[57] The offense of tearing off a woman's headdress was also punishable by substantial penalties under secular law.[58] Such attacks on women may often have been motivated by greed rather than malice; women's hats, necklaces, and earrings could be valuable. Even when the victim was not sexually abused in the course of the robbery, the assault was deemed *nasil'stvo* (rape) and *bezčest'e* (dishonor).[59]

Protection of Women's Honor   *Greakord*

Provisions to protect women's honor abounded in Slavic codes, and especially in Russian ones. In the Code of Jaroslav, laws dealing with false accusation of harlotry and unjust divorce closely resemble those for rape in the forms of sexual imposition (*pošibati*), kidnapping (*oumčiti*), and seizure (*zasjadeti*).[60] The same fines were ordered, without distinction as to whether the attack was verbal or physical. A man could be

---

victim] is to be believed; but by the same token only twenty-five character witnesses have to swear, putting their hands on the book, concerning the rape and against the accused." Only female character witnesses were permitted on the woman's behalf. If any witness's testimony was proven to be fallacious, the accused rapist went free. See Butler, 88–89.

55. Quaife, 172–173. English law in the seventeenth century also required that the woman report the rape at the time it occurred, and she must have had no previous sexual contact with the rapist. Neither of these provisions is found in the Slavic world. For a study based in an earlier period, see John Marshall Carter, *Rape in Medieval England* (New York, 1985). For a summary of the evolution of canon law on rape in the Roman Catholic Church, see James A. Brundage, "Rape and Seduction in Medieval Canon Law," in Brundage and Bullough, 141–148.

56. Grbaljski Zakonik, art. 113, in Novaković, *Zakonski sponmenici*, 114.

57. Jaroslav's Ustav, art. 44, in *DKU*, 97.

58. Treaty between Novgorod, Lubeck, and Gotland, 1189–1192, S. N. Valk, *Gramoty velikogo Novgoroda i Pskova* (M./L., 1949), 58. A thirteenth-century Croatian code contains a similar provision: Vindolski Zakon, art. 27, in Butler, 86–89. According to this code, the fine for a woman who committed the same offense was a mere token.

59. See, e.g., nos. 18, 63, and 86 in RIB, 25:19, 72–73, 100–102; nos. 230 and no. 284 in RIB, 14:552–553, 643–648. In the last instance, the attackers beat up the woman, who was pregnant at the time, and she miscarried the child. These are petitions to secular and ecclesiastical authorities to protest the robbing of women. In both cases the women suffered physical assault in addition to the loss of their attire, but there is no suggestion of sexual imposition.

60. Arts. 2–4, 7, 31, in *DKU*, 94, 96.

prosecuted for verbal insults to a woman, even if no physical attack took place. In northern Russia in 1653, for example, Luka Jur'ev filed charges against Ivan Belov, accusing him of standing under his mother's window and calling her a whore. The complaint was accepted.[61] Similarly, Pavlik Esipov accused Pjatko Čerepanov of *nasil'stvo* against his wife when he called her a whore and a bitch and slapped her ears.[62]

No man had a right to slander a woman by wrongly accusing her of adultery, not even her husband. A miracle attributed to the icon of the Virgin of Hilandar illustrates the importance of a husband's respect for his wife. The tale, set in Russia, begins with the unusual birth to a princess of a black child. Her husband concluded that he could not have fathered the baby, and he accused his wife of adultery with his Saracen retainer. He expelled the princess and her child from his home. When she could find no refuge anywhere, she went to the river to drown herself and the child. The Virgin intervened, rescued the princess, and changed the child from black to white as a sign of innocence. The prince then invited his wife back, but she refused to overlook his insult and chose to become a nun instead.[63]

The provisions on kidnapping concerned only real abduction, not the capture games that were part of pagan marriage rituals, which did not dishonor a woman.[64] According to one provision, a man who abducted a maiden was guilty only if he did so without her parents' permission.[65] If the families agreed to the "kidnapping," church marriage was permitted, although there might be a penance because of the inappropriate pagan form of the earlier ceremony. For a real abduction and rape by

---

61. No. 359 in RIB, 14:766–767. Penitential questionnaires inquired about the sin of insulting a person by impugning his mother's behavior. See, e.g., VAT-Bor. 15, f. 48r.

62. No. 234 in RIB, 14:558–559, dated to 1605. Compare these cases with similar suits concerning sexual slander in England: Ingram, 292–319.

63. BNL 740, ff. 82v–85r. See also the case of Ana in birchbark document no. 531 (Arcixovskij et al., 7:130–134), discussed in chap. 4.

64. Art. 2 of Jaroslav's Ustav (*DKU*, 94) refers to "kidnapping or raping" ("*oumčit' děv'ku ili ponasilit'*"), indicating that abductions with consent were not covered by this provision. The *ustav* of Prince Rostislav and Bishop Manuil of Smolensk also distinguished between real and ritual abduction. The prince and the bishop shared jurisdiction when a maiden was abducted. When a married woman was kidnapped, the bishop alone judged the offenders. Given the strong tradition of treating all cases of rape equally, regardless of the victim's marital status, the provision becomes understandable only as an attempt to distinguish between real and ritual abductions. In the latter case, the "abductor" was married to the "victim," and only the church needed to be concerned, because of the inappropriate form of wedding. In the former case, both the prince and the church needed to be involved to apprehend and punish a person guilty of raping a young girl. See Beneševič, *Sbornik pamjatnikov po istorii cerkovnago prava*, 104–105.

65. See Smirnov, *Materialy*, 47, which assumes that *mučit'* (torture) in this case was a miscopying of *umčit'* (kidnap).

force, four years of public penance were imposed.[66] Because of the survival of abduction games as part of the popular wedding ceremony, Serbian epics condemned only the abduction of married women.[67]

When a pagan ritual did cause a woman embarrassment, it was forbidden; witness this odd article in the Code of Jaroslav: "If cheese is cut for a maiden, for the cheese the fine is a *grivna*, and three *grivny* to the maiden for her shame; and she shall be compensated for whatever was lost. The metropolitan shall receive six *grivny*, and the prince shall punish the offender."[68] The provision makes sense when it is understood that cheese was a pagan symbol of fertility; it was one of the ritual foods consumed at harvest festivals, which under Christianity were absorbed into the celebration of the Nativity of the Virgin. To cut cheese for a maiden was to suggest that she was not a virgin. For that reason, she was entitled to compensation "for her shame." A person who dishonored a woman was punished by both ecclesiastical and secular authorities. Thus the prince was authorized to punish the offender, and the metropolitan received a fine. Although in most cases of insult to women, the fine to the bishop was equal to the compensation to the victim, in this case the six-*grivny* fine reflected the usual penalty for pagan activity. Because Orthodox Christians were not supposed to eat foods that had been used in pagan rites, the maiden was also entitled to reimbursement for the cheese that had been ruined. Although a similar law was not recorded among the South Slavs, Serbian epic poetry treated slander of a bride at her wedding as an unforgivable sin, worse than incest with a godparent.[69]

The protection of maidens' honor developed further in seventeenth-century Russia. Because aristocratic girls remained in the *terem* out of public view, even casting aspersions on a young woman's beauty became a punishable offense. According to the émigré courtier Kotošixin, when

66. GIM, Sin. 227, ff. 188v–189r. This is a reworking of the provision on elopement. Real kidnappings were not always for the purpose of rape; young women were a valuable commodity on the slave market. A seventeenth-century victim was a Tatar maiden, entrusted by her father to compatriots who were to escort her on a short trip. She ended up as a slave of the Bashkirs, and her father appealed to the Russian authorities, claiming that her escorts had abducted and sold her. They countered that the Bashkirs had raided their camp and kidnapped the girl. See no. 14 in A. A. Titov, ed., *Kungurskie akty (1668–1699 g.)* (SPb., 1888), 30–32.

67. Brkić, 90–91. The author misunderstands the import of his data here. He argues that the only instances of abduction in medieval Serbia involved maidens in wedding rituals; wives, he says, were never kidnapped. In fact, the epics are quite clear: the ritual abduction of a maiden as part of a wedding did not constitute an insult to the family; kidnapping and raping a wife expressed disdain for her, her husband, and their family.

68. Jaroslav's Ustav, art. 36, in *DKU*, 97. N. L. Puškareva suggested in an unpublished paper that this article refers to a broken engagement.

69. Brkić, 59–60. The author argues unconvincingly that the motif of slandering the bride was an innovation of the Ottoman period.

a proposed marriage did not materialize, the bridegroom might take his revenge by spreading rumors about the bride's ill-favored appearance. Such a report would discourage prospective suitors almost as much as open insinuations about her chastity. In recognition that real injury had occurred, the patriarch's court might order the author of the insults to marry the girl, ugly or not. Or, if he had since married someone else, he could be forced to pay compensation for dishonor.[70]

Women's honor was highly valued. A woman who had been dishonored, like a man who had suffered an insult, received monetary compensation. This money went to the woman herself, not to her male relatives. The compensation and fines for rape or insult to women were among the highest levied. In sixteenth-century Russia, the payment for dishonoring a man's wife or daughter (termed *bezčest'e*) was double the amount due to a dishonored man. In the seventeenth century, the daughter's *bezčest'e* payment was raised to four times the amount collected by her father.[71] In keeping with Russian standards, the actual amount varied by the woman's social status, but even women of dubious reputation, such as fortune-tellers, were entitled to protection of their honor. These codes did not specify a method by which a woman could be dishonored; it could be assault, sexual innuendo, or verbal insult. In this way, Russian codes deemphasized sexual contact between rapist and victim as the grounds for prosecution. The provisions reflect recognition of a social reality: an attack on a woman's reputation damaged her standing in society as much as a physical attack.

Both the Russians and the South Slavs recognized a particular sort of verbal insult against a woman: a slander intended to coerce her compliance in illicit sex. The church imposed a penance of three years with 100 to 200 prostrations a day on a person who attacked a married woman in this manner. If the target was a maiden and she consequently succumbed to the slanderer, the penance was raised to ten years.[72]

Powerless Women and Sexual Coercion

Slavic canon law gave special consideration to situations in which the female victim was not in a position to resist sexual advances. The first such situation was that of statutory rape—that is, sexual congress with a

70. Buslaev, 312.

71. *Sudebnik* of 1550, art. 16, in *Sudebniki XV–XVI vekov* (M., 1952), 148; *Uloženie* of 1649, chap. 10, art. 99, in *PRP*, 6:92.

72. BAN-S 48, n.p.; Hil. 378, f. 175r. Almazov, 3:284–285, lists the penance for an unsuccessful rumor as one year.

girl who was under the legal age of consent. In the Byzantine models for
Slavic legislation, a man who engaged in sexual intercourse with a girl
under the age of thirteen, even with her consent, was considered guilty
of rape and was punished accordingly.[73] South Slavic canons changed
the age of consent to twelve years, in order to match the legal age of
marriage, and substituted a penance of twelve years for the fines and
corporal punishment listed in Byzantine civil law.[74] Russian sources
revealed a different approach to statutory rape. The usual laws for rape
applied when violence or coercion was used. If the girl gave her consent,
the penance was three to five years. Even this penalty was waived if the
man later married her. If he neither repented of his sin nor married his
victim, however, he was to be turned over to the civil authorities for
exaction of a substantial fine.[75] In essence, there was no minimum age of
consent to sexual activity under this law. By the seventeenth century, the
Russians adopted the South Slavic conception of statutory rape, as revealed by the inclusion of such a provision in Russian codes and the
omission of earlier rules permitting marriage after the seduction of a
young girl.[76]

War captives constituted another group of powerless women subject
to rape. The church recognized that victims of wartime rape were in no
way responsible for their degradation, and specifically denied the need
to put them under penance.[77] In seventeenth-century Russia, state and
church authorities acted together to give some protection to women
during time of war. Penitential questionnaires for aristocrats made it
clear that raping captives—even infidels—was not acceptable behavior
in the eyes of the church.[78] A secular statute of 1649 punished soldiers
who raped civilian women during war with death.[79]

The risks of rape in wartime were real; this passage from the Novgorodian chronicle describing the conquest of Toržok by Prince Michael of
Tver in 1372 was typical: ". . . good women and girls drowned themselves in the river, seeing for themselves ravishment from the Tverians;
for they tore off their clothes to complete nakedness—even the pagans
do not do this. And these women from shame and misfortune drowned

73. Pavlov, "'Knigi zakonnyja,'" 74; arts. 12–13 in ZSL-P, 141. The similar provision in
the short redaction lists the age of consent as 20; see ZSL-K, 37. It is possible that this reading
reflects a scribal error.

74. E.g., Hil. 628, f. 16r.

75. Smirnov, *Materialy*, 66; Almazov, 3:285.

76. Kiev 191, f. 683v; Hil. 302, f. 76r.

77. Smirnov, *Materialy*, 91, 102.

78. Almazov, 3:172, 208.

79. *Uloženie* of 1649, chap. 7, art. 30, in PRP, 6:57. See also the provision against trampling
a woman and causing a miscarriage, chap. 22, art. 17, in ibid., 432–433, repeated in the
Zakonodatel'stvo o sude of 1669, art. 103, in ibid., 7:428.

themselves in the water."[80] A woman who was raped received compensation not for suffering or physical injury but "for her shame." If the victim could not obtain compensation to restore her integrity (and, in practical terms, make up for her loss in value as a marriage partner), she remained permanently dishonored. In such a state, death might be preferable.

The protection against wartime rape was intended for innocent female bystanders rather than for the womenfolk of enemies. When a man deserved dishonor and execution for treason, his wife, mother, or daughter might suffer also, and her dishonor could take the form of rape. Jerome Horsey, who visited the court of Ivan IV of Muscovy in the sixteenth century, described the execution of Prince Boris Tulupov. He was impaled, and his mother was raped to death. "And she, a goodly matronly woman, upon like displeasure given to one hundred gunners, who defiled her to death one after the other; . . . the emperor at that sight saying, 'Such I favor I have honored and such as be traitors will I have thus done unto.'"[81]

Fiction confirms the existence of the custom of extracting vengeance against an enemy by raping his womenfolk. The *bylina* of Mixailo Potok depicted the people of Kiev as handing the hero's wife over to the Mongols during a dispute with him.[82]

Slaves constituted a third category of women who needed special consideration in the matter of rape. As we have seen slave women were considered a more or less acceptable sexual outlet for bachelors. The sexual use of slaves could take the form of casual occasional intercourse or a permanent and semirecognized concubinage. Churchmen taught that it was sinful for an unmarried man to engage in sex with any woman, regardless of her social class, but they granted the likelihood of violations, and strove only to limit bachelors' sexual contacts to appropriate classes of women and non-Lenten periods. Leniency did not extend to married men, who had a licit sexual outlet. But in deciding how to deal with men's infidelities with slaves, churchmen had to consider the women's sexual sin as well.

The Byzantine inheritance included two approaches. First, Byzantine civil law, adopted in Bulgaria in the Zakon Sudnyj Ljudem, called for harsh treatment of a man who violated his marriage vows with his slave: he could be subjected to corporal punishment, and the slave was sold

---

80. Novgorod I chronicle, Komissionyj manuscript, in *Novgorodskaja pervaja letopis'*, 371–372.

81. Lloyd E. Berry and Robert O. Crummey, eds., *Rude and Barbarous Kingdom* (Madison: University of Wisconsin Press, 1968), 279.

82. Tixonravov and Miller, 27–28, based on a seventeenth-century prose version of the tale.

abroad so as not to tempt him further.[83] The slave woman's consent—
or lack of it—did not enter into the balance. She was not compensated
at all for the offense against her. Instead, she was viewed as nothing
more than the instrument of continuing temptation to her master. But
the Church Fathers, such as St. Basil and Nicephoros of Constantinople,
had been more sympathetic to the slave woman. They tried to distinguish between a slave woman who slept with her master willingly and
one who was constrained. In the first instance, she was to be punished
for her sin, undergoing the penance for illicit fornication. In the second,
she was to be judged guiltless.[84]

Slavic codes did not replicate the first provision from Byzantine secular law, preferring the alternative ecclesiastical regulations. Numerous
Slavic texts repeated the rulings of the Church Fathers.[85] Unlike their
Byzantine forebears, some Slavic churchmen recognized that slave wom-
en acted under constraint; they did not have the right to refuse their
masters' advances. As one author put it, the slave woman belonged to
her master, body and soul; for that reason, he had to bear full responsibility if he initiated a sexual relationship with her.[86] By this reckoning,
the slave woman was never responsible for illicit sexual activity with her
master; consequently, he would be ordered to undergo a penance, but
she would not.[87]

In this vein, the dominant tradition in Slavic canon law directed that a
slave woman who bore her lord a child be freed, while the lord was
placed under penance for a year. There are many indications that this
policy was not followed, even though it appeared often enough in the
nomocanon.[88] Were this the case, there would have been no need for the
provision in Russkaja Pravda to free a slave mistress and her children
upon the death of the master. Bishop Nifont granted that canon law
mandated release of a slave woman from bondage after she bore the
master a child, but acknowledged that Russian custom was different.[89]
If a nonbelieving slave concubine who had an exclusive relationship
with her master decided to convert to Orthodoxy, the priest was permitted to accept her without requiring that she extricate herself from the
illicit sexual relationship first.[90] In this way some Slavic clerics indicated

83. E.g., *Xristomatija po starobŭlgarska literatura*, 133; ZSL-K, 36; ZSL-P, 140; Pavlov, "'Knigi zakonnyja,'" 72–73; Peć 77, f. 115v.
84. E.g., GIM, Sin. 117, f. 192v; Kiev 191, f. 687r; Hil. 305, f. 28v.
85. E.g., SANU 123(28), f. 34v.
86. Rila 1/20(48), ff. 89v–90r; Hil. 302, f. 80v.
87. Smirnov, *Materialy*, 75.
88. E.g., Smirnov, *Materialy*, 48, 51; VAT-Bor. 15, f. 477v; BNL 251(200), f. 128r; Hil. 167, f. 223v.
89. Voprosy Kirika, art. 70, in RIB, 6:42.
90. Hil. 378, f. 150v.

that they deemed a slave woman who slept with her master to be innocent of wrongdoing.

By granting that the slave woman might be an innocent victim, Slavic
churchmen put themselves in a quandary. Slaves owed their masters
obedience, under both secular and ecclesiastical law; yet, obedience in
this case meant acquiesence in sin. If churchmen turned a blind eye to
coerced sex, they would be ignoring a serious violation of principles of
canon law. If they prosecuted the sexual exploitation of slaves in the
same way as the rape of free women, they encouraged disobedience to
superiors. Neither approach was satisfactory; churchmen tried to compromise by excusing the slave woman while not punishing her master
severely.

The master's rights of sexual imposition on slave women were not
limited to rape. Penitential literature also declared it a sin for a master to
force a slave into an unwanted marriage or to prohibit a slave to contract a desired union.[91]

Russian secular law revealed the same sympathy for the slave woman
victimized by her master, while still acknowledging that such relations
were to be expected. Although a slave mistress and her children were not
entitled to any share of the master's estate, they were to be freed at his
death.[92] Trade treaties with the Hansa provide further information. A
slave woman who was raped could demand her freedom, according to
one treaty; in another, she was entitled to a ruble in compensation.[93] To
prevent slave women from making false accusations of rape in order
to win their freedom, they, unlike free women, had to produce witnesses
to the crime.[94] The secular *Uloženie* of 1649 retained earlier procedures
for a slave to sue her master for rape in an ecclesiastical court, although
in general slaves could not bring suit.[95] Such suits were in fact brought
to trial.[96] Despite these provisions, it is clear that rape of a slave was not
considered a great offense.[97]

When the rapist was a man other than the slave woman's master, the
situation became more complicated. Slavic law copied the inspiration of
the Byzantine in this case: the offense was deemed more against the

91. Almazov, 3:172; Smirnov, *Materialy*, 68.
92. Russkaja Pravda, art. 98, in *PRP*, 1:118.
93. *PRP*, 2:62, 126.
94. Treaty between Smolensk and Riga, art. 12, in ibid., 2:62.
95. *Uloženie* of 1649, chap. 20, art. 80, in *PRP*, 6:350.
96. Richard Hellie, *Slavery in Russia, 1450–1725* (Chicago, 1982), 494–495. See also
Hellie's valuable discussion of sexual imposition on Russian slaves in a comparative perspective, 115–117.
97. Almazov, 3:144, 147. The tsar, having supreme authority over all men and women in his
realm, was likewise adjured not to force women, as indicated in penitential questions written
specially for him; see Almazov, 3:174.

woman's master than against the woman herself. Under Byzantine secular law, a man who slept with another man's slave was to pay compensation to her owner for the offense.[98] If a man dared to marry a slave
woman without her master's permission, he too could be enslaved.[99]

In this way, regulations for the rape of slave women balanced the need
to discourage sexual intercourse outside of the parameters authorized by
the church with the greater need to maintain the authority of masters
over slaves. Consequently, a master's sexual exploitation was punished
with greater or lesser severity, depending less on his use or nonuse of
force than on his marital status. The protection of the slave woman from
sexual exploitation by her master was twice limited. First, the "protection" afforded by canon law consisted of excusing the victim from
culpability rather than punishing the offending master severely. Second,
the slave woman had to demonstrate that she was forced against her will
into sexual intercourse, even though it is questionable whether any sexual involvement between slave and master could truly be considered
without constraint, because the slave woman was not free to reject her
master's advances without risk of punishment. The greatest protection
of women slaves from sexual imposition among medieval Orthodox
Slavs was found not in ecclesiastical canons but in Russian secular law.

Slavic churchmen recognized that when a superior coerced an inferior,
the inferior was not always a woman. Although rape per se involved a
male attacker, men could also be forced to engage in sex against their
will, either by another man or by a female superior. Two variations
entered into the canons. The first concerned an aristocratic woman who
took her male slave as her lover. Byzantine secular law ordered severe
punishment of both the woman and the slave, and they were forbidden
to marry.[100] The Code of Stefan Dušan followed in the same vein, punishing both the woman and her bondsman by mutilation.[101] Russian
canon law similarly regarded sexual contact between mistress and slave
as inappropriate. No provision of canon law considered the possibility
that the slave might have acted unwillingly, complying with his mistress's demands only out of fear of punishment. The second variation
concerned an aristocratic servitor who engaged in illicit sex with the
ruler's wife, "either willingly or unwillingly, for the sake of honors in
this transient life."[102] As the wording of this penitential question suggests, a sexual relationship with one's suzerain's wife could have definite

98. Pavlov, "'Knigi zakonnyja,'" 73.
99. Rila 1/20(48), f. 97v; SANU 124(29), f. 86v.
100. Pavlov, "'Knigi zakonnyja,'" 69–70.
101. *Zakonik cara Stefana Dušana*, Athos version, art. 53, 176.
102. Almazov, 3:173.

political advantages. The dangers, however, were greater still; adultery in this case also constituted treason. The anonymous author of this question was aware that a servitor could be constrained into a sexual relationship; to refuse could be to risk the jilted princess's hostility. Even so, the man was deemed at fault for agreeing to illicit sex. Thus Slavic canon law did not recognize that men as well as women could be forced into unwanted sexual intercourse.

The Context of Rape

The strictures in canon and secular law against rape did not prevent occurrences. Indeed, certain aspects of medieval Slavic society promoted the sexual abuse of women, despite condemnations of it by clerical authorities. Literary texts and actual court records of rape cases (from seventeenth-century Russia) illuminate the social context in which rapes took place.

Churchmen did not challenge the idea that sexual intercourse, even if unwanted, defiled the woman who engaged in it. It constituted an insult not only to the woman but also to her relatives. According to the Novgorod chronicle, the rape of native women by the Varangian mercenaries based in Novgorod became a *causus belli*.[103] An anonymous Dutch observer reported that one of the most serious complaints against the False Dmitri in early-seventeenth-century Russia was his failure to prosecute a Polish nobleman for raping a Russian girl.[104] The same theme is found in a tale in the Bulgarian *paterikon*: in order to discredit the holy monk Markel, the Devil took his form and coerced pious women into illicit sex:

> He forced them to fornicate with him, and conversed with them with improper conversation, and taught them that there is no sin in fornicating thus. The demon did this not once or twice but many times. . . . The women came and told their husbands, and word carried throughout the entire city. The men gathered on Sunday in the church, and the prince called the women, and asked them if he had been told the truth. There were more than twenty women, and they told him, "It was not once or twice, but many times that he forced us to fornicate with him."[105]

103. Novgorod I chronicle, in *Novgorodskaja pervaja letopis'*, 174–175; Novgorod V chronicle, *PSRL*, 5:108–109.
104. "The Reporte of a Bloudie and Terrible Massacre in the City of Mosco . . . ," in Howe, 82–85.
105. Nikolova, 256–258.

The unsuspecting monk Markel was beaten and confined to his cell in punishment before the Devil's role was uncovered. The lessons of this tale were twofold: First, rape was a serious offense, deserving of public outrage and princely investigation. Second, accusers should make sure of their identification of the rapist before taking action.

In all of the published court cases dealing with rape, the attacker was identified by name. It should not be assumed, however, that the victim usually was acquainted with the man who assaulted her. Rather, a woman would be unlikely to publicize her victimization unless she could demand compensation and punishment of the man who offended her—an unlikely eventuality if the rapist was a stranger.

If the woman decided to press charges, her first step was to petition the ecclesiastical or secular authorities to intervene. The widow Marija Mixailova *doč'* Trufanova petitioned Metropolitan Varlaam of Rostov, Jaroslavl', and Ustjug, accusing Andrjuška Kolokolnicyn, nicknamed Parnjug, of raping her. The attack occurred in the evening, after Marija returned home from a visit with her brother. Andruška Parnjug ripped the lock from her door, forced his way into the house, raped Marija, and robbed her. Then he ran off. By filing an official complaint, Marija could enlist the assistance of the authorities in locating Parnjug and returning him to the scene to face charges—a necessary first step in gaining compensation. Unfortunately, further information about this case is lacking.[106]

Other documents tell about how the ecclesiastical courts dealt with accusations of rape. In theory and in practice, the burden of proof was on the accused, as the case of Tanka Ivanova *doč'* Zybova illustrates. Tanka had been married, but her husband had abandoned her more than three years earlier. Since that time, Tanka had lived with her parents at a saltworks owned by the priest Aleksej. When her pregnancy became obvious, she first accused the priest's Cossack boarder, Aleška Lukijanov *syn* Žigulev, of raping her during Lent. After the rape, she stated, she had slept with him willingly. Aleška had since run away and could not be located. Three days after making this initial accusation, Tanka changed her story. Now she accused the priest Aleksej of raping her while he was drunk. Three weeks after that (the delay was due to the birth of the baby), Tanka again changed her testimony, accusing a neighbor youth, Timoška, of raping her also on a separate occasion. The priest Aleksej denied raping Tanka, and named the absent Aleška as the father of the child. Timoška similarly denied raping Tanka. Tanka then

106. No. 93 in RIB, 25:113–114, dated to 1632. See also another rape case, no. 249, in ibid., 25:340–341, dated to 1675–1676.

admitted the truth, that no rape had occurred at all. She had slept with Aleška willingly and had become pregnant by him. Her spurious accusations of rape were motivated by a desire to find an excuse for her illicit pregnancy and, if possible, to force someone to support her child. She had accused the priest because, after learning of the extra-marital affair, he had told Aleška to leave. The accusation against Timoška was also revenge; Timoška had made fun of Tanka, teasing her about Aleška's vanishing act. Ultimately the court waived the fines against Tanka for illegitimate birth, ordered her flogged for perjury, and sent her home.[107] Tanka's contradictory statements were obviously false, but the behavior of the court is noteworthy: each accusation was given due consideration, as though Tanka were a reliable plaintiff. Because it was considered to be defiling to the victim, rape had to be treated as a serious offense, and one not difficult to prove.

A petition by a bailiff of the ecclesiastical court of Ustjug, Matvej Lobanov, gives insight into the treatment of rapists after conviction. After the court collected any fine or compensation for the victim and inflicted any corporal punishment, the convict was returned to the community. Long prison sentences were not usually handed down in seventeenth-century Russia, because of the expense of incarcerating malfeasants. Instead, the criminal was placed on a sort of parole: his relatives had to swear *poruka* for him, guaranteeing his future conduct. Lobanov's duty was to collect the *poruka* documents from the convicted rapist Kozma Terent'ev *syn* Žilin and to enforce the other terms of the parole. Kozma was forbidden to leave Ustjug, and he was forbidden to marry without the consent of the court. However, Kozma's aunt and cousins refused to cooperate with Lobanov, beat him up, and helped Kozma to flee from the authorities.[108] Inadequate supervision of parolees is a universal problem of criminal justice systems; its appearance in medieval Russia should elicit no surprise. Nor would it be reasonable to expect the convict's aunt to go against her nephew's interests, despite common bonds of gender between her and the rape victim. The court's prohibition of marriage for Kozma, however, is notable: it reveals an understanding that rapists are dangerous to all women, and that a wife would not be safe in Kozma's household. Further, it reveals that medieval Russians did not believe that rape occurred because the rapist could not find alternative licit sexual outlets.

Perhaps because the plaintiff was readily believed, several of the surviving rape cases were settled out of court. For example, Fevronija

---

107. No. 245 in RIB, 12:1144–1154, dated to 1695.
108. No. 176 in RIB, 25:228–229, dated to 1640.

Stefanova *doč'* petitioned Archbishop Aleksandr of Ustjug on July 12, 1686, accusing Danilo Ivanov Malkov and his friend Grigorij of robbing her house, threatening her with death, and raping her. Danilo and Grigorij denied all charges, but Fevronija produced responsible witnesses. The accused then hastened to settle out of court in the hope of avoiding a judgment against them. Thus on July 16—only four days after the original charge was filed—Fevronija and the defendants petitioned together to have the case dropped. The erstwhile defendants were left to pay the court costs, as well as whatever Fevronija extracted as a condition for dropping the suit.[109] A similar case in the same year was sent to secular authorities, as it concerned soldiers in a border region. Ofimica Ivanova *doč'* Aleška *žena* Artem'eva accused the soldier Grigorij Ščetkin of ripping her dress and forcing oral sex on her. Grigorij countered with an accusation of slander. As the testimony against him increased, Grigorij tried to get Ofimica to drop charges in exchange for a half-measure of grain. At first she refused. Ultimately he must have offered her sufficient compensation, because the two petitioned together that the charges be dropped.[110]

Because rape dishonored a woman, and by extension her family, it was popularly viewed in medieval Russian secular literature as an acceptable way of taking revenge on a woman who ridiculed a man. The earliest example of this attitude may be found in the highly fictionalized chronicle account of Rogneda. Grand Prince Vladimir asked Princess Rogneda of Polotsk to marry him, but she refused, insulting his parentage. In revenge, Vladimir seized her during her wedding to his half-brother Jaropolk and forced her to become his concubine.[111] The *byliny* presented this same view of rape as proper revenge in a later period. In one version of the *bylina* of Xoten Bludovič, the hero told the girl who rejected his proposal of marriage:

> Young Čajna Časovična!
> If you come out with honor, I will take you for myself.
> If not, I will take you for my comrade,
> For my beloved servant.
> Your teeth will be scattered, Čajna,
> Your hair will be unbraided, Čajna,
> Your legs will be spread, Čajna . . .[112]

109. No. 166 in RIB, 12:724–730.
110. No. 48 in Titov, 112–114.
111. Novgorod IV chronicle, in *PSRL*, 4, pt. 1, vyp. 1, pp. 53–55.
112. Variant LXIV, ll. 137–143, in Smirnov and Smolickij, 280.

This text can be interpreted only as a threat of rape, made with the full approval of the narrator. Čajna deserved rape because she and her mother rudely rejected his respectable proposal of marriage with insults against his parentage and abilities. Similarly, in another *bylina*, Vasilij Buslaev threatened to rape an old woman who criticized him for bathing nude in the holy Jordan River. In another version of the tale, Vasilij ripped the clothing off a woman who disparaged the bravery and fighting skill of his retinue.[113]

In seventeenth-century secular literature, rape was also permissible to initiate a maiden into a sexual relationship and gain her support. In the "Tale of Frol Skobeev," the hero, an adventurer from the lower aristocracy, wished to marry the wealthy and noble Annuška. She was beyond his reach by conventional means, so he proceeded by a less honorable route. As we saw in Chapter 4, Frol joined in the girls' game of "wedding" in the guise of a girl and violated Annuška. After the rape, Annuška eagerly joined forces with Frol to outwit her father.[114] The narrator seems to consider Frol's behavior naughty but not offensive. Annuška was not an injured innocent, but saucy, opportunistic, and larcenous, rather like Frol Skobeev. The two deserved each other, and ultimately lived happily ever after. The forcible seduction disturbed the author and the audience not at all.

A woman who was drunk was likewise asking for trouble. The Orthodox Church railed against intoxication, considering it to be an intensifying factor in any crime. A woman who was raped while she was drunk shared responsibility for her victimization.[115] A man who committed rape while he was under the influence of alcohol was condemned as much for drunkenness as for his other crimes; it was overindulgence in liquor that led him into evil.[116] The German envoy to seventeenth-

---

113. Variants II, ll. 224–233, and XIV, ll. 153–172, in ibid., 16, 72. These themes are repeated in folktales, which cannot be dated accurately; see Yury Perkov, trans., *Erotic Tales of Old Russia* (Oakland, Calif., 1980), 59–61, 87–88.

114. "*Prinuždeniem razstlil děvičestvo*": Gudzij, 418 and *passim*. The idea that a rape makes the victim more responsive to later sexual contact with the rapist (or leads her to fall in love with him) is a common theme in Western literature to this day; see Brownmiller, 290, 314–315, 344–345. Certainly courts in Renaissance Venice accepted the idea that a long-term sexual liaison could begin with rape. By forcing the woman once, a man could gain her acquiescence to further sexual contact either by threatening to expose her unchastity or by promising to retrieve her honor through marriage. See Ruggiero, 156. This theme does not appear in Russian literature before the seventeenth century, and the tale of Frol Skobeev belongs to a genre that is first documented in that period. It is possible that the motif of a "happy rape" was a borrowing from the West.

115. Almazov, 3:169.

116. See, e.g., the didactic tale "The Legend about Saint John Chrysostom," in Butler, 146–148.

century Muscovy, Adam Olearius, included this report of the rape of an intoxicated woman:

> . . . a drunken woman came out of the tavern, collapsed in the street nearby, and fell asleep. Another drunken Russian came by, and seeing the partly exposed woman lying there, was inflamed with passion, and lay down with her to quench it, caring not that it was broad daylight and on a well-peopled street. He remained lying by her and fell asleep there. Many youngsters gathered in a circle around this bestial pair and laughed and joked about them for a long time, until an old man came up and threw a robe over them to cover their shame.[117]

In this incident, nobody intervened to prevent abuse of the woman, and her predicament elicited little sympathy, even from the critical foreign observer. When such cases came to the attention of public authorities, however, they were investigated as rigorously as any other serious offense. A report roughly analogous to that recounted by Olearius survives in state archives:

An unknown woman was found in Dmitrovskaja village, badly beaten and raped. The villagers denied any complicity in the crime. A few identified the woman as a stranger named Tanka, who came from the Streltsy (infantry) garrison nearby. Several reported that they had seen her lying drunk in the street. Suspicion immediately fell on the soldiers who were being quartered in the village. One of these soldiers, Pronka Vysockij, known by the nickname Šilo, claimed to have seen two drummers, Sofonko and Senka, beating the woman, pulling a wattle fence over her, and walking on top. In his first statement, Pronka Šilo accused a soldier, Savost'ka, of participating, but then credited him with driving the two drummers away. All three of those implicated in Šilo's testimony denied involvement, but their statements conflicted. In order to resolve the conflicts, the court ordered all those implicated, including Pronka Šilo, to undergo torture by hot iron. Under torture, the ranks of the implicated grew to include others, including a soldier, Vaska, and Pronka Šilo's landlord, Eremka Andreev. Meanwhile, the woman had recovered consciousness, named Šilo as her attacker, and died. Investigators sent by the court uncovered additional evidence. First, the nurses who cared for the dying woman reported that her anus was bruised, an indication of rape. Second, the woman was identified definitively. She was the wife of a soldier, and had been publicly flogged for adultery in the past. Third, Pronka Šilo's original testimony against Sofonko and Senka was discredited when an investigator reported that the scene of

117. Olearius, 143.

the crime was not visible from Pronka's yard, and the fence in question was overgrown with grass and had obviously not been moved. Under torture, little by little the truth came out. Pronka Šilo had found Tanka drunk and had had sex with her, along with Savost'ka and Vaska. All three claimed that Tanka had been willing. Later that day, Tanka went to Pronka Šilo's lodging to protest. The landlord, Eremka Andreev, refused to let her in, and kicked her down. Pronka then dragged her out of the house, raped her again, and beat her with a birch rod.

The medieval Russian system of trial did not require conviction on a specific charge. In this case, it was clear that a crime had been committed: the woman was dead, and the three soldiers had had illicit sex with her. Although the victim was hardly a credit to society, the court could not ignore the offense against her. Pronka, Savost'ka, and Vaska were imprisoned for ten months and then returned to their regiments. Šilo, the most culpable, was flogged before his release.[118] Ultimately, it was more important to state authorities to get service out of the soldiers than to punish them for insult and injury to an adulterous woman.

Wife Abuse

The case of Pronka Šilo and the popular attitudes toward rape suggest that medieval Slavic society had a high level of tolerance for violence against women. The sixteenth-century German traveler Baron von Herberstein reported that Russian women were abused: locked up in their houses with no control over their lives and abysmally treated by their kinsmen. Russian women, he said, like other servile Russians, considered beating to be a sign of affection.[119] Adam Olearius, who prepared for his trip to Russia by reading Herberstein's memoirs, dismissed the notion that Russian women *liked* to be beaten, but he conceded that the practice was common, and in his opinion it was well deserved, because Russian women were lewd-tongued, drunken, and adulterous.[120] Samuel Collins also described the tradition of wife-beating, symbolized by the whip presented to the husband in the popular wedding ceremony, but noted that the wife's natal family would intervene to

118. No. 19 in *Moskovskaja delovaja i bytovaja pis'mennost' XVII veka* (M., 1968), 277–285. By the standards of the time, ten months' imprisonment was fairly long; sentences were rarely more than a year, because of the cost of maintaining prisoners.
119. Sigismund von Herberstein's source for this peculiar conclusion seems to have been a German blacksmith living in Moscow, who ultimately murdered his Russian wife. See his *Description of Moscow and Muscovy* (London, 1966), 40–41.
120. Olearius, 170 and *passim*.

prevent gross abuse.[121] Despite this reputation for indifference to the mistreatment of women, Russian canon law—unlike that of the South Slavs—contained provisions to protect women from violent husbands.

Russian sources confirm that husbands beat their wives and daughters; but there were limits to this violence. First, only a husband or father could beat a woman; even a father-in-law or brother-in-law could not beat his kinswoman with impunity. Unless they could show just cause, they could be subjected to the same punishment as any outsider.[122] A son was not permitted to strike his mother for any reason.[123] A woman who felt ill treated could appeal to the bishop's court. In one record of the seventeenth century, the widow Kapilica Grigor'eva *doč'* accused her father-in-law of abusing her and refusing to support her. Although he denied the charge, the father-in-law found it prudent to settle with Kapilica out of court.[124] Similarly, a fourteenth-century Novgorodian woman sent a birchbark letter to the archbishop's procurator to protest a beating by her stepson.[125]

The church granted the husband the right to chastise his wife when she committed some wrong, but undue violence was not encouraged. In the sixteenth-century manual on housekeeping *Domostroj*, husbands were admonished not to use wooden or iron rods on their wives, or to beat them about the face, ears, or abdomen, lest they cause blindness, deafness, paralysis, toothache, or miscarriage. Wives were to be beaten only in private, without anger, for a "great offense," such as disobedience or inattention.[126] The existence of such instructions suggests that men could not be counted on to show restraint. The legal restrictions on wife-beating were considerably weaker. A husband did not have to show just cause to beat his wife. She could protest the treatment only if it were "evil" (*kakoe zloe dělo*) or endangered her life. Under those circumstances, she was entitled to a divorce.[127] A husband who injured his pregnant wife and caused her to miscarry was guilty of a sin, but the wife received no compensation and was not freed from the marriage.[128]

---

121. Collins, 8–10. Best, 373–375, also reported the wedding ritual with the whip.
122. Jaroslav's Ustav, Markelovskij izvod, art. 41, in *DKU*, 102.
123. Jaroslav's Ustav, art. 45, in *DKU*, 47.
124. No. 194 in RIB, 12:918–922.
125. No. 415 in Arcixovskij et al., 7:21–22. The identification of the addressee, Feliks, as the archbishop's procurator is tentative because the letter itself does not include a title, but V. L. Janin here makes a strong case for this interpretation.
126. *Domostroi*, 108.
127. *Stat'i o razvodax*, expanded version, arts. 10–11, in *DKU*, 207. The conditions under which a husband could beat his wife were similar in medieval Bohemia; see Klassen, "Marriage and Family," 269–270.
128. Almazov, 3:154, Voprosy Ilji, art. 16, in RIB, 6:60.

A woman could obtain a divorce if her husband threatened her economic well-being by building up massive debts, selling himself and her into slavery, or being a habitual drunkard. If the husband both committed adultery and beat his wife, she could divorce him after a warning.[129] Neither adultery nor wife-beating alone constituted sufficient cause.

Despite this legal limitation on the wife's right to seek release from an abusive husband, surviving ecclesiastical court records indicate that women indeed did petition successfully for divorce on grounds of physical abuse. In this way, the provision in canon law to permit divorce in cases of marital rape was extended to nonsexual types of *nasilie*.[130]

A woman, Irinka, and her father, Griška Filipov Popov, petitioned against her husband, Vedenij, and his father, Arist Kondratov. Irinka's right arm had been so injured by her husband's beatings that she could no longer work. Fearing for her life, Griška took his daughter home. Irinka wanted to become a nun, and demanded that her husband and father-in-law buy her a cell and provide a pension. At first Arist denied beating Irinka at all; Vedenij said that he had only "instructed her because of her disobedience." Irinka's injuries, they claimed, were the result of an act of God, not their maltreatment. Neighbors testified on Irinka's behalf that she had been a chaste wife and a hard worker, and that the beating had not been warranted. Faced with this evidence, Vedenij and Arist settled out of court. It was arranged that Irinka would live apart from her husband, with "good people" who would care for her injuries. Vedenij would provide her with an annual income of a measure of rye, half a measure each of millet and oats, a *pud* of salt, and four *altyny* for clothing.[131]

In a similar case, Tatjanica and her father, Eroška Ivanov, won a judgment against her former husband, Gavrilko the hatmaker. During six years of marriage, Gavrilko had beaten Tatjanica and threatened to cut off her nose and sell her into slavery. Two years earlier, Gavrilko had forced Tatjanica, who was then pregnant, to take vows as a nun. Gavrilko immediately remarrried. Tatjanica did not mind escaping her abusive husband, but demanded that he return her dowry and provide her with a private cell and pension in the convent. The archbishop ordered an investigation, ruling that, if Tatjanica's case were substantiated, Gavrilko would have to pay her what she asked.[132]

The case of Annica Alekseeva *doč'* is most notable in regard to the court's protection of women from severe domestic violence. Annica's

129. Voprosy Kirika, art. 92, in RIB, 6:48; Smirnov, *Materialy*, 70.
130. Compare these Russian cases with English cases of the same period: Ingram, 183–184.
131. No. 183 in RIB, 12:866–875, dated to 1687.
132. No. 206 in ibid., 2:946–949.

husband, Vaska Kyčkin, first petitioned Metropolitan Pavel of Siberia for a divorce on the grounds of her adultery; he caught her with her lover. The metropolitan, finding Vaska's evidence incontrovertible, was prepared to grant his request, but Annica testified that she had been living apart from Vaska for almost a year because she feared that he would murder her. Thus the metropolitan had to decide between two grounds for divorce: the wife's adultery and the husband's attempted murder. He chose the latter, indicating his view that wife abuse was the more significant and serious offense.[133]

Though only the woman herself could demand a divorce, relatives who were concerned about her treatment could alert ecclesiastical and secular authorities to the problem. The relatives' petitions would describe the mistreatment, voice dire fears for the life and safety of their kinswoman, and point the finger at the likely culprit in case of her unnatural death. The statements to this effect were formulaic, and in some cases obvious overstatements; their purpose was to spur the ecclesiastical court into initiating an investigation.[134] The widow Oksin'ja Leontiev *doč'* Gurieva had to petition secular authorities to force the local ecclesiastical court to accept her warnings about the maltreatment of her daughter. Oksin'ja complained that her son-in-law and his uncle beat her daughter Natal'ja and deprived her of food and clothing. She feared that Natal'ja would be killed without a chance for a final confession and spiritual comfort. This sort of ill treatment Oksin'ja termed *nasilie*, even though there was no evidence that Natal'ja's husband abused her sexually.[135] Oprosin'ica Timofeeva *doč'* warned that her daughter Anjutka was being abused by her husband, father-in-law, and mother-in-law. The purpose of the daily beatings in this case was to persuade Anjutka to become a nun so that her husband could remarry.[136] In defense against an accusation of wife abuse, the widower Aleška Akpostanov petitioned to report the accidental death of his wife, Sulibija. He stated that as she was walking on the ice over the Syla River, drunk, she fell in. He offered the word of the other villagers to back up his testimony. The purpose of the petition was to forestall a suit against him by his wife's relatives.[137]

133. Nikolaj Kalačov, *Akty otnosjaščiesja do juridičeskago byta drevnej Rusi*, vol. 2 (SPb., 1864), 641–643, dated to 1683.

134. For an example of an obviously fallacious warning of imminent death, see no. 46 in RIB, 25:48–50. The author of the petition, Vaska Ivanov *syn* Skornjakov, is objecting to his brother-in-law's support of his wife's divorce action. He warns of the possibility of his wife's imminent death at the hands of her brother, which would seem, on the basis of evidence provided in the petition, to be most unlikely. This document is discussed in chap. 2.

135. No. 34 in RIB, 6:36, dated to 1627. No. 207 in ibid., 24:272–273, dated to 1655, is similar.

136. No. 183 in ibid., 25:236–237, dated to 1644.

137. No. 9 in Titov, 19, dated to 1670.

The husband who was condemned in a divorce action did not always accept the court's ruling with equanimity, as the petition by the nun Evpraksija attests. She appealed to Archimandrite Lavrentij of Ustjug to protect her from her former husband, Semen Kondrat'ev *syn* Vologžanin. Clearly Semen was outraged by the criticism of his conduct which Evpraksija's divorce implied. He came to the convent where she was residing, attacked Evpraksija with a knife, and injured her severely. Although Evpraksija did not mention forced sex, she did term her husband's attack *nasil'stvo*. Semen also took her valuables; one purpose of the petition was to recover them. Two laywomen who lived in the convent abetted Semen in his attack on Evpraksija, feeling him to be in the right. Another nun, Domnika, witnessed the crime, and ran to the metropolitan's court for help. The metropolitan's bailiffs came, took Semen's knife, and expelled him. Evpraksija then took refuge with her daughter and son-in-law and his father, fearing that Semen would come to the convent to attack her again. Semen found her anyway and threatened her protectors. In this case, the formulaic warnings about a life-or-death situation may well have been accurate.[138]

Some victims of wife-beating abandoned their husbands without a formal divorce. A petition to Metropolitan Varlaam by Kuzma Ivanov *syn* Popov describes such a situation. Kuzma charged that his stepdaughter Aleksandra Evsiv'eva *doč'* Kyzemkina suffered from such ill treatment at the hands of her husband and father-in-law that she ran away. At the time he filed the complaint, Kuzma had not located his stepdaughter.[139] Cases of runaway wives are not uncommon in the records of seventeenth-century Russian ecclesiastical courts.

When a wife left her husband, he had to report her absence to the ecclesiastical authorities. Of course, no husband admitted to abusing his wife. The aim of the petition was rarely to have the errant wife returned; most often the husband wished only to report his wife's disappearance so that he would not be subjected to ecclesiastical penalties for failure to cohabit with his legal spouse. The petition would also open the way to legal remarriage for the abandoned husband.[140] In some cases, the husband petitioned for the purpose of recording serious charges against his absent wife, as a defense against any future claims she might bring against him. One irate husband, the icon painter Loginko Mixajlov, accused his wife, Ofimka, of adultery and desertion while he had been in jail. He had been imprisoned as a result of Ofimka's charges against him, and had to assert that they were really still married despite this past history of court-ordered separation.[141]

138. No. 105 in RIB, 25:128–131, dated to 1632.
139. No. 99 in ibid., 25:123, dated to 1632.
140. Nos. 5, and 26 in ibid., 6–7, 27–28; no. 10 in Titov, 19–20, dated to 1670.
141. No. 156 in RIB, 25:205, dated to 1638.

Naturally, there would be a strong suspicion that only an extremely undesirable situation would motivate a wife to leave the security of her husband's home for an uncertain future. For this reason, one petitioner, the priest Pavel, stated explicitly that his runaway daughter-in-law Annica Kirjanova *doč'* had not been beaten or abused. Other facts in his petition suggested that Annica had reasonable grievances: she had left her husband three times previously to return to her natal family, who refused to order her to return to him.[142] It is unlikely that a mother, who presumably helped to arrange the marriage, would encourage her daughter to abandon it without cause.

Relatives who helped a wife to abandon her lawful husband became liable to a countersuit by the husband and his family. Nikita Piminov *syn* Lunev gathered a group of friends and took his daughter back from Ivaška, the son of Miška Stepanov *syn* Eloxin. He then petitioned the ecclesiastical court of Ustjug, apparently on his daughter's behalf. Miška retaliated by petitioning Tsar Aleksej to charge Nikita with assault against him and his family, asking that the secular authorities direct the church of Ustjug to record the countersuit.[143] Considerable violence could result when the woman's natal family intervened on her behalf. Biljaiko Artem'ev *syn*, for example, accused six members of his father-in-law's family of attacking him and his friends with arrows and spears, severing his arm and inflicting other injuries.[144]

When the wife's natal family did not support her attempt to gain release from an abusive husband, she had little recourse. After all, wives were expected to tolerate physical punishment from their husbands, provided he had "just cause" and did not cause permanent injury. Matrena Klimantova *doc'* ran away from her husband, Stenka, because he and his father, Anofrejko Ivanov, beat her. Her brother, Evdokim, was interested in preserving the marital alliance, and joined forces with Anofrejko and Stenka to have Matrena located and returned. Meanwhile, Matrena found shelter with one Ivaško Pečatin in another village and bore him an illegitimate child. She then wandered from village to village, earning her own living. In a distant place she entered into an illegal second marriage with Miška Čertopoloxov and became pregnant by him. The ecclesiastical court that heard the case insisted upon returning Matrena to her lawful first husband, Stenka, who was instructed not to beat her. Ivaško was given custody of Matrena's illegitimate child by him; presumably Miška was given custody of the second child. The

142. No. 174 in ibid., 226–227, dated to 1640. No. 117 in ibid., 146, dated to 1633, is very similar.
143. No. 243 in ibid., 329–331, dated to 1665.
144. No. 264 in ibid., 14:608–609, dated to 1612.

priest who baptized Ivaško's child without demur and the priest who married Matrena and Miška were placed under archiepiscopal review.[145]

Restrictions on violence against wives extended to forced sex. Medieval Slavic writings on marriage contained no equivalent to the Western concept of conjugal debt, which justified sexual intercourse as a duty to one's spouse. The belief that sex originated with the Devil justified a woman in refusing sexual intercourse at any time, even with her husband. Canon law permitted a wife to seek a divorce if her husband "pillaged her clothing," a euphemism for attempted rape.[146] In penitential literature, the priest was instructed to give a heavy penance to a man who forced his wife to engage in anal sex. Some versions of this provision were purposely vague, permitting the priest to intervene whenever the wife complained about her husband's "evil rape."[147] For a man even to lay a hand on his wife in sexual desire without her consent was a sin, carrying a penance of six days.[148] These provisions against marital rape may seem remarkably advanced, but it should be remembered that the motivation was not protection of the woman's autonomy—after all, a husband could beat his wife, within moderation, with impunity. Rather, the motivation may be found in the Slavic belief that lust was improper, even in marriage, and should not be encouraged.

False Accusations of Rape

The ease with which a charge of rape could be accepted was not always conducive to the triumph of justice. The records of a few rape cases, such as that of Tanka Ivanova *doč'* Zybova, indicate that women sometimes filed spurious charges. In most societies, false accusations of rape would seem to be unlikely, because the victim is often subject to scorn and disbelief.[149] However, the tendency of medieval Russian courts to grant credence to accusations of rape provided a much different context for false accusations. Furthermore, the women who were most likely to make spurious charges were those whose illicit sex was

145. No. 180 in ibid., 12:856–860, dated to 1687. As we saw in chap. 2, Matrena tried unsuccessfully to argue against the validity of her marriage to Stenka on the grounds of his failure to consummate it.
146. "*Porty sja grabiti načnet'*": Voprosy Kirika, art. 92, in RIB, 6:48. A later version of this ruling in the "Pravilo 'ašče dvoženec'" (Smirnov, *Materialy*, 70) rewrites this provision to make the grounds for divorce theft of the wife's clothing (for the purpose of paying the husband's debts).
147. "Ašče že nasilstvuet" zol" muž", togda žena da izvestit" duxovnym", tii že sovet" blag" dadut"": Pavlov, *Nomokanon pri Bol'šom Trebnike*, 168.
148. Almazov, 3:275.
149. Brownmiller, 386–388.

already public knowledge. A woman in seventeenth-century Russia was better off claiming to be a victim of rape than admitting herself to be an adulteress.

An unmarried girl, Pelagija Prokop'eva *doč'*, gave birth to a daughter on February 5, 1690. When the local priest questioned her, Pelagija named the blacksmith's servant boy, Evdokimko Elizarev *syn*, as the father. She accused him of having raped her in the bathhouse during Lent. Pelagija admitted to sleeping with Evdokimko willingly after that. Evdokimko denied everything. Faced with conflicting testimony, the court ordered both to be flogged in the hope of eliciting the truth. Although neither confessed to perjury, the two agreed to a settlement. Evdokimko acknowledged paternity by paying court costs and a sum for the support of the child. Pelagija dropped the charge of rape but refused the court's offer to insist that Evdokimko marry her.[150] In this case, the court had every reason to disbelieve Pelagija. She had not reported the supposed rape when it occurred, and had engaged willingly in illicit sex. Furthermore, a little arithmetic suggests that the child, born on February 5, had not been conceived during Lent. It is likely that Pelagija invented the rape in order to force Evdokimko to take responsibility for the child and to acquit herself of culpability in illicit fornication. The ploy worked only because the court was predisposed to take the accusation of rape seriously.

Because a rape charge was so serious, even the threat of one was to be feared, but such a charge could backfire. In 1626 Natal'ja Bobina threatened to accuse Mitka Emel'janov *syn* Xodutin if he did not marry her. Natal'ja chose Mitka as her prospective husband, he claimed, because she owed him two rubles and did not want to have to repay him. Mitka rebuffed her, and she proceeded to make public accusations against him. Her father arrived on the scene to disavow responsibility for his daughter's charges, saying that she was insane.[151]

The motivation to file a false charge of rape is usually clear. By claiming to be the unwilling victim of assault, a woman avoided a fine or penance for engaging in illicit sex. The man who fathered her child could be forced to provide for it financially. If he refused to admit responsibility, the woman could, through a spurious charge of rape, constrain some

150. No. 212 in RIB, 12:988–990. Because Russian canon law did not regard marriage as a "cure" for rape, Pelagija could not have used the charge as a means of forcing Evdokimko to marry her. In Renaissance Venice, where a rapist could be required to marry his victim, women were widely believed to make false accusations of rape to force marriage with reluctant men. Venetian authorities, suspicious of young women's accusations of rape, punished offenders very lightly. See Ruggiero, 98.

151. No. 22 in RIB, 25:23.

other man to take responsibility instead. The woman had nothing to lose by this maneuver—her pregnancy already testified to her misconduct in the eyes of the church. Women could also use accusations of rape as revenge against men who displeased them. Because the courts regarded a charge of rape soberly, regardless of the reputation of the woman who filed it, an accusation of this type was a sure way of getting an obnoxious man into a great deal of trouble.

It is clear that medieval Slavic society simultaneously censured rape in its legal and ecclesiastical norms and sanctioned attitudes and structures that justified it. While both ecclesiastical and secular authorities deplored the social disruption caused by rape, physical violence, and insult to women, the protection of women in subordinate positions was accorded lower priority than the preservation of the social order. For that reason, an attack on a woman of a lower class or of poor reputation was punished less severely than an attack on an aristocratic woman. It was more important to social stability to retain masters' authority over their slaves than to uphold slave women's chastity. Women were supposed to defer to their husbands and accept chastisement unless it was exceptionally brutal and unprovoked. In order to escape from an abusive marriage, de facto if not de jure a wife needed the support of her natal family. When a woman did not conduct herself in a manner appropriate to her place in society—if she insulted men, for instance, or got drunk— rape was popularly considered appropriate retaliation.

In the ecclesiastical view, rape served as evidence of evil active in the world: the uncontrolled expression of lust, which threatened the purity and ultimately the salvation of the community. Secular society regarded rape as a crime of violence, the ultimate insult against a woman and her family in a society that valued honor highly. The victim of rape might be blameless, but she was still defiled as a consequence of engaging in illicit sex, and, especially in the South Slavic tradition, was treated as a repentant sinner. But on balance rape law and its prosecution in the courts worked to the victim's advantage. The penalties, if the victim was blameless, were substantial. The victim's prior sexual conduct, while an issue, did not imply automatic consent. The court did not assume the woman's complicity; on the contrary, the veracity of the woman's testimony was accepted until the overwhelming weight of the evidence indicated otherwise. Consequently, women could use false accusations of rape to manipulate and pressure men.

Despite the strong position of women before the law in the case of rape, in general women's autonomy was sharply constrained. Women did not appear freely in public, did not participate openly in the institutions of political power, and did not choose their own husbands. Despite women's important economic role in the family, they were socially and often physically subject to their husbands. Women had recourse against rapists because rape constituted an insult to the family's honor and a violation of public morality. A woman whose family "deserved" insult, in return for an insult given or resistance in time of war, lost her right to protection. A woman who herself violated public morality by drunkenness or adultery lost any claim to popular sympathy. Medieval Slavs accepted the use of violence by superiors against inferiors and lawbreakers; this was the natural order of a sinful world. In these societies, as in any other that authorizes violence and subordinates women to men, rapes were bound to occur.

CHAPTER 6

Sex and the Clergy

The clergy played a dual role in the enforcement of the Orthodox sexual standard. First, clerics—and in particular parish priests—were expected to teach their spiritual children about the requirements of the Christian life and to impose penances for sins. Second, they were expected to practice what they preached, so to speak, by living their own lives according to the rules of the church. In this way, clerics could serve as examples of proper conduct.

The Orthodox Church presented two versions of Christian sexual conduct through the models of its clergy. The first consisted of monasticism. It was considered superior to other lifestyles, both ecclesiastical and laic, because of its exclusive devotion to prayer, works of charity, and asceticism. Monks and nuns not only did not marry but ideally had no sexual contact. The parish clergy embodied the second model of the Christian life. As a rule, they were married, and were supposed to live in exclusive and chaste Orthodox wedlock with their spouses.

The Slavic Orthodox churches were deeply concerned about the sexual behavior of their clergy, whether celibate or married. A cleric's sexual impropriety affected more than his soul and that of his partner. In spiritual terms, his entire community, either monastery or parish, was endangered by his lapse. Inappropriate sexual activity at an inopportune time could threaten the sanctity of the sacraments. In practical terms, a cleric's violation made enforcement of the rules among the laity exceedingly difficult. The populace could readily point the finger at erring clerics, and argue that the standard was impossibly high if even churchmen fell into sin. Further, they could accuse churchmen of hypocrisy for teaching one standard and living by another. The anonymous author of one version of rules for priests wrote: "Be afraid, you priests, who have heard how Christ cannot find a place among you, because of the stench of fleshly desire. You lose the blessing of the Holy Spirit through your profligacy. How will you teach the common people purity and fear of God, when you do not restrain yourselves? How will you teach those who receive the body and blood of the Lord from you?"[1] For the spiritual well-being of the community, as well as the maintenance of ecclesiastical authority, it was necessary for hierarchs to regulate carefully the sexual expression of their subordinates.

In Slavic Orthodox countries, as elsewhere in medieval Christian Europe, the church people enjoyed immunity from prosecution by secular powers. In granting this immunity, the state did not intend that offenders within the church should escape punishment. On the contrary, by stating specifically that clerics who erred were subject to ecclesiastical courts, the secular authorities indicated that they expected ecclesiastical authorities to prosecute clerical violators.[2]

The rules for the sexual conduct of the clergy were more extensive and more stringent than those for the laity. Certain behaviors permissible for the laity were forbidden to the parish clergy. A high standard of sexual purity was a requirement for entry into the priesthood. Penalties for violations tended to be more severe, especially for individuals in the higher ranks. The penances listed in *trebnici* and nomocanons represented recommendations rather than mandates; the erring cleric's superior was empowered to impose any penalty he saw fit. As for the laity, the penalty could include extra fasts, prayers, and exclusion from communion; for priests, it could also include a prohibition on administering the sacraments for a limited period or permanently.

Parish Clergy

Clerical Marriage

According to Orthodox canon law and custom, parish clergy who lived "in the world," ministering to the spiritual needs of lay people, had to be married. This position was an outgrowth of early church policy, which permitted married men to serve as priests. In the West, married status was never a requirement for parish service, and ultimately celibacy became the rule. In the Orthodox world, celibacy was mandated for monastic life and for the upper levels of the hierarchy, but not for parish priests and deacons. Canons of the Eastern church forbade a priest to

---

1. Smirnov, *Materialy*, 98; see also 110.
2. See, e.g., Jaroslav's Ustav, art. 46, in *DKU*, 97.

marry after ordination; a man who was single at that time had to remain celibate. However, a married man could be ordained a priest, and he was under no obligation to repudiate his marriage.[3] As celibacy became the rule in the Roman Catholic Church, Orthodox polemicists seized upon this point of difference between Western and Eastern Christianity to insist that marriage was not only permissible for parish clergy but advisable.[4] Those who insisted on celibacy were anathematized.[5]

The Eastern church did not officially require all parish clergy to be married, but in this matter custom took the force of law. It became a virtual requirement for parish clergy to marry before ordination. Orthodox hierarchs feared that the temptations of living side by side with women would prove too great for parish clergy, and felt that marriage would keep them from sin. Clerics who wished to remain celibate were channeled into monastic service. Those who intended to marry had to do so before ordination, often while serving a sort of apprenticeship in the rank of reader or chanter. Marriage for deacons fell into a gray area of canon law. Although some canons categorized them with priests, and thus forbade them to marry after achieving that rank, an alternative tradition permitted marriage for a deacon, provided he had informed the bishop of his desire to marry before ordination.[6] Metropolitan Ioann II of Russia espoused the first view, requiring subdeacons who intended careers in the "white" clergy to marry before ordination, and forbidding marriage afterward.[7]

The Orthodox acceptance of married clergy was based more on practical than on theoretical considerations. Married clerics resided more comfortably in the lay community, where they could provide a living model of Christian life "in the world." Married priests were easier to recruit, and they tended to provide their own replacements, in their sons. They were also less likely to seek illicit sexual outlets if they had wives. Married clergy clearly appealed to Tsar Boris of Bulgaria in the ninth

---

3. Peć 77, ff. 224v–225r; NBS 48, ff. 40, 147v–148r; Hil. 300, f. 42r–v; Hil. 466, f. 51v; GIM, Sin. 227, f. 300r; *Sintagmat*, 160; *Dejanija moskovskix soborov*, synod of 1667, 88v. The Eastern church's policy on clerical marriage was set at the Council of Constantinople in 692; see Bullough, *Sexual Variance*, 320–321. The issue of clerical celibacy first rose to prominence at the Council of Elvira in the early fourth century. The council recognized chastity as a mark of Christian life which the clergy, as the moral elite, should follow. The council also expressed concern to protect the sacraments from ritual defilement by priests' contact with sex. See Brundage, *Law, Sex, and Christian Society*, 69–70.
4. NBS 48, f. 149r–v; *Sintagmat*, 158. For an example of a polemic put in the form of a discussion of "Jewish" custom, see Hil. 301, f. 122v.
5. BAN-S 48, n.p.; Hil. 378, f. 166r–v; Peć 77, ff. 264v–265r; *Kormčaja*, 245, citing Gangre Council, art. 4.
6. NBS 48, f. 63r–v; GIM, Sin. 227, ff. 82v–83r.
7. Beneševič, *Sbornik pamjatnikov po istorii cerkovnago prava*, 112.

century; he specifically asked Pope Nicholas I about the Roman Catholic stand against them.[8]

The conferring of ecclesiastical rank on married men did not simultaneously indicate official endorsement of marital sexuality. On the contrary, clerical sexual activity, even within the acceptable confines of marriage, constituted a threat to the sanctity of the sacraments.

Abstinence in Clerical Marriages

To insist that the cleric and his wife refrain from sexual intercourse entirely would defeat the purpose of having married clergy and would be tantamount to embracing an aspect of the Latin heresy. In order to maintain ritual purity, married clerics were expected to abstain from conjugal relations during fasts and on days when they would serve in the church.[9] Weekly days of observance for priests, as for all Christians, included all Wednesdays, Fridays, Saturdays, and Sundays, as well as the special fast days.[10] Clerics usually served in the church on those days, so conjugal relations were prohibited for that reason also. In addition to following the rules for the laity, clerics were to abstain from sex on the day preceding performance of the liturgy, in order to prepare spiritually for the rite: if a priest held services on Wednesdays and Fridays, sexual intercourse was proscribed for him on Tuesdays and Thursdays in addition. Should he need to serve on a Tuesday, Monday was eliminated as well. Bishop Nifont proposed a compromise, recognizing that a demand for abstinence all week would lead to violations of the rule: if the priest could not forgo sex altogether, he could sleep with his wife "between days"—that is, before sunrise on Monday morning.[11] Less understanding canonists ruled that the priest and his wife would have to exercise restraint in this situation.[12] The priest and his wife were not only forbidden to engage in marital intercourse on the night preceding performance of the liturgy, but they were not even allowed to share the same bed.[13]

Hierarchs were not so naïve as to assume that their instructions on abstinence would always be followed. Most ordered that priests who slept with their wives at night refrain from performing the liturgy the

---

8. *Izvori za bŭlgarskata istorija*, 7:109.

9. NBS 48, f. 149v. Arts. 4 and 25 of the Carthaginian Council were cited in defense of this position; see *Kormčaja*, 313, 328–329. While married clergy remained in the West, they also were under prohibitions in order to prevent their defiling the sacraments by marital sex. See Brundage, *Law, Sex, and Christian Society*, 150.

10. Almazov, 3:184–185.

11. Voprosy Kirika, arts. 29, 77, in RIB, 6:31, 45.

12. Smirnov, *Materialy*, 137.

13. SANU 124(29), f. 32v.

following day. Those who violated this rule could be placed under penance for forty days or even a year.[14] On the other hand, Bishop Nifont of Novgorod permitted the priest to serve in this case, but he had to bathe first and recite prayers of purification, and then read the Gospel outside the sanctuary, and could not take communion himself.[15] His motivation for this liberal view was apparently a desire to make sure that lay parishioners were not deprived of the sacraments because of the priest's weakness. If a priest engaged in conjugal relations with his wife after performing the liturgy, the usual penance was forty days or six weeks of fasting. The offense was condemned as a form of blasphemy; the priest had consumed the body and blood of Christ, and it behooved him to refrain from indulging in bodily pleasures as long as the holy gifts were inside him.[16] One late-fifteenth-century Russian text of unusual severity mandated abstention from marital sex for a year.[17]

Medieval Slavic episcopal letters include considerable discussion of the question of sexual abstinence for priests during fasts. The discussion paralleled that on abstinence for that laity. Archbishop Ilja of Novgorod espoused the most liberal view, ordering priests to give communion on Easter to those who engaged in marital intercourse during Lent. He inquired sardonically of the conservatives who demanded strict observance, "And you, being priests, how many of you want to serve, and on how many days do you separate yourselves from your wives?"[18] Bishop Nifont argued that restraint was recommended for the "white," or secular, clergy, if not for the laity, in imitation of Christ's fast, but it was not essential.[19] The most conservative view required total abstinence for clergy and laity alike during the forty days of Great Lent. Although this view originated among the Greek Fathers, it was not included in the Greek nomocanons. The compilers of the Slavic version deliberately added it.[20] This strict interpretation of the Lenten rules for the parish clergy became dominant in the Slavic Orthodox tradition in the sixteenth and seventeenth centuries.

The rules prohibiting marital sex on the eve of church rituals could not prevent involuntary nocturnal emissions, termed "demonic temptation." Extensive rules were formulated concerning the circumstances under which a parish priest might still serve despite having experienced

14. Hil. 305, f. 116r; Almazov, 3:277; Smirnov, *Materialy*, 99, 105; *Sintagmat*, 200–201.
15. Voprosy Kirika, arts. 27–28, in RIB, 6:30–31. See also art. 29, p. 31.
16. E.g., BNL 246(103), f. 157r; BNL 251(200), f. 127r; Rila 1/20(48), f. 189r; Hil. 169, f. 71r; Smirnov, *Materialy*, 82, 98, 99, 105, 110, 132.
17. "Voprosy i otvety pastyrskoj praktiki," art. 31, in RIB, 6:863.
18. "Poučenie arxiepiskopa Ilja," art. 18, in RIB, 6:365.
19. Voprosy Kirika, art. 52, in RIB, 6:37–38.
20. Pavlov, *Nomokanon pri Bol'šom Trebnike*, 166–167.

this mark of diabolical attention. The weight of clerical opinion held that it was better for a priest not to perform the sacraments on the day he experienced a nocturnal emission, especially if he had brought it upon himself by masturbation or lustful thoughts. However, if there was no one else to serve, and the parishioners would be left without access to the sacrament, he was permitted to serve, after he bathed and recited penitential prayers.[21] A few codes also imposed a penance of seven or ten days.[22] When a priest noticed semen on his clothing but did not recall a "temptation," he was permitted to serve, after he had changed into a clean robe.[23] Special rules concerned instances when a priest or deacon fell asleep in the church and experienced the "temptation" there; the penance consisted of seven days of fasting and a hundred prostrations a day.[24] When the incident occurred in the sanctuary, the penance was raised to forty days, and the altar had to be sprinkled with holy water. A similar procedure, with a penance of three hundred prostrations, was prescribed for the same occurrence in the choir loft. If the priest failed to purify the choir loft before reading the liturgy, the penance was raised to six hundred prostrations.[25]

As a further step to safeguard the sacred from contamination by sexuality, deacons were warned against permitting evil and lustful thoughts to enter their minds while assisting in the liturgy. Priests and deacons were also warned to bathe after engaging in marital sex and before putting on vestments or entering the sanctuary for nonliturgical duties.[26] Although canonists ruled that a priest could continue to wear his cross while engaging in marital relations with his wife, the existence of the ruling indicates that some clerics had reservations about the practice.[27] The extent of these rules, which far surpass the requirements for the laity's, indicates the level of concern for the sanctity of the priest's office.

Limitations on Clerical Marriage

Orthodox canonists needed to ascertain that married clergy confined their sexual activity to licit intercourse with their wives. A certain leeway might be permitted for laymen, but the clergy were supposed to be

21. E.g., BNL 684, f. 161r–v; Rila 1/20(48), ff. 34v, 190r; SANU 124(29), ff. 32v, 35r, 38r; Voprosy Savy, art. 17, and "Voprosy i otvety pastyrskoj praktiki," art. 58, in RIB, 6:55–56, 867; Almazov, 3:185. Bathing for pleasure was prohibited to a priest before or after reading the liturgy; see Almazov, 3:277; Smirnov, *Materialy*, 99.
22. Dečani 68, f. 277v, and 69, f. 108v.
23. Smirnov, *Materialy*, 44.
24. Sinai 37, f. 104v.
25. Hil. 304, ff. 111v–112r; Dečani 70, f. 255r–v.
26. Almazov, 3:181, 184; Smirnov, *Materialy*, 94, 103, 106.
27. Smirnov, *Materialy*, 118.

beyond suspicion, a model of purity and piety. In order to have a priestly class of reputable people, church hierarchs forbade ordination to candidates who had committed serious sins. Some offenses that contraindicated ordination were religious, such as participation in pagan rites or the practice of sorcery. Others were grave civil offenses, such as murder and brigandage. But the first-named and most numerous sins were sexual.

Clerical marriages had to be of unquestionable validity. A candidate for the priesthood or deaconate was permitted only the one marriage, fully in accordance with canon law. A marriage contracted within a prohibited degree of kinship, between underaged individuals, or otherwise in violation of canon law made a candidate ineligible for ordination. The "dispensation" of a second union was not available to a man who intended to present himself as a model to the community.[28] Even a previous legal marriage made a man ineligible for the priesthood or any other clerical position, according to biblical prescriptions.[29] For purposes of entry into the priesthood, a betrothal counted as a marriage. A candidate who had been betrothed to another woman before his marriage could be automatically disqualified, even though the first union had not been consummated.[30] A few codes permitted ordination provided the union had ended in the death of the fiancée while she was still a virgin.[31] An exception could be made if the first fiancée broke off the engagement, and the betrothal had lasted less than six years.[32]

A proper marriage was celebrated in accordance with church canons. A man who took a wife through a clandestine wedding or by force was ineligible for the parish priesthood.[33] Some canonists made exceptions, however. One allowed the candidate the option of taking monastic vows and being ordained a "black" priest after three years.[34] Another permitted ordination after the common law union was solemnized in church.[35]

The same criteria for ordination to the priesthood were applied to candidates for the lesser positions of deacon and sexton.[36] A man who entered into a second marriage was ineligible to become a sexton in a secular parish, although it was permissible for him to serve in that capacity in a monastery, after taking vows as a monk.[37]

28. Sreznevskij, *Svedenija i zametki*, 152.
29. Kiev 191, f. 773v, citing St. Basil. See 1 Tim. 3:2 for the biblical rule.
30. Smirnov, *Materialy*, 86.
31. Ibid., 58, 118; Tixonravov, *Pamjatniki otrečennoj russkoj literatury*, 1:295.
32. *Sintagmat*, 190–191.
33. BNL 251(200), f. 130v.
34. Rila 1/20(48), f. 39r.
35. Smirnov, *Materialy*, 117.
36. "Otvety mitropolita Kipriana igumenu Afanasiju," in RIB, 6:259.
37. "Tri svjatitel'skija poučenija," in RIB, 6:924.

Extramarital Sex   [handwritten: No Liturgy for Men who desired to be priest]

The candidate's extramarital sexual behavior came under scrutiny. Although most Slavic hierarchs were willing to forgive bachelors their peccadilloes, this leniency did not extend to men who planned careers in the church. Premarital sex with anyone or anything made a man ineligible to become a priest. Prohibited activities included even one instance of illicit fornication before marriage; the woman partner's status was not relevant.[38] A candidate was disqualified even if his sole premarital sexual experience was with his fiancée, on the grounds that he had "stolen the marriage."[39] If he was already a reader in the church, he was permitted to remain in that function, after a hiatus of a year in penance. All roles as "server" (*služitel'*) were barred to him, including the subdeaconate.[40] Bestiality, "with something unclean or with cattle," also made a candidate ineligible for ordination.[41]

Homosexual relations sometimes made a man ineligible to become a priest; the ruling depended on the method of intercourse and the opinion of the canonist. According to St. John the Penitent, a boy who had been the passive or active partner in intercrural homosexual relations could still be admitted to the priesthood, after confession and penance. He reasoned that intercrural intercourse did not constitute a "complete fall." Anal penetration was regarded as more defiling than intercrural intercourse; in this case both active and passive partners were barred from ecclesiastical service. St. John did not regard the passive partner as more guilty in anal than in intercrural penetration; he could not be held fully accountable for his sins before reaching maturity. However, submission to anal intercourse was "defiling" even when it was involuntary, and a "defiled" man could not become a priest.[42] This view accorded with general canons on homosexuality and ancient Greek attitudes. In this case, the suitability of the candidate for ordination was determined not by his own actions, but by his standing before the community: a man who had submitted to anal penetration had lowered himself to the position of a subordinate or a woman.

Patriarch Evtimij of Bulgaria did not explicitly disagree with the teachings of St. John the Penitent, who, he said, "had revealed himself to

38. Kiev 191, ff. 773v–774r, and the decisions of the church council at Vladimir in 1274, in RIB, 6:90–91, include a complete listing of sins that preclude admittance into the priesthood.
39. E.g., Hil. 628, f. 18r; NBS 10, f. 29r.
40. Peć 77, ff. 224r–225r; *Sintagmat*, 162, 187. GIM, Sin 227, f. 195v, adds the condition that the reader must have had a formal betrothal to qualify even for this leniency.
41. Hil 302, f. 23v; Rila 1/20(48), f. 16r–v.
42. E.g., Troicki, 69–70; Pavlov, *Nomokanon pri Bol'šom Trebnike*, 334; BNL 684, f. 171v; SANU 123(28), ff. 59v–60r; Kiev 191, f. 774r–v; Hil. 628, f. 38v; similar: SANU 129(24), f. 16v. See Zaozerskij and Xaxanov, 55, for a different version of this rule.

be the most compassionate and the most merciful to the human race,"
but he did not entirely share the saint's generosity to those who engaged
in masturbation and intercrural homosexual relations. "If the great St.
Paul expels men from the Kingdom of God for masturbation," Evtimij
wrote, "what can be said about those who sin with another person?" He
personally advised that a bishop might overlook one or two incidents of
masturbation in determining a candidate's eligibility for ordination, but
nothing further. In particular, he considered the active partner in intercrural relations to be defiled.[43] Following Evtimij's interpretation, an
occasional Bulgarian code forbade ordination to either the active or the
passive partner in youthful homosexual relations.[44]

Like intercrural homosexuality, masturbation alone did not preclude
a candidate's ordination. If he committed this sin without knowing it to
be one, he could still be admitted to the priesthood, once he was educated and repentant.[45] The candidate had to confess these sins fully and
undergo penance before he could become a priest.[46] If he continued to
masturbate after receiving instruction, he was banned from clerical
ranks above that of reader.[47]

The candidate's conduct after his marriage also came under scrutiny.
Ordination was forbidden to a man who engaged in "unnatural" intercourse with his wife or any other woman after marriage.[48] A candidate
who had committed any one of these sins could no more become a
priest, according to St. Basil, than the dead could be resurrected in this
world.[49]

Most codes were unequivocal in their prohibition of ordination to the
priesthood of any deacon who had engaged in extramarital sex, though
apparently he was allowed to continue in his rank.[50] Some codes added
a penance of four years, sometimes with a diet of bread and water.[51] A
reader was also permitted to keep his rank after an extramarital affair,
undergoing a four-year penance.[52] A less common tradition mandated
that the offending deacon be deposed. In this case, he was not placed
under any other penance or excluded from communion, on the grounds

43. Kaluzniacki, 222–223.
44. BNL 324(520), ff. 2v–3v.
45. BNL 684, ff. 171v–172r; Hil. 628, f. 19r; Hil. 301, f. 86r.
46. BNL 324(520), f. 3v.
47. SANU 124(29), f. 17r.
48. BNL 24(520), ff. 2v–3r; BNL 684, f. 162v; Kiev 191, f. 683v; Hil. 301, f. 85r; NBS 654, f. 110v.
49. E.g., Troicki, 78; BNL 324(520), ff. 2v–3v; Hil. 301, f. 107v.
50. E.g., Hil. 167, f. 227v; Smirnov, *Materialy*, 86, 100; VAT-Bor. 15, f. 478r; BNL 246(103), f. 160r, 161v, 165r; BNL 251(200), f. 129v; Dečani 68, ff. 279r, 282r.
51. E.g., Dečani 68, ff. 279r, 282r; BNL 246(103), ff. 160r, 161r, 165r.
52. BNL 246(103), f. 160r, and 251(200), f. 129v; Hil. 171, f. 255v; Dečani 69, f. 110r.

that loss of the deaconate was sentence enough.[53] This leniency did not apply to deacons who had engaged in adultery (that is, extramarital sex with a married woman), homosexuality, bestiality, or rape, or to those who fathered illegitimate children.[54] Officially, the deacon who committed these offenses was barred from the priesthood and removed from his rank.

Despite the stringency of these rules, hierarchs apparently were willing to overlook certain deficiencies, sexual and otherwise, provided the candidate was otherwise suitable for ordination. Sins committed before a man was baptized as a Christian did not preclude his entry into the priesthood after his conversion.[55] Early church canons permitted a man to remain in an incestuous marriage after accepting baptism and still enter into clerical rank.[56] According to one anonymous Russian hierarch, only four conditions precluded ordination: illiteracy, manslaughter (literally, the "destruction of a soul"), theft, and his wife's unchastity. All other violations could be healed with a penance before the candidate assumed priestly rank.[57] He did not make the candidate's personal sexual behavior an absolute condition for ordination, and some of his compatriots agreed. Metropolitan Kirill of Russia, in an encyclical to the bishops, implied that only premarital sex "with many" would make a man ineligible for clerical rank. He also excused thefts committed in childhood.[58] Bishop Nifont was asked whether a bachelor who had fathered a single illegitimate child could be ordained a deacon. He refused permission, not on the grounds that the single incident made the candidate unfit but because he doubted that he sinned only once. In another case, he ordered that a priest or deacon who had an illicit affair with only one woman be removed from his office, but allowed a subdeacon in the same circumstance to continue in his rank. When asked about the possibility of ordaining a man who had deflowered one maiden and married another, Bishop Nifont's response was surprisingly vague: "Don't ask me about this: both of them must be pure."[59] A few Russian codes did not entirely bar the offending deacon from ordination. According to one code, he would be subject to this penalty only if he engaged in illicit sex while already under penance.[60] The Russians were

53. Hil. 378, f. 153r; Peć 77, ff. 200v–202r; NBS 48, f. 177r; Hil. 378, f. 153r; ZSL-P, 145; *Kormčaja*, 466–467, citing St. Basil, art. 3.
54. E.g., BNL 684, f. 157r; Hil. 171, f. 261r–v; Peć 77, f. 112r–v; Kiev 191, f. 775r; Smirnov, *Materialy*, 101; *Sintagmat*, 461.
55. Peć 77, f. 157r–v.
56. NBS 48, f. 209r.
57. Smirnov, *Materialy*, 119. On murder as an absolute obstacle, see ibid., 121.
58. VAT-Bor. 15, f. 482r–v.
59. Voprosy Kirika, arts. 79, 84, 80, in RIB, 6, 45–47.
60. Smirnov, *Materialy*, 39, 116.

lenient on the issue of literacy also: the Stoglav Council discussed the reasons why illiterate priests had been ordained.[61]

Certain conditions not of the candidate's own making also precluded his entry into the priesthood, although Slavic Orthodox clerics were not in complete agreement. According to a seventeenth-century Russian text, blindness or deafness made a candidate ineligible for ordination. An ordained priest who became blind or deaf was reassigned from liturgical duties to private prayer. In one view, a man born of a semilegal third marriage or an incestuous relationship was also forbidden to enter the priesthood. Any bishop who dared to ordain such a person was deposed from his office.[62] Other codes of canon law took the opposite point of view, and permitted the ordination of a worthy candidate despite his untoward birth.[63] A marginal comment, "Look!" in one manuscript of the *zakonik* indicates that this rule was not uniformly accepted in medieval Slavic society.[64] Although a man who castrated himself was forbidden to enter the priesthood, this restriction did not apply to someone who had been made a eunuch in childhood, or was born with a genital defect.[65] A final condition of ordination was the character of the priest's wife.

The person who ordained the priest was responsible for determining his suitability for the post. To ordain a man in violation of the canons was to ensure damnation: "Do not dare to testify for him to be a priest, for you will both burn. Be attentive to this with all your strength, so that you do not inherit the eternal fire, and you will not be like Judas, because you bestowed the priesthood on one who was not worthy."[66] To prevent the ordination of an unworthy candidate, hierarchs were urged to examine the future priest and his wife carefully in advance.[67] A priest who had successfully concealed his sins until after ordination was deposed from the priesthood, according to one version of the canons; another version, relating specifically to clandestine sexual sins, ruled that he was forbidden to read the liturgy, but he could continue in his rank.[68]

---

61. *Stoglav*, 91–92. See the discussion of the Stoglav ruling on illiterate priests in Jack E. Kollmann, 66–68.

62. Hil. 302, f. 24r.

63. See articles attributed to Nicetas, metropolitan of Iraklia, and Nicephoros of Constantinople, in Troicki, 75; also, Hil. 627, f. 29v; Peć 77, f. 286r–v.

64. Hil. 301, f. 117v. SANU 123(28), f. 120r–v, includes a question but no answer, either by accident or by design. In SANU 122(47), f. 47r, this provision was added to the text later.

65. Peć 77, ff. 159v–160v; Hil 378, f. 142r–v; Sreznevskij, 3:253.

66. Kiev 191, f. 774r; NBS 10, f. 52r.

67. Hil. 302, f. 98r. See "Svidetel'stvo duxovnika o stavlenike," in RIB, 6:909–910, for an example of the questions asked of a candidate at the time of ordination.

68. Hil. 628, f. 38r–v; Peć 77, f. 271r–v.

sin after marriage. Defrocked

If a priest later committed any of the sins that precluded ordination, he was defrocked. Slavic codes drawing on the rules of St. Basil specifically listed adultery, homosexuality, bestiality, "unnatural" intercourse with his wife, and sorcery as grounds to depose a priest.[69] Many also imposed a lengthy penance on the deposed priest: five to seven years for adultery, ten years for "sodomy."[70] Penances varied widely for bestiality, from two years to fifty years, sometimes varying with the cleric's age and marital status.[71] Coitus from the rear was a more serious offense, for which a priest or deacon could be removed from his rank.[72] Incest with any relative, including a third cousin, brought loss of rank, and frequently a penance of eight to ten years, depending on the degree of consanguinity.[73]

Several traditions arose for ways of dealing with a priest who engaged in extramarital sex. A few codes distinguished between a partner who was married and one who was not, in the manner of provisions for laymen. According to one code, if the priest had only one, unmarried woman as his mistress, he was subject only to loss of rank; if he kept several women, or if his mistress was married, he was placed under penance also.[74] Under another code, a priest lost his rank only if his extramarital partner was herself married; otherwise, he underwent a penance but kept his rank.[75]

Usually the penalty was the same regardless of the priest's choice of lover, and the sin was classified as "illicit fornication" (*blud*) rather than adultery. Many codes ordered that a priest who engaged in extramarital sex be deposed from his rank.[76] Some canonists considered loss of rank sufficient punishment, and permitted the erstwhile priest to continue to

69. E.g., Rila 1/20(48), f. 35r; BNL 324(520), f. 3v; BNL 684, f. 162v; Kiev 191, f. 683r; Hil. 628, f. 15r–v; Smirnov, *Materialy*, 90, 101, 136. "Unnatural" marital sex could be either anal intercourse or vaginal intercourse from the rear.

70. E.g., Sinai 37, f. 101r; Hil. 167, f. 225r; BNL 246(103), f. 160r–v; BNL 251(200), f. 129v; Smirnov, *Materialy*, 137.

71. Penances for bestiality by unmarried priests are not consistently lower or higher than for the same offense by married priests. To complicate determination of the penances, scribes sometimes misread the age specification in older manuscripts as the length of penance, creating a new tradition of extremely long periods of contrition. See, e.g., Sinai 37, f. 103r (10 years if unmarried and 30 years old, 13 years if married); BNL 684, ff. 156v–157r (2 years if unmarried and 30–40 years old, 10 years if married, including 3 on bread and water); Hil. 378, f. 166r (30 to 40 years if unmarried, 15 years if married, including 13 on bread and water); Hil. 171, f. 256v (30 to 50 years whether married or not); BNL 246(103), f. 160v (5 years, including 3 on bread and water); BNL 251(200), f. 130r (6 years if 30–40 years old).

72. Smirnov, *Materialy*, 64–65.

73. Codes specifically mention incest with a stepmother, mother-in-law, sister, and cousin: BNL 684, ff. 161v–162r; Rila 1/20(48), f. 35v; SANU 124(29), f. 33r–v.

74. Smirnov, *Materialy*, 137, 147; Zaozerskij and Xaxanov, 53–55.

75. SANU 124(29), ff. 23v–24r, 32v–33r.

76. Ibid., f. 14r–v; SANU 122(47), f. 11v; Smirnov, *Materialy*, 86, 131; Suvorov, 420; ZSL-P, 145.

receive communion without a penance, albeit as a layman.[77] Harsher codes imposed a penance in addition to loss of rank, varying from one year to nine.[78] A more liberal set of canons placed the offending priest under penance with a strict fast, usually for three to seven years, and curtailed his duties.[79] According to one fourteenth-century Russian code, a priest who engaged in illicit fornication underwent a dry fast for a mere seven days, with accompanying prostrations and prayers, and then resumed regular service.[80] If a married priest deflowered a virgin, he was ordered to refrain from reading the liturgy until he found a husband for the maiden, and then to fast for three years. Although he was to continue with careful observance of fasts and prayers for the rest of his life, apparently he was permitted to resume his priestly duties in full.[81]

Until the offender had been convicted in the metropolitan's court, it was permissible for laymen to receive communion from him; hierarchs emphasized, perhaps to a dubious populace, that the sacraments were still holy despite the sins of the priest who performed them. The church did not wish the laity to judge the worthiness of their priests by themselves; it would be too easy to deny clerical authority that way. Once the bishop had officially barred the priest from serving, it became a sin for anyone to receive the sacraments from him.[82]

If a priest committed a sexual sin that did not bar ordination, the penalty usually did not include permanent loss of rank. According to one code of canon law, a priest who engaged in masturbation was required to refrain from reading the liturgy for a year and to receive the usual forty-day penance and additional prostrations for the sin. If he gave up his sin, he was then allowed to resume his position. A priest who persisted in masturbating was defrocked.[83] One code mandated defrocking if the priest engaged in masturbation knowing it to be sinful; the year's suspension applied only if he had not known masturbation to

77. NBS 48, f. 40r; Peć 77, ff. 160v–161r; Almazov, 3:286.
78. Hil. 305, f. 116v (1 year); Smirnov, *Materialy*, 131 (6 years); SANU 124(29), f. 35r (9 years).
79. E.g., Sinai 37, f. 101v (3 years, or 5 years with 3 on bread and water if the priest was married); BNL 251(200), ff. 129v (7 years on bread and water), 129v–130r (3 years, 1 on bread and water); Hil. 171, f. 255v (4 years on bread and water); Dečani 68, ff. 279r (7 years, 3 on bread and water), 279v (5 years, 3 on bread and water, 100 prostrations).
80. Smirnov, *Materialy*, 137.
81. Rila 1/20(48), f. 35r–v; similar, SANU 124(29), f. 33r.
82. Smirnov, *Materialy*, 121. Tsar Boris raised this issue with Pope Nicholas I and received a similar response; see *Izvori za bŭlgarskata istorija*, 7:109–110.
83. E.g., BNL 684, ff. 161v, 172r; Hil. 627, f. 15r; Hil. 301, f. 86r; SANU 124(29), f. 33r. See also Pavlov, *Nomokanon pri Bol'šom Trebnike*, 184, for a comparison of the Slavic and Greek versions of this provision. Rila 1/20(48), which is more liberal on priests' sexual sins, omits the provision on defrocking for this sin (f. 35r).

be a sin—an interesting comment on the level of knowledge of some priests.[84] Another code, attributed to St. John the Penitent, reduced the priest to the rank of reader for this sin, but only on the second or third offense.[85] Mutual masturbation between a cleric and another man was treated in the same manner as masturbation alone: a year's suspension for the first offense, and reduction in rank upon the second or third repetition.[86] In keeping with the Greek and medieval Slavic traditions, homosexual relations that did not include anal penetration were not regarded as a serious offense. The sources were not in complete agreement whether self-castration required loss of rank. An eleventh-century code mandated only three years on bread and water.[87] Later canonists seem to have rejected this view in favor of treating self-castration as analogous to murder. One scribe crossed out the three-year penance and inserted a provision for loss of clerical rank.[88]

A deacon who often kissed women lustfully was barred from aiding in the performance of the liturgy until he overcame this defilement, but was permitted to continue to receive communion with the other deacons.[89] Other sexual activities that resulted in temporary removal from clerical duties included the practice of open-mouthed kissing, coitus interruptus, and non-vaginal intercourse as part of marital relations.[90] In such cases, the priest or deacon was forbidden to perform the liturgy while under penance.

Thus the strict requirements of sexual purity demanded of the clergy in theory could be eased in actuality. Canonists consistently barred from parish clergy only those men whose sexual sins were so serious and notorious that they would be held up to public ridicule. The persisting shortage of priests might have provided the primary motivation for leniency.[91]

Standards for Clerics' Wives

Principles of Slavic canon law established that a man who lived with an unchaste woman himself became an adulterer, regardless of his own conduct. For that reason, the moral status of the wife of a candidate for the priesthood became even more of an issue than the character of the

84. E.g., Kiev 191, f. 686r; Hil. 302, f. 79v; Rila 1/20(48), ff. 21v–22r; Hil. 305, f. 27r–v.
85. *Sintagmat*, 358.
86. Troicki, 67.
87. Sinai 37, f. 102r.
88. NBS 48, ff. 39v–40r; see also Peć 77, ff. 159r–160r; Dečani 68, f. 280r, and 69, f. 110v.
89. Peć 77, f. 225v.
90. Voprosy Kirika, art. 78, in RIB, 6:45.
91. Backus, 85–86.

candidate himself. Canon law established the appropriate choice of
spouse for a candidate for the priesthood or deaconate. To forestall later
problems, readers and chanters who wished to proceed to ordination
were required to gain approval of their choice of spouse.[92]

The wife of a parish priest was required to be a virgin at the time of
their marriage.[93] The manner in which she had lost her virginity was not
taken into consideration; it made no difference whether she had engaged
in premarital sex with her husband or with another man, or whether she
had been previously married and widowed. Even a prior betrothal made
a maiden an inappropriate choice for a prospective priest, because it was
the religious ceremony rather than consummation that validated a marriage.[94] If his wife was not a virgin at the time of marriage, a man could
enter the priesthood only after divorcing her.[95] Since marriage was in
actuality a requirement for the secular clergy, in such circumstances a
man could become only a monastic priest.

The prohibition of a prospective priest's marriage to a woman who
had violated canons of sexual conduct is understandable: if the priesthood was to present a model of the Christian life to the community, the
priest's wife had to be as respectable as her husband. Consequently,
Orthodox canons ruled that certain classes of women of low repute,
such as slaves, barmaids, actresses and dancers, were improper wives for
clerics.[96] If a priest discovered after his marriage and ordination that his
wife had been in a forbidden category, he was to cease serving in his
office, so that his parishioners would not have "festering thoughts."[97]
The prohibition of marriage to a widow is less understandable in this
context; the church did grant recognition, albeit reluctantly, to second
marriages. But because a second marriage was viewed as a dispensation
for human weakness, church hierarchs hesitated to permit it for a priest,
who was supposed to be spiritually stronger than the laity. Furthermore,
hierarchs were aware of the biblical precept forbidding the ancient He-
brew priestly class (the *kohanim*) to marry widows or divorcees.

Candidates for ordination were also expected to observe the mandated degrees of consanguinity carefully. Although a layman might be

92. *Kormčaja*, 66, citing Apostles' Canon, art. 26.
93. BNL 324(520), ff. 2v–3r; Smirnov, *Materialy*, 86; Sreznevskij, 252. Cf. Roman law,
which forbade priests of Jupiter to marry widows. Even after the establishment of celibacy in
the Roman Catholic Church, Gratian permitted the ordination of a man who had been married
to one virgin bride, but prohibited it if his wife had previously had sex with another man. See
Brundage, *Law, Sex, and Christian Society*, 36–37, 252.
94. Hil. 301, f. 94v.
95. *Voprosy Kirika*, art. 81, in RIB, 6:46; VAT-Bor. 15, f. 478r; Hil. 305, ff. 116v–117r;
Hil. 170, f. 90r.
96. Hil. 378, f. 142r; Peć 77, ff. 157v–158r; NBS 48, f. 39r; *Sintagmat*, 162.
97. Hil. 378, f. 158r.

No frmly 7/18

permitted to marry a woman related to him in the seventh degree (that is, a second cousin once removed), a candidate for the priesthood could not.[98] If a priest was found in an incestuous marriage, he was removed from his rank, along with the hierarch who had sponsored him. If he had known that his union was improper, he was also barred from communion. The same held when the priest's wife was a former nun.[99]

The wives of clerics were also considered to be clergy, and were subject to special rules. The wife of a cleric was expected to uphold the same high standard of sexual conduct as her husband; her lapses had serious consequences for her husband's career. If a candidate's wife committed adultery after their marriage but before he became a priest, he became ineligible for ordination, despite his own righteous conduct.[100] Some codes permitted him to seek ordination, but only after divorcing his erring wife.[101]

Once he was ordained, the situation became more complicated, because hierarchs were unsure whether to hold the priest fully responsible for his wife's misconduct:

> If the wife of a priest commits adultery, but he did not know about it, he may serve the liturgy. If someone tells him about her, he should refrain from reading the liturgy until he investigates. If it is true about her and he saw it with his own eyes, he should divorce her. He should remain patient [i.e., not remarry] and continue to serve. If he divorces his wife and marries another, he may not serve the liturgy, but he is not forbidden to take communion with lay people. If he keeps his wife, he is placed under penance, but upon his death he may be buried as a simple pious priest. If his wife dies before him, and he does not join with another woman, then he may serve as a priest without a penance. If she is still alive, and he cannot catch her with the man he was told about, then he should serve and he should not divorce her.[102]

According to most codes, mere suspicion of misconduct was not sufficient to justify a divorce in the case of a cleric. Only one code authorized the priest to separate from his wife because she traveled with other men.[103]

98. SOCH 197, f. 14r. See Hil. 171, f. 281r, for an example of regulations on consanguinity which permitted such a union.

99. Hil. 300, f. 48r–v.

100. E.g., BNL 324(520), f. 3r; Kiev 191, f. 775r; Hil. 302, f. 98r; Hil. 628, ff. 39v–40r; GIM, Sin. 227, f. 85v; Rila 1/20(48), f. 21r; *Dejanija moskovskix soborov*, 88.

101. SANU 124(29), f. 16v.

102. Hil. 302, f. 24r–v; similar, BNL 684, f. 163r–v; Rila 1/20(48), f. 17v; Hil. 169, f. 73r–v. This ruling was developed from Neocaesarian canon 8; see NBS 48, f. 70r.

103. BNL 246(103), ff. 161v–162r.

Great cost to woman who was adulterous

Once the wife's adultery was proven, the priest could continue to serve in his office only if he divorced her.[104] The same was true for a deacon.[105] Like a priest whose wife had died, he could then enter a monastery and become a "black" priest, ministering to monks. Even this career option was questionable. A rule attributed to Basil the Great barred a deacon from sacramental duties if his wife committed adultery with a pagan. Even if he divorced her and she married the pagan and converted him to Christianity, the deacon still could not return to his rank. St. Basil gave as his reason not the wife's adultery but her second marriage.[106]

Because adultery by a priest's, deacon's, or reader's wife made further pursuit of his career impossible, canonists enacted exceptionally stringent penalties for this violation. The adulterous wife had, in effect, "killed" her husband, because he could no longer serve in his capacity as priest while remaining in the marriage with her.[107] Some codes set the penance at sixteen years for both the erring wife and her lover, and the offense was sometimes equated with incest.[108] Russian codes tended to follow the usual rules for adultery in the codes of St. Basil (fifteen years) or John the Penitent (three years).[109] Lest wishes lead to actions, a man who lusted after a priest's or deacon's wife was subjected to a penance of six weeks.[110]

Because of the emphasis on chastity for the wives of clerics, even involuntary infidelity raised questions. A priest asked Metropolitan Ioann II whether he should receive his wife back after she had been "defiled" while a captive of a pagan tribe. The metropolitan replied that a woman who was raped was innocent, and to divorce an innocent wife made her and her husband adulterers; yet one manuscript variant implied that the priest should divorce her anyway, in order to avoid possible impurity.[111] The cleric's wife was allowed special leeway in preserv-

---

104. E.g., Troicki, 68; Pavlov, *Nomokanon pri Bol'šom Trebnike*, 341; BNL 684, f. 163r–v; Kiev 191, f. 775r; VAT-Bor 15, f. 478v; Hil. 305, f. 116r; *Dejanija moskovskix soborov*, 88. The decisions of the Council of Elvira in the West required a priest to repudiate his adulterous wife. Failure to do so meant excommunication; even brief delay meant exclusion from the church for ten years. See Brundage, *Law, Sex, and Christian Society*, 72.

105. *Voprosy Kirika*, art. 82, in RIB, 6:46; Smirnov, *Materialy*, 100.

106. *Sintagmat*, 461.

107. Zaozerskij and Xaxanov, 53; Suvorov, 381, 427–428.

108. Peć 77, f. 235r. SANU 124(29), f. 53v, records the 16-year penance, but f. 35r contains an erroneous 10 years. NBS 10, f. 31v, includes the marginal notation "Look!" next to this provision. Byzantine codes mandated mutilation as a civil penalty (see Pavlov, "'Knigi zakonnyja,'" 73), but in Slavic countries the church had exclusive jursidiction over priests' wives.

109. "Voprosy i otvety pastyrskoj praktiki," art. 38, in RIB, 6:864–865; Almazov, 3:149, 283.

110. Almazov, 3:280.

111. "Kanoničeskie otvety," art. 26, in RIB, 6:14–15; Benešević, *Sbornik pamjatnikov po istorii cerkovnago prava*, 118.

ing her chastity. Canons permitted the wife of a cleric who engaged in extramarital sex to divorce him in order to avoid defilement through contact with him. She was not permitted to remarry, however, and she was commanded to remain in the marriage if he gave up his illicit affair.[112]

Because parish clergy were expected to be married in order to forestall sexual sin and innuendo, when a priest's marriage ended, he was encouraged to relinquish his post. Mutually agreed-upon separation so that both spouses could live in abstinence had to be permitted, however, as a higher good: "If the wife of a priest wants to leave him for the sake of her virtue [*celomudrie*] so that she does not defile herself with him, she is free to do so, as long as she does not look for another husband. But if that priest will be left to illicit fornication, then he should remain with his wife, and a deacon and a reader also."[113] Analogous rules deterred a priest from entering a monastery unless his wife agreed to remain celibate also. If she remarried later, according to some hierarchs, the priest was forbidden to serve. A layman who gave up married life to become a "black" priest was similarly ineligible if his wife remarried.[114] Metropolitan Ioann II of Russia disagreed with this ruling, arguing that it was not the priest who had sinned, but his wife's new husband—better to bar *him* from the priesthood![115] Because of the possibility of abuse, one eleventh-century code refused to permit clerics to divorce their wives in order to accept higher posts in the church, and imposed penances of seven to ten years for the offense.[116] A priest who drove his wife out without cause was similarly forbidden to serve, even if he did not enter into an illicit second marriage. If he continued to refuse to take his wife back, he was deposed.[117] This rule applied equally in the case of a priest who was involuntarily separated from his wife.[118]

Widowed Priests

Early church canons forbade widowers to marry again after ordination, classifying remarriage with illicit fornication and adultery.[119] The

---

112. Hil. 302, f. 24v; Rila 1/20(48), f. 18r; NBS I-14, f. 273v.

113. BNL 684, ff. 163v–164r; SANU 124(29), f. 2v–3r.

114. E.g., Hil. 302, f. 24v; Hil. 305, f. 115v; Smirnov, *Materialy*, 137.

115. Beneševič, *Sbornik pamjatnikov po istorii cerkovnago prava*, 113. See also the similar ruling for deacons in Smirnov, *Materialy*, 58.

116. Sinai 37, f. 101v.

117. Rila 1/20(48), ff. 32v–33r; Hil. 378, f. 140r; NBS 48, f. 37v; Smirnov, *Materialy*, 243; *Kormčaja*, 63, citing Apostles' Canon, art. 5.

118. NBS 48, ff. 208v–209r.

119. Ibid., ff. 146v–147r; GIM, Sin. 227, f. 84v. The *Sintagmat* (163) records Byzantine civil law as permitting young clerics to remarry because of human weakness, but this view did not enter into the mainstream of Slavic canon law.

same prohibition applied to deacons and subdeacons, but readers were exempt.[120]

No canons from the Church Fathers required a widowed priest to leave his secular duties for monastic life. Two views on this question developed in the Slavic Orthodox world. The stricter interpretation strongly discouraged widowed clerics from remaining in the lay community. When a priest was widowed, hierarchs feared that he would not be able to restrain himself from sin, and urged him to seek the monastery. Even if the priest himself was of strict moral character, his widowed status left him open to unsavory insinuations. It was better for the church's image that clerics without wives retire from the world.

The fourteenth-century Russian metropolitan Peter of Moscow was a prime proponent of the restrictive view: "I have often written to you [the clergy] about this: If a priest's wife dies, he shall enter a monastery and retain his clerical rank. If he remains in weakness and the love of worldly pleasures, he shall not perform the liturgy. If he does not obey my commands, he will not be blessed—and also those who associate with him."[121] While the metropolitan's tone was harsh, he actually demanded only that the widowed priest curtail his liturgical activities. In reality, the church chose not to force widowed priests into monasteries, and instead established guidelines for their continued service in their parishes. In 1504, Ivan III of Russia ordered that widowed priests who lived chastely could stand in the wings of the sanctuary and receive communion with priests, but not perform the liturgy. They were entitled to a pension of one quarter of parish income.[122] The Stoglav Council enacted similar rules, forbidding widowed priests and deacons to perform the liturgy, hear lay confessions, or have female visitors other than close relatives in their homes.[123] Thus the church hierarchy discouraged widowed clerics from remaining in their parishes by denying them most of their previous income as well as some of their authority and responsibilities. A priest who entered a monastery, in contrast, was permitted to continue his sacerdotal functions.

Proponents of the moderate view argued that early church canons required priests to live chastely but did not insist that they be married in order to serve "in the world." Citing "ancient law," the Moscow Synod of 1667 ruled that widowed priests of good character should be permitted to continue in all duties except reading the liturgy. It was not widow-

---

120. Hil. 300, f. 43v; GIM, Sin. 277, f. 300r.

121. "Poučenie mitropolita Petra," in RIB, 6:161.

122. *Drevnjaja rossijskaja vivliofika*, 14:206–210. The German ambassador Herberstein also reported this policy. He was under the impression that the prohibition on performance of the liturgy was of recent date. See his *Notes upon Russia*, 56.

123. *Stoglav*, chap. 81, cited in Beneševič, *Sbornik pamjatnikov po istorii cerkovnago prava*, 74.

hood but intemperance that made a priest ineligible to serve. Further-more, only those who were accused of misconduct by responsible witnesses were to be forced to leave priestly duties.[124] The victory of the moderate position over the strict one might best be explained on practi-cal rather than theoretical grounds. Ultimately, the shortage of parish priests argued in favor of allowing widowers to serve, provided they conducted themselves appropriately, and did not take second wives or concubines.[125]

An ecclesiastical court case in late-seventeenth-century Russia illus-trates the problem of allowing widowed priests to remain in the secular world. The court of the archbishop of Ustjug was called upon to investi-gate charges of attempted rape filed against the widowed priest Ivan Andreev *syn* Sergin. The author of the complaint, surprisingly enough, was his daughter-in-law. Fekla, the wife of his son Gerasim, charged that he repeatedly attempted to rape her during the six months of her marriage. The first attempt, she testified, occurred on Tuesday of the first week of Lent. Ivan was prevented from carrying out his intentions only because his daughter Matrena intervened. After that Ivan came to her bed many times, and Fekla was hardly able to escape him. The second attempt came in late June, another fast period. Once again Fekla's cries brought a rescuer, this time the servant girl Paraskov'ja. At that time, Fekla reported the attack to the priest's spiritual father, who ordered him to desist. But her father-in-law made a third attack, this time attempting rear intromission. Fekla fled to the neighbors. When Father Ivan was interrogated, he denied the charges and threw himself on the mercy of the court.

The case was settled in six days. Fekla submitted her petition on July 22; Father Ivan was summoned to court the next day. The archbishop handed down his decision on July 25. By July 28, Ivan had been re-manded to a monastery.[126] The court decided not to call witnesses to confirm Fekla's accusations. There are two possible explanations for this decision. The court may have reasoned that extensive testimony on a priest's misconduct, whether true or false, would be embarrassing to the church. Or perhaps the court felt that Fekla's testimony alone was sufficiently damning. She accused her father-in-law of a large number of attempted crimes: rape, incest, sex during Lent, intercourse from the rear, and disobedience to his superior.

Fekla wished to be sure that her testimony cleared her of any sus-picion of complicity. If Gerasim intended a career in the church, follow-

124. *Dejanija moskovskix soborov*, 86v–88r.
125. Jack E. Kollmann, 72–74.
126. RIB, 14:1280–1284.

ing in his father's footsteps, it was essential that his wife's sexual purity be above question. As she averred that none of the attempted rapes succeeded, she could still claim to be a chaste wife. Because she always cried out for help and found rescuers, she passed the tests for innocence established by canon law. Perhaps she was telling the unadorned truth, but the skeptical reader will note inconsistencies and clichés in her story. Did she augment her report of the attacks with statements sure to win the court's quick approval of her petition? Or maybe Father Ivan actually succeeded in raping his daughter-in-law, but they tacitly agreed to keep it secret: Fekla to protect her good name and her husband's career, Father Ivan to minimize his offense. Another—albeit remote—possibility is that Fekla fabricated the charges in order to force her father-in-law to enter a monastery, leaving the parish and its income to his son. Whatever the case, it was in the interest of the archbishop to preserve the church from scandal by removing Father Ivan from the parish and confining him in a monastery.

The problem lay in the fact that many widowed priests violated the conditions under which they could remain "in the world." Such skeptics as Joseph of Volokalamsk warned that many widowed clerics failed to uphold high standards of conduct. Tsar Ivan IV personally raised the issue at the Stoglav Council. "Many widowed priests and deacons have strayed from the truth," he complained, "having forgotten the fear of God. They engage in misconduct: after their wives [have died] they keep concubines, and perform sacerdotal functions that they are unworthy to perform." To compound the problem, some widowed clerics settled in distant places, passed their concubines off as wives, and continued in their ecclesiastical role. The council ruled that widowed priests and deacons who persisted in living in sin should be deprived of all ecclesiastical rank and protection.[127]

Churchmen were divided on the issue of priestly remarriage. The dominant position required remarried clerics to give up sacramental service, allowing them to remain in the world without penalty and to take communion as laymen.[128] Some codes specifically denied the need for a penance; although second marriages usually carried a penance of two to four years, the loss of priestly rank was deemed penalty enough. Other canonists imposed a penance of three years, as for any remarriage.[129] This leniency on remarriage did not hold if the new wife was

---

127. *Stoglav*, 239–240.
128. Smirnov, *Materialy*, 129; Beneševič, *Sbornik pamjatnikov po istorii cerkovnago prava*, 82.
129. E.g., Hil. 302, f. 23v; Rila 1/20(48), f. 15v; SANU 124(29), f. 35v.

not marriageable—if, for example, she had been a nun.[130] Lest the priest attempt to evade the prohibition on remarriage by merely taking a concubine, canon law condemned this practice as worse than a second marriage, even to the point of anathematizing those who remained in such relationships.[131]

An even more permissive view competed for a time in Russia. Metropolitan Simon in the early sixteenth century even went so far as to permit twice-married priests to serve in sacerdotal functions, but this ruling was not widely accepted. Another contemporary liberal view permitted remarried priests to continue with all duties except the liturgy.[132] Ultimately the Russians conformed to tradition. The Stoglav Council and the Moscow Synod of 1667 reiterated the established canons, ordering that priests and deacons who took second wives be deposed. The hierarchs of the synod were not unsympathetic to young widowers, however, and authorized their economic support by the church and their service as readers and chanters in the event of their remarriage. Those who chose to pursue careers in state service (where there was great need of literate men) were free to do so, provided they did not enter the military.[133]

Although the moderate view permitting churchmen to remarry, albeit with loss of clerical status, became dominant, there was a strong dissenting opinion. In the view of some hierarchs, a widowed priest's remarriage constituted betrayal of the church and of God. A sixteenth-century Serbian apocrypha depicted Jesus as equating remarried priests with "destroyers of souls" and consigning them to eternal torment.[134] According to a fourteenth-century Russian code, a priest who remarried lost his rank and was placed under penance for thirty-seven years.[135]

Metropolitan Fotij of Russia was particularly vociferous in condemning clerical remarriage. He justified this stand by reference to the New Testament teaching that husband and wife constitute "one body." A cleric who remarried, he wrote, "gives half his dead body to the earth," and thus insults his calling to God's service.[136] When God had taken a

130. NBS 48, f. 147r–v.
131. Hil. 378, ff. 141v–142r; Smirnov, *Materialy*, 57; *Dejanija moskovskix soborov*, 88v.
132. Jack E. Kollmann, 69–72.
133. Beneševič, *Sbornik pamjatnikov po istorii cerkovnago prava*, 82.
134. Novaković, "Apokrifi kijevskoga rukopisa," 91. Serbian epic poetry likewise depicted remarried priests as damned; see Brkić, 53.
135. Smirnov, *Materialy*, 136.
136. "Gramota mitropolita Fotija v Pskov" (1422/1425), in RIB, 6:430. This passage, which became the basis for the Augustinian doctrine of conjugal debt in lay marriages, went almost unnoticed in the Slavic Orthodox world except as the linchpin of a justification prohibiting remarriage for clerics. It appears in BNL 684, f. 164r, as part of a set of rules on priestly marriages.

priest's wife, "half their body was dead," and it behooved the widowed priest to retire to a monastery and pray for the remission of his sins. If his spiritual father considered it appropriate, the former "white" priest could continue to serve as a "black" priest in the monastery. Fotij knew that his orders in this matter would not be popular, because many priests and deacons continued to serve in their parishes after the death of their wives.[137]

Fotij's interpretation of the apostolic doctrine of "one body" could reasonably be applied to all married couples, yet he did not intend to prohibit second marriages for the laity, much as improper unions concerned him.[138] He did not even insist that the widow of a cleric refrain from a second union, although he considered her remarriage "not nice." It was better for her to "preserve the purity of her single body with her first husband." Fotij did object to the marriage of a widowed priest with another priest's widow, and ordered them to divorce.[139] Other hierarchs permitted the widow of a priest or deacon to remarry, but with a penance for both her and her new husband.[140] Even though canon law fell short of prohibiting a second union for the widow of a priest, other ecclesiastical texts categorized it with illicit fornication by nuns and adultery. A twelfth-century apocryphal tale describing the Virgin's descent into hell depicted remarried priests' widows as consigned to torture by fire and snakes.[141]

In the final reckoning, it was in the practical interest of the church to make remarriage possible for the clergy, however strong the theological arguments against it. While remanding widowed priests to monasteries might cut down (but not eliminate) the possibilities of illicit sexual behavior, a parish priest might be ill suited to cenobitic life. If he were widowed young, he might have underaged children, who needed their father. But widowed clerics who remained in the secular community became a potential source of embarrassing sexual violations. Furthermore, they drained income from the parish while performing only limited services; in many cases their successors could not have been pleased to have them remain. It may well have seemed that the best solution was to permit and even subtly encourage them to remarry. They could be expected to do well in the lay community: men with their skills and education could find numerous opportunities in state service.

---

137. "Gramota mitropolita Fotija v Pskov" (1422/1425), in RIB, 6:434–435.
138. On lay marriage, see ibid., 281; "Poslanie mitropolita Fotija v Novgorod," in RIB, 6:272–273.
139. "Gramota mitropolita Fotija v Pskov" (1422/1425), in RIB, 6:430, 433.
140. "Voprosy i otvety pastyrskoj praktiki," art. 64, in RIB, 6:868.
141. Gudzij, 94–95; Karanov, 268.

Clerical Propriety

The ability of the clergy to inculcate Christian morality in the community was directly related to their respectability in the eyes of the laity.[142] Sexual purity was a prime consideration. Canon law revealed considerable concern for maintaining the appearance of propriety. As models of the sober Christian life, clerics were expected to abstain from secular amusements. To avoid possible temptation and rumor, priests were expected to be circumspect in their dealings with women. They were instructed to avoid female conversation and female company. Any cleric who joined in dancing (with its sensual and pagan overtones), played chess or other games, drank to excess, or consorted with *skomoroxi* (entertainers) was deposed if he refused to desist. So was a priest who encouraged prostitution or visited taverns.[143] Metropolitan Ioann II of Russia stopped short of forbidding priests to attend laymen's feasts, even when women were in attendance, provided the guests were "God-fearing and honorable." He regarded such parties as a "great temptation," however, and warned clerics to absent themselves when dancing, "demonic" singing, and sexual joking started.[144] He would have agreed with the advice of a later churchman: "A priest ought to attend a meal with fear, and eat and drink in moderation, for he is God's servant. And laymen also."[145]

So great was the concern for sexual propriety that innocent associations between clerics and women raised questions. Early church canons prohibited priests from going alone to visit widows or unmarried girls, except upon explicit instruction from the bishop.[146] Clerics in particular were barred from bathing with women.[147] To avoid any hint of scandal, priests were to hear women's confessions in the anteroom to the church, with the doors left open, rather than in front of the altar, as for men. The risk of compromising the confidentiality of women's confessions was preferable to a potentially compromising situation.[148] Even the most

---

142. The problem of gaining popular respect for parish clergy remained in Russia in the nineteenth century. For a priest's understanding of the problem, see I. S. Belliustin.

143. Hil 302, f. 24r; Smirnov, *Materialy*, 133; Rila 1/20(48), f. 35r; Družinin, 78–84; Almazov, 3:285; *Sintagmat*, 465; Smirnov, *Materialy*, 147, 243; Mošin, "Vlastareva sintagma," 84. Priests were also forbidden to associate with pagans—either to eat, drink, or converse with them or to bring crosses to their homes to bless them: Almazov, 3:184.

144. "Kanoničeskie otvety," arts. 16, 24, in RIB, 6:8–9, 13–14. See also Almazov, 3:181, 183, 184.

145. Almazov, 3:283–284.

146. *Kormčaja*, 339, citing Carthaginian Canons, art. 38.

147. Smirnov, *Materialy*, 43; *Kormčaja*, 273, citing Laodichaean Council, art. 30.

148. See, e.g., "Poučenie arxiepiskopa Ilji," art. 3, in RIB, 6:353–354. It is likely that women were more reluctant to confess to personal misdemeanors in such a setting. Perhaps that is why instructions to confessors warn that it was more difficult for women to confess than for men.

tangential contacts were challenged. Hierarchs had to rule specifically that both a husband and his wife could confess to the same priest.[149] Bishop Nifont was asked whether a priest could dress in clothing remade out of a woman's robe. He replied in the affirmative, but the question itself indicates the concern in the ranks of the clergy for observance of propriety.[150]

Serious questions arose as to the propriety of a priest's serving priestly functions with members of his family, especially his wife. In addition to concern over the priest's objectivity in these circumstances, there was also concern about violations of the canons on sexuality and familial relationships. For that reason, priests were discouraged from ministering to their own families, including siblings and in-laws, if another priest were available. The greatest reluctance was shown for the priest's wife.[151] Otherwise identical codes divided on this issue.[152] According to early church canons, it was anathema to suggest that it was improper for a priest to give communion to his wife.[153] Despite this early ruling, Slavic clerics remained uncertain as to the propriety of a priest's ministering to his wife, and questions to this effect arose quite often. "If a priest's wife wants to receive communion and there is no other priest, the priest himself may give it to her. If someone says that it is not proper, answer that that is not in the law."[154] Metropolitan Ioann II noted that among the Greeks, it was not permitted for a priest to provide the sacraments to his wife. He would allow it in Russia, but only when no other priest lived nearby.[155] Certain codes—especially those that tended to severity—ruled that a priest must refrain from giving communion to his wife or blessing her. It was considered particularly inappropriate for a priest to recite the prayers for purification after childbirth over his wife.[156] When no other priest was available, however, or in case of great need, priests were permitted to fulfill sacerdotal functions with their relatives.[157] Due precautions were recommended to prevent violations

149. Smirnov, *Materialy*, 117.
150. Voprosy Savy, art. 6, in RIB, 6:53.
151. "Voprosy i otvety pastyrskoj praktiki," art. 39, in RIB, 6:865; Smirnov, *Materialy*, 85, 99.
152. See, e.g., two variants of "Zapoved ko ispovedajuščimsja synom i dščerem," in Smirnov, *Materialy*, 119.
153. Hil. 628, ff. 31v–32r; Hil. 305, f. 42r; SANU 123(28), ff. 50v–51r, quoting Trulla Council.
154. SANU 124(29), f. 87r. Smirnov, *Materialy*, 147, is similar.
155. "Kanoničeskie otvety," arts. 19–20, in RIB, 6:29.
156. SANU 124(29), f. 36r; Smirnov, *Materialy*, 39; "Voprosy i otvety pastyrskoj praktiki," arts. 55 and 56, in RIB, 6:867.
157. See, e.g., the autobiography of the archpriest Avvakum in George P. Fedotov, ed., *A Treasury of Russian Spirituality* (New York, 1965), 160. He describes ministering to his family while they were in exile, but he felt it inappropriate to give his wife communion.

of canon law. A priest was permitted to baptize his own child, for example, but he had to be sure that another person presented the child for baptism. If the priest presented the child himself, he became its godfather, and in effect his wife's *kum*. Then, to prevent incest, the priest and his wife would have to separate.[158] Hierarchs recommended that a priest baptize his own child only in case of its imminent death.[159] In Serbia, where the witness to a wedding also became a *kum*, a priest could bless his son's marriage only if another person took on the role of marriage *kum*.[160] Metropolitan Fotij of Russia did not permit a priest to preside at his own child's wedding at all.[161]

Slavic churchmen retained the Church Fathers' concern about propriety in living arrangements, especially for unmarried clergy. They were forbidden to share their dwellings with any women other than their mothers, sisters, and daughters. Other relatives were specifically excluded from the domicile, perhaps because of the custom of passing off a mistress as a cousin or niece. Slave women were also prohibited, because of their vulnerability to sexual exploitation.[162] Hierarchs recognized that the arrangement might be innocent in some cases, but even so, bishops were advised to instruct priests, who might be ignorant of this rule, about the prohibition.[163]

Because a cleric's career depended on his sexual purity, he was susceptible to slander. A didactic tale in a Serbian collection was intended to discourage women from making false accusations of sexual impropriety against clerics. The story told of a dishonest maiden who found herself pregnant out of wedlock. She named an innocent reader as the father, and he was summoned before the bishop for misconduct. Although he did not admit responsibility, he was forced to marry the girl. Of course, since she was not a virgin at the time of their marriage, the reader became ineligible for the priesthood. However, truth won out in the end: the girl was unable to give birth to the child until she admitted her double sin of illicit fornication and slander.[164] In fact, the church, which had charge of all cases of illicit pregnancy, was not so likely to believe accusations against clerics. One authority ruled that the testimony of a woman of poor reputation was not to be believed unless respectable

158. SOCH 197, f. 65r–v; Smirnov, *Materialy*, 119, 137.
159. "Voprosy i otvety pastyrskoj praktiki," art. 12, in RIB, 6:859.
160. Hil. 627, f. 21r.
161. "Poslanie mitropolita Fotija pskovskomu duxovenstvu," in RIB, 6:411.
162. Sreznevskij, 257.
163. Rila 1/20(48), ff. 32v–33r; Peć 77, ff. 236v–238v; SANU 124(29), f. 30v. There were similar objections in the West to clerics' sharing of living quarters with women. See Brundage, *Law, Sex, and Christian Society*, 150.
164. Hil. 278, ff.134v–137v.

witnesses could be found to confirm her complaint. He recognized that the woman could be telling the truth about the priest's misconduct, but he was content to consign him to God's judgment and the woman to her fate. In any case, he advised that the priest be reassigned to a different parish in order to avoid scandal.[165]

An attempt to incite a man of God to commit a sexual sin was a punishable offense, even if he did not succumb. Anyone who brought a widow to a priest with the intent of encouraging an illicit affair between them was subject to a penance of three years.[166] A didactic tale tells of a beautiful woman of an important family who conceived a great lust for the pious bishop Vikentij. To attract his notice, she feigned illness and called him to her bedside. She then took advantage of the situation to reveal her nakedness to him. The embarrassed bishop fled from the house, and God made the woman fall truly sick.[167]

Through confessional questions centering on sexual behavior, the clergy promoted the view that sexual chastity was the mark of propriety and ultimately of salvation. After condemning others for their sexual sins, the priest could not expect public toleration of his misconduct, real or imagined. Despite the church's efforts to protect the reputations of its clergy, clerics, and particularly parish priests, became the butts of smutty jokes and stories. Russian penitential questionnaires provided for a penance of twelve days for any layman who made fun of a priest, monk, or nun.[168] Attributing misbehavior to enforcers of the law is a common motif in literature. Because Slavic clerics emphasized proper sexual conduct, it is not surprising that they were frequently depicted as perpetrators of sexual offenses in folklore.[169] Few anticlerical texts were written down as long as the church monopolized book publishing. An occasional seventeenth-century tale survives, and folktales recorded later provide ample examples.

In "The Tale of Karp Sutulov," the merchant Karp goes on a business trip to Lithuania, leaving his beautiful young wife, Tatiana, behind alone. He instructs his friend Afanasij Berdov to provide her with a hundred rubles if she needs it. After three years, Tatiana asks Afanasij for the money, but he agrees to turn it over to her only if she will sleep

165. Troicki, 74; Hil. 167, f. 270r–v; (Peć 77, ff. 260v–261r, 271v, is similar), NBS 48, f. 357r–v. The author's name is given variously as Metropolitan Nikita of Iraklia and Metropolitan Ilja of Tyre.
166. Smirnov, *Materialy*, 31.
167. Deržavina, 228–229.
168. Almazov, 3:282.
169. Perkov, 19–22, 29–32, 49–53, 62, 71–72, 75–78, 94. Although the parish clergy was the main butt of jokes, monks and the hierarchy did not escape altogether. Claude Carey recorded a number of obscene proverbs featuring "black" clergy, see pp. 46, 48.

with him. Tatiana is confused by this demand from a man her husband trusts, and asks the advice of her confessor. The duplicitous priest offers her two hundred rubles if she will sleep with him instead. Still more perplexed by this turn of events, Tatiana consults the archbishop. He urges her to forget the offers of the merchant and the priest and go to bed with *him*, in exchange for three hundred rubles. No longer confused, Tatiana invites all three to come and fulfill their desires the same night. Each suitor arrives, pays Tatiana the promised sum, and is hurriedly hidden in a trunk when the next visitor comes to the door. She then calls in the *voevoda* (military commander), who is convinced of the truth of her accusations when she opens the trunks to reveal the three prominent citizens in a state of undress; the archbishop, to his further shame, is clad not in his vestments but in Tatiana's dress.[170]

The lessons of this tale are many. The wife is repaid for her wisdom and loyalty: she keeps the rubles the three suitors have given her and shares the fines for misconduct which the *voevoda* levies against the miscreants. Virtue, it seems, need not be its own reward. It is not accidental that clerics are cast as two of the villains; the author makes a number of gratuitous jests at their expense. For example, when Tatiana expresses concern about eternal punishment for the sin of adultery, the archbishop blithely promises her absolution. Later she is prompted to ask her confessor, "Are you, Father, the righteous judge? Do you have the power to send me to Torment or to Paradise?" In this way the author confirms the legitimacy of the church's teachings on sexual morality while criticizing the clergy for their failings. Furthermore, it is the secular authorities rather than the ecclesiastical ones who uphold moral standards in this story, a reflection of the state's increasing role in the regulation of personal conduct in seventeenth-century Muscovy.

Proskurnici

The women who baked the bread for communion constituted another class of clergy. A *proskurnica* had to be a widow of good character, so insinuations of misconduct were particularly dangerous for such women. The *proskurnica* Avdot'ja Filipova *doč'*, for example, petitioned Tsar Michael of Russia in 1626 to restrain her neighbor from making false accusations that she was selling spirits.[171]

Any prior sexual sin made a woman ineligible to serve in this capacity.

---

170. Gudzij, 425–430.
171. No. 9 in RIB, 25:10–11. Marija countersued, accusing Avdot'ja of defamation of character, see no. 10, pp. 11–12.

A prospective *proskurnica* could have been married only once.[172] In fact, exceptions could be made. One churchman ruled that a widow whose first marriage had not been celebrated in church could bake the bread if she was old and had undergone a penance for her youthful offense.[173] It is possible that unusual circumstances prompted this leniency; the author of the inquiry was the Russian bishop in the Mongol capital of Sarai. The sacred character of the *proskurnici's* work demanded that they observe high standards of purity. They were forbidden to bake the bread while they were menstruating. If a menstruating woman happened to touch the bread after it was prepared, however, it still could be used.[174] According to one code, a menstruating *proskurnici* was to abstain from baking communion bread for twenty days.[175] This rule virtually required that the position be filled by postmenopausal women. They also were ordered to abstain from eating meat while performing their spiritual service. The rules for *proskurnici* seem to have been adapted from early canons related to deaconesses. Like this vanished class of female clerics, *proskurnici* had to be mature, that is, over forty years of age, and they were forbidden to remarry, on the grounds that widows who remarried "followed not spiritual wisdom but the flesh."[176] If they engaged in illicit fornication, they were forbidden to continue their work.[177] A *proskurnica's* lover was given the maximum penance for adultery under the rules of St. John the Penitent.[178]

Enforcement

It was almost as difficult to get the clergy to obey the rules of sexual behavior as it was to impose conformity on the laity. The church relied upon its supervision and community pressure to enforce proper conduct among the clergy, but ultimately a cleric's righteousness depended on his own sense of morality. Clerics were no more immune to illicit sexual desires than any other group. Indeed, they were not always well enough educated to know what sort of behavior was prohibited. As long as a sin remained private, a cleric may well have preferred not to confess it,

---

172. "Otvety mitropolita Kipriana igumenu Afanasiju," in RIB, 6:259; "Tri svjatitel'skija poučenija," in ibid., 922–923.

173. "Otvety na voprosy sarajskogo episkopa Feognosta," in RIB, 6:137–138.

174. Voprosy Kirika, art. 98, in RIB, 6:50; Smirnov, *Materialy*, 85, 99.

175. Smirnov, *Materialy*, 59.

176. "Gramota mitropolita Fotija v Pskov" (1422/1425), in RIB, 6:433. On deaconesses, see *Kormčaja*, 119, citing the Council of Chalcedon, art. 15.

177. Voprosy Ilji, art. 12, in RIB, 6:59.

178. Almazov, 3:283.

fearing the consequences. Loss of rank meant not only public humiliation but also loss of livelihood. At the same time, the clergy would be
more likely than laymen to take seriously the exhortation to full confession and repentance, on pain of eternal damnation. In order to encourage clerics to admit their sins and gain salvation through repentance,
Archbishop Ilja of Novgorod reassured them that loss of rank would not
result in destitution.

> Now, if anyone has committed some sin, do not say to yourselves, "If we
> leave the priesthood, we will die of hunger." God forbid that that should
> happen to my brothers! The Cathedral of St. Sophia is not poor; we are
> capable, and will take you into the Church and give you sustenance. I will
> not cut off income to anyone, or to your wives or children, or send you into
> exile.[179]

Church hierarchs did not rely solely on the clerics to report their
misconduct. In order to forestall public outrage and preserve the moral
authority of the parish clergy, the church established a supervisory hierarchy. Each priest had a spiritual father, to whom he confessed his sins.
The spiritual father, usually another "white" priest with more experience and seniority, judged whether he was worthy of serving in his rank.
The spiritual father was to report any noncompliance to the bishop, but
he was not to be overly stringent with the clerics under his supervision,
as a sinful priest in the parish was better than no priest at all.[180]

The upper ranks of the hierarchy were filled not by the parish clergy
but by the monastic clergy. Early canons required that bishops, metropolitans, and patriarchs be celibate. If a bishop-elect was married, he
and his wife had to agree to separate. To prevent a scandal, the wife was
to enter a distant convent.[181] It was not unknown in the annals of
church history for a man who aspired to the episcopate to divorce his
wife against her will in order to attain the post. Consequently, penitential questions prepared for Russian patriarchs inquired whether the prelate had expelled his wife without cause.[182] To prevent this sort of
scandal, it became customary to seek candidates for the episcopate from
the ranks of the monastic clergy.

The moral standing of a candidate for the post of bishop was of great
importance, because he was charged with enforcing rules on sexual
expression among clergy and laity both. A cleric who had engaged in
fornication was considered ineligible for the episcopate.[183] A bishop

179. "Poučenie arxiepiskopa Ilji," art. 14, in RIB, 6:361.
180. "Tri svjatitel'skija poučenija," in RIB, 6:926.
181. NBS 48, f. 157v.
182. Almazov, 3:185.
183. NBS 688, f. 44r.

who engaged in fornication after ordination lost his rank and was placed under penance for ten years.[184] Because bishops cooperated with the secular authorities (at least in theory) in the promotion of law and order, the bishop's sexual sins attracted notice in the secular realm. For this reason, the Code of Stefan Dušan ordered that any bishop who engaged in fornication be punished under civil law, suffering mutilation.[185]

Monastic Clergy

Monasteries developed as a means to allow men and women to devote their lives to prayer, meditation, and works of charity without worldly distractions and temptations. Orthodox theologians described the monastery as "heaven on earth"; to become a monk was to take on "angelic form." But if the monastery was to fulfill its function as a spiritual center, reflecting the divine order of the heavenly kingdom, the inhabitants had to separate themselves from earthly desires, including sexual ones. Orthodox churchmen did not underestimate the difficulty of this task, given the Devil's ability to tempt even holy men away from the path of righteousness (fig. 15).

The Challenge of Celibacy

Orthodox churchmen, well aware of the difficulty of celibacy, urged that all men who expressed an interest in becoming monks be questioned carefully about their ability to live without women.[186] The Moscow Synod of 1667 issued a ruling requiring all candidates for the monastic life to undergo a waiting period of three years to determine whether they could sustain it. In case of "need" (not defined), this period might be shortened to a year and a half. Children could not be admitted as novices, because too many young people later abandoned vows immaturely made.[187]

The Devil, churchmen warned, particularly wished to disrupt the pious life of monks by attacking them with lustful desires at inopportune moments. The Russian saint Nil Sorskij recommended a means of resistance to such an attack:

> When we are harried by the temptation to fornication, I believe that it is salutary also to think of our monastic state; for we have assumed the form

184. E.g., Sinai 37, f. 101v; BNL 251(200), f. 129r; Peć 77, f. 109r; Smirnov, *Materialy*, 133, 136; ZSL-P, 145.
185. Art. 53, in NBS 688, f. 138v.
186. NBS 48, f. 181r.
187. *Dejanija moskovskix soborov*, 25v.

15. The Ladder. Monks attempting to ascend the ladder to spiritual reward are distracted by demons. A face appears on the groin of the demon at lower right, to indicate concentration on the sensual; he holds a glass of wine. Miniature, Russian (sixteenth century), from *Drevnerusskaja miniatjura* (Moscow, 1933), no. 50.

of angels, and how can we trample on our conscience and defile this holy form with such an abomination? We may likewise picture to ourselves the shameful and scandalous example that we should present to the eyes of men, and this too might help us to resist these unworthy thoughts. . . . When the assault is particularly violent, however, we should rise to our feet, and lifting our eyes and extending our arms, we should pray, as Gregory of Sinai instructs us, and God will disperse these evil imaginings. . . . Avoid all conversation with women, and indeed the very sight of them; shun youthful, beardless and effeminate faces, for the devil lays these snares for monks. If it can possibly be avoided, never be alone with such persons, however necessary it might seem.[188]

In keeping with the perceived threat in contact between the sexes, hierarchs frowned even on nonsocial contacts between monks and laywomen. Monasteries were not to employ women servants, either slave or free.[189] Only monks in "virtuous old age" were permitted to hear women's confessions; better, the penitent was to confess to a married parish priest.[190] This policy was not in accord with Byzantine tradition, in which only monastic priests heard lay confessions. The South Slavs had originated the practice of having parish priests hear confessions, perhaps because of a shortage of monks in the early centuries after the adoption of Christianity, and the Russians adopted the practice from them.[191] Despite regulations prohibiting monks to serve as spiritual guides for laywoman, however, they continued to do so throughout the history of the Slavic Orthodox churches. Patristic tales promoted it, describing the spiritual benefits laywomen received from their monastic confessors.[192]

To forestall sexual sins, the leaders of the early church insisted on separate monastic institutions for men and women. If men and women shared the same dwelling, the temptation to sin would be great, and the less charitably minded in the community might assume unchastity even if all was well. Early church canons thus forbade mixed-sex monasteries.[193] Women were not to spend the night in male institutions, and vice versa, even on a temporary basis.[194] It was also prohibited for women to live in male institutions dressed as men, on the grounds that

188. Fedotov, *Treasury of Russian Spirituality*, 112–114.
189. GIM, Sin. 227, f. 78v; Sreznevskij, 273, citing art. 18 of the Seventh Ecumenical Council.
190. NBS I-14, f. 264r.
191. Smirnov, *Drevne-russkij duxovnik*, 13–17.
192. Nikolova, 188–190.
193. GIM, Sin. 227, f. 78r–v; *Kormčaja*, 225–226, citing art. 20 of the Second Nicaean Council; Sreznevskij, 266, citing art. 47 of the Sixth Ecumenical Council.
194. NBS 48, f. 157v.

women should not attempt to change their nature.[195] Numerous saints'
lives directly contradicted this ruling. The heroines were canonized precisely because they lived out their lives doing deeds of humility, self-
denial, and good works in male disguise.[196]

Despite numerous canons prohibiting monks and nuns from living in
the same monastery, the practice continued. Metropolitan Fotij of Russia in 1410 found it necessary to order nuns to leave institutions that
originally were male, and vice versa.[197] The Moscow Synod of 1667
again addressed the problem of mixed-sex institutions, arguing forcefully, if not accurately, that in the early days of Christianity, houses for
monks were not even located in proximity to those for nuns, lest temptation result. Monks of any age or rank were not permitted to associate
with nuns; to do so was "hazardous and not nice."[198]

Even when monks and nuns lived in separate institutions, hierarchs
persistently complained about inappropriate association. Metropolitan
Ioann II was distressed by raucous parties held in monasteries:

> What do we do if feasts are held in monasteries frequently, inviting men
> and women together, and competing with each other to see who can ar-
> range the best feast? They are zealous not about God, but their zeal is for
> devilish things, and they go by the right-handed lie; and the model of mercy
> and spiritual comfort they see and destroy. . . . The bishop should forbid
> such things with all his strength, teaching that drunkenness is evil, and they
> are losing the Heavenly Kingdom, because drunkenness leads to other
> evils: lack of self-control, impurity, fornication, swearing, profanity, not to
> mention evildoing such as this, and bodily illness.[199]

Metropolitan Ioann was not alone in his concern. The Bulgarian-born
metropolitan Kiprian of Russia had the same objection, and also complained that monks were usurping the functions of the parish clergy:

> It is not appropriate to do anything secular in a monastery, whether for
> men or women, or to remember secular matters. . . . If anyone has repudi-

195. Peć 77, f. 266r; NBS 48, f. 72v. Cross-dressing was a sin for the laity also, largely
because it occurred in the context of carnival festivals of pagan origin: SANU 124(29), f. 40v;
Almazov, 3:283; Smirnov, *Materialy*, 54.

196. See, e.g., the tale of Andronik and Afanasija in Hil. 458, f. 380r. Even outside of
monastic life, didactic literature lauded women who showed male characteristics. St. Philothea,
according to Patriarch Evtimij, "through the fulfillment of the Holy Spirit, took masculine
strength in her feminine nature": Kaluzniacki, 79. The Russian saint Olga was similarly praised
for overcoming her femininity: N. K. Nikol'skij, *Materialy*, 93. The princess Dinara was said to
have donned armor to lead the army to victory over the Persians, aided by the Virgin: *Pamjatniki starinnoj russkoj literatury*, 1:373–376.

197. "Poslanie mitropolita Fotija v Novgorod," in RIB, 6:275–276; "Gramota mitropolita
Fotija v Pskov," in ibid., 284–285.

198. *Dejanija moskovskix soborov*, 27.

199. "Kanoničeskie otvety," art. 29, in RIB, 6:16–17.

ated the world, father and mother, brothers and sisters, wife and children, and all worldly concerns, and then in the monastery he sees and does the same things, of what use is withdrawal from the world? For this reason, it is not appropriate to hold marriages in the monastery, or betrothals, or for women to come in and tempt the brothers. It is not appropriate for an abbot or a monk to perform a marriage; this is the job of secular priests, not monastic ones. The same for baptizing a child, except in case of great need.[200]

Kiprian's successor, Metropolitan Fotij, went further: he forbade abbots and monks to hear the confessions of laywomen, recite prayers of purification after childbirth, or celebrate marriages.[201]

Kiprian also objected to ownership of property by individual monks, not on any theoretical grounds of monastic poverty but because the administration of estates brought monks in contact with the laity. He was particularly concerned that monks would receive women visitors.[202] Neither Kiprian nor his successors were able to eliminate the practice. Nearly three centuries later, Metropolitan Evfimij of Novgorod reported the same problem: monks received visitors of both sexes and all ages in their cells and even invited them to remain overnight. This practice, he admonished, was "very indecent and contrary to order," because it led to "lustful desire." He ordered that no women be permitted in private cells, without exception, "not only not to spend the night, but not even for a short time." Women, including close relatives, were to be entertained in guest salons only. The metropolitan held the abbots responsible for enforcing these rules, threatening them with the severest punishment, including loss of rank, in case of violations.[203] The Moscow Synod of 1667 went even further, ordering the excommunication of both lay and clerical offenders.[204]

Convents

In its overt forms, monastic life for nuns paralleled that for monks. Nuns took the same vows as their male counterparts. The same sevice marked their entry into the religious life, with the substitution of references to female rather than male saints.[205] Orthodox churchmen regarded women who took monastic vows favorably. A woman who rejected worldly pleasures and honors to become a "bride of Christ" was

200. "Otvety mitropolita Kipriana igumenu Afanasiju," in RIB, 6:253–254.
201. "Gramota mitropolita Fotija v Pskov" (1422/1425), in RIB, 6:431.
202. "Otvety mitropolita Kipriana igumenu Afanasiju," in RIB, 6:263.
203. No. 312 in *Akty sobrannye v bibliotekax i arxivax Rossijskoj imperii*, 4:463–464.
204. *Dejanija moskovskix soborov*, 27.
205. "Otvety mitropolita Kipriana igumenu Afanasiju," in RIB, 6:256.

praised, especially if she did so while still a virgin. In practical terms, monasticism offered women an alternative to the obligations of marriage and family life. Convent life was not without restriction, of course, but it promised women ecclesiastical protection and high social status. Because of the appeal of monastic life for women, churchmen were concerned that girls would make a vow of celibacy before they knew whether they could keep it. For that reason, it was recommended that maidens not take vows until they had reached mental adulthood, defined as over age sixteen or seventeen.[206]

Much as hierarchs approved of female monasticism, the task of meeting the spiritual needs of communities of unmarried women presented problems. The gender roles imposed by church and society guaranteed that communities of women could not function without contact with men. Nuns could take on certain religious duties usually the domain of men—they were permitted, for example, to enter the sanctuary of a church, even one outside their convent, in order to light candles and decorate the altar[207]—but the liturgy, penance, and all other sacraments had to be administered by male clerics.

Hierarchs were wary about authorizing interactions between nuns and male clergy, lest improprieties result. For that reason, young hieromonks (monk-priests) were forbidden to minister to nuns or give them communion.[208] "White" priests whose wives were living were the preferred spiritual fathers for nuns.[209] The practice of Orthodoxy, however, required deacons, clerks, sextons, and lay servants—all of whom were featured as potential sexual partners in the penitential questions for nuns.[210] Tales and saints' lives described the freedom of male clerics to enter convents in order to minister to the religious needs of the residents. One lively Bulgarian story told of a bandit who disguised himself as a monk in order to gain access to a convent and its wealth. When the nuns crowded around him to ask for his blessing and spiritual advice, the bandit was so moved that he forsook his evil ways and adopted the religious life in earnest.[211]

The societal role played by convents increased the interaction of nuns with male outsiders. Administration of convent property required the assistance of men. Nuns, like their lay sisters, needed to rely on men to

206. GIM, Sin. 227, ff. 187r–v, 194v.
207. Troicki, 76; Hil. 302, f. 80r–v.
208. Troicki, 77; Hil. 628, f. 23v.
209. "Poučenie Petra Mitropolita," in *Pamjatniki starinnoj russkoj literatury*, 4:186–188; "Poslanie mitropolita Fotija v Novgorod," in RIB, 6:276; Order of Ivan III (1504), in *Drevnjaja rossijskaja vivliofika*, 14:206–210; *Dejanija moskovskix soborov*, 46.
210. Almazov, 3:179, 180.
211. Nikolova, 204–205.

travel to distant holdings and represent them in court. Furthermore, convents served as refuges for women who had lost their husbands' support through death or divorce and as places of detention for female wrongdoers. Consequently, many residents of convents felt no monastic calling. Slavic nuns were not cloistered in the Western European sense. Widows and innocent divorced women who took up residence in the monastery could purchase their own cells and retain independent income,[212] and they came and went with relative freedom.

The administration of private and monastic income required that convent residents be permitted to receive male visitors, often in the privacy of their cells. Sexual violations resulted. Penitential questions for nuns inquired about sexual contact with a whole range of relatives: brothers, cousins, nephews, godbrothers, brothers-in-law, stepfather, godfather, child's godfather, and even ex-husband.[213] The abbess Ul'janija of the Monastery of the Transfiguration in Ustjug petitioned Metropolitan Varlaam in 1630 to complain about just such goings-on. The nun Marem'jana Ozgixina and her daughter Ovdot'ja Ivanova had been violating convent rules by entertaining male visitors overnight. The abbess seems to have been complaining more about the drunken guests' noise and unruliness than about the possibility of sexual impropriety.[214] When there was real suspicion of sexual immorality, the result was public outrage. Rumors spread about the False Dmitri's visits to a convent where his wife was staying on retreat; the impostor was reported to have engaged in drinking, dancing, and illicit sex with the nuns.[215]

The Treatment of Sexual Violations

Canonists recognized that it was not possible to isolate men and women religious completely. They also realized that the absence of regular contact with members of the opposite sex did not suffice to eliminate sexual temptations. The persistence of sexual desires even in a holy setting proved Satan's strength. And despite the injunctions on monastic life, monks and nuns had ample opportunity to sin. The penitential questions addressed to monks in a Russian *trebnik* of 1651 shows the range of sexual sins conceivable even in monastic life.

> My lord brother and son: Did you not transgress your monastic vow? Did you not defile your monastic form? As a monk, did you not fall with

212. Marie A. Thomas, "Muscovite Convents in the Seventeenth Century," *Russian History* 10, no. 2 (1983): 230–242.
213. Almazov, 3:179, 180.
214. No. 82 in RIB, 25:96–97.
215. Reported by an anonymous Dutch merchant, in Howe, 58.

someone, either with women, or with maidens, or with nuns, or with *skimnicy*, or with widows, or with priests' wives, or with deacons' wives, or with youths, or with clean animals or with unclean animals? Did you not destroy maidens' virginity by rape or sorcery? Did you not defile someone with fornication, while he slept or was drunk? Did you not think something improper about a holy icon? Did you put someone on top of yourself? Did you not fornicate in your hand, or in another's? Did you not ejaculate, having looked with desire on a woman or anyone else? Did you not think with lust about young monks or youths, or women, or girls? Did you not enter the church while you were unclean from fornication, or from a nocturnal temptation, or in a dirty cassock? Did you not fall with your sister, or with a close kinsman from your family or your in-laws? Did you not fall with your brother or kinsman? Did you not fornicate with one woman or maiden?[216]

This catalogue includes the full range of sexual sins named in penitential questionnaries for laymen: illicit fornication, adultery, homosexuality, bestiality, rape, incest, masturbation, lustful thoughts, and nocturnal emissions. The questions for nuns covered the same range of violations and several others apparently thought to be exclusively female concerns: contraception, abortion, infanticide, prostitution, use of cosmetics.[217] Further canons admonished nuns not to assist others in committing adultery or infanticide, warning that they could be punished equally with the actual perpetrators of these offenses.[218]

The provisions for dealing with violations of the rules of sexual conduct for monastic clergy differed somewhat from those for laity. First, monastic rules tended to evaluate nonsexual sins in terms of sexual sins. A monk who engaged in drunkenness, theft, slander, or insubordination, for example, was judged "as a fornicator."[219] Second, the rules of St. Basil, with their longer penances, were usually preferred over those of St. John the Penitent. St. Basil was one of the "founders" of cenobitic monasticism, and the prestige of his rules was virtually unequaled. Further, monastic clergy already followed a regimen of fasting and prayer; unlike laymen, they could not shorten a penance by taking on an ascetic discipline that they practiced in any case.

Judging by the lengths of the recommended penances, sexual sins were among the most serious for monastic clergy, equaled only by murder. The monastic rules of St. Basil dictated that any illicit sexual intercourse by a monk or nun deserved the fifteen-year penance associated with the

216. Kiev 191, f. 169r–v; cf. Almazov, 3:175–177.
217. Kiev 191, f. 173r–v; Almazov, 3:180.
218. Hil. 167, f. 268r, quoting St. Basil's Rule, art. 71.
219. "*S' bloudnykom' osouždaem',*" Peć 77, ff. 281v–282r.

sin of adultery. The ruling was justified, especially in the case of a virgin nun, on the grounds that she had betrayed her bridegroom, Christ; the venerable St. John the Penitent also espoused this view.[220] This provision inspired rules governing the conduct of monks in some Serbian *trebnici*, resulting in a peculiar depiction of Christ as the "bridegroom" of monks.[221] An alternative tradition, traced to the Sixth Ecumenical Council, directed that a monk guilty of fornication undergo no more than the usual penance for laymen.[222]

Combining these contradictory teachings, the tradition that came to prevail in Slavic canon law differentiated between requirements for monks and nuns of the "lesser form" and those prescribed for religions of the "greater form," or *skimnici*. The *sxima*—a vow of extreme asceticism—was taken only by the most pious of religious, or upon one's deathbed. A sexual sin by a monk of the "lesser form" merited the usual penance for fornication, that is, seven years. A *skimnik* who committed the same offense was deemed more guilty, and underwent the fifteen-year penance for adultery.[223] Following the guidelines laid down by St. John the Penitent, a few Slavic compilers reduced the penances to five years for *skimnici* and two years for other monks, or seven years and three years.[224]

The penances for nuns who violated their vows of celibacy differed from those for monks. An "adulterous" *skimnica* received a penance of twelve years, rather than the fifteen suffered by a male counterpart. For a nun of the lesser form, one tradition recommended a penance of nine years, considerably longer than that for a male counterparts.[225] Other codes, especially common in Russia, imposed the same penances on nuns as on monks, ranging from two to seven years.[226]

The worst form of fornication for a nun was intercourse with a monk. Because monks and nuns were "brothers and sisters in Christ," sexual intercourse between them was incest. Consequently, harsh penalties were imposed. The usual penance consisted of a dry fast for twelve

220. Zaozerskij and Xaxanov, 83; NBS 48, ff. 180v, 188v. Some versions of the syntagma order a sixteen-year penance; see Troicki, 67.
221. Peć 77, ff. 261v–262r; SANU 124(29), f. 54v.
222. Troicki, 67.
223. E.g., Hil. 302, ff. 84r, 126r–v; Hil. 628, ff. 22r, 24v, 69v; Rila 1/20(48), f. 185r–v.
224. BNL 648, f. 157r; BAN-S 48, n.p.; Peć 77, f. 111r (but not in the code on f. 236r); Dečani 68, f. 281r; Almazov, 3:271, 279; Smirnov, *Materialy*, 32. SANU 123(28), ff. 37r, 107v, reduced the penances for the respective ranks to 3 years and 1 year and 2 months. The 4-year penance in Sinai 37, f. 101v, probably reflects a scribe's misreading of the word *č'tec*, "reader," for *černec*, "monk"; it also appears in Peć 77, f. 109r, and Dečani 68, f. 279r.
225. Kiev 49, ff. 660v–661r; Hil. 169, ff. 79v–80r; SANU 124(29), f. 73r; NBS I-14, f. 260v. Dečani 69, f. 111r recommends a dry fast of 5 years with 300 prostrations for a *skimnica*.
226. Almazov, 3:271; Smirnov, *Materialy*, 30, 32.

years, accompanied by 150 prostrations a day, and a prohibition against setting foot inside a church for that period.[227] In one manuscript tradition, the twelve-year penance applied when the woman was a *skimnica*; when the nun had taken the lesser vow, the penance was nine years.[228]

Because "black" priests enjoyed the dignity of both monastic and priestly rank, their sexual sins were regarded as correspondingly serious. Rules that came out of the tradition of St. John the Penitent recommended a penance of three years and loss of rank.[229] A monastic priest who committed incest was demoted to the rank of a simple monk and placed under penance for fifteen years; the maximum penance for a "white" priest was ten years.[230] When the "black" priest's partner was a nun, he fasted the same length of time as a simple monk, but the number of daily prostrations was raised substantially, varying from 500 to an impossible 20,000.[231]

Church canons officially did not differentiate between casual fornication by a monk or nun and an illegal marriage.[232] In both situations, the offender received a penance of seven years. Only a *skimnik* underwent a fifteen year penance (on bread and water).[233] A somewhat lighter penance of five years was imposed on a monk who abandoned his vows of celibacy and dietary abstinence under constraint while a captive of the infidels.[234]

Monks and nuns who decided that they could not maintain monastic celibacy did not have the option of returning to "the world" and marrying. Immunity charters granted to the Russian church established that men and women who had forsaken their monastic vows still legally fell under the jurisdiction of the church.[235] The canons of St. Basil declared that such a union "should be judged not marriage but fornication." One version of canon law imposed a penance of seven years on a monk or nun who returned to the religious life after an illicit marriage, reserving the fifteen-year penance for a former religious who repented but nevertheless remained with his or her spouse.[236] This provision de facto

227. E.g., BNL 684, f. 157r; Hil. 378, f. 167r; Almazov, 3:283. A few Russian codes recommend a penance of 15 years; see Almazov, 3:272; Smirnov, *Materialy*, 34. ZSL-P, 146, orders life imprisonment.

228. This tradition is preserved only in the regulations regarding monastic priests; see Rila 1/20(48), f. 47v; Hil. 305, f. 82r; SANU 123(28), f. 98v, and 124(29), f. 140v.

229. E.g., Hil. 302, f. 120v; Rila 1/20(48), f. 47v; Hil. 305, f. 81v; SANU 125(154), f. 84v.

230. Rila 1/20(48), f. 47v; SANU 124(29), f. 140v.

231. E.g., Hil. 302, f. 121v; Rila 1/20(48), f. 47v; Hil. 305, f. 82r.

232. NBS 48, f. 156v, quoting art. 44 of the Sixth Ecumenical Council at Trulla.

233. Hil. 302, f. 126r–v. See Pavlov, *Nomokanon pri Bol'šom Trebnike*, 225, for a comparison between the Slavic and the Greek versions of this rule.

234. Rila 1/20(48), f. 50v.

235. "Pravosudie mitropolič'e," art. 37, in *DKU*, 211.

236. NBS 10, ff. 33r–34v, in accordance with art. 44 of the rules of the Sixth Ecumenical Council at Trulla.

No escape to marriage

permitted a person to leave the monastic life, although the long penance tended to discourage the practice. A more common provision dictated that the only acceptable course was for the former religious to forsake the illegal marriage and return to the monastery. Upon repentance, the offenders underwent a penance of fifteen years, as for adultery. If they continued to live in sin until they died, they were denied Christian burial.[237] The rule of Nicephoros of Constantinople, included in some versions of the syntagma, was even harsher: it anathematized a monk who left the monastery and took a wife, and directed that he be returned to monastic life by force if necessary.[238] The code of Stefan Dušan contained a provision for the enforcement of this rule, ordering that a monk who abandoned his calling be confined in a dungeon until he agreed to return to his monastery. The Beogradska Krmčija demonstrates the Slavic preference for the stricter interpretation: the scribe first described the marriage of a nun as "fornication" (*blud*), then crossed out that word and replaced it with "adultery" (*ljubodějanie*).[239]

The taking of deathbed monastic vows complicated the rules governing the sexual conduct of monks and nuns. The custom was widespread in the Orthodox world, owing in large part to the belief that people left their sins behind them when they entered the religious life and took a new name.[240] Men and women might take the *sxima* when they believed themselves to be at death's door, then recover after all. The church regarded monastic vows as irreversible, especially when the *skimnik* had experienced a seemingly miraculous cure. However, the *skimnik*, restored once more to health and vigor, might be unwilling or unable to uphold the vow made in a moment of physical or emotional weakness. Perhaps this was the group the anonymous compiler of the twelfth-century Russian Efremovskaja Kormčaja had in mind when he recommended compassion for maidens who violated vows of chastity. Such young women should be treated gently, he wrote, and placed under penance for only a year, as for a second marriage. He was less sympathetic toward widows who broke promises not to remarry, presumably in an effort to guarantee their inheritance rights.[241] In the fifteenth century, Metropolitan Fotij of Russia was presented with such a case: a deacon had married a *skimnica*. The union violated at least two regulations: a nun was not permitted to marry, and Fotij disapproved of

---

237. E.g., Kiev 191, f. 688r; Hil. 301, f. 87v.; Hil. 305, f. 30r–v; Hil. 302, ff. 81v–82r, citing St. Basil's Rule, art. 6. See also the comparison of Greek and Slavic versions in Pavlov, *Nomokanon pri Bol'šom Trebnike*, 199. SANU 125(154), ff. 25v–26r; 122(47), f. 18r; and 123(28), ff. 36r–37r, contain both the more liberal and the stricter provisions.

238. Troicki, 78.

239. NBS 48, f. 177v.

240. Novaković, *Primeri književnosti i jezika*, 528.

241. GIM, Sin. 227, ff. 186v–187r.

marriage after ordination. Despite his usual harshness, Fotij did not require the couple to separate, though he gave them a heavy penance.[242] The Moscow Synod of 1667 tried to discourage the practice of taking vows in anticipation of death. It forbade young married persons to take monastic vows, even in sickness, without the permission of the spouse and parents. Only old people, and those without spouses and children, should take vows when they were ill.[243]

Canon law recommended other approaches in addition to penitential fasts, prostrations, and exclusion from communion, depending on the circumstances. If the source of a sinful monk's temptation was located close at hand, the abbot was instructed to send him to a distant monastery, with a letter recounting his conduct.[244] A document of this sort survives from seventeenth-century Russia. Patriarch Filaret wrote to the abbot of the isolated Nikolskij monastery in Karelia to tell him to expect the monk Nafanailo. Nafanailo had been apprehended in fornication. The patriarch ordered the abbot to ascertain that the disobedient monk was never released from the monastery or permitted to get drunk. He was also to be denied communion until the hour of his death, although he could associate with the rest of the monks otherwise. Filaret also required the abbot to supply him with a report on Nafanailo's conduct after a year.[245]

Slavic canons frequently included special provisions for laypeople who engaged in illicit sex with clerics. Canonists did not always advocate increased penalties when the partner was a cleric. One code recommended an unusually heavy penance of five years of fasting for a laywoman who engaged in sex with a monk. The reasoning seems to have been that interfering with the piety of a man of God was an especially serious offense. Another code, however, imposed an unusually light penance of one year, perhaps with the understanding that the woman might have acquiesced out of deference to his authority.[246] A layman who slept with a nun of either the greater or lesser form could be placed under penance for as little as two years or as much as fifteen.[247] It was a sin, carrying a

242. "Gramota mitropolita Fotija v Pskov" (1422/1425), in RIB, 6:433.
243. *Dejanija moskovskix soborov*, 26.
244. Rila 1/20(48), f. 52r–v; SANU 124(29), f. 144v; Hil 468, f. 245v.
245. No. 142 (dated to 1631) in RIB, 14:359–360.
246. Almazov, 3:160, 163.
247. E.g., ibid., 149 (2 years if with one nun, 4–6 years if with many, 5 years if with a *skimnica*), 277 (2 years' dry fast or 5 years if with a *skimnica*), 287 (7 years, 600 prostrations twice daily on Mondays, Wednesdays, and Fridays); Smirnov, *Materialy*, 54 (5 years on bread and water), 151 (15 years); Peć 77, f. 109r (3 years on bread and water); Hil. 167, ff. 225v (3 years, 1 on bread and water), 235v (8 years standing outside church); Rila 1/20(48), f. 195v (8 years, 150 prostrations); Kiev 49, ff. 660v–661r (9 years for sex with a *skimnica*, rape, or removal of the nun from her convent; otherwise 5 years); "Voprosy i otvety pastyrskoj praktiki," art. 38, in RIB, 6:864–865 (10 years); NBS I-14, f. 260v (12 years, 300 prostrations).

penance of seventeen days, for a layman even to think lustfully about a nun.[248] The wide diversity in penances and the absence of any recognizable manuscript tradition point to a high degree of scribal selection. Scribes evidently agreed that sexual intercourse with a nun constituted a special category of sin but varied in their estimation of its relative seriousness. The heavy, forty-*grivny* fine imposed by the Code of Jaroslav placed this offense in the same category as incest within the nuclear family and rape of a noblewoman.[249]

Associations between monks and women were discouraged even when no sexual intercourse took place. Monks were forbidden to kiss women (or boys, for that matter), including their own mothers. Embracing a woman or a boy carried a penance of forty days, according to one tradition, and 600 prostrations according to another.[250] It was somewhat less serious for a monk to kiss his mother; the penance then consisted of 300 prostrations.[251] In another tradition of monastic rules, it was a more serious offense for a monk to kiss a woman than a boy, particularly if he was "tempted," perhaps meaning that he experienced an erection.[252]

It was similarly forbidden for a monk to sit on a woman's lap (including his mother's); the penance consisted for forty days of exclusion from communion and from the company of other monks at meals.[253] It was a violation of monastic rules for a monk to go anywhere with a woman, although the penance was minor, consisting of only a hundred prostrations.[254] Conversation with a woman merited twenty-five prostrations.[255] A monk who attended a party in the company of a woman "willingly defiled his mind and his heart," because "even looking at

248. Almazov, 3:280.

249. *DKU*, 95. Under Byzantine law, civil penalties, such as mutilation, could also be levied against a man who defiled a "bride of Christ's Church." See Hil. 466, f. 144r; Pavlov, "'Knigi zakonnyja,'" 73; *Sintagmat*, 177; *ZSL-P*, 140.

250. E.g., Hil. 302, ff. 85r, 126v; Hil. 167, f. 220r; Hil. 304, ff. 38r, 92v; SANU 125(154), ff. 31r, 95v; Almazov, 3:272. Pavlov traced the rule with the 40-day penance to the code of Theodore the Studite; see *Nomokanon pri Bol'šom Trebnike*, 230.

251. E.g., Hil. 302, f. 126v; 304, f. 92v; 305, ff. 35r; Kiev 191, f. 690v. Other versions made an exception for a monk's mother; see BAN-S 48, n.p.

252. A monk who kissed a male and was "tempted" underwent a fast of 20 days; if he was not "tempted," the penance was 500 prostrations. If the monk was "tempted" by a woman, the penance was 40 days; if he avoided "temptation" while kissing her, the penance was 2 days: Hil. 628, f. 86r; SANU 122(47), f. 44r. Another version of this rule concerned only embracing a woman. A lustful kiss earned the usual penance of 40 days, while the penalty was halved for a passionless one. Rila 1/20(48), f. 199v; Peć 77, f. 282v. An alternate version mandated the lower, 20-day penance for a monk who was "tempted" by a woman; see Dečani 70, f. 255r.

253. E.g., BAN-S 48, n.p.; Rila 1/20(48), f. 201v; Hil. 167, f. 220r; Almazov, 3:272.

254. E.g., Rila 1/20(48), f. 201v; Hil. 167, f. 220v; Dečani 69, f. 106v; Kiev 191, f. 690r; Hil. 302, f. 126r.

255. Almazov, 3:273.

women, much less eating and drinking with them, is foreign to the way of monks."[256] Despite the harsh language, the usual penance for merely attending a feast was minor—seven days of exclusion from communion or twenty-four prostrations.[257] The penance increased dramatically, to three years and 1,060 prostrations a day, if the monk engaged in dancing and profane language.[258] Other forbidden activities were singing "demonic songs"; playing musical instruments, chess, or dice; and associating with prostitutes and slave women.[259] The presence of women at a feast was not crucial to condemnation, however: it was sufficient for a monk to attend with laymen, too, for "God will call him a bear." A monk became a "dog" in God's sight for looking at a woman.[260] However, it was not prohibited for monks to serve food to male and female visitors to the monastery.[261]

Monastic Homosexuality

For a monk, sex with a male was equated with sex with a female; the sin lay in the sexual contact rather than in the choice of partner. Both equally represented a temptation by Satan.[262] The danger inherent in women could be eliminated by strict control over their comings and goings. The spiritual center at Mount Athos banned women—and female animals—from the peninsula entirely. It was not possible, however, to isolate monks from the sexual temptation of other men. The structure of medieval Slavic society encouraged homosexuals to seek a monastic vocation. Laymen were expected to be married. For men who did not find women sexually appealing, the monastery was the only alternative to wedded life.

The extent of homosexuality in monasteries has long been a matter for aspersive speculation. Hierarchs have traditionally been reluctant to admit to the laity such a major incongruity with established principles of pious conduct. Nor could they tolerate it with equanimity. Consequently, monastic rules contain a large number of provisions designed to prevent sexual interactions between monks. Two penitential traditions

256. Rila 1/20(48), f. 54r; SANU 124(29), f. 146v; Hil. 468, f. 246r.
257. E.g., Hil. 305, f. 89r; SANU 125(154), f. 31r; Almazov, 3:273; Smirnov, *Materialy*, 38.
258. SANU 124(29), f. 146v.
259. Almazov, 3:176–177. The Slavic prohibition on monks' attendance at lay social functions is based on art. 15 of the Carthaginian Council, see Sreznevskij, 287.
260. Dečani 69, f. 106v; Smirnov, *Materialy*, 36; similar: Hil. 305, f. 34r; NBS 10, f. 37r; SANU 125(154), f. 31r.
261. GIM, Sin. 227, f. 80r–v.
262. Hil. 302, f. 29v.

existed for dealing with homosexual anal intercourse. The milder code imposed a penance of eight years on both offenders; the harsher one, a penance of sixteen years. Both codes imposed the same penances for bestiality.[263] Specific rules prohibited a monk from showing his genitals to another monk or sharing a bed with another (except on the abbot's instruction); both behaviors were classified as fornication, on the presumption that the intent was present.[264] When specific penances were named for these offenses, however, they frequently fell far short of the usual seven years mandated for fornication. A monk who grasped his genitals in public, for example, was excluded from communion and common meals for only a day.[265] The penance for a monk who shared a bed with another brother might be as minor 500 prostrations or as great as a fast of three years.[266] In one tradition, it was barely an offense even for a *skimnik* to kiss another monk: the penance was merely a hundred prostrations.[267]

Hierarchs did not underestimate the complexity of the problem. In early-sixteenth-century Russia, the anonymous author of an epistle to monks warned, "Youths are worse for monks than women!" So great was his concern that he was even willing to dispute the rule of Basil the Great, who permitted boys of sixteen or seventeen to take monastic vows, and church canons that permitted the taking of vows at age ten. He cited St. Isaac's admonition that monks "preserve themselves from association with youths, so that they do not defile their minds with lustful thoughts." Even the argument that many of the saints began their pious careers with early entry into the religious life failed to sway him. Young monks, he averred, should live in a separate monastery, apart from the older brothers, so as not to tempt them. And to discourage misconduct among the novices, the abbot should place them under a strict regime: fasting, little water, limited rest, no beds (they could sleep on the floor), prayer, singing of psalms, reading of holy writ, and work. Another contemporary author, recognizing that a separate monastery for the young was not a viable solution, urged that they keep their heads well covered by their cowls so as not to tempt others to sin.[268]

263. Manuscripts with an 8-year penance: Hil. 167, f. 221r; Dečani 69, f. 107r, Almazov, 3:273; Smirnov, *Materialy*, 37. Manuscripts with a 16-year penance: Hil. 302, f. 126v; Hil. 628, f. 69r–v; NBS 10, f. 98r. SANU 123(28), f. 107v, applied to monks the 15- or 3-year penance of the code for laymen.

264. E.g., BAN-S 48, n.p.; Dečani 69, f. 106v; Hil. 167, f. 220v; Kiev 191, f. 690v; Smirnov, *Materialy*, 35.

265. Rila 1/20(48), ff. 55v–56r; Hil. 468, f. 246v. A seventeenth-century Russian code labels this offense "fornication" but lists no penance; see Almazov, 3:272.

266. Prostrations: NBS 10, f. 37r; SANU 123(28), f. 41r. Fast: Almazov, 3:272.

267. Dečani 69, f. 107r.

268. Družinin, 89–92, 96.

Masturbation usually did not carry a longer penance for a monk than for a layman; forty days was deemed sufficient. However, the monk was expected to follow a strict dry fast during this period in order to eliminate his lustful passion, and perform 300 prostrations a day.[269] Another tradition mandated a dry fast of sixty days for a simple monk who sinned in this manner.[270] The penance was raised to two years for a monastic priest, and he was forbidden to perform the liturgy.[271] It was also forbidden for a monk to hold or look at his own genitals.[272]

For monks as for other men, a nocturnal emission signified a test for weakness by the Devil. Nil Sorskij warned that Satan would try to disrupt the lives of men devoted to God.[273] A variety of traditions existed on how to handle an "unclean dream."[274] In one, the unfortunate monk was supposed to confess his sin to the other brothers, who would pray to God for his forgiveness. According to one code, he was also excluded from communion for that day, and had to complete the usual prostrations and recitations of prayers.[275] A monastic priest was forbidden to perform the liturgy, even in the event of great need.[276] Another code imposed additional prayers, forty-nine prostrations, and exclusion from communion for seven days. A third imposed a fast of twenty days followed by exclusion from communion for six months.[277]

Monastic Discipline

The maintenance of monastic discipline was the responsibility of the abbot. The abbot was empowered to judge the monks under his authority, in accordance with the canons and his own conscience. The abbot's authority became a particular issue when the laity learned of a monk's misconduct. One canon concerned the abbot's responsibility when a monk was caught in flagrante delicto with a married woman, and either he or the husband was killed. In the case of this "multiplication of sins," an investigation was to be made to determine whether the abbot was at fault for failing to supervise the monk properly. If the abbot had tried to instill morality in the monk but had been disobeyed, he was exoner-

269. Rila 1/20(48), f. 62v.
270. NBS 10, f. 30r.
271. Rila 1/20(48), f. 48r. The 12-year penance mandated by SANU 124(29), f. 141r, is doubtless a copyist's error.
272. Hil. 167, f. 220r; Dečani 69, f. 106v.
273. Fedotov, 112–113.
274. NBS 24, f. 7r–v.
275. Rila 1/20(48), ff. 52v–53r, 62r–v, Smirnov, *Materialy*, 176.
276. Hil. 302, f. 121v; Rila 1/20(48), f. 47r–v; SANU 123(28), f. 98v.
277. Peć 77, f. 282r; Dečani 70, f. 255r.

ated.[278] The abbot's refusal to abide by canons prohibiting women from living in a monastery was considered sufficient grounds for a monk to leave without his superior's permission.[279] The abbot could be removed from his position merely for discussing matters with women.[280]

Penitential questions for abbots reveal that they, too, could fall into sexual sin. Potential partners included, first of all, young monks, but also married women, widows, slaves, maidens, and nuns—all of whom might reasonably dwell in a monastic complex.[281] Because of the abbot's position of authority and respect, special care had to be taken in the case of his sexual sin. If he was rumored to be a fornicator, he was not to be confronted in front of the community. Instead, two or three of the most senior monks were to gather to discuss the situation. Then each was to go singly to visit the abbot in his cell, tell him humbly of the concern of the brethren, and beg him to give up his sin. If he did not repent, the monks were free to go to another monastery, but only God had the right to judge the abbot.[282] It was more important to uphold the abbot's prestige and authority in the monastery than to punish his offenses.

Churchmen faced an even more serious problem than the maintenance of discipline within monasteries: what was to be done about self-proclaimed monks and nuns who lived outside of ecclesiastical institutions? The early Christian tradition included many hermits of both sexes. Some became saints, and the tales about them filled didactic collections. With this sort of precedent, it was difficult for hierarchs to condemn individual eremitism in general, but they were wary because of the problems of maintaining discipline among such people.

Some canonists were lenient, and permitted women—usually widows—to adopt the monastic life in their homes, provided they took formal vows and placed themselves under the supervision of an elder nun.[283] It was a practical alternative for a widow, who might wish to follow the religious life without neglecting her young children. By taking monastic vows, she made a commitment never to remarry, thus guaranteeing her right to inherit a share of her late husband's property. A woman who lived as a nun in her own home was not bound by the restrictions on movement and property ownership of monastic life. All

278. Rila 1/20(48), f. 52v; SANU 124(29), ff. 144v–145r; Hil. 468, f. 245v. It is not clear from the text who would carry out the investigation, but it would probably be the archimandrite, who oversaw all of the monasteries in a region.
279. Hil. 305, f. 36r; Hil. 167, f. 272v, quoting the rules of Nicephoros of Constantinople.
280. Hil. 302, f. 125v; Hil. 305, f. 88r; Rila 1/20(48), f. 48v.
281. Almazov, 3:183.
282. SANU 124(29), ff. 139v–140r.
283. Hil. 302, ff. 82v–83r; Hil. 305, ff. 31v–32r.

in all, it was an appealing alternative for widows, especially in sixteenth- and seventeenth-century Russia, where women enjoyed substantial inheritance rights but significant constraints on personal activity.

The *vita* of Juliana Lazarevskaja, written by her son, epitomizes the life of the pious woman who followed the monastic life in her home even though she was not a widow. Juliana had wished to become a nun from childhood, her son wrote, but obeyed her parents' desire for her to marry. After bearing children to her husband, she expressed a desire to enter a convent, but agreed instead to remain with her children at home, living as a nun in their midst. She removed herself from the bedroom, gave up all sexual contact with her husband, and devoted her life to prayer, acts of self-denial, and works of charity.[284]

The Serbian saint Peter Koriski lived for a time as a monk in his own home. After his father's death, Peter wished to enter a monastery, but his mother dissuaded him, reminding him of his duty to support her and his young sister. She agreed to refrain from arranging a marriage for him, and to allow him to fast and pray at home. Peter's pursuit of monastic asceticism and spirituality at home impressed his sister, who eventually rejected marriage to become a nun.[285]

Many hierarchs forbade men and women to take up the monastic life on their own, either in the wilderness or in a town. The temptation to abandon monastic discipline was too great. The Code of Stefan Dušan espoused this view, requiring all monks and nuns to live in cenobitic communities under the authority of an abbot or abbess.[286] Metropolitan Fotij of Russia agreed. A proper nun had to live in an ecclesiastical institution, under the supervision of an abbess; she also had to dress in a nun's habit, rather than in lay clothing.[287] Later hierarchs issued similar rulings, including the Moscow Synod in 1667 and Metropolitan Pitrim of Novgorod in 1668. Nuns and monks who had left monasteries were to return to them, and those who had remained in lay residences were to take up cenobitic life. Even sick persons who had taken deathbed vows had to be moved into religious institutions. Furthermore, in order to guarantee that a new monk or nun would be supervised by an abbot or abbess, only specially appointed "black" priests could officiate at the taking of monastic vows.[288] The elder Serapion, investigating the

284. Gudzij, 345–351. For a study of the *vita* of Juliana Lazarevskaja, see T. A. Greenan, "Iulianiya Lazarevskaya," *Oxford Slavonic Papers* n.s. 15 (1982): 28–45.

285. Novaković, *Primeri književnosti i jezika*, 340.

286. *Zakonik cara Stefana Dušana*, 100 (Struški version), 168–170 (Atonski version); Burr, 201.

287. "Gramota mitropolita Fotija v Pskov" (1422/1425), in RIB, 6:431; " Voprosy i otvety pastyrskoj praktiki," art. 65, in ibid., 868.

288. *Dejanija moskovskix soborov*, 47r, 72v–73r; no. 162 in *Akty sobrannye v bibliotekax i arxivax Rossijskoj imperii*, 4:214–216.

Old Belief for Tsar Aleksei in seventeenth-century Russia, complained about the influence exercised by the heretical *Raskolniki* among women who followed the religious life at home. He noted that these self-proclaimed nuns refused to attend church or receive the sacraments, and followed the tutelage of an Old Believer monastic priest. When confronted by ecclesiastical authorities, they fled to another place. Monasticism in the home was popular among Old Believers, who believed that the world stood on the brink of the Apocalypse.[289]

In its regulation of the sexual expression of the clergy, the Slavic Orthodox churchmen had a variety of imperatives, not all of them compatible. The first was to protect the church from satanic intrusion, revealed in the form of sexuality. To this end, clerics who had engaged in any sort of sexual activity, voluntarily or involuntarily, could not partake of the sacraments or administer them. An exception could be made only in cases of "great need"—usually interpreted to mean the lack of a substitute on an important occasion. Although sensual actions were more defiling, sexual desire alone indicated susceptibility to demonic influence.

The second imperative was to present living models of the Christian life: celibate monks and nuns, chaste clergy and their wives. Monasticism was the superior form, marked by self-restraint and devotion to prayer and works of charity. Monks and nuns tried to take on "angelic form"—and angels were asexual beings. Any expression of sexual interest, even something far short of fornication, indicated a failure to achieve the primary goal of monastic life. Clerical marriage permitted limited sexual expression. It included the same constraints on sexuality as lay marriage: restriction of all sexual activity to marriage, at a time when religious duties would not be compromised. Because clerics had extensive ecclesiatical duties, their conjugal relations were correspondingly curtailed. Churchmen were less understanding of human frailty in clerics than in the laity. For that reason, clerics were expected to observe periods of abstinence more strictly than laymen, and they were forbidden the dispensation of remarriage.

In order to serve as models of Orthodox piety, both "black" and "white" clergy had to avoid public violations of sexual norms. A third imperative of the church was to maintain the reputations and the authority of clerics in the eyes of the laity. To this end, hierarches had first to scrutinize candidates for ordination and for ecclesiastical offices to ascertain their moral character, judged primarily by their sexual behavior. Second, hierarchs were prepared to remove offending clerics

289. Barskov, 78, 82–83, 121.

from their posts, especially when their violations became public knowledge. Third, they tried, albeit unsuccessfully, to discourage the circulation of scurrilous reports about clerics' conduct. And fourth, they established that clerical offenders would be subject exclusively to ecclesiastical rather than secular authorities.

Finally, churchmen wished to uphold the authority of hierarchs within ecclesiastical institutions. To satisfy this imperative, they bestowed upon bishops and abbots the right to judge their subordinates as they saw fit, within the diverse traditions of canon law. They also established procedures for removing bishops and abbots guilty of misconduct from their positions. In these procedures, however, it was more important to uphold the prestige of the office, despite the current holder's unworthiness, than to castigate him for his sins. Often it was the secular powers who intervened to depose hierarchs for misconduct, which was sometimes defined by political expediency.

The enforcement of the standards of sexual morality for all of medieval Slavic society rested on the knowledge and vigilance of the clergy. A necessary precondition for fulfillment of this role was the propagation of these standards within the ranks of the church.

Conclusion

The medieval Orthodox Slavs regarded sexual expression as a public rather than a private matter, with consequences for the welfare of society. Behind the moralizing tone of ecclesiastical writings lay social realities. Violations of rules of sexual conduct endangered familial and community stability. In a society organized primarily around relationships defined through familial and quasi-familial ties, any sexual activity either confirmed or threatened existing bonds. Regulations on incest, divorce, remarriage, and concubinage ensured that familial relationships would remain unambiguous and that bonds of responsibility would be clear. Prohibitions on premarital and extramarital sex protected the sanctity of marriage, which formed the basis of political and economic alliances between families. If couples who married out of obligation rather than emotional or physical attraction found themselves to be sexually incompatible, restrictions on marital intercourse minimized their difficulties. Thus rules reinforced the authority of families over individuals, masters over servants, men over women, and the clergy over their parishioners.

The church, the state, and the community all had a stake in maintaining order. Hence they cooperated in the inculcation and enforcement of the standards of sexual behavior. Nobody expected the complete elimination of sin, but they hoped to require those who deviated to acknowledge their mistakes and the validity of the norms of conduct. To this end, the secular authorities, the clergy, the community, the family, and the individual all had to cooperate.

The secular authorities had the least direct influence over the sexual behavior of the population. Unlike Byzantium, the Slavic states granted complete authority over morality and intrafamilial matters to the church, and for the most part allowed the church to operate without

interference in its governing of sexual behavior. Provisions for the enforcement of sexual standards in Byzantine civil law were transferred
into the realm of canon law in Slavic countries. Churchmen frustrated
by violations of canon law might call upon the secular authorities to
help them enforce the rules, but such appeals were rarely heeded. Conversely, rulers might bring persistent problems to the attention of the
church, but the hierarchs were generally already aware of them. The
state also wanted the clergy, its major tool of social control, to command respect, and it could initiate the removal of undesirable clerics
from their offices. Finally, the secular rulers invoked canon law, accurately or inaccurately, as justification for policies advantageous to the
state.

The secular authorities concerned themselves with sexual behavior
only when it directly threatened peace and order. Rape was one such
case, because it was a crime of violence more than a sexual misde-
meanor. The state had an interest in determining the validity of marriages only insofar as secular matters, such as inheritance, were at stake.
Civil authorities did not enforce ecclesiastical provisions requiring
church weddings, despite the appeals of generations of prelates. When
princes directed the formation of policy on sexuality, as Stefan Dušan
did in his law code and Ivan IV did at the Stoglav Council, they acted in
their capacity as tsar, fulfilling the Byzantine emperor's traditional role.
No medieval Slavic prince sought to remove oversight of sexual behavior from the church's purview.

Although there were many sources of conflict between church and
state, sexual morality was rarely counted among them. Political goals
sometimes required divorce, remarriage, intermarriage, incestuous
unions, or other violations of canon law. Even as princes transgressed
the rules of sexual behavior, they upheld their validity by arguing that
only their special extenuating circumstances—*raisons d'état*—justified
their actions. Usually churchmen concurred, seeing the advantages in
having an heir or constructing a new foreign alliance, and did not challenge their princes. When the church did protest, the primary objection
was usually to the policy the ruler was pursuing. In the main, religious
and secular authorities had the same goal: the restriction of uninhibited
sexual expression, which threatened spiritual well-being and the social
order alike.

The clergy had the primary responsibility for the promotion of sexual
morality. They used three methods: example, education, and penaliza-
tion. By living in celibacy or chaste marriage, the clergy demonstrated
that the minimum requirements of canon law were workable, albeit not
easy. Sexual violations by the clergy threatened the structure of society

considerably more than the same offense by the laity. The laity would view a cleric's failure to uphold the standard as license to sin, or worse, as justification for disobedience to a hypocritical priest. In the interest of maintaining clerical authority if not morality, the church hierarchy had to prosecute clerical offenders vigorously. At the same time, certain moderate prelates recognized that priests who made excessive demands on themselves and on their parishioners also endangered the church's authority. Consequently, they sought to inculcate in parish clergy sympathy for human weakness and advocated leniency for sexual offenses that caused little social disruption.

There were two major obstacles to the building of a parish clergy that observed and taught the sexual standard established by the church. First, the priests were not always knowledgeable. Most learned their profession through a sort of apprenticeship and had minimal formal education. The only saving grace was that ignorant priests usually ministered to an equally untutored laity, who would not be likely to notice their lapses. The parish clergy tended to share the perspectives of the community in which they were born, grew up, lived, and served, including their attitudes on sexuality. When the hierarchy of the Russian church in the sixteenth and seventeenth centuries attempted to improve the training of priests and mark them as a social group distinct from the laity, they made the job of the parish clergy more difficult. The villagers would be less likely to cooperate with a priest whom they perceived as an outsider, who was inflexible and unresponsive to the community's needs and values. Second, the parish clergy depended on the goodwill of their parishioners, who were neighbors and a major source of income. A priest who made unpopular demands would find himself ostracized and impoverished. The long toleration of irregular marriages, divorces, and remarriages may best be explained by the local priests' unwillingness to challenge their parishioners. As a result, the church had substantial motivation to develop and enforce a sexual standard that was compatible with popular sensibilities.

In the absence of widespread formal education, instruction in sexual behavior had to come from the local clergy in the context of religious rites. The *vitae* of saints and the didactic tales presented the norms of sexual conduct. The saints represented the ideal, albeit an unreachable one: complete abstinence from physical sex, a successful struggle against desire. Tales and sermons illustrated the awful consequences of sexual misconduct: the sinner condemned to eternal torment, shamed before the community; the community condemned to war and other "natural" disasters because of its toleration of evil. Repentance followed by a life of abstinence and contrition was the only way to avert the wages of sin.

By presenting the rewards of sexual virtue and the adversities attendant on sexual sin in graphic form, the clergy hoped to persuade the laity to practice self-restraint.

Confession presented an additional means of educating the populace about proper sexual conduct. By concentrating on sexual matters almost to the exclusion of other sins, penitential questionnaires conveyed a strong message that sexual righteousness was the determining factor in an individual's standing before God and the community. Because even violations committed in ignorance would be harmful to the soul and to society, the church preferred to provide detailed information on them. Slavic priests long ago addressed the modern issue of whether educating young people about responsible sexual expression incited them to misconduct, and concluded that it did not.

The use of penance as the primary vehicle for the enforcement of the standard of sexual behavior implies community cooperation. The community took an active interest in the sexual behavior of its members. Neighbors reported violations to the ecclesiastical authorities, especially when the welfare of the society was threatened. Popular shaming procedures complemented ecclesiastical strictures. Persons who refused to desist from violation found themselves ostracized from church and community. Although confession itself was private—at least insofar as the requirements of propriety permitted—fulfillment of the penance was usually public, to some degree. Fasts and prayers were carried out in view of the family; exclusion from communion placed the penitent in public view. The ban on entering the church building placed on those who committed serious sins made the severity of their offenses still more obvious. Though the parishioners might not know the nature of the penitent's sin, the penance surely provided grounds for speculation. By carrying out the penance, the sinner reaffirmed the community's standard of sexual behavior and his or her personal failing. The combination of community and ecclesiastical sanctions was effective against all but the most marginal and the most recalcitrant persons.

Each family was charged with regulation of the behavior of its members. The husband was responsible for his wife, and the parents for their children. The parents selected marriage partners for the children, giving priority to potential political and economic gains rather than personal attraction. A volatile relationship between husband and wife could interfere with the functioning of the agreement between families. Thus it was in the interest of the families to discourage excessive passion as well as infidelity and gross abuse.

The Orthodox Slavs, unlike Christians in the West, paid little attention to the emotional component of sexual behavior. Slavic churchmen did not ponder whether procreative intent made conjugal sex sinless; they looked only at procreative achievement, measured by the birth of a viable child. The Orthodox Slavs cared little what emotion motivated sexual intercourse, or what pleasure or satisfaction participants derived from it. They evaluated the quality of the sexual act solely by its form and its circumstances. The principle of Western canon law that "marital affection" sufficed to validate a marriage was alien to the Orthodox Slavs. Although husbands and wives ideally grew to feel devotion for each other, their emotional relationship was irrelevant to the validity of their union. Neither affection nor attraction was deemed an appropriate motivation to marry, or to engage in a nonmarital sexual relationship.

In short, the medieval Slavs saw no link between physical and emotional intimacy. This perception had two main ramifications. First, Eastern and Western European ideas about love and sexuality increasingly diverged. The idea of romantic love, which became dominant in Western literature and ultimately in legal and popular conceptions of marriage, remained unfamiliar in the East. It is not accidental that the great romances of the later Middle Ages, such as the tale of Tristan and Isolde, were not reworked in the Slavic Orthodox world. The depth of the cultural gulf between East and West in matters of male–female relationships may be seen in the disdain foreign visitors expressed for Orthodox Slavic women and the suspicion eighteenth- and nineteenth-century Slavic peasants felt for the Westernized lifestyle of their aristocratic landlords.

Second, the conception of sex and love as antithetical meant that medieval Slavs looked to nonmarital relationships for emotional fulfillment. Arranged marriages were more palatable in the East than in the West, because young people entered them hoping only for consideration and cooperation, as in a business transaction. Even when one spouse became unfaithful, the other could not feel emotionally betrayed. The strongest emotional bond was between a mother and her children, in particular the sons, who would not leave the household even as adults. Friends were another source of emotional support, and such relationships were confirmed through ceremonies of adoption and spiritual kinship. The result was exceptionally strong ties between generations and between allies.

Although the requirements for proper conduct were stringent, the Orthodox Slavs did not worry about the attitudes and intentions behind behavior. People were made responsible only for controlling their actions, not for controlling their thoughts and feelings. Further, the repressiveness of the sexual standard was balanced by realistic expectations about levels of observance.

Scholars of the medieval West have suggested that the masses of the laity were amoral in sexual matters—that is, they did not worry about the spiritual value of their actions; they were concerned only about the possible consequences. The church, meanwhile, tried to control sexual behavior on the basis of morality—that is, by reference to abstract principles of theology. This view of the dichotomy between people and church parallels the dominant theory about religion in the medieval Slavic world: the masses of the population continued to practice paganism, covering it with a thin veneer of Christianity in an effort to delude the clergy, while the church struggled to impose its alien theology.

The study of Orthodox Slavic sexuality suggests that this view overstates the difference between church and community. At least in sexual matters, the gap between ecclesiastical and community norms was not great. The church's approach to sexuality was eminently practical. It rightly regarded sexuality as a potential threat to the social order. It labeled most manifestations of sexual expression as unambiguously illicit. The severity of the punishment for offenses roughly matched the degree to which that behavior disrupted social stability, in the form of established hierarchies and gender roles. Allowance was made for extenuating circumstances, such as youth, ignorance, or advantage to the community. Finally, the church had realistic expectations about the level of observance of the rules, and developed methods to deal with violations. The population violated the rules frequently enough, but cooperated in punishment for offenses and in their enforcement. In general, the laity accepted the church's teachings on what constituted sexual sin and its perception of proper sexual conduct as essential to spiritual well-being.

The sexual standard that resulted from this harmony between ecclesiastical and popular attitudes was extraordinarily stable. It lasted through periods of political upheaval and foreign conquest. Even heretics tended to reinforce the norms of sexual conduct while challenging other aspects of ecclesiastical institutions and theology. If the medieval standard did not survive the introduction of Western ideas of sexuality, it died not because those ideas were superior or more natural but because they were better suited to the new way society was organized. When the state rather than the church and the community oversaw personal conduct, when political and economic connections did not follow family ties, the old rules of sexual conduct ceased to be practical. The medieval Slavic experience suggests strongly that the most successful standards of sexual behavior are those that are most compatible with social realities.

Bibliography

Manuscripts and Early Printed Books

An asterisk (*) indicates that the works listed are available on microfilm at the Hilandar Research Library, Ohio State University, Columbus.

BAN-L: Library of the Academy of Sciences, Leningrad
16.14.14   Mineja službenaja. Russian, fifteenth century.
*BAN-S: Bulgarian Academy of Sciences, Sofia
48   Missal and *trebnik*. Serbian, mid-fourteenth century.
*BNL: Bulgarian National Library, Sofia
245(103)   *Trebnik*. Serbian, sixteenth century.
251(200)   *Trebnik*. Bulgarian-Serbian, 1641.
275   *Zbornik*. Bulgarian, nineteenth century.
309   *Zbornik*. Serbian, seventeenth century.
324(520)   *Zbornik*. Bulgarian-Serbian, eighteenth century.
612(17)   *Trebnik*. Serbian, fifteenth–sixteenth century.
684   *Zbornik*. Serbian, seventeenth century.
740(168)   "Miracles of the Virgin." Church Slavonic, eighteenth century–
           1812.
Dečani: Dečani Monastery, Yugoslavia
67   *Trebnik*. Serbian, mid–fourteenth century.
68   *Trebnik*. Serbian, 1422.
69   *Trebnik*. Serbian, 1390–1400.
70   *Trebnik*. Serbian, first quarter seventeenth century.
*GBL: Lenin Library, Moscow
F. 304   "Sbornik slov i poučenij." Russian, twelfth–thirteenth century.
no. 12
GIM, Sin.: State Historical Museum, Moscow, Sinodal'nyj Collection
227   "Kormčaja Efremovskaja." Russian, twelfth century.
598   *Služebnik*. Russian, fourteenth century.
707   *Sestodnev*. Russian, fifteenth century.
997   Velikij minej čet'i. August, Russian, sixteenth century.

GPB: Saltykov-Ščedrin Library, Leningrad
FnI44   *Pčela.* Russian, fourteenth–fifteenth century.
Sof. b-ka,   Stisnoj prolog. Russian, twelfth–thirteenth century.
  no. 1324
Solov.   "Sbornik žitij svjatyx." Russian, sixteenth–seventeenth century.
  183/183
SPbDA, no.   "Skazanie o rossijskix svjatyx." Russian, sixteenth–seventeenth
  280   century.
*Hil.: Hilandar Monastery, Mount Athos, Greece
  167   *Trebnik.* Serbian, second quarter fifteenth century.
  169   *Trebnik.* Serbian, last quarter fifteenth century.
  170   *Trebnik.* Serbian, 1656.
  171   *Trebnik.* Serbian-Vlah, 1580.
  172   *Trebnik.* Serbian, mid-seventeenth–eighteenth century.
  227   *Zbornik.* Bulgarian, second quarter fifteenth century.
  278   *Zbornik.* Serbian, mid–fifteenth century.
  300   *Zakonik.* Serbian, first quarter fifteenth century.
  301   *Zakonik.* Serbian, 1620.
  302   *Sbornik.* Russian, 1631.
  304   Nomokanon Epitimijni. Serbian, mid–seventeenth century.
  305   Nomocanon. Serbian, seventeenth century.
  378   *Trebnik.* Serbian, fifteenth century.
  458   *Zbornik.* Bulgarian, second half fourteenth century.
  466   *Zbornik.* Serbian, second quarter fifteenth century.
  468   *Zbornik.* Serbian, c. 1400.
  477   *Zbornik.* Serbian, c. 1400.
  485   *Zbornik.* Russian-Moldavian, 1547.
  627   Nomocanon. Serbian, 1610–1620.
  628   Nomocanon. Serbian, first decade seventeenth century.
  Mogila, Peter *Trebnik.* Kiev, 1646. Printed book.
*Kiev: Slavonic books from Kiev, University of Toronto
  49   *Trebnik.* Kiev, 1606. Printed book.
  127   *Trebnik.* Moscow, 1637. Printed book.
  136   *Potrebnik Mirskoj.* Moscow, 1639. Printed book.
  191   *Potrebnik.* Moscow, 1651. Printed book.
*Lavra: Great Lavra Monastery, Mount Athos, Greece
  GL-9   *Zbornik.* Mixed recension, first half sixteenth century.
  GL-36   *Zbornik.* Bulgarian, second half fourteenth century.
NBS: National Library of Serbia, Belgrade
  10   Nomokanon Epitimijni. Serbian, 1615–1625.
  24   *Trebnik* (fragment). Serbian, 1480s.
  41   *Trebnik.* Serbian, first quarter sixteenth century.
  48   *Kormčaja.* Serbian, third quarter fifteenth century.
  51   *Trebnik.* Serbian, 1690–1700.
  52   *Trebnik.* Serbian, c. 1666.
  654   *Trebnik.* Serbian, c. 1666.
  688   *Zakonik.* Serbian, mid–sixteenth century.

I-14   *Trebnik.* Serbian, 1546. Printed book.

I-39   *Trebnik-Molitvenik.* Serbian-Vlah. Venice, 1635. Printed book.

Nov. Mus.: Novgorod State Museum, Novgorod, USSR

  10923   *Sbornik.* Russian, nineteenth century.

PD: Institute of Old Russian Literature (Puškinskij Dom), Leningrad

  Pinež. 2   "Sbornaja rukopis'." Russian, eighteenth century.

  Koll. Pereca,   "Sbornik bogoslužebnyj." Russian, 1405.
    no. 21

  Op. 24, no.   "Sbornik slov i žitij." Russian, nineteenth century.
    18

Peć: Peć Monastery, Yugoslavia

  77   *Trebnik.* Serbian, mid-fifteenth century.

*Rila: Rila Monastery, Bulgaria

  1/20(48)   Nomocanon. Serbian, seventeenth century.

  2/1(51)   *Trebnik.* Serbian, seventeenth century.

SANU: Serbian Academy of Sciences and Arts, Belgrade

  122(47)   Nomocanon. Serbian, sixteenth–seventeenth century.

  123(28)   Nomocanon. Serbian, seventeenth century.

  124(29)   Nomocanon. Serbian, seventeenth century.

  125(154)   Nomocanon. Serbian, sixteenth–seventeenth century.

*Sinai: Mount Sinai Monastery, Egypt

  17(17)   *Trebnik.* Serbian, fourteenth century.

  37   *Trebnik.* Old Church Slavonic, Glagolitic, eleventh century.

*SOCH: Serbian Orthodox Church of Hungary, Szentendre

  197   Nomocanon. Serbian, 1754.

TsGADA: Central State Archive of Ancient Acts, Moscow

  F. 181

    No. 332   *Pčela.* Russian, fifteenth century.

    No. 370   *Pčela.* Russian, fourteenth century.

  F. 381

    No. 39   "Lestvica Ioanna Lestvičnika." Russian, fourteenth century.

    No. 45   *Časoslov.* Russian, fourteenth century.

    No. 131   Mineja prazdničnaja. Russian, twelfth century.

    No. 133   Mineja prazdničnaja. Russian, fifteenth century.

    No. 162   Prolog. Russian, fourteenth century.

    No. 163   Prolog. Russian, 1356.

    No. 173   Prolog. Russian, thirteenth–fourteenth century.

*Uppsala: Uppsala University Library, Sweden

  Slav-70   "Apokalipsis." Russian, seventeenth–eighteenth century.

  Slav-71   *Sbornik.* Russian, seventeenth–eighteenth century.

*VAT-Bor: Vatican Library, Borgiani Illirici Collection

  15   *Trebnik.* Russian, 1541.

Other Works Cited

Adrianova-Peretc, V. P. "Drevnerusskie literaturnye pamjatniki v jugoslavjanskoj pis'mennosti." *Trudy otdela drevnerusskoj literatury* 19 (1963): 5–27.

Akty juridičeskie. St. Petersburg, 1838.

Akty sobrannye v bibliotekax i arxivax Rossijskoj imperii. Vol. 4. St. Petersburg, 1836.

Akty xolmogorskoj i ustjužskoj eparxij. Russkaja istoričeskaja biblioteka, vols. 12, 14, 25. St. Petersburg, 1890, 1894, 1908.

Alekseev, Konstantin. "Ob otnošenie suprugov po imuščestvu v drevnej Rossi i v Pol'še." In *Čtenija obščestva istorii i drevnostei rossijskix pri Moskovskom universitete,* bk. 2, pp. 1–108. Moscow, 1868.

Almazov, A. *Tajnaja ispoved' v pravoslavnoj vostočnoj cerkvi.* 3 vols. Odessa, 1894.

Amundsen, Darrel W., and Carol Jean Diers. "The Age of Menarche in Medieval Europe." *Human Biology* 45 (1973): 363–369.

—— and ——. "The Age of Menopause in Medieval Europe." *Human Biology* 45 (1973): 605–612.

Angelov, Bonju St. "Iz istorijata na ruskoto kulturno vlijanie v Bulgarija (XV–XVIII v.)." *Izvestija na Instituta za Bulgarska istorija* 6 (1956): 291–325.

Angelov, Dimitar. "Man through the Middle Ages of Bulgaria." *Bulgarian Historical Review* 10, no. 2 (1982): 66–80.

Angelov, Dimitŭr. *Bogomili.* N.p., 1961.

Anna Comnena. *The Alexiad.* Trans. Elizabeth A. S. Dawes. New York: Barnes & Noble, 1967.

Arcixovskij, A. V., et al., eds. *Novgorodskie gramoty na bereste.* 7 vols. Moscow, 1953–1976.

Ariès, Philippe, and André Béjin, eds. *Western Sexuality: Practice and Precept in Past and Present Times.* New York: Basil Blackwell, 1985.

Atkinson, Dorothy. "Society and the Sexes in the Russian Past." In Atkinson et al., *Women in Russia,* 3–24. Stanford: Stanford University Press, 1977.

Backus, Oswald P. "Evidences of Social Change in Medieval Russian Religious Literature." In Andrew Blaine, ed., *The Religious World of Russian Culture,* 75–99. The Hague: Mouton, 1975.

Baldziev, V. T. "Studija vŭrxu našeto personalno supružestvenno pravo." *Sbornik za narodni umotvorenija, nauka i knižnina* 4 (1891): 156–93, 5 (1891): 187–203, 7 (1892): 111–58, 8 (1892): 194–215, 10 (1894): 236–67.

Barskov, Ja. L. *Pamjatniki pervyx let russkago staroobrjadčestva.* St. Petersburg, 1912.

Barsukov, Nikolaj. *Istočniki russkoj agiografii.* St. Petersburg, 1882.

Baumgarten, N. de. *Généalogies des branches regnantes des Rurikides du XIIIe au XVIe siècle.* Orientalia Christiana, vol. 35. Rome: Pontifical Institute, 1934.

——. *Généalogies et mariages occidentaux des rurikides russes du Xe au XIIIe siècle.* Orientalia Christiana, vol. 9. Rome: Pontifical Institute, 1927.

Begunov, Ju. K. *Kozma Presviter v slavjanskix literaturax.* Sofia, 1973.

——. "Povest' o vtorom brake Vasilija III." *Trudy otdela drevnerusskoj literatury* 25 (1970): 105–118.

Belliustin, I. S. *Description of the Clergy in Rural Russia.* Ithaca: Cornell University Press, 1985.

Beneševič, V. N. *Drevne-slavjanskaja kormčaja XIV titulov bez tolkovanij.* St. Petersburg, 1906.

——. *Pamjatniki drevne-russkago kanoničeskago prava.* Russkaja istoričeskaja biblioteka, vol. 6. St. Petersburg, 1908.

——. *Sbornik pamjatnikov po istorii cerkovnago prava.* Petrograd, 1915.

——. *Sinagoga v 50 Titulov i drugie juridičeskie sborniki Ioanna Sxolastika.* St. Petersburg, 1914.

Berry, Lloyd E., and Robert O. Crummey, eds. *Rude and Barbarous Kingdom.* Madison: University of Wisconsin Press, 1968.

Best, Robert. "The Voyage Wherein Osepp Napea . . . " *Hakluyt Society Works* 73 (1886): 355–377.

Boswell, John. *Christianity, Social Tolerance, and Homosexuality.* Chicago: University of Chicago Press, 1980.

Božilov, Ivan. *Familijata na Asenevci: Genealogija i prosopografija.* Sofia, 1985.

Bozoky, Edina, ed. *Le Livre secret des cathares.* Paris, 1980.

Brjusova, V. G. *Russkaja živopis' 17 veka.* Moscow, 1984.

Brkić, Jovan. *Moral Concepts in Traditional Serbian Epic Poetry.* Slavistic Printings and Reprintings, vol. 24. The Hague: Mouton, 1961.

Brooke, Christopher N. L. "Aspects of Marriage Law in the Eleventh and Twelfth Centuries." In *Proceedings of the Fifth International Congress of Medieval Canon Law, Salamanca, 21–25 September 1976,* pp. 333–344. Monumenta Iuris Canonici, ser. C: Subsidia, vol. 6. Vatican, 1980.

——. "Marriage and Society in the Central Middle Ages." In R. B. Outhwaite, ed., *Marriage and Society: Studies in the Social History of Marriage,* 17–34. London: Europa, 1981.

Brown, Judith C. *Immodest Acts: The Life of a Lesbian Nun in Renaissance Italy.* New York: Oxford University Press, 1986.

Brownmiller, Susan. *Against Our Will.* New York: Simon & Schuster, 1975.

Brundage, James A. "Carnal Delight: Canonistic Theories of Sexuality." In *Proceedings of the Fifth International Congress of Medieval Canon Law, Salamanca, 21–25 September 1976,* 361–385. Monumenta Iuris Canonici, ser. C: Subsidia, vol. 6. Vatican, 1980.

——. "Concubinage and Marriage in Medieval Canon Law." *Journal of Medieval History* 1, no. 1 (1975): 1–17.

——. *Law, Sex, and Christian Society in Medieval Europe.* Chicago: University of Chicago Press, 1987.

——. "Let Me Count the Ways: Canonists and Theologians Contemplate Coital Positions." *Journal of Medieval History* 10, no. 2 (1984): 81–93.

——. "Sumptuary Laws and Prostitution in Late Medieval Italy." *Journal of Medieval History* 13, no. 4 (1987): 343–355.

—— and Vern L. Bullough. *Sexual Practices and the Medieval Church.* Buffalo: Prometheus Books, 1982.

Buffière, Felix. *Eros adolescent: La Pédérastie dans la Grèce antique.* Paris: Belles Lettres, 1980.

Bugge, John. *Virginitas: An Essay in the History of a Medieval Ideal.* The Hague: Martinus Nijhoff, 1975.

Bŭlgarija prez vekovete. Sofia, 1982.

Bullough, Vern L. *Sexual Variance in Society and History.* New York: Wiley, 1976.

Burr, Malcolm. "The Code of Stephan Dušan." *Slavonic and East European Review* 28 (1949–1950): 198–217, 516–539.

Buslaev, Fedor. *Russkaja xrestomatija: Pamjatniki drevnej russkoj literatury.* Slavistic Printings and Reprintings, vol. 222. 1904; The Hague, Mouton, 1969.

Butler, Thomas, ed. *Monumenta Serbocroatica*. Ann Arbor: Michigan Slavic Publications, 1980.

Buxarev, I. *Žitija vsex svjatyx prazdnuemyx pravoslavnoju greko-rossijskoju cerkoviju*. Moscow, 1896.

Byčkova, M. E. *Rodoslovnye knigi XVI–XVII vv*. Moscow, 1975.

Byrnes, Robert F., ed. *Communal Families in the Balkans: The Zadruga*. Notre Dame, Ind.: University of Notre Dame Press, 1976.

Cambridge Medieval History: The Byzantine Empire. Vol. 4, pt. 1. Cambridge: Cambridge University Press, 1966.

Carey, Claude. *Les Proverbes érotiques russes*. The Hague: Mouton, 1972.

Carter, John Marshall. *Rape in Medieval England*. New York: University Press of America, 1985.

Clements, Barbara Evans. *Bolshevik Feminist: The Life of Aleksandra Kollontai*. Bloomington: Indiana University Press, 1979.

Colfer, A. Michael. *Morality, Kindred, and Ethnic Boundary: A Study of the Oregon Old Believers*. New York: AMS Press, 1985.

Collins, Samuel. *The Present State of Russia*. London, 1671.

Cross, Samuel H., ed. and trans. *The Russian Primary Chronicle*. Cambridge, Mass.: Medieval Academy, n.d.

Cvetkova, Bistra A., ed. *Frenski putepisi za Balkanite XV–XVIII v*. Sofia, 1975.

Daly, Mary. *The Church and the Second Sex*. New York: Harper & Row, 1968.

Dauvillier, Jean, and Carlo de Clercq. *Le Mariage en droit canonique oriental*. Paris: Sirey, 1936.

Dejanija moskovskix soborov 1666 i 1667 godov. Slavistic Printings and Reprintings, vol. 190. 1893; The Hague: Mouton, 1970.

Demina, Evgenija I. *Tixonravovskij Damaskin: Bolgarskij pamjatnik XVII v*. Sofia, 1971.

Deržavina, O. A. *"Velikoe Zercalo" i ego sud'ba na russkoj počve*. Moscow, 1965.

Dewey, Horace W., and Ann M. Kleimola. "Suretyship and Collective Responsibility in Pre-Petrine Russia." *Jahrbücher für Geschichte Osteuropas* 18 (1970): 337–354.

—— and ——. *Zakon Sudnyj Ljudem (Court Law for the People)*. Michigan Slavic Materials, no. 9. Ann Arbor: University of Michigan Press, 1973.

Dinekov, P. "Iz istorii russko-bolgarskix literaturnyx svjazej XVI–XVIII vv." *Trudy otdela drevnerusskoj literatury* 19 (1963): 318–329.

Dinkov, K. *Istorija na bŭlgarskata cŭrkva (četiva)*. Sofia, 1954.

Ditrix, Marija Nikolaevna. *Russkaja ženščina velikoknjažeskago vremeni*. St. Petersburg, 1904.

Dmitriev, L. A. *Žitijnye povesti russkogo severa kak pamjatniki literatury XIII–XVII vv*. Moscow, 1973.

Dobrjakov, Aleksandr. *Russkaja ženščina v do-mongol'skij period*. St. Petersburg, 1864.

Domostroi. Letchworth: Bradda, 1971.

Donahue, Charles, Jr. "The Policy of Alexander the Third's Consent Theory of Marriage." In *Proceedings of the Fourth International Congress of Medieval Canon Law, Toronto, 21–25 August 1972*, 251–281. Monumenta Iuris Canonici, ser. C: Subsidia, vol. 5. Vatican, 1976.

Dover, Kenneth J. *Greek Homosexuality.* Cambridge: Harvard University Press, 1978.

Drevnerusskaja knižnaja miniatjura iz sobranija gosudarstvennoj publičnoj biblioteki imeni M. E. Saltykova-Ščedrina. Leningrad, 1980.

Drevnjaja rossijskaja vivliofika. Slavistic Printings and Reprintings, vol. 250/13–14. 1790; The Hague: Mouton, 1970.

Družinin, V. G. *Neskol'ko neizvestnyx literaturnyx pamjatnikov iz sbornika XVI-go veka.* Letopis' zanjatij imperatorskoj arxeografičeskoj kommissii za 1908 god. St. Petersburg, 1909.

Dubakin, D. N. *Vlijanie xristianstva na semejnyj byt russkago obščestva.* St. Petersburg, 1880.

Duby, Georges. *Medieval Marriage: Two Models from Twelfth-Century France.* Baltimore: Johns Hopkins University Press, 1978.

Dujčev, I. "Centry vizantijsko-slavjanskogo obščenija i sotrudničestva." *Trudy otdela drevnerusskoj literatury* 19 (1963): 107–129.

24 Stenopisa ot Rilskija manastir. Sofia, 1983.

Dworzaczek, Wodzimierz. *Genealogia.* Warsaw, 1959.

Eck, Alexandre. "La Situation juridique de la femme russe au moyen âge." *Recueils de la Société Jean Bodin pour l'histoire comparative des institutions* 12 (1962): 404–420.

Elnett, Elaine. *Historic Origin and Social Development of Family Life in Russia.* New York: Columbia University Press, 1926.

Evrejski izvori za obščestveno-ikonomičeskoto razvitie na balkanskite zemi. 2 vols. Sofia, 1960.

Fedotov, George P. *The Russian Religious Mind.* 2 vols. [1946.] Belmont, Mass.: Nordland, 1975.

———, ed. *A Treasury of Russian Spirituality.* New York: Harper & Row, 1965.

Fine, John V. A. *The Early Medieval Balkans.* Ann Arbor: University of Michigan Press, 1983.

———. *The Late Medieval Balkans.* Ann Arbor: University of Michigan Press, 1987.

Flandrin, J.-L. "Repression and Change in the Sexual Life of Young People in Medieval and Early Modern Times." In Robert Wheaton and Tamara K. Harevin, eds., *Family and Sexuality in French History,* 27–48. Philadelphia: University of Pennsylvania Press, 1980.

———. "Sex in Married Life in the Early Middle Ages: The Church's Teaching and Behavioural Reality." In Philippe Ariès and André Béjin, eds., *Western Sexuality: Practice and Precept in Past and Present Times,* 114–129. New York: Basil Blackwell, 1985.

———. *Le Sexe et l'Occident: Évolution des attitudes et des comportements.* Paris: Seuil, 1981.

———. *Un Temps pour embrasser: Aux origines de la morale sexuelle occidentale (VIe–XIe siècle).* Paris: Seuil, 1983.

Fletcher, Giles. *Of the Russe Commonwealth.* Ed. Richard Pipes. Facsimile ed. Cambridge: Harvard University Press, 1966.

Florovsky, Georges. "The Problem of Old Russian Culture." In Michael Cherniavsky, ed., *The Structure of Russian History.* New York: Random House, 1970.

Foucault, Michel. *The History of Sexuality.* Vol. 1, *An Introduction.* New York:

Vintage, 1980. Vol. 2, *The Use of Pleasure.* New York: Vintage, 1985. Vol. 3, *The Care of Self.* New York: Pantheon, 1986.

Franklin, Simon. "Literacy and Documentation in Early Medieval Russia." *Speculum* 60, no. 1 (1985): 1–38.

Gal'kovskij, N. M. *Bor'ba Xristianstva s ostatkami jazyčestva v drevnej Rusi.* Vol. 1, Kharkov, 1916; vol. 2, Moscow, 1913, as Zapiski Moskovskogo arxeologičeskogo instituta, no. 18.

Gaudemet, Jean. "Recherche sur les origines historiques de la faculté de rompre le mariage non consommé." In *Proceedings of the Fifth International Congress of Medieval Canon Law, Salamanca, 21–25 September 1976,* 309–331. Monumenta Iuris Canonici, ser. C: Subsidia, vol. 6. Vatican, 1980.

——. *Sociétés et mariage.* Strasbourg: Cerdic, 1980.

Georgieva, Ivanička. "The Bulgarian Kinship System." *Ethnologia Slavica* 3 (1971): 151–157.

Goehrke, Carsten. "Die Witwe im Alten Russland." *Forschungen zur osteuropaischen Geschichte* 38 (1986): 64–96.

Golubinskij, E. *Istorija russkoj cerkvi.* 2 vols. Moscow, 1901, 1904.

Goodich, Michael. *The Unmentionable Vice: Homosexuality in the Later Medieval Period.* Santa Barbara: ABC Clio, 1979.

Gottlieb, Beatrice. "The Meaning of Clandestine Marriage." In Robert Wheaton and Tamara K. Hareven, eds., *Family and Sexuality in French History,* 49–83. Philadelphia: University of Pennsylvania Press, 1980.

Greenan, T. A. "Iulianiya Lazarevskaya." *Oxford Slavonic Papers* n.s. 15 (1982): 28–45.

Grossman, Joan D. "Feminine Images in Old Russian Literature and Art." *California Slavic Studies* 11 (1980): 33–70.

Gudzij, N. K. *Xrestomatija po drevnej russkoj literature XI–XVII vekov.* Moscow, 1962.

Guilland, R. "Les Noces plurales à Byzance." *Byzantinoslavica* 9 (1947–48): 9–30.

Hadrovics, Ladislas. *Le Peuple serbe et son église sous la domination turque.* Paris, 1947.

Halle, Fanina W. *Woman in Soviet Russia.* London, 1933.

Halperin, Charles J. *Russia and the Golden Horde.* Bloomington: Indiana University Press, 1985.

——. "Sixteenth-Century Foreign Travel Accounts to Muscovy: A Methodological Excursus." *Sixteenth Century Journal* 6 (October 1975): 89–111.

Hammarberg, Gitta. "Eighteenth-Century Narrative Variations of 'Frol Skobeev.'" *Slavic Review* 46 (1987): 529–539.

Hammel, E. A. "The Zadruga as Process." In Peter Laslett and Richard Wall, eds., *Household and Family in Past Time,* 334–373. New York: Cambridge University Press, 1972.

Hellie, Richard. *Slavery in Russia, 1450–1725.* Chicago: University of Chicago Press, 1982.

Herberstein, Sigismund von. *Description of Moscow and Muscovy.* Ed. Bertold Picard. Trans. J. B. C. Grundy. London: Dent, 1966.

——. *Notes upon Russia (1517).* Hakluyt Society Works 10 (London, 1851): 53–95.

Horak, Stephen M. "The Kiev Academy: A Bridge to Europe in the 17th Century." *East European Quarterly* 2, no. 2 (1968): 117–137,

Howe, S. E. *The False Dmitri—A Russian Romance and Tragedy*. London, 1916.

Hubbs, Joanna. *Mother Russia: the Feminine Myth in Russian Culture*. Bloomington: Indiana University Press, 1988.

Hynkova, Hana. "Putepisni izvori ot XV i XVI v. za bita i kulturata na Bŭlgarskija narod." *Sbornik za narodni umotvorenija i narodopis* 55 (1976): 145–273.

Ingram, Martin. *Church Courts, Sex, and Marriage in England, 1570–1640*. New York: Cambridge University Press, 1987.

Istoričeskie i juridičeskie akty XVII–XVIII stoletij. Čtenija obščestva istorii i drevnostei rossijskix. Bk. 4. Moscow, 1869.

Ivanov, Jordan. *Bogomilski knigi i legendi*. Sofia, 1925.

———. *Starobŭlgarski razkazi*. Sofia, 1935.

Ivić, Aleksa. *Rodoslovne tablice srpskih dinastija i vlastele*. Novi Sad, 1928.

Izbornik 1076 goda. Moscow, 1965.

Izvori za bŭlgarskata istorija. Vol. 7: *Latinski izvori za bŭlgarskata istorija*. Sofia, 1960.

Jagić, V. "Opisi i izvodi iz nekoliko južnoslovinskih rukopisa: Srednovječni liekovi, gatanja i vračanja." *Starine* 10 (1878): 81–126.

Janin, V. L. "Berestjanye gramoty i problema proizxoždenija novgorodskoj denežnoj sistemy XV v." *Vspomogatel'nye istoričeskie discipliny* 3 (1970): 150–179.

———. *Denežno-vesovye sistemy russkogo srednevekovija*. Moscow, 1956.

———. *Novgorodskaja feodal'naja votčina*. Moscow, 1981.

Jochens, Jenny M. "The Church and Sexuality in Medieval Iceland." *Journal of Medieval History* 6 (December 1980): 377–392.

Kagan-Tarkovskaja, M. D. "Slovo o ženax dobryx i zlyx v sbornike Evfrosina." In *Kul'turnoe nasledie Drevnej Rusi*, 382–386. Moscow, 1976.

Kaiser, Daniel H. *The Growth of the Law in Medieval Russia*. Princeton: Princeton University Press, 1980.

———. "The Transformation of Legal Relations in Old Rus' (Thirteenth to Fifteenth Centuries)." Ph.D. dissertation, University of Chicago, 1972.

Kalačov, Nikolaj. *Akty otnosjaščiesja do juridičeskago byta drevnej Rusi*. Vol. 2. St. Petersburg, 1864.

Kaluzniacki, Emil. *Werke des Patriarchen von Bulgarien Euthymius*. [1901.] London: Variorum Reprints, 1971.

Kantor, Marvin. *Medieval Slavic Lives of Saints and Princes*. Ann Arbor: University of Michigan Press, 1983.

Karanov, E. "Pametnici ot Kratovo." *Sbornik za narodni umotvorenija nauka i knižnina* 13 (1896): 266–281.

Karlen, Arno. "The Homosexual Heresy." *Chaucer Review* 6 (Summer 1971): 44–63.

Katić, Relja. *The Chilandar Medical Codex N. 517*. Belgrade: National Library of Serbia, 1980.

Kavelin, K. D. "O sostojanii ženščin v Rossii do Petra Velikago: Istoričeskoe izsledovanie Vitalija Šul'gina." 1850. In *Sobranie sočinenij*, vol. 1, 1030–1044. St. Petersburg, 1897.

Kazakova, N. A., and Ja. S. Lur'e. *Antifeodal'nye eretičeskie dviženie na Rusi XIV–načala XVI veka*. Moscow/Leningrad, 1955.

Keuls, Eva C. *The Reign of the Phallus*. New York: Harper & Row, 1985.

Kinsey, Alfred C. *Sexual Behavior in the Human Female*. Philadelphia: W. B. Saunders, 1953.

———. *Sexual Behavior in the Human Male*. Philadelphia: W. B. Saunders, 1948.

Klassen, John M. "The Development of the Conjugal Bond in Late Medieval Bohemia." *Journal of Medieval History* 13, no. 2 (1987): 161–178.

———. "Marriage and Family in Medieval Bohemia." *East European Quarterly* 19, no. 3 (1985): 257–274.

Kleimola, Ann M. "Law and Social Change in Medieval Russia: The Zakon Sudnyj Ljudem as a Case Study." *Oxford Slavonic Papers* n.s. 9 (1976): 17–27.

Ključevskij, V. O. *Drevnerusskija žitija svjatyx kak istoričeskij istočnik*. Moscow, 1871.

Kollmann, Jack E. "The Stoglav Council and the Parish Priests." *Russian History* 7, nos. 1–2 (1980): 65–91.

Kollmann, Nancy Shields. *Kinship and Politics: The Making of the Muscovite Political System, 1345–1547*. Stanford: Stanford University Press, 1987.

———. "Kinship and Politics: The Origin and Evolution of the Muscovite Boyar Elite in the Fifteenth Century." Ph.D. dissertation, Harvard University, 1980.

———. "The Seclusion of Muscovite Women." *Russian History* 10, no. 2 (1983): 170–187.

Kosanović, Sava, ed. "Beleška o bogomilima." *Glasnik Srpskog učenog društva* 37 (1873): 179–188.

Kovalevsky, Maxime. *Modern Customs and Ancient Laws of Russia*. London, 1891.

Kožančikov, D. E., ed. *Stoglav*. St. Petersburg, 1863.

Krstić, Nikola. "Razmatranja o starim srbskim pravima." *Glasnik društva srbske slovesnosti* 11 (1859): 222–224.

LaPorte, Jean. *The Role of Women in Early Christianity*. New York: Edwin Mellen, 1982.

Laslett, Peter. *Family Life and Illicit Love in Earlier Generations*. New York: Cambridge University Press, 1977.

——— and Marilyn Clarke. "Houseful and Household in an Eighteenth-century Balkan City: A Tabular Analysis of the Listing of the Serbian Sector of Belgrade in 1733–4." In Peter Laslett and Richard Wall, eds., *Household and Family in Past Time*, 375–400. New York: Cambridge University Press, 1972.

Le Vasseur, Guillaume, sieur de Beauplan. "A Description of the Ukraine." In *A Collection of Voyages and Travels*. London, 1732.

Levin, Eve. "Infanticide in Pre-Petrine Russia." *Jahrbücher für Geschichte Osteuropas* 34, no. 2 (1986): 215–224.

———. "Novgorod Birchbark Documents: The Evidence for Literacy in Medieval Russia." In *Medieval Archeology*, ed. Charles Redman, 127–137. Medieval and Renaissance Texts and Studies, vol. 60. Binghamton, N.Y., 1989.

———. "The Role and Status of Women in Medieval Novgorod." Ph. D. dissertation, Indiana University, 1983.

Lewitter, L. R. "Women, Sainthood, and Marriage in Muscovy." *Journal of Russian Studies* 37 (1979): 3–11.

Likhachev, D. S. "The Type and Character of the Byzantine Influence on Old Russian Literature." *Oxford Slavonic Papers* 13 (1967): 14–32.

Lynch, Joseph H. *Godparents and Kinship in Early Medieval Europe*. Princeton: Princeton University Press, 1986.

Macdonald, John. *Czar Ferdinand and His People*. New York: Arno Press, 1971.

McNally, Susanne J. "From Public Person to Private Prisoner: The Changing Place of Women in Medieval Russia." Ph.D. dissertation, SUNY-Binghamton, 1976.

Makowski, Elizabeth M. "The Conjugal Debt and Medieval Law." *Journal of Medieval History* 3 (June 1977): 99–114.

Maksimović, L. "Georgije Paximer." In *Vizantijski izvori za istoriju naroda Jugoslavije*, vol. 6, 1–62. Belgrade, 1986.

Mandel, William M. *Soviet Women*. Garden City, N.Y.: Anchor/Doubleday, 1975.

Mansvetov, I. *Mitropolit Kiprian v ego liturgičeskoj dejatel'nosti*. Moscow, 1882.

Matossian, Mary. "In the Beginning, God Was a Woman." *Journal of Social History* 6 (Spring 1973): 337–338.

Medlin, William K. "Cultural Crisis in Orthodox Rus' in the Late 16th and Early 17th Centuries as a Problem of Socio-Cultural Change." In Andrew Blaine, ed., *The Religious World of Russian Culture*, 173–188. The Hague: Mouton, 1975.

Miège, Guy. *A Relation of Three Embassies from His Sacred Majestie Charles II to the Great Duke of Muscovie, the King of Sweden, and the King of Denmark*. London, 1669.

Miklosich, Fr. *Monumenta Serbica spectantia historiam Serbiae Bosnae Ragusii*. Vienna, 1858.

Mogila, Peter. *Trebnik*. Kiev, 1646.

Morgan, Edmund S. "The Puritans and Sex." *New England Quarterly* 15 (1942): 591–607.

Mošin, Vladimir. "Balkanskata diplomatija i dinastickite brakovi na kralot Milutin." In *Spomenici za srednovekovnata i ponovata istorija na Makedonija*, vol. 2, 89–213. Skoplje, 1977.

——. "O periodizacii russko-južnoslavjanskix literaturnyx svjazej X–XV vv." *Trudy otdela drevnerusskoj literatury* 19 (1963): 28–106.

——. "Vlastareva sintagma i Dušanev zakonik u Studeničkom 'Otečniku.'" *Starine* 42 (1949): 7–93.

Moskovskaja delovaja i bytovaja pis'mennost' XVII veka. Moscow, 1968.

Mursten, Bernard I. *Love, Sex, and Marriage through the Ages*. New York: Springer, 1974.

Musallam, B. F. *Sex and Society in Islam: Birth Control Before the Nineteenth Century*. New York: Cambridge University Press, 1983.

Nicol, Donald M. "Mixed Marriages in Byzantium in the Thirteenth Century." In *Byzantium: Its Ecclesiastical History and Relations with the Western World*, 160–172. London: Variorum Reprints, 1972.

Niketić, Svetozar. "Istorijski razvitak Srpske crkve." *Glasnik srpskog učenog društva* 27 (1870): 81–163; 31 (1871): 45–88.

Nikolov, Jordan. "Pravoslavnata cŭrkva prez epoxata na feodalizma (IX–XIV v.)." In *Pravoslavieto v Bŭlgarija (teoretiko-istoričesko osvetlenie)*, 101–124. Sofia, 1974.

Nikolova, Svetlina. *Pateričnite razkazi v bŭlgarskata srednovekovna literatura*. Sofia, 1980.

Nikol'skij, Konstantin. *Posobie k izučenie ustava bogosluženija pravoslavnoj cerkvi.* St. Petersburg, 1865.

Nikol'skij, N. K. *Materialy dlja istorii drevnerusskoj duxovnoj pismennosti.* Sbornik otdelenija russkago jazyka i slovesnosti imperatorskoj akademii nauk, vol. 82. St. Petersburg, 1907.

Noonan, John T., Jr. *Contraception: A History of Its Treatment by the Catholic Theologians and Canonists.* 2d ed. Cambridge: Harvard University Press, 1986.

——. *Power to Dissolve: Lawyers and Marriages in the Courts of the Roman Curia.* Cambridge: Harvard University Press, 1972.

Novaković, Stojan. "Apokrifi kijevskoga rukopisa." *Starine* 16 (1884): 89–96.

——. *Matije Vlastara Sintagmat.* Zbornik za istoriju, jezik i književnost srpskog naroda; prvo odeljenje: Spomenici na srpskom jeziku, vol. 4. Belgrade, 1907.

——. *Primeri književnosti i jezika staroga i srpsko-slovenskoga.* Belgrade, 1904.

——. *Zakonik Stefana Dušana.* Belgrade, 1898.

——. *Zakonski spomenici srpskih država srednjega veka.* Belgrade, 1912.

Novgorodskaja pervaja letopis' staršego i mladšego izvoda. Moscow/Leningrad, 1950.

Obolensky, Dmitri. *The Bogomils.* Cambridge: Cambridge University Press, 1948.

Olearius, Adam. *The Travels of Olearius in Seventeenth-Century Russia,* ed. Samuel H. Baron. Stanford: Stanford University Press, 1967.

Onclin, W. "L'Age requis pour le mariage dans la doctrine canonique mediévale." In *Proceedings of the Second International Congress of Medieval Canon Law, Boston College, 12–16 August 1963,* 237–247. Monumenta Iuris Canonici, ser. C: Subsidia, vol. 1. Vatican, 1965.

Pamjatniki drevnerusskoj cerkovno-učitel'noj literatury. St. Petersburg, 1897.

Pamjatniki literatury drevnej Rusi, XII vek. Moscow, 1980.

Pamjatniki literatury drevnej Rusi, XIII vek. Moscow, 1981.

Pamjatniki literatury drevnej Rusi, XIV–seredina XV veka. Moscow, 1981.

Pamjatniki russkogo prava. 8 vols. Moscow, 1953.

Pamjatniki starinnoj russkoj literatury. 4 vols. Slavistic Printings and Reprintings, vol. 97. 1860–1862; The Hague: Mouton, 1970.

Pankratova, N. P. "Ljubovnye pis'ma pod'jaščego Arefy Malevinskogo." *Trudy otdela drevnerusskoj literatury* 18 (1962): 364–369.

Pantazopoulos, N. J. *Church and Law in the Balkan Peninsula during the Ottoman Rule.* Thessaloniki: Institute for Balkan Studies, 1967.

Pantelić, Nikola. "Snahačestvo in Serbia and Its Origin." *Ethnologia Slavica* 3 (1971): 171–180.

Pascu, St., and V. Pascu. "Le Remariage chez les orthodoxes." In J. Dupaquier et al., eds., *Marriage and Remarriage in Populations of the Past,* 61–66. New York: Academic Press, 1981.

Pavlov, A. S. "'Knigi zakonnyja' soderžaščija v sebe v drevne-russkom perevode vizantijskie zakony zemledel'českie, ugolovnye, bračnye i sudebnye." *Sbornik otdelenija russkago jazyka i slovestnosti imperatorskoj akademii nauk* 38, no. 3 (1885): 1–92.

——. *Nomokanon pri Bol'šom Trebnike.* Odessa, 1872; Moscow, 1897.

——. *Pervonačal'nyj slavjano-russkij Nomokanon.* Kazan, 1869.

Payer, Pierre J. "Early Medieval Regulations Concerning Marital Sexual Relations." *Journal of Medieval History* 6 (December 1980): 353–376.

———. *Sex and the Penitentials: The Development of a Sexual Code, 550–1150.* Buffalo: University of Toronto Press, 1984.

Perkov, Yury, trans. *Erotic Tales of Old Russia.* Oakland, Calif.: Scythian Books, 1980.

Petrovskij, N. M. "Pis'mo patriarxa Konstantinopol'skago Feofilakta carju Bolgarii Petru." *Izvestija otdelenija russkago jazyka i slovesnosti imperatorskoj Akademii nauk* 18, no. 3 (1913): 356–372.

Picchio, Riccardo. "Models and Patterns in the Literary Tradition of Medieval Orthodox Slavdom." In Victor Terras, ed., *American Contributions to the Seventh International Congress of Slavists,* vol. 2, 439–67. The Hague: Mouton, 1973.

Pixoja, R. G. "Cerkov' v drevnej Rusi (konec X–pervaja polovina XIII v.): Drevnerusskoe pokajannoe pravo kak istoričeskij istočnik." Avtoreferrat, Sverdlovsk, 1974.

Polnoe sobranie russkix letopisej. Vol. 4, St. Petersburg, 1848; Petrograd, 1915. Vol. 5, Leningrad, 1925. Vol. 8, St. Petersburg, 1859.

Popruženko, M. G. "Sinodik carja Borila." *Bŭlgarski starini* 8 (1928).

Puech, Henri-Charles, and André Vaillant. *Le Traité contre les Bogomiles de Cosmas le prêtre.* Paris, 1945.

Puškareva, N. L. "Imuščestvennye prava ženščin na Rusi (X–XV vv.)." *Istoričeskie zapiski* 114 (1986): 180–224.

———. "Ni svjaščennika čtjat, ni boga sja bojat . . . " *Nauka i Religija,* 1986, no. 1: 15–18.

———. "Pravovoe položenie ženščiny v srednevekovoj Rusi: Voprosy prestuplenija i nakazanija." *Sovetskoe gosudarstvo i pravo* 1985, no. 4: 121–126.

———. "Rjadnaja gramota Fedora Onkifoviča s Matfeem Ivanovičem XV v. (Spornye voprosy germenevtiki pamjatnika nasledstvennogo prava)." In *Issledovanija po istočnikovedenija istorii SSSR dooktjabrskogo perioda,* 37–50. Moscow, 1982.

——— and Eve Levin. "Ženščina v srednevekovom Novgorode XI–XVvv." *Vestnik Moskovskogo Universiteta, Serija Istorija* 1983, no. 3: 78–89.

Quaife, G. R. *Wanton Wenches and Wayward Wives: Peasants and Illicit Sex in Early Seventeenth-Century England.* New Brunswick, NJ: Rutgers University Press, 1979.

Ritzer, K. *Le Mariage dans les églises chrétiennes du Ier au XIe siècle.* Paris, 1962.

Rogov, A. I. "Russko-bol'garskie kul'turnye svjazi v konce XII–XIII vv." *Etudes balkaniques* 17, no. 3 (1981): 86–91.

Roman, Stanislaw. "Le Statut de la femme dans l'Europe orientale (Pologne et Russie) au moyen âge et aux temps modernes." *Recueils de la Société Jean Bodin pour l'histoire comparative des institutions* 12 (1962): 389–403.

Romanov, B. A. *Ljudi i nravy drevnej Rusi.* 2d ed. Leningrad, 1966.

Ruggiero, Guido. *The Boundaries of Eros: Sex Crime and Sexuality in Renaissance Venice.* New York: Oxford University Press, 1985.

Russkaja istoričeskaja biblioteka. Vol. 2 (1875); vol. 6: *Pamjatniki drevne-russkago kanoničeskago prava* (1908); vol. 12: *Akty xolmogorskoj i ustjužskoj eparxii, časť pervaja, 1500–1699 gg.* (1890); vol. 14: *Akty xolmogorskoj i ustjužskoj eparxii, časť vtoraja* (1894); vol. 25: *Akty xolmogorskoj i ustjužskoj eparxii, kniga treť ja* (1908). St. Petersburg.

Rybakov, B. A. *Jazyčestvo drevnej Rusi.* Moscow, 1987.

———. *Jazyčestvo drevnyx slavjan*. Moscow, 1981.
Šafarik, J. "Život despota Stefana Lazarevića, velikog kneza srpskog." *Glasnik srpskog učenog društva* 28 (1870): 363–428.
Šaškov, S. S. *Istorija russkoj ženščiny*. St. Petersburg, 1879.
Savva, V. I., S. F. Platonov, and V. G. Druzinin. *Vnov' otkrytyja polemičeskija sočinenija XVII veka protiv eretikov*. Letopis' zanjatij imperatorskoj arxeografičeskoj kommissii za 1905 god, vol. 18. St. Petersburg, 1907.
Sbornik starinnyx bumag xranjaščixsja v muzee P. I. Ščukina. Moscow, 1898.
Ščapov, A. P. "Položenie ženščiny v Rossii po do-Petrovskomu vozzreniju." 1873. In *Sočinenija*, vol. 2, 105–153. St. Petersburg, 1908.
Ščapov, Ja. N. "Brak i sem'ja v drevnej Rusi." *Voprosy istorii* 1970, no. 10: 216–219.
———. *Drevnerusskie knjažeskie ustavy*. Moscow, 1976.
Sharenoff, Victor N. "A Study of Manichaeism in Bulgaria with Special Reference to the Bogomils." Ph.D. dissertation, Columbia University, 1927.
Slijepčević, Djoko. *Istorija srpske pravoslavne crkve*. Vol. 1: *od pokrštavanja Srba do kraja XVIII veka*. Munich: Iskra, 1962.
Slovo Daniila Zatočnika po redakcijam XII i XIII vv, i ix peredelkam, podgotovil k pečati M. N. Zarubinim. Leningrad, 1932.
Smirnov, Ju. I., and V. G. Smolickij. *Novgorodskie byliny*. Moscow, 1978.
Smirnov, S. "Baby bogomerzkija." In *Sbornik statej posvjaščennyx Vasiliju Osipoviču Ključevskomu*, 217–243. Moscow, 1909.
Smirnov, S. I. *Drevne-russkij duxovnik*. Moscow, 1913.
———. *Materialy dlja istorii drevnerusskoj pokajannoj discipliny*. Čtenija obščestva istorii i drevnostei rossijskix pri Moskovskom universitete, vol. 3. Moscow, 1912.
Snegarov, Ivan. *Duxovno-kulturni vružki meždu Bŭlgarija i Rusija prez srednite vekove (X–XV v.)*. Sofia, 1950.
Soliday, Gerald L., et al., eds. *History of the Family and Kinship: A Select International Bibliography*. Millwood, N.Y.: Kraus International, 1980.
Solovjev, A. "Svetosavski nomokanon i njegovi novi prepisi." *Brastvo* 26 (1932): 21–43.
Spisi o istoriji pravoslavne crkve u dalmatinsko-istrijskom vladičanstvu od XV do XIX vijeka. Vol. 1. Zadar, 1899.
Sreznevskij, I. I. *Svedenija i zametki o maloizvestnyx i neizvestnyx pamjatnikov*. 3 vol. St. Petersburg, 1867.
Stafford, Pauline. *Queens, Concubines, and Dowagers*. London: Batsford, 1983.
Stern, Mikhail, with August Stern. *Sex in the USSR*. New York: Times Books, 1980.
Strotmann, D. T. "Quelques aperçus historiques sur le culte marial en Russie." *Irénikon* 32 (1959): 178–202.
Struys, John. *The Voyages and Travels of John Struys*. London, 1684.
Stuard, Susan Mosher. "Women in Charter and Statute Law: Medieval Ragusa/Dubrovnik." In Stuard, ed., *Women in Medieval Society*, 199–208. Philadelphia: University of Pennsylvania Press, 1976.
Sŭbev, Todor. *Samostojna narodnostna cŭrkva v srednovekovna Bŭlgarija*. Sofia, 1987.
Sudebniki XV–XVI vekov. Moscow, 1952.
Šul'gin, Vitalij Jakovlevič. *O sostojanii ženščin v Rossii do Petra Velikogo*. Kiev, 1850.

Suvorov, N. "Verojatnyj sostav drevnejšago ispovednago i pokajannago ustava v vostočnoj cerkvi." *Vizantijskij vremennik* 8, nos. 3–4 (1901): 357–434.

Szeftel, Marc. "Le Statut juridique de l'enfant en Russie avant Pierre le Grand." *Recueils de la Société Jean Bodin pour l'histoire comparative des institutions* 36 (1976): 635–656.

Tentler, Thomas N. *Sin and Confession on the Eve of the Reformation.* Princeton: Princeton University Press, 1977.

Thomas, Marie A. "Muscovite Convents in the Seventeenth Century." *Russian History* 10, no. 2 (1983): 230–242.

Titov, A. A., ed. *Kungurskie akty (1668–1699 g.)* St. Petersburg, 1888.

Tixomirov, M. N. "Pravosud'e mitropolič'e." In *Arxeografičeskij ežegodnik za 1963 god*, 32–55. Moscow, 1964.

———, ed. *Merilo pravednoe po rukopisi XIV veka.* Moscow, 1961.

Tixonravov, Nikolaj. *Letopisi russkoj literatury i drevnosti.* Moscow, 1863.

———. *Pamjatniki otrečennoj russkoj literatury.* 2 vols. St. Petersburg, 1863.

——— and V. O. Miller. *Russkija byliny: Staroj i novoj zapisi.* Slavistic Printings and Reprintings, vol. 204. 1894; The Hague: Mouton, 1970.

Troicki, Sergije V. *Dopunske članci vlastareve sintagme.* Srpska akademija nauka, Posebna izdanja, vol. 268; Odeljenje društvenix nauka, vol. 21. Belgrade, 1956.

Valk, S. N. *Gramoty velikogo Novgoroda i Pskova.* Moscow/Leningrad, 1949.

Vasica, J. "Collectio 87(93) Capitulorom dans les Nomocanons slaves." *Byzantinoslavica* 20 (1959): 1–8.

Velikija minei četii, sobrannyja vserossijskim mitropolitom Makariem; Oktjabr', dni 4–18. St. Petersburg, 1874.

Veyne, Paul. "Homosexuality in Ancient Rome." In Philippe Ariès and André Béjin, eds., *Western Sexuality: Practice and Precept in Past and Present Times*, 26–35. New York: Basil Blackwell, 1985.

Voyce, Arthur. *The Art and Architecture of Medieval Russia.* Norman: University of Oklahoma Press, 1967.

Vryonis, Speros, Jr., "Religious Changes and Patterns in the Balkans, 14th–16th Centuries." In Henrik Birnbaum and Speros Vryonis, eds., *Aspects of the Balkans: Continuity and Change*, 151–176. The Hague: Mouton, 1972.

Weeks, Jeffrey. *Sex, Politics, and Society: The Regulation of Sexuality since 1800.* New York: Longman, 1981.

Xristomatija po starobŭlgarska literatura. Sofia, 1967.

Zabelin, I. E. "Iz knigi 'Zlatoust.'" In *Opyty izučenija russkix drevnostej i istorii*, vol. 1, 179–188. Moscow, 1872.

———. "Ženščina po ponjatijam starinnyx knižnikov." *Russkij vestnik* 9 (1857): 5–46.

Zakon Sudnyj Ljudem: Kratkoj redakcii. Moscow, 1961.

Zakon Sudnyj Ljudem: Prostrannoj i svodnoj redakcii. Moscow, 1961.

Zakonik cara Stefana Dušana. Belgrade, 1975.

Zakonodatel'nye akty russkogo gosudarstva vtoroj poloviny XVI–pervoj poloviny XVII veka. Leningrad, 1986.

Zaozerskij, N. A., and A. S. Xaxanov. *Nomokanon Ioanna Postnika v ego redakcijax: Gruzinskoj grečeskoj i slavjanskoj.* Čtenija obščestva istorii i drevnostej rossijskix pri Moskovskom universitete, no. 2. Moscow, 1903.

Zguta, Russell. *Russian Minstrels*. Philadelphia: University of Pennsylvania Press, 1978.

Zimin, A. A. "Vypis' o vtorom brake Vasilija III." *Trudy otdela drevnerusskoj literatury* 30 (1976): 132–148.

Zlatarski, V. N. "Žitie i žizn' prepodobnago otca našego Feodosij." *Sbornik za narodni umotvorenija, nauka, i knižnina* 20, no. 5 (1904): 1–41.

Žužek, P. Ivan. *Kormčaja Kniga: Studies on the Chief Code of Russian Canon Law*. Orientalia Christiana Analecta, no. 168. Rome: Pontifical Institute, 1964.

Index

Names of participants in lawsuits who are otherwise unidentifiable are omitted from the index.